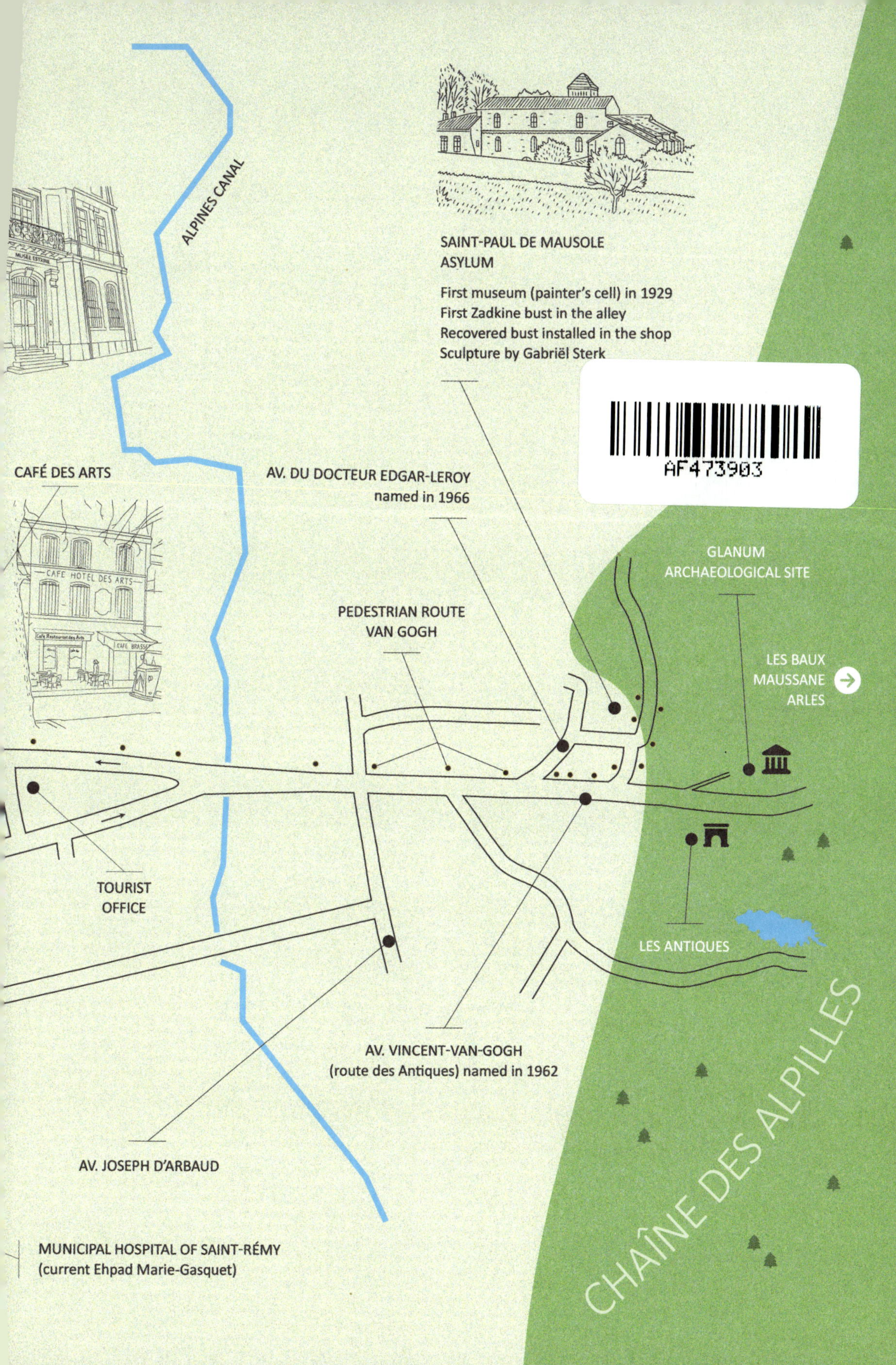

ALPINES CANAL
SAINT-PAUL DE MAUSOLE
ASYLUM
First museum (painter's cell) in 1929
First Zadkine bust in the alley
Recovered bust installed in the shop
Sculpture by Gabriël Sterk
CAFÉ DES ARTS
CAFE HOTEL DES ARTS
AV. DU DOCTEUR EDGAR-LEROY
named in 1966
GLANUM
ARCHAEOLOGICAL SITE
PEDESTRIAN ROUTE
VAN GOGH
LES BAUX
MAUSSANE
ARLES
TOURIST
OFFICE
LES ANTIQUES
AV. VINCENT-VAN-GOGH
(route des Antiques) named in 1962
AV. JOSEPH D'ARBAUD
CHAÎNE DES ALPILLES
MUNICIPAL HOSPITAL OF SAINT-RÉMY
(current Ehpad Marie-Gasquet)

VINCENT VAN GOGH
in Saint-Rémy-de-Provence

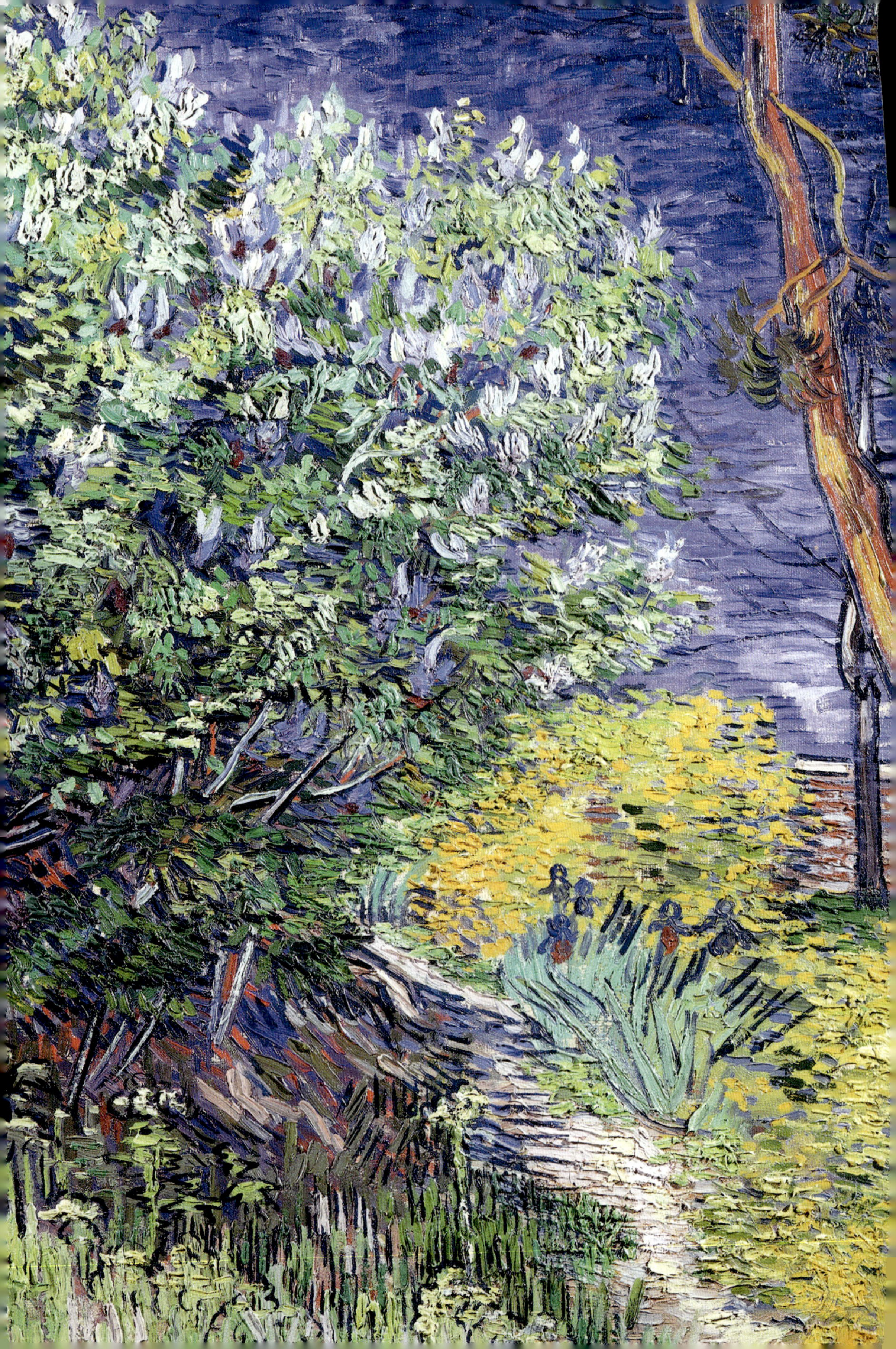

VINCENT VAN GOGH
in Saint-Rémy-de-Provence

SilvanaEditoriale

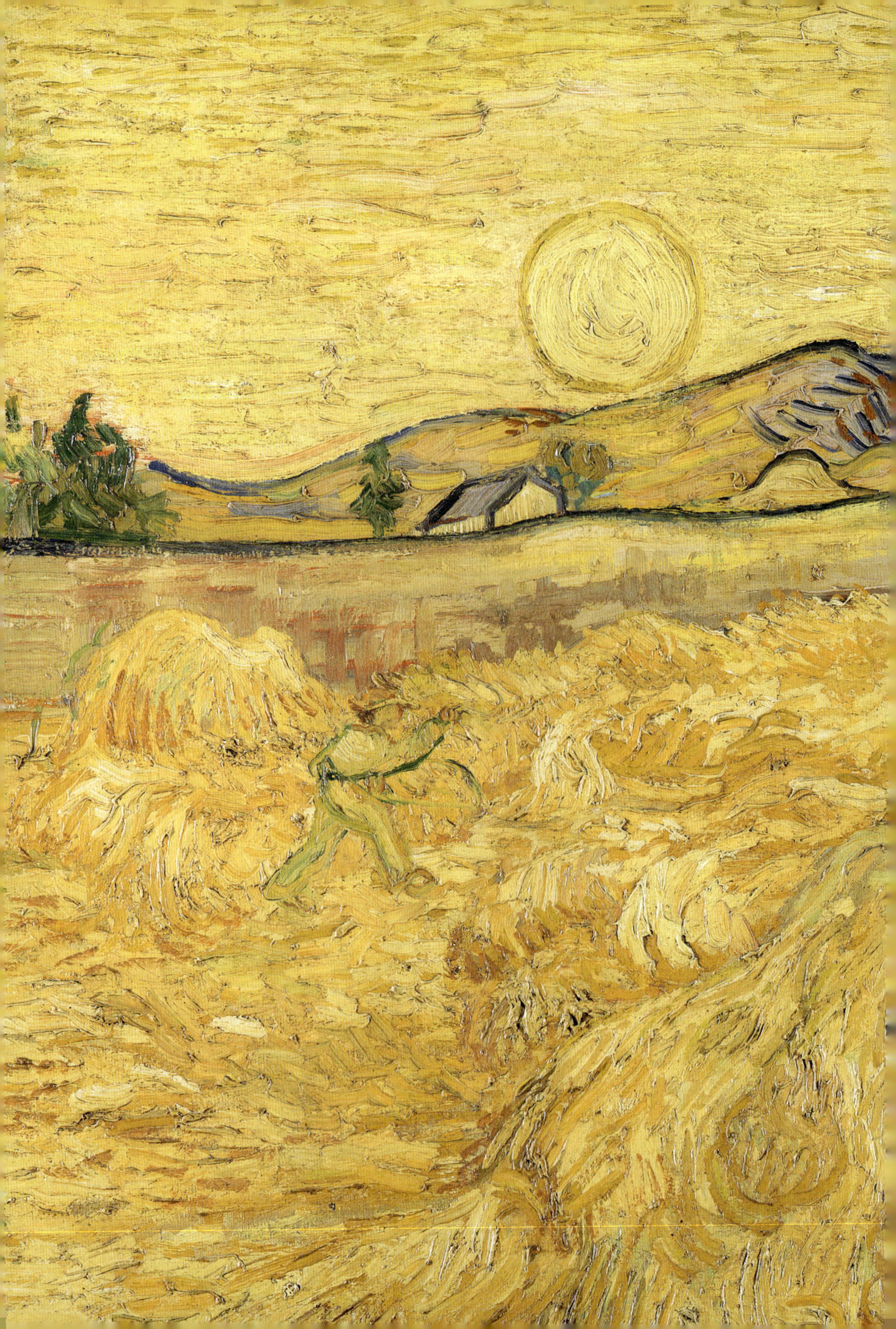

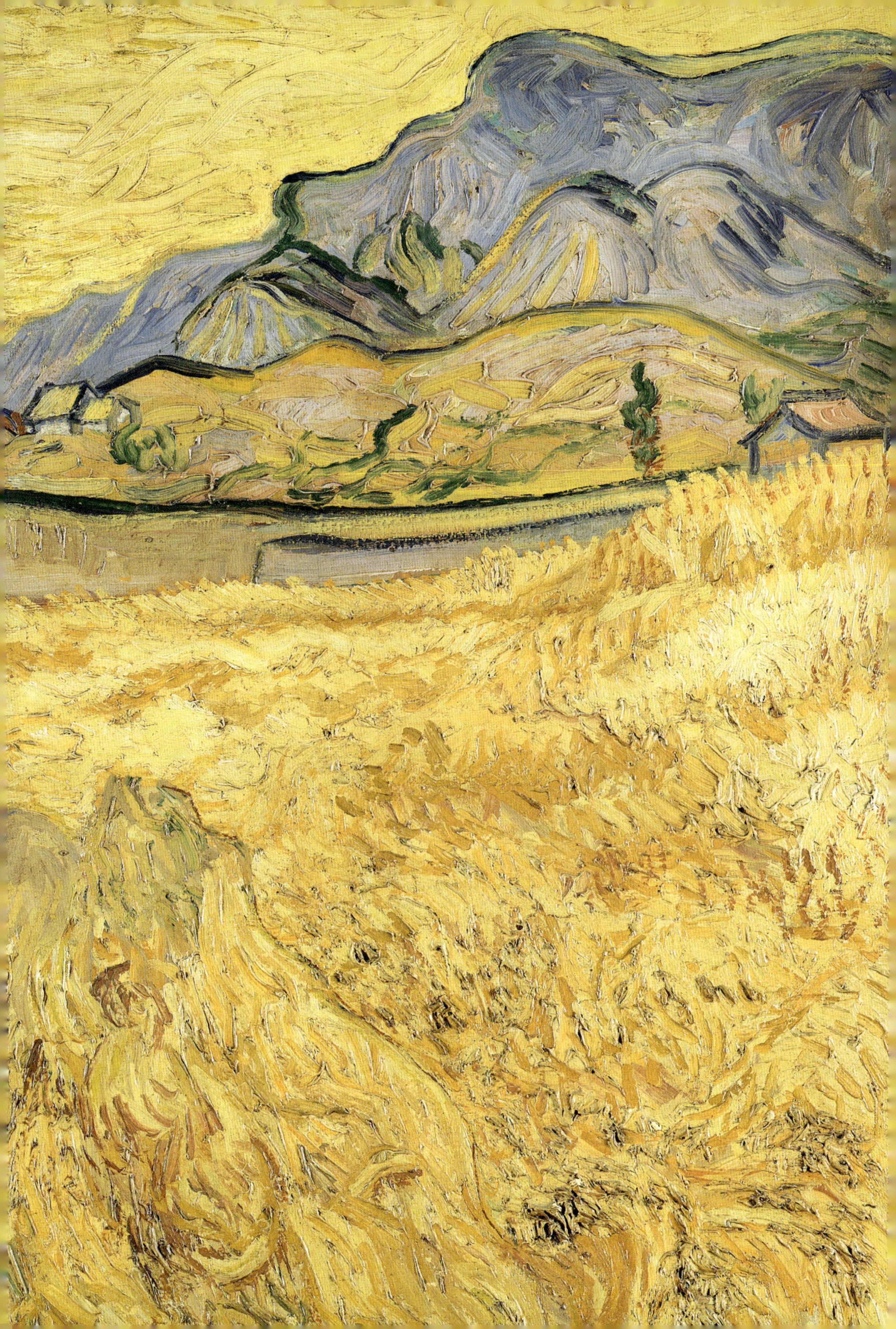

Hervé Chérubini

Mayor of Saint-Rémy-de-Provence
President of the Vallée des Baux-Alpilles Community of Municipalities

More than a century ago, the village of Saint-Rémy housed Vincent van Gogh in the utmost anonymity, within the Saint-Paul de Mausole healthcare institution, then still known as the "Saint-Paul Asylum". After his death, the artist would become the most famous painter in the world and dramatically increase the international renown of Saint-Rémy. The painter and the town share destinies that are intimately intertwined, for if Van Gogh gave immensely to this land, the territory in turn contributed, in its own way, to unleashing his artistic creativity and genius.
At the end of the 19th century, Van Gogh took advantage of the progress offered by the Provençal village, which was rapidly developing thanks to improvements in transportation and the postal service. Above all, he was faced with the beauty of the Alpilles landscapes, whose colours he managed to magnify. The care and watchful attention provided by Doctor Peyron and his team at Saint-Paul de Mausole further enhanced the benefits the painter enjoyed during his stay.
Despite the countless works written on the artist, none has been devoted to the relationship between the painter and Saint-Rémy-de-Provence. Yet the town has been very successful in promoting the painter's stay, as early as in 1929 with the first museum of reproductions of Van Gogh's canvases, an initiative of Doctor Edgar Leroy; then in 1951 with a double exhibition of original works by Van Gogh, organised by the mayor of the time, Charles Mauron, together with the Réattu Museum in Arles; and finally, in 1989, with the creation of the Musée Estrine – Vincent van Gogh Interpretation Centre. Since then, it has never ceased to pay tribute to the man who, in the end, spent but a single year of his life in these lands; a year, nevertheless, of extraordinary prolific production, creating nearly one hundred and fifty paintings, among his most celebrated, marvellous "ambassadors" of our town throughout the world. Today, Saint-Rémy-de-Provence has become a place of "pilgrimage" for all lovers of the artist's work who come to walk in his footsteps, visit the place where he lived, and seek in the local museums answers about what his life in the heart of Provence truly was.
It is thus only natural that we should wish to pay him a new tribute, by evoking all that binds us through a rich and abundant history. This publication is not merely another book on Van Gogh. It gathers a collective memory and marks the gratitude of an entire community towards the man who transformed its destiny forever.
Although, regrettably, none of Van Gogh's paintings has been preserved within the town, his trace appears in the asylum's admission register, kept in the modern municipal archives, with the mention of his name recorded upon his arrival on the 8th of May 1889.
We would like to extend our warm thanks for their contributions to the authors: Adrien Bosc, Jean-Marc Boulon, Élisa Faran, Jacqueline Leroy, Jean-Pierre Luminet, Claude Mauron, Virginie Olier, and Alexandra Roche-Tramier, who, through their research as well as their personal sensibilities, have succeeded in conveying the profound bond between Van Gogh and Saint-Rémy. Our thanks also go to the publisher Silvana Editoriale, who immediately believed in this project, and to all those who, directly or indirectly, took part in it.
More than one hundred and thirty years later, this fine collective undertaking contributes to keep alive the magnificent legacy left by Van Gogh.

The Authors

Adrien Bosc
Writer

Jean-Marc Boulon
Psychiatrist – Clinical Medical Director Saint-Paul – Head of the Vincent van Gogh Cultural Centre

Élisa Farran
Art Historian, Director of the Musée Estrine

Jacqueline Leroy
Honorary Chief Curator

Jean-Pierre Luminet
Astrophysicist, Emeritus Research Director at the CNRS

Claude Mauron
Professor Emeritus at Aix-Marseille University

Virginie Olier
Director of the Musée des Alpilles

Alexandra Roche-Tramier
Head of Heritage, Archives, and Provençal Culture for the City of Saint-Rémy-de-Provence

Table of Contents

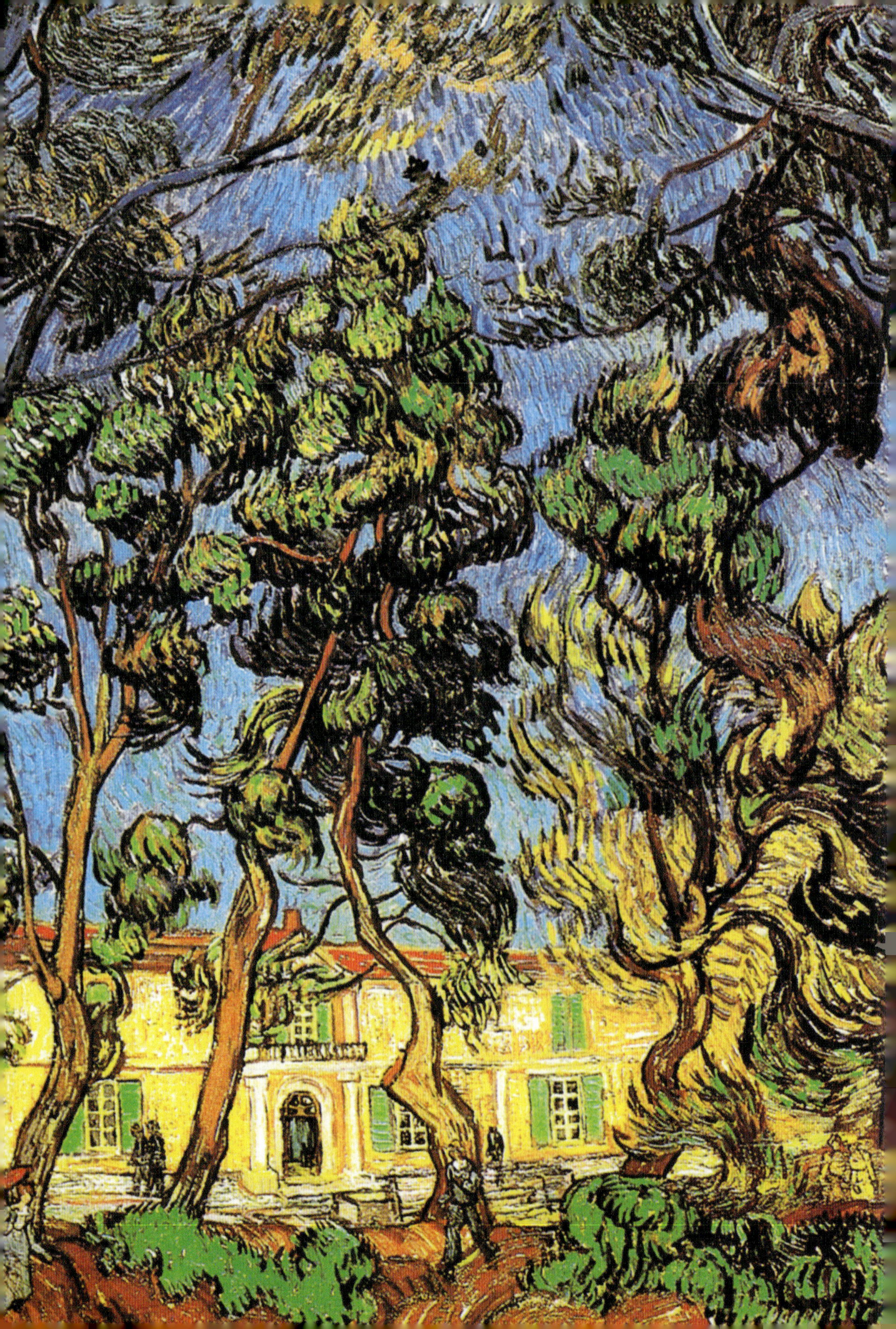

Jean-Marc Boulon

Saint-Paul de Mausole and Vincent van Gogh

From Monastery to Asylum

The buildings of Saint-Paul de Mausole possess a long religious and social history beginning in the 10th century, and later taking on a medical function from the 19th century onwards (fig. 1). After the Augustinian canons, followed by the archdeacons, the Observant monks received "in their convent those who have the misfortune of falling into madness, and even those who are confined by *lettres de cachet*".[1]

In 1790, the Constituent Assembly decreed the suppression of religious orders. The mayor of Saint-Rémy once again supported the monks' asylum: "Saint-Paul is a refuge for the poor insane, a house of charity entirely devoted to the wretched whose reason has gone astray, situated in the countryside one mile from the town, in a most fortunate location, governed by Cordelier monks long practised in this charitable work, and who are the honourable custodians of the trust of numerous families afflicted by this grievous illness."

Despite this support, the monks were expelled, and the monastery's garden and land were seized and subsequently sold at auction in 1791. The new owners intended "to devote themselves to the same kind of service for which the place had earned and obtained the public's trust, and to continue receiving and treating those who, through unfortunate circumstances, had lost their reason".

In 1807, Dr Mercurin became the owner, director, and physician.

At the dawn of the 19th century, there were few institutions for troubled minds wandering about: they were either taken in by convents or left to sleep in poorhouses. Without any understanding of their disorders, they often found themselves in the company of the destitute, the

1 Evelyne Duret, *Un asile en Provence. La maison Saint-Paul à Saint-Rémy du XVIIIe au XIXe siècle*, Aix-en-Provence: Presses universitaires de Provence, 2020.

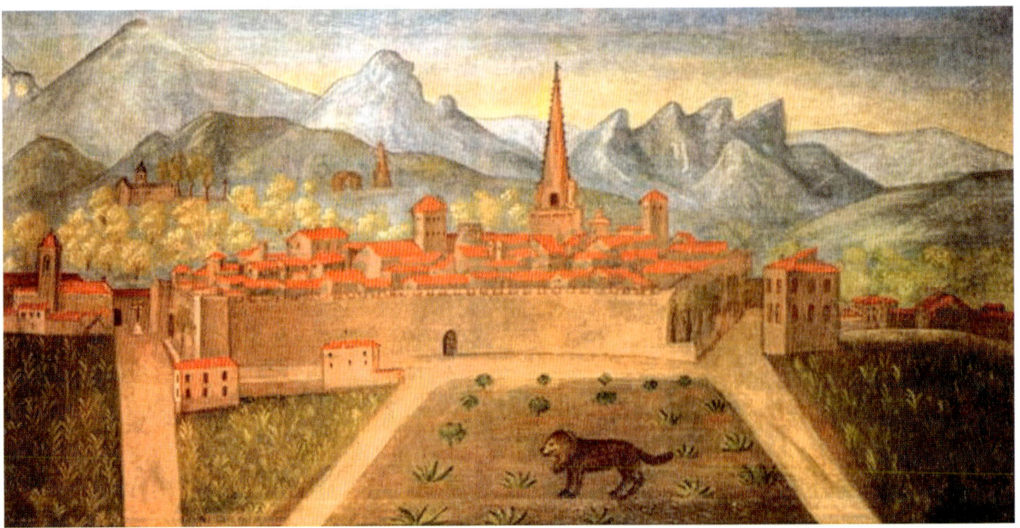

Fig. 1
Saint-Rémy in the 17th century, Saint-Rémy-de-Provence, Musée des Alpilles – *L'Œil et la Mémoire*. Saint-Paul appears in the background on the left at the foot of the hill

vagrants, and outlaws, and became social outcasts barred from managing their own affairs. In certain wretched places of repression, isolation, and coercion, they were not merely unfortunate, but also mistreated, locked in cells, chained, sometimes subjected to cold showers, and even beaten.

The Emergence of Moral Treatment

Philippe Pinel, renowned for having freed mental patients from their chains at the Bicêtre Hospital, introduced the concept of "moral treatment", which was founded upon respect for the alienated individual, careful clinical observation, and the belief that mental disorder is curable.
Article 64 of the 1810 Penal Code established a distinction between criminals to be punished and the mentally ill to be treated, defining the state of lunacy at the time of the act.
The law of June 30, 1838 laid down the procedures for admitting individuals suffering from mental disorders: open wards, locked wards for voluntary or compulsory admission. It had a dual purpose: to protect those afflicted by mental disorders and to preserve public order. "A house for the insane is an instrument of cure in the hands of a skilful physician" it declared, requiring each county council to establish a public asylum to which many mentally ill patients, previously dispersed across various locations such as hospices and prisons, were to be transferred.
Alienists adopted a hybrid approach, combining therapeutic care with measures of social control. Their limited therapies relied upon natural substances, empirical remedies, or traditional pharmacopoeia, often derived from plants or rudimentary chemical compounds: opium for the agitated, chloral hydrate for insomnia, camphor and valerian for the nervous, potassium bromide and silver nitrate for convulsions. Stimulant substances

included quinine, caffeine, and theine. Medicines were prescribed in vague terms for agitation, anxiety, or depression, yet they carried serious side effects, ranging from dependence to toxicity.
Some practitioners supplemented their methods with physical interventions such as bloodletting, purgatives, dietary regimens, the rotating chair, cold-water jet showers, isolation, and restraint devices in bathtubs, employed more to neutralise patients than to heal them, with the attendant risks of hypothermia, exhaustion, or even drowning.
When Napoleon restored the regular clergy, in certain asylums physicians refused to admit any religious personnel, whereas in others they greatly valued "the experience of the sisters, their availability, and their reputation for dedication, order, and morality, which provided an advantage in contrast to the mediocrity of the secular staff, who were less stable, untrained, and unmotivated".
Arriving at Saint-Paul in 1847, the Sisters of Saint Vincent de Paul gradually came into conflict with the directors. These tensions would reverberate through the asylum for a decade.
From 1850 onwards, four wards were arranged for men and an equal number for women, distinguishing patients as "under treatment", "convalescent", "agitated", and "senile" (figs. 2 and 3).
In 1855, the Prefect of Bouches-du-Rhône issued a decree stipulating that "the Saint-Paul establishment shall remain authorised as a private asylum, dedicated solely to the insane, for 50 men and 50 women".
In 1857, Dr Charrière informed the Prefect of "his inability to act fully due to the influence of the Sisters of Saint Vincent."

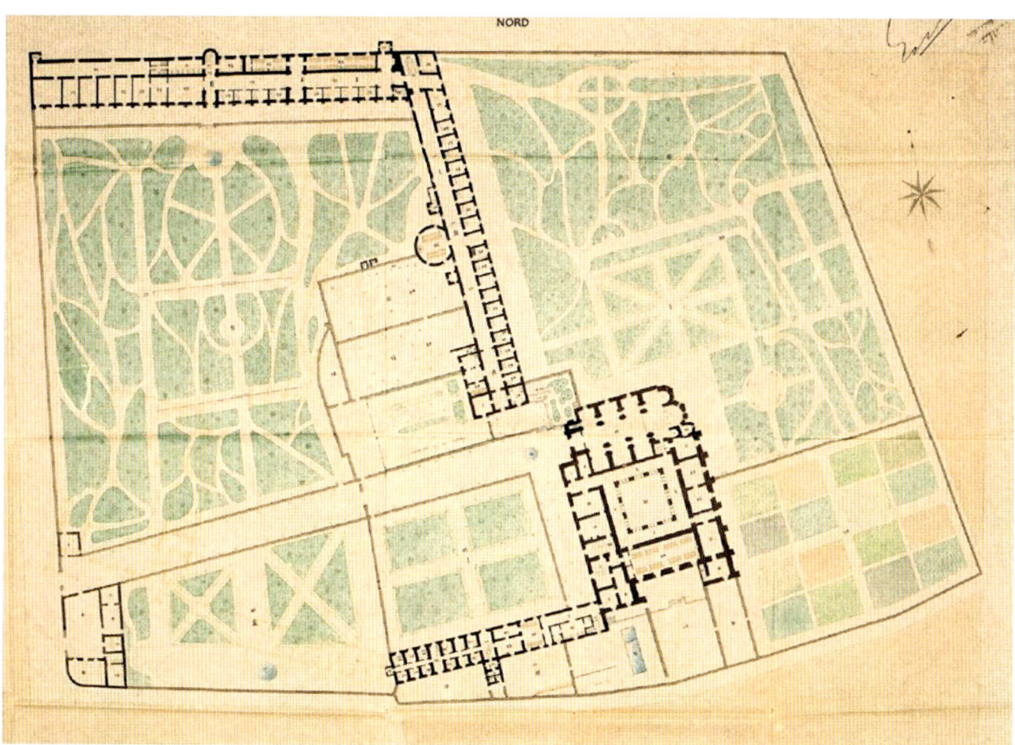

Fig. 2
Plan of Saint-Paul in 1855, Departmental Archives of Bouches-du-Rhône, 5 X 138

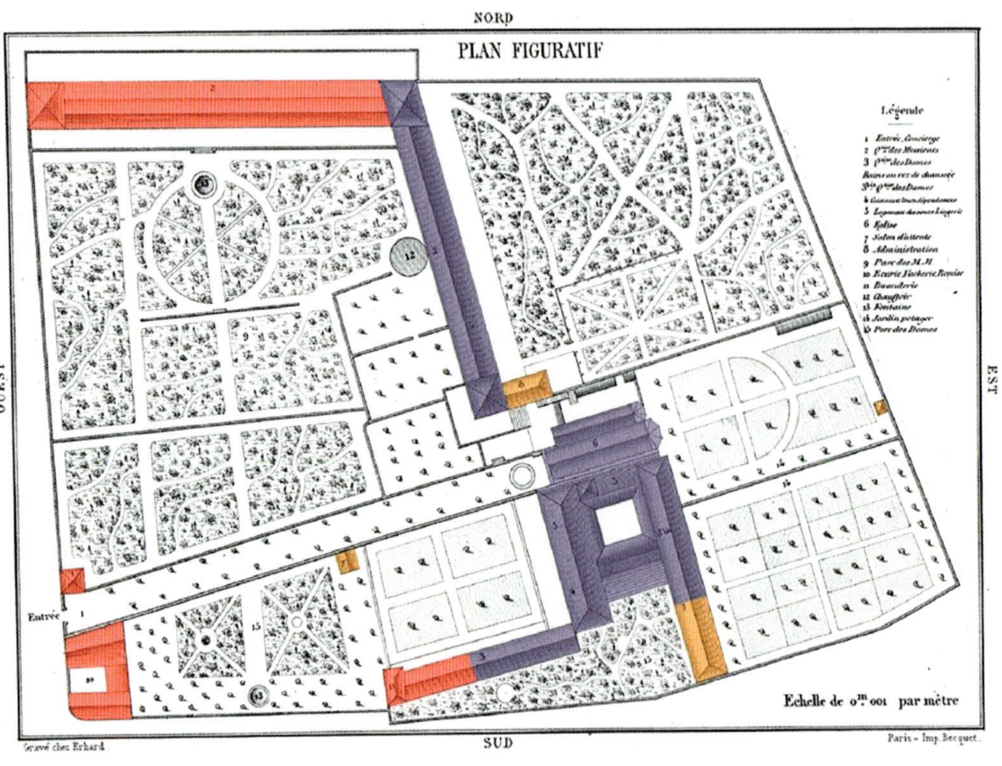

Buildings existing on the 1829 cadastral map

Expansions shown on the 1855 map

Expansions between 1855 and 1866

Fig. 3
Saint-Paul Health Center in 1866; phases of expansion, Saint-Rémy-de-Provence, Musée des Alpilles

After 1860, the fusion of the roles of director and prefect-approved physician eased the tensions.
In 1865, Dr Arnoux reorganised the asylum to bring it into compliance with regulations and to restore the Sisters of Saint Vincent de Paul to their legitimate position, while keeping the Prefecture informed. "The sisters were able to render great services in this establishment, yet their unlimited powers, unchecked, were unduly continued to the point of giving rise to the most glaring abuses. In short, their governance of the house rested solely upon falsehood, hypocrisy, deceit, denunciation, and terror […]. Moreover, the sisters refused to follow the director's instructions." The Minister of the Interior expressed concern, while the Prefect supported the director.
The Sisters of Saint Vincent departed from the establishment in 1866. They were succeeded by five sisters of the Order of Saint Joseph of Vesseaux, accompanied by four novices and six orphans.
An agreement established their position

within the hierarchy under the authority of the physician and the director. Their role would prove pivotal in ensuring the quality and humanity of care at Saint-Paul. Sister Épiphane joined them, becoming the chief superior of the women's ward. The spiritual and human support she fostered proved to be of crucial positive influence on Van Gogh (fig. 4). Drawing upon six years' experience at the public asylum for the insane in Marseille, Dr Théophile Peyron distinguished himself through numerous acts of generosity, such as arranging accommodations for the most destitute during the cholera epidemic of 1866 and financing the establishment of a free dispensary in Marseille.

Upon his arrival at Saint-Paul in 1874, he brought a stability which, together with Sister Épiphane's rigor and compassion, created a complementary and balanced management between collegiality and responsibility. This steadfast duo played an essential role in fostering the calm environment that, a few years later, would enable Van Gogh's creativity to flourish. Van Gogh referred to him as "the good Mr Peyron", spoke of "his humanity and clemency", and described him as "attentive to his patients".

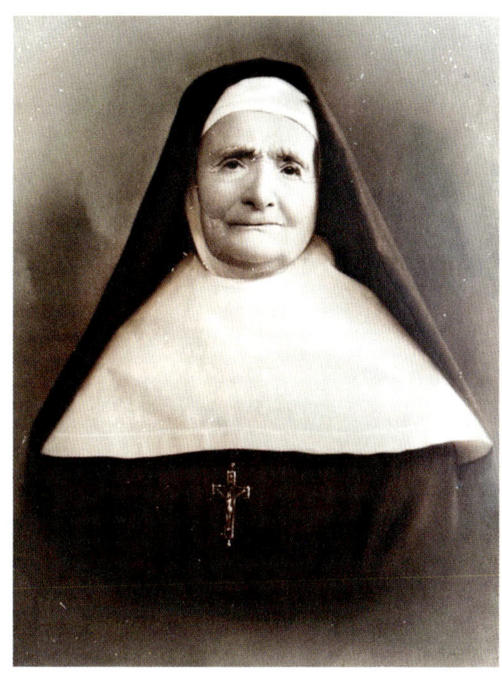

Fig. 4
Sister Épiphane, photograph, Saint-Paul de Mausole Archives

Van Gogh at Saint-Paul de Mausole

Medical Reasons

The Arles period corresponds to a phase of psychiatric decompensation. On December 23, 1889, Van Gogh cut off part of his left ear with a razor and presented it to Rachel, a prostitute at House of Tolerance No. 4, requesting her "to keep this object carefully".

The following morning, the police found him at the Yellow House, bloodied and lying on the floor, his mind in turmoil. Rushed to Arles Hospital, the young intern Dr Rey suspected a form of epilepsy, characterised by hallucinations and episodes of confused agitation, with crises precipitated by excessive alcohol consumption.

On December 29, the Mayor of Arles received the following letter:

> Enclosed is the certificate from Dr Urpar, chief physician of the hospital, noting that Monsieur Vincent, who on the 23rd of this month cut off his ear with a razor, is afflicted with mental insanity.
> The care this unfortunate individual is receiving in our establishment being insufficient to restore him to reason, I beg you to take the necessary measures to have him admitted to a specialised asylum.

On January 2, 1889, Van Gogh wrote:

> My dear Theo,
> to put your mind completely at ease regarding me, I write these few words from the office of Mr Rey, the intern Rey. [...] I shall remain here at the hospital for a few more days – then I dare to hope to return home very quietly.

Van Gogh was discharged, but he was soon readmitted following further behavioural disturbances.
Neighbours and shopkeepers in the vicinity of the Yellow House, alarmed by his unpredictable conduct, submitted a petition to the mayor in February 1889, requesting his detention:

> He does not enjoy the full use of his mental faculties, indulges in excessive drinking, after which he becomes so agitated that he no longer knows what he is doing or saying, and is highly unpredictable for the public, causing concern for all the residents of the neighbourhood, and especially for women and children...

Dr Delon, summoned by the mayor, certified:

> He is in a state of complete exaltation, seized by a real delirium, with incoherent speech and auditive hallucinations, which accuse him, and a fixed idea that he is the victim of a poisoning attempt... The condition of this patient appears most serious and seems to require vigilant supervision and treatment in a specialised asylum, for his mental faculties are profoundly impaired.

Van Gogh was then compulsorily admitted to the Hôtel-Dieu in Arles.

Van Gogh's Christian Roots and Pastor Salles

From birth, Christian culture and faith held a significant place in Van Gogh's life. His paternal lineage included a dynasty of Protestant pastors spanning several generations, among them his father, grandfather, uncles, and great-uncles.
He would remain profoundly rooted in this family tradition, maintaining a deep connection with Christianity. It shaped his spiritual and moral sensibilities and, by extension, influenced his artistic sensibility, both literary and pictorial.
This path led him, in Arles, to establish a relationship with Pastor Frédéric Salles, a respected figure known for his dedication to the most destitute.
Van Gogh expressed to Salles his wish to be treated in an asylum. He assisted him in planning his admission to Saint-Paul Asylum, for which various sources noted that "its situation on the slope of a hill, a spacious building in a favourable position, the tranquillity that prevails there, the enclosed and ample gardens, convenient baths, pure air, and wholesome waters, justify its purpose, and bring to the souls of the unfortunate who inhabit it consolations and aids that soothe their suffering or help them overcome it". Furthermore, they attested to "the efficacy, for certain nervous diseases, of the ferruginous spring waters rising from the Saint-Clergue valley, the large gardens pleasantly wooded and flowered, and the visitor lounges for families" (fig. 5).
Theo took up his pen to request the voluntary admission of his brother to Saint-Paul:

> Sir Director,
> With the consent of the person concerned, who is my brother, I beg to request the admission to your

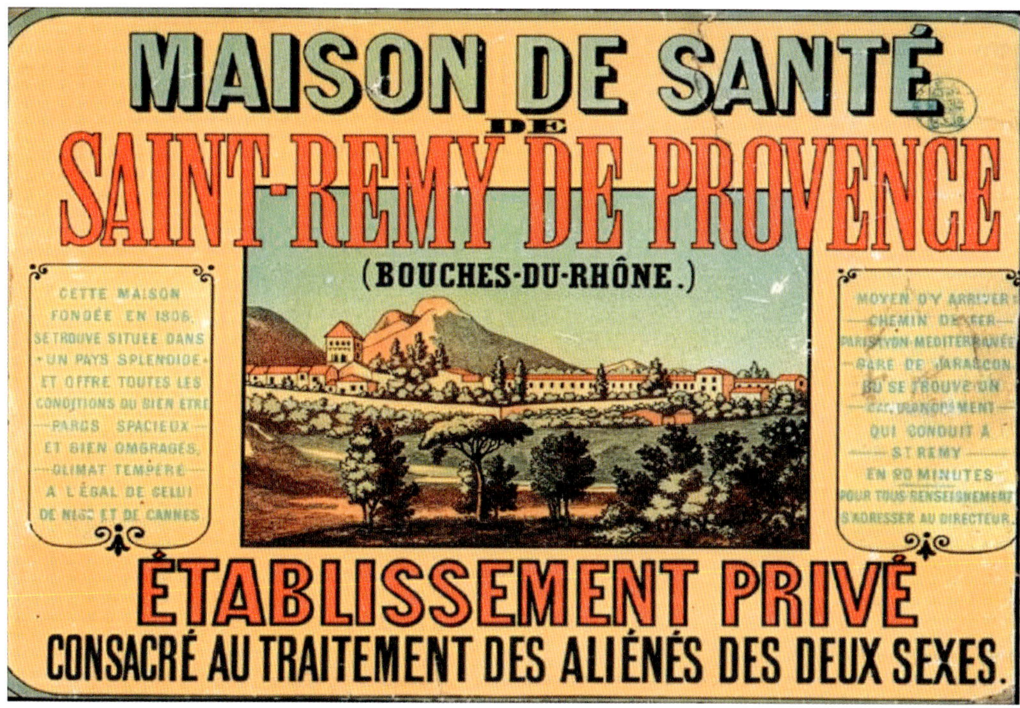

Fig. 5
Advertising leaflet for Saint-Paul, around 1875, Saint-Rémy-de-Provence, Musée des Alpilles

establishment of Vincent Willem van Gogh, a painter aged thirty-six. I kindly ask that he be admitted with your third-class boarders.
As his admission is requested more to prevent the recurrence of past crises than because his mental state is currently impaired, I hope you will find no objection to allowing him the freedom to paint outside the establishment whenever he wishes. Moreover, without insisting upon the care he may require, which I trust is provided with equal diligence to all your boarders, I would be grateful if you would allow him at least half a litre of wine with his meals.
Please accept, Sir Director, the assurance of my highest consideration.
Theo van Gogh
8, Cité Pigalle, Paris

Dr Peyron responded:

Sir,
Yesterday, Mr Salles, the Protestant minister of Arles, delivered to me your letter, which also serves as a request for the admission of your brother, a painter in Arles; he also conveyed the conditions you wish for your patient during his stay at the house. Among these conditions, there are some which I shall be pleased to grant him, but there is one which I cannot accept in advance: that of allowing him to leave the establishment whenever he wishes. I trust you will understand that, under such circumstances, my responsibility would be greatly compromised, as I could not properly oversee him.
What I can assure you in advance is that, after observing your patient for some time and gaining certainty that he can enjoy greater freedom without detriment, I shall be the first to grant it to him.

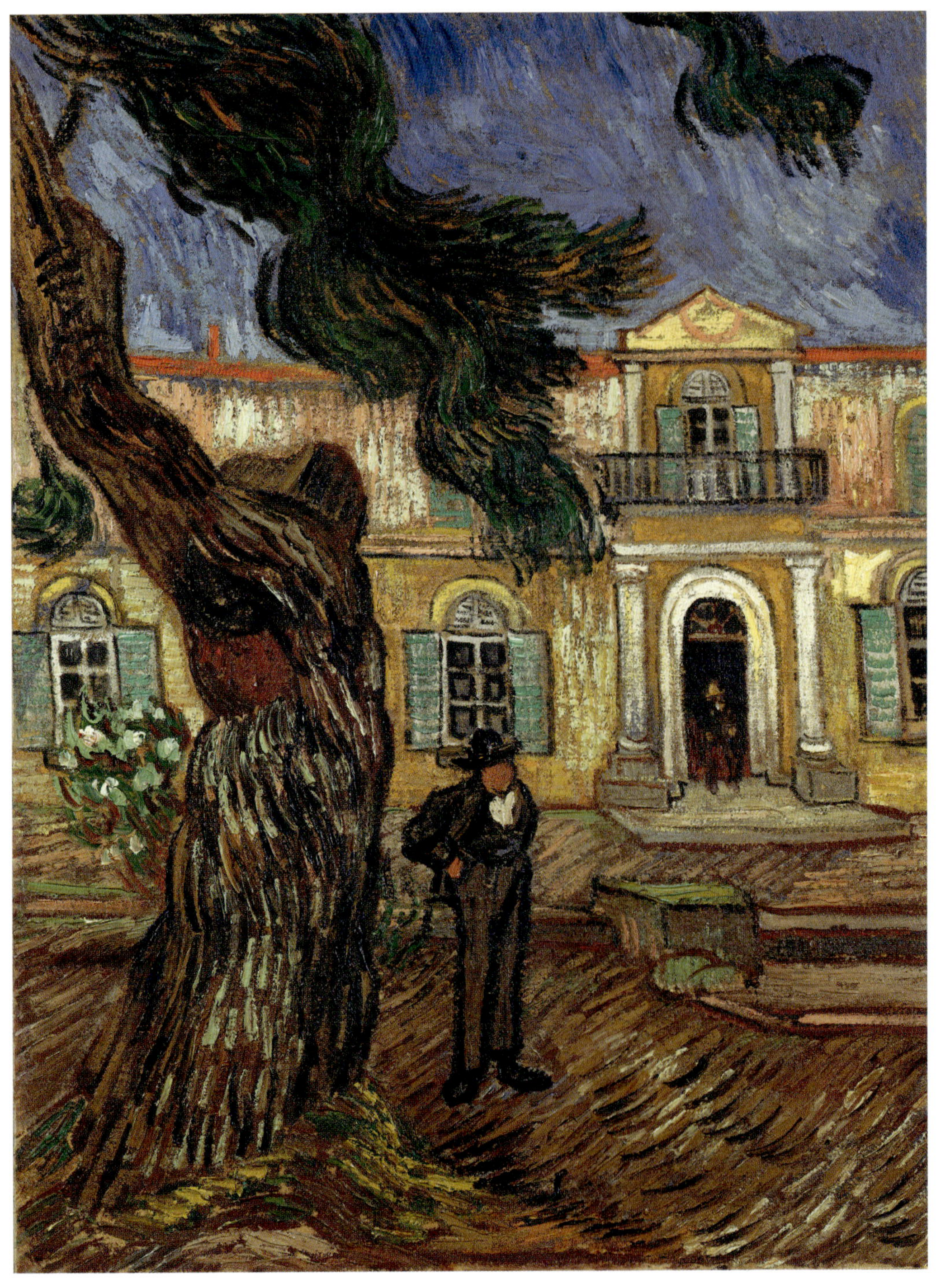

Fig. 6
Saint-Paul Asylum, Saint-Rémy, November 1889, oil on canvas, 58 × 45 cm, Paris, Musée d'Orsay

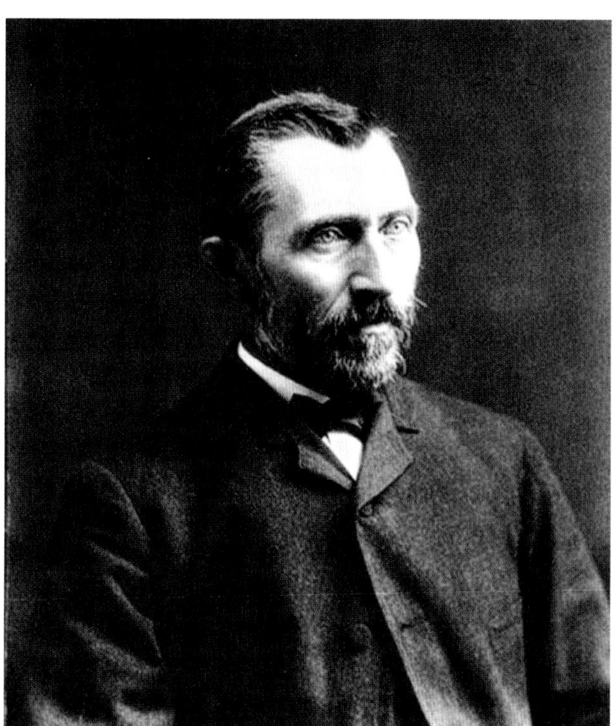

Fig. 7
Vincent van Gogh, photograph, Atelier Victor Morin, Archives

As for painting and not being confined within the establishment, I promise that we shall provide him with every means to indulge his natural inclinations and, within the house, to allow him the greatest freedom compatible with his mental condition.
In the same way, we shall permit him wine at all his meals, particularly as all my patients partake daily. I must inform you that under these conditions the board remains fixed at 100 francs per month, and it would be impossible for me to offer any reduction. I should also add that you will be required to pay, for the first month only, a supplementary ten francs for the medical certificate from the physician appointed by the administration to oversee patient admissions; this expense is payable for the first month alone.
Medical care is provided with the same diligence to all classes of patients.
His birth certificate will be required upon admission. As for his clothing needs, necessary to maintain the cleanliness of patients, I have arranged this with Mr Salles, who will accompany him to Saint-Rémy.
Yours faithfully,
Dr Th. Peyron

On May 8, 1889, Van Gogh and Pastor Salles took the train from Arles to Tarascon, then the local tram to the Saint-Rémy station, and finally travelled in the carriage sent for them by Saint-Paul (fig. 6). Upon their arrival, Dr Peyron welcomed them, showing kindness to the newcomer, who responded with lucidity and calm, identifying himself as a painter, though he had never sold anything in his life except a few early watercolours (fig. 7).
The physician was aware of: Theo's letter; the benevolent recommendation of Pastor Salles, supporting a person in great social difficulty, homeless, without income, and

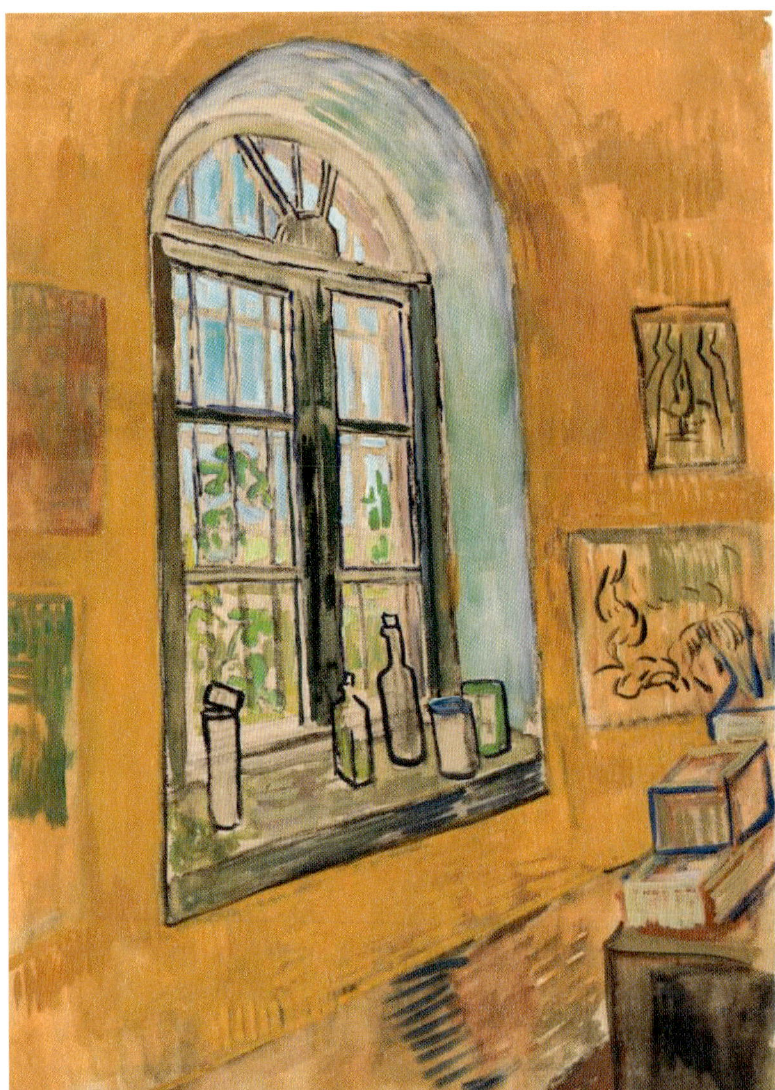

Fig. 8
Window in the Studio, September-October 1889, chalk, brush, oil paint and watercolour on paper, 62 × 47.6 cm, Amsterdam, Van Gogh Museum

dependent on his brother; the strained relations with numerous acquaintances and behavioural disturbances in Arles; the self-mutilation; the petition; the confinement for public order disturbances; and the patient's state of advanced malnutrition and fatigue.
Under such circumstances, other alienists might have opted for initial supervision in a locked room, transferring him to a cell in the event of disturbing behaviour. In contrast, Dr Peyron provided him with one room to sleep in, another to use as his studio, a third to store his paintings, and also permitted him to paint freely in the park (fig. 8).
He then recorded the following words in the register book:

> I, the undersigned, Doctor of Medicine and Director of the Maison de Santé of Saint-Rémy, certify that the individual named Vincent van Gogh, aged thirty-six, a native of Holland, and currently residing

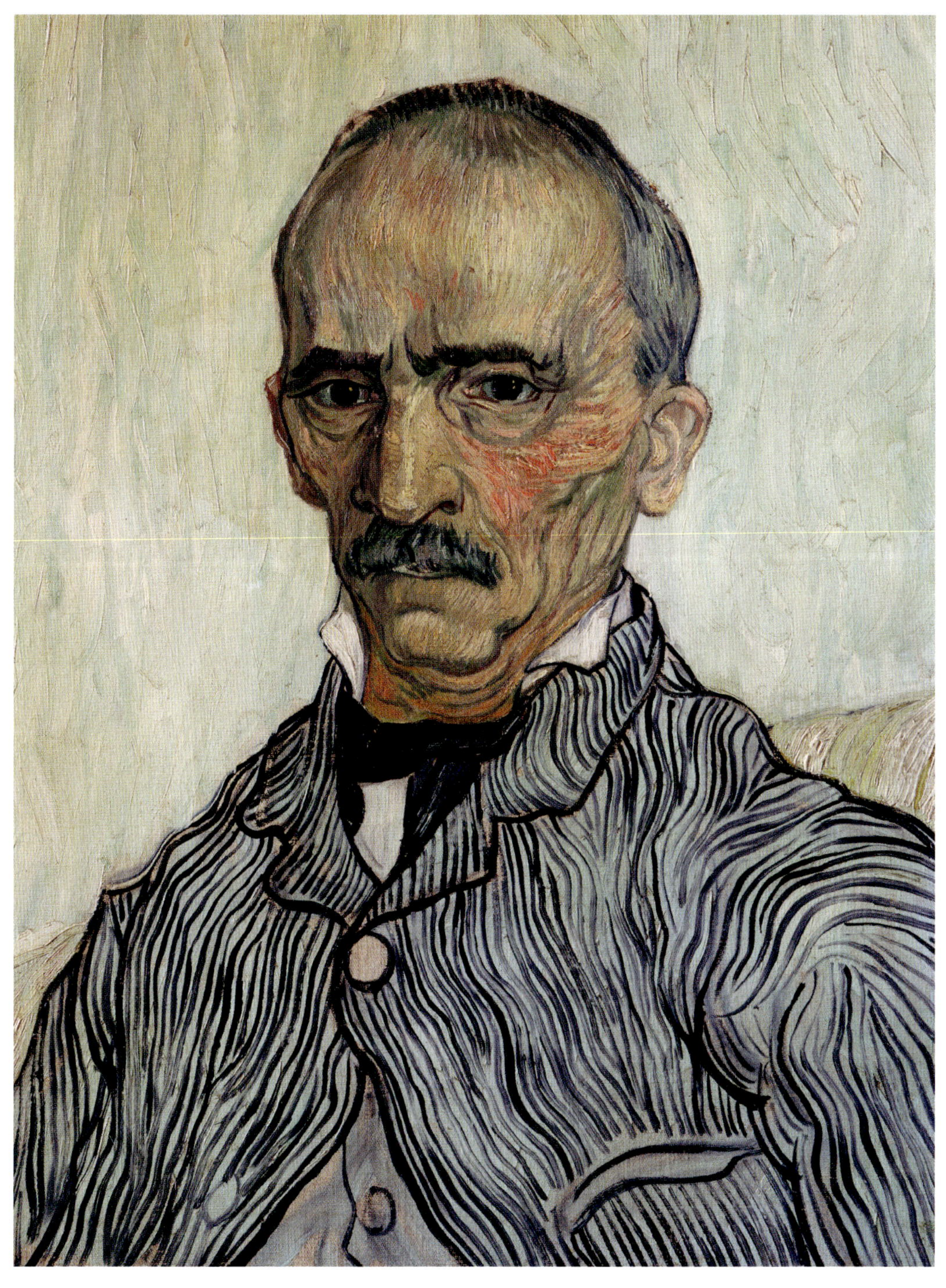

Fig. 9
Portrait of Superintendant Trabuc, September 1889, oil on canvas, 61 × 46 cm, Solothurn, Kunstmuseum Dübi-Müller-Stiftung

in Arles (Bouches-du-Rhône), undergoing treatment at the hospital of this city, has suffered from acute mania, with visual and auditory hallucinations that led him to self-mutilate by cutting off his ear. Today, he appears to have regained his reason, yet he feels neither the strength nor the courage to live freely and has himself requested admission to the house. Consequently, in view of all the foregoing, I consider that Mr Van Gogh is subject to epileptic attacks, widely spaced apart, and that he should be placed under prolonged observation within the establishment.

The First Days

The following day, Van Gogh discovered a daily routine governed by the house regulations. Rising times were set according to the season, between five and seven in the morning, with lights out between eight o'clock and nightfall. Lunch was served at half past ten, and dinner at five in the afternoon.
Half an hour each morning was devoted to personal hygiene. Clothing, sheets, and linens were to be kept clean and well maintained (fig. 10). Beards were trimmed once a week, or twice for higher-class boarders, and hair was cut monthly.
Work formed an integral part of the therapy. Men took care of the gardens, carried out cleaning duties, or attended to the lavatories, while women engaged in needlework. Walks and religious services were held outdoors on Saturdays, Sundays, and feast days, though the sexes remained separate, even in the chapel.
Leisure activities were offered: games, music, reading, billiards, or piano. Gambling was strictly forbidden.
Powdered or smoking tobacco was provided but allowed only during recreation hours, and solely for those already accustomed to its use.
Religious services were conducted by a chaplain, who could speak to patients only with the doctor's consent. The doctor carried out his visits under escort.
Prescribed medicinal preparations and treatments were dispensed by the local pharmacist in accordance with the rules of the Codex.
The diet was determined according to the boarder's class (fig. 11). No permission to make fires was granted.
Morning and evening prayers, as well as those before and after each meal, were recited aloud by a patient, an attendant, or a nun.
Visits from relatives were allowed only with medical approval, in the visiting room, the garden, or, exceptionally, in the bedrooms.
The introduction of food, alcohol, sharp objects, or newspapers deemed harmful was strictly prohibited.

The Encounter with the Sisters of Saint Joseph

Each morning, before dawn, the sisters would get up in the silence of the asylum to pray. At the heart of their lives, their spiritual practices, such as participation in liturgical services, imparted profound meaning to everything they did.
Upon leaving the chapel, they immersed themselves in a demanding daily routine of service, care, and humility. They took care of the patients with devotion, washing bodies, treating wounds, and soothing anxieties. Alternating between the roles of nurses and maternal figures, they slept in each dormitory of the women's ward.
They watched day and night over the dignity of those considered lost. Despite their modest means, they displayed immense patience, also overseeing all the

Fig. 10
Residents' kit approved in 1866

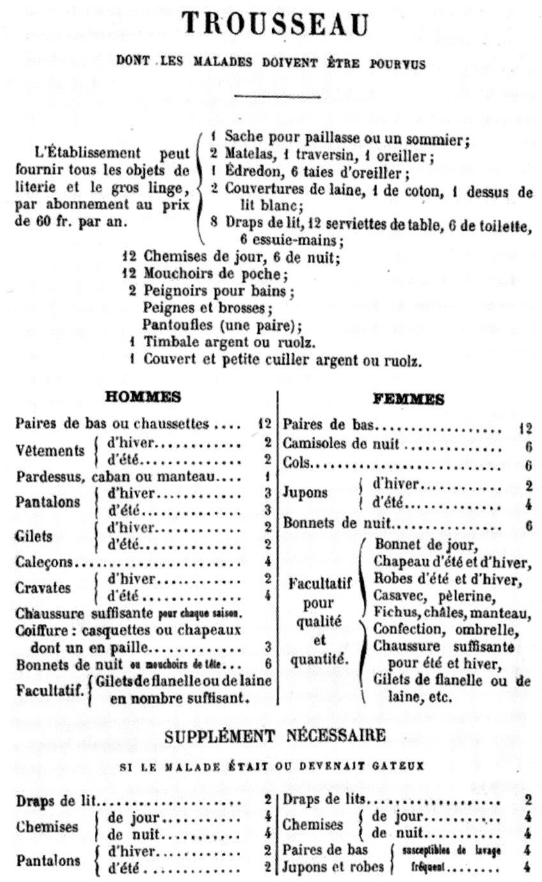

TROUSSEAU

DONT LES MALADES DOIVENT ÊTRE POURVUS

L'Établissement peut fournir tous les objets de literie et le gros linge, par abonnement au prix de 60 fr. par an.	1 Sache pour paillasse ou un sommier; 2 Matelas, 1 traversin, 1 oreiller; 1 Édredon, 6 taies d'oreiller; 2 Couvertures de laine, 1 de coton, 1 dessus de lit blanc; 8 Draps de lit, 12 serviettes de table, 6 de toilette, 6 essuie-mains;

12 Chemises de jour, 6 de nuit;
12 Mouchoirs de poche;
2 Peignoirs pour bains;
Peignes et brosses;
Pantoufles (une paire);
1 Timbale argent ou ruolz.
1 Couvert et petite cuiller argent ou ruolz.

HOMMES		FEMMES	
Paires de bas ou chaussettes	12	Paires de bas..................	12
Vêtements { d'hiver............	2	Camisoles de nuit	6
Vêtements { d'été.............	2	Cols...........................	6
Pardessus, caban ou manteau....	1	Jupons { d'hiver............	2
Pantalons { d'hiver............	3	Jupons { d'été..............	4
Pantalons { d'été..............	3	Bonnets de nuit................	6
Gilets { d'hiver............	2	Facultatif pour qualité et quantité. { Bonnet de jour, Chapeau d'été et d'hiver, Robes d'été et d'hiver, Casavec, pèlerine, Fichus, châles, manteau, Confection, ombrelle, Chaussure suffisante pour été et hiver, Gilets de flanelle ou de laine, etc.	
Gilets { d'été.............	2		
Caleçons.......................	4		
Cravates { d'hiver............	2		
Cravates { d'été.............	4		
Chaussure suffisante pour chaque saison.			
Coiffure : casquettes ou chapeaux dont un en paille............	3		
Bonnets de nuit ou mouchoirs de tête...	6		
Facultatif. { Gilets de flanelle ou de laine en nombre suffisant.			

SUPPLÉMENT NÉCESSAIRE

SI LE MALADE ÉTAIT OU DEVENAIT GATEUX

Draps de lit....................	2	Draps de lits..................	2
Chemises { de jour..........	4	Chemises { de jour..........	4
Chemises { de nuit..........	4	Chemises { de nuit..........	4
Pantalons { d'hiver...........	2	Paires de bas { susceptibles de lavage	4
Pantalons { d'été............	2	Jupons et robes { fréquent........	4

Fig. 11
Residents' weekly menu

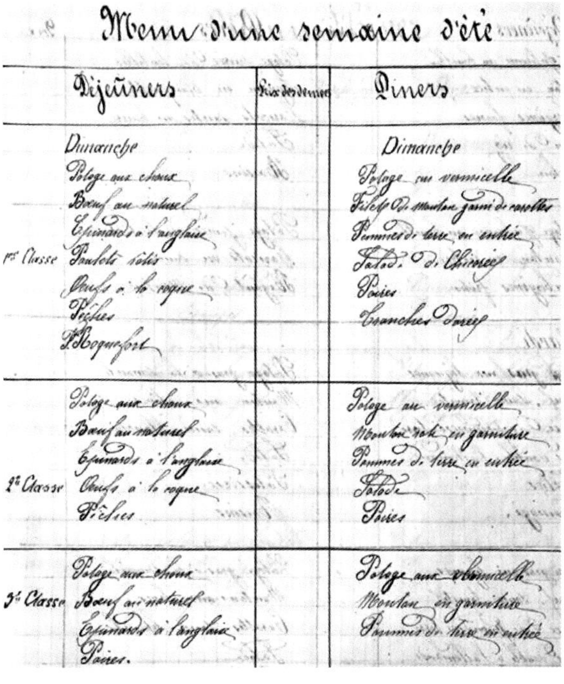

Menu d'une semaine d'été

	Déjeuners	Prix des denrées	Dîners
1re Classe	Dimanche Potage aux choux Bœuf au naturel Épinards à l'anglaise Poulets rôtis Oeufs à la coque Pêches Roquefort		Dimanche Potage au vermicelle Filets de mouton garni de carottes Pommes de terre en entrée Salade de chicorée Poires Tranches d'oies
2e Classe	Potage aux choux Bœuf au naturel Épinards à l'anglaise Oeufs à la coque Pêches		Potage au vermicelle Mouton rôti en garniture Pommes de terre en entrée Salade Poires
3e Classe	Potage aux choux Bœuf au naturel Épinards à l'anglaise Poires.		Potage au vermicelle Mouton en garniture Pommes de terre en entrée

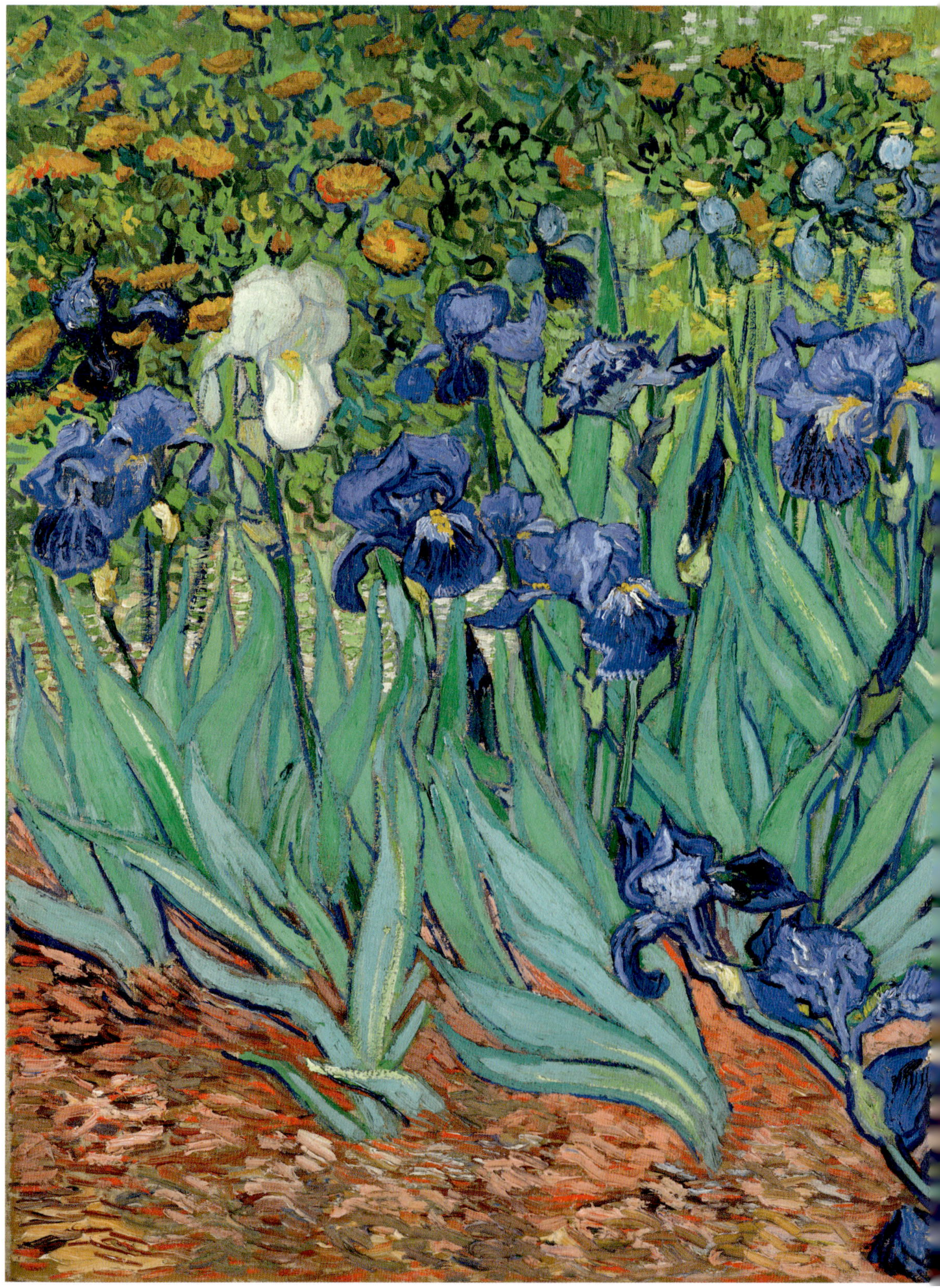

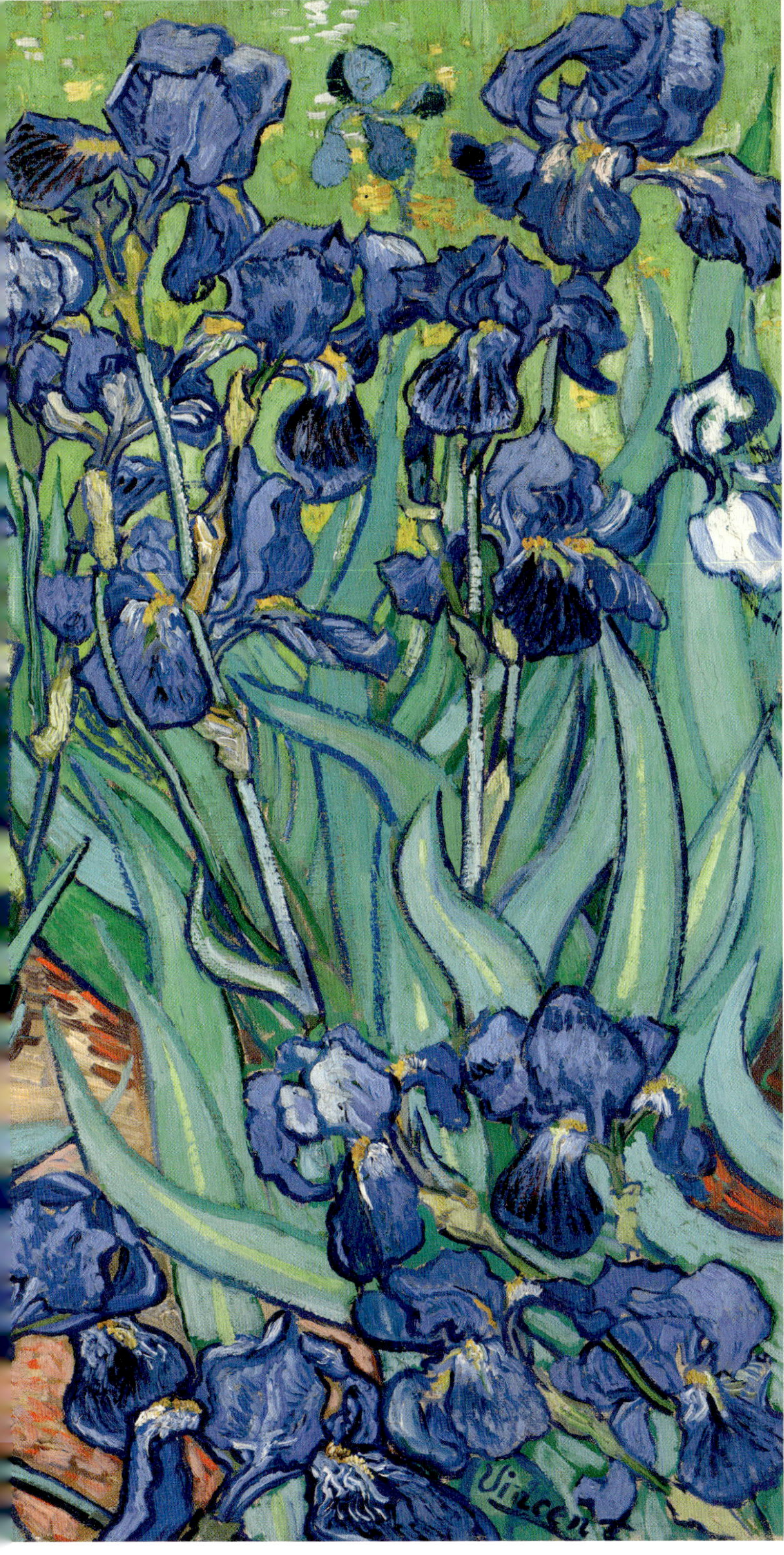

Fig. 12
Irises, May 1889, oil on canvas, 71 × 93 cm, Los Angeles, Getty Museum

material operations of the establishment. Kitchen work, cleaning, laundry, sewing, dormitory supervision—nothing escaped their care. And for those entrusted with it, they took charge of the education of orphaned or rescued girls. Life was harsh, the days long, yet there was no complaint. Their strength derived from the community, their faith, and the certainty that every action was a form of living charity.

At a time when the secular staff were poorly trained and often unstable, the comforting and steadfast presence of the sisters provided an essential balance to the asylum. They were seldom seen, rarely heard, yet their silent work sustained Saint-Paul de Mausole. They were its discreet, profoundly humane soul, and without them nothing would endure. The day after his admission, Vincent wrote his first letter to his brother.

> My dear Theo,
> Thank you for your letter. You are quite right to say that Mr Salles has been exemplary throughout this, and I owe him a great debt. I wanted to tell you that I believe I did well to come here [...].
> I have two other paintings in progress—purple irises and a lilac bush, both motifs taken from the garden (fig. 12).

Executed during a period of great psychological instability, these irises carry a strong symbolic and emotional charge: their rhizomes lend permanence to the plant, while the solitary white iris amidst the purple flowers may represent the solitary self, his experience of marginality, and the green of the foliage the hope of a springtime renewal.

The curves of the stems and the liveliness of the petals evoke, through them, a dynamic world. Their fluidity conveys a sense of vital energy despite the physical and psychological confinement the painter describes in his letters. Finally, the softened colours reflect a moment of tranquillity.

Van Gogh maintained an intense relationship with mysticism, showing compassion and love for humanity, without adhering to dogma, despite his criticisms of his native Church: "I am a painter, yet in truth I remain profoundly a man of faith."

The reading of the painting can be spiritual. Van Gogh was well acquainted with Christian symbols: the iris is often associated with the Virgin Mary, as is the lily. The white lily evokes purity, the purple iris the suffering of Mary at the foot of the cross; their blade-shaped leaves suggest the sword piercing the heart foretold in the Gospel of Luke ("And a sword will pierce your own soul also"); the majestic spring bloom symbolises renewal and hope after hardship. This bed of irises became, for Van Gogh, an allegorical work evoking his solitude, his suffering, his faith, his compassion, and the restorative support offered by Saint-Paul Asylum, Sister Épiphane, and Dr Peyron.

Devi Ormond, a painting restorer at the Getty Museum in Los Angeles, conducted research in 2024 to determine whether the current purple hues of the irises are those originally applied by Van Gogh. Chemical imaging studies revealed that the colour used for the flowers comprised a mixture of geranium lake (a red pigment), cobalt blue, and ultramarine blue. Over time, exposure to light had faded the geranium lake, leaving only the blues visible on the petals. Each spring, the original purple reappears in the irises growing at Saint-Paul from the rhizomes dating back to Van Gogh's time.

On May 22, 1889, his friend, the postman Roulin, encouraged Van Gogh by letter:

> Continue your paintings; you are in a beautiful region, the soil is very well tended. You will find a great difference in the cultivation there; you will not see gardens resembling cemeteries as in Arles. With the goodwill you possess, you will succeed in creating very fine paintings. You live in the garden of Bouches-du-Rhône; the models that nature provides will not be lacking.

Van Gogh was captivated by the enchanting beauty of the park around the pond. The incessant ballet of life that surrounded him fascinated and inspired him—the simple insects and other small creatures, the dense bushes, the most rustic of flowering plants, the majestic pines of the park—all gave him the impression of a nature almost untamed (figs. 13-19).

Van Gogh produced several paintings with biblical themes. Eugène Delacroix's *The Good Samaritan* (figs. 20 and 21) alludes, on one hand, to the New Testament parable employed by Christ to illustrate his conception of "love for one's neighbour", and, on the other hand, may also serve as

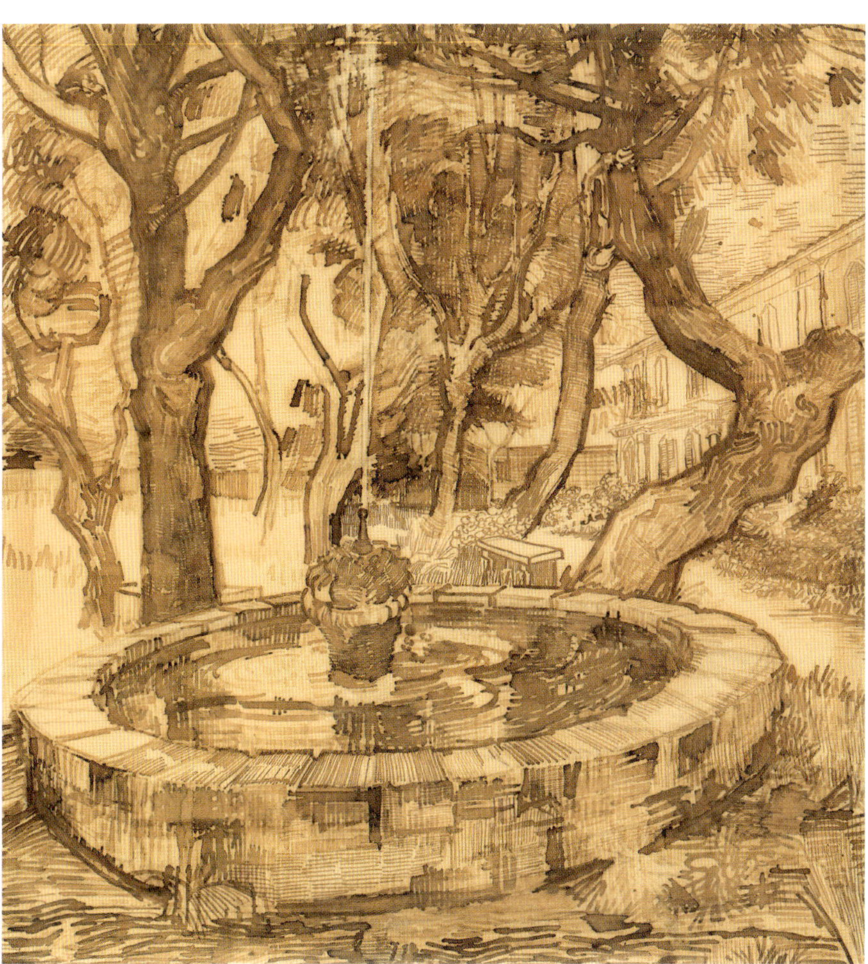

Fig. 13
Fountain in the Garden of the Asylum, May-June 1889, chalk, pen and Indian ink on paper, 49.8 × 46.3 cm, Amsterdam, Van Gogh Museum

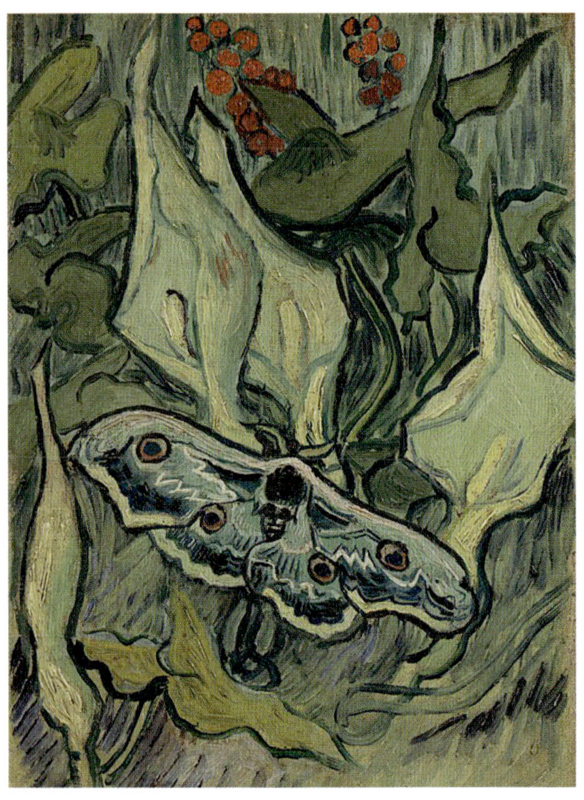

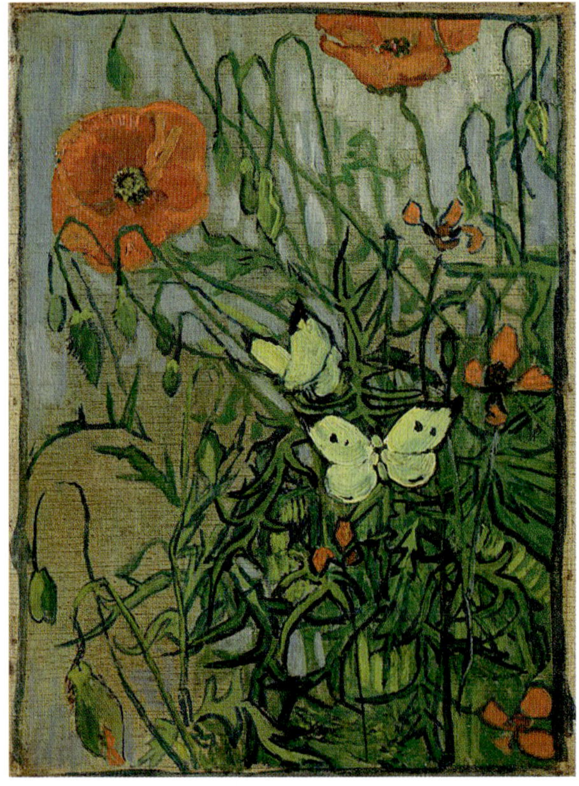

Fig. 14
Butterflies, May-June 1889, oil on canvas, 33.5 × 24.5 cm, Amsterdam, Van Gogh Museum

Fig. 15
Butterflies and Poppies, May-June 1889, oil on canvas, 35 × 25.5 cm, Amsterdam, Van Gogh Museum

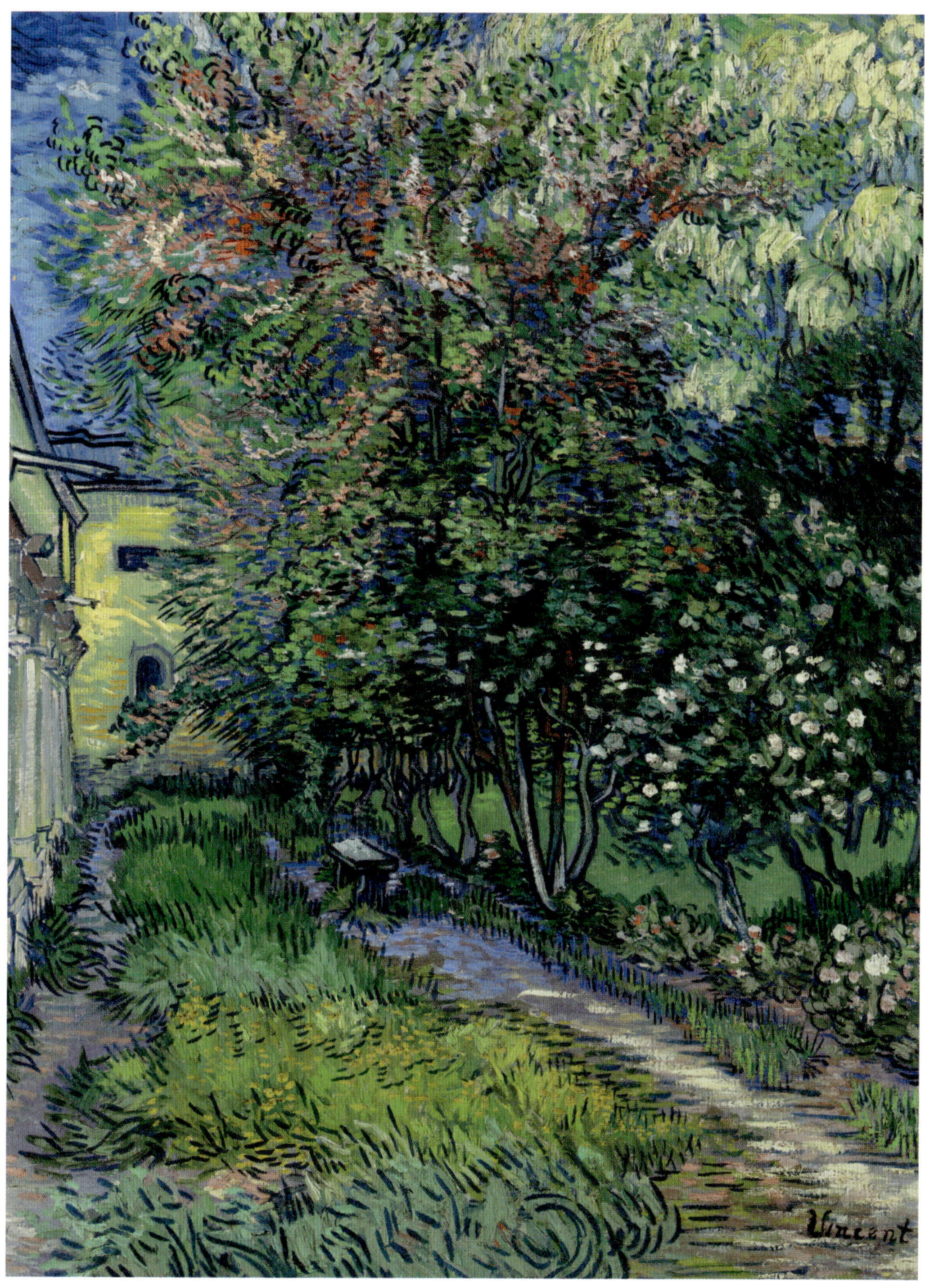

Fig. 16
The Garden of the Asylum at Saint-Rémy, May 1889, oil on canvas, 95 × 75.5 cm, Otterlo, Kröller-Müller Museum

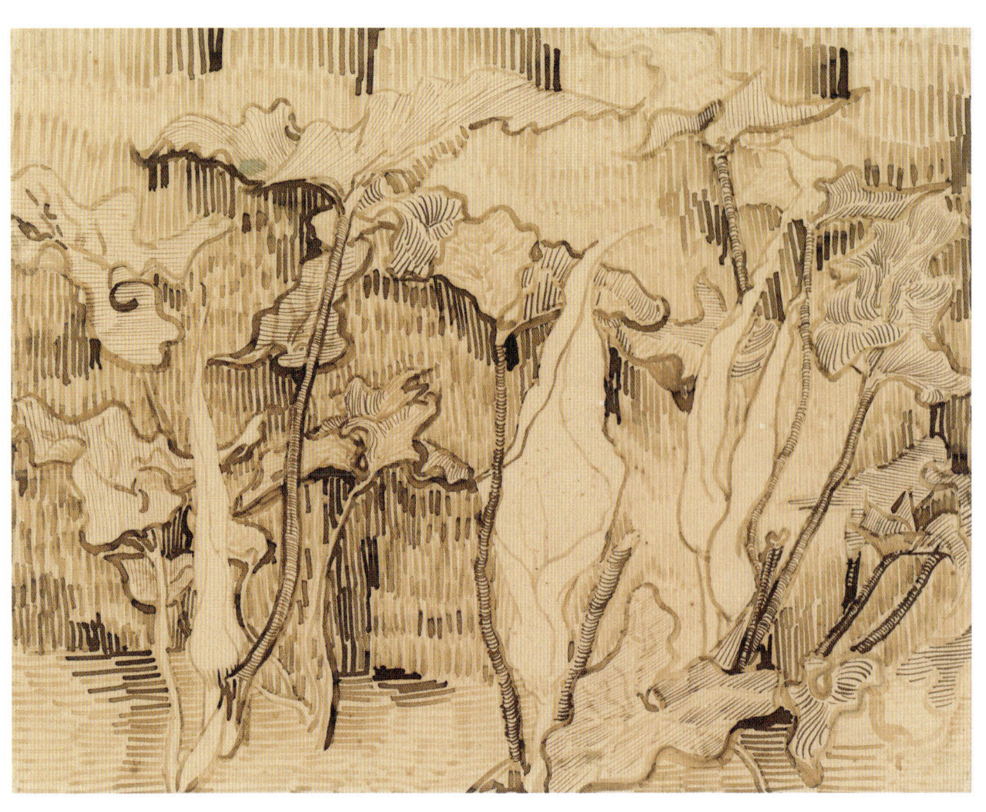

Fig. 17
Arums, May-June 1889, pen and Indian ink on paper, 31.4 × 41.3 cm, Amsterdam, Van Gogh Museum

Fig. 18
Undergrowth, July 1889, oil on canvas, 73 × 92.3 cm, Amsterdam, Van Gogh Museum

Fig. 19
Meadow in the Garden of Saint-Paul Hospital, May 1890, oil on canvas, 65 × 81 cm, London, National Gallery

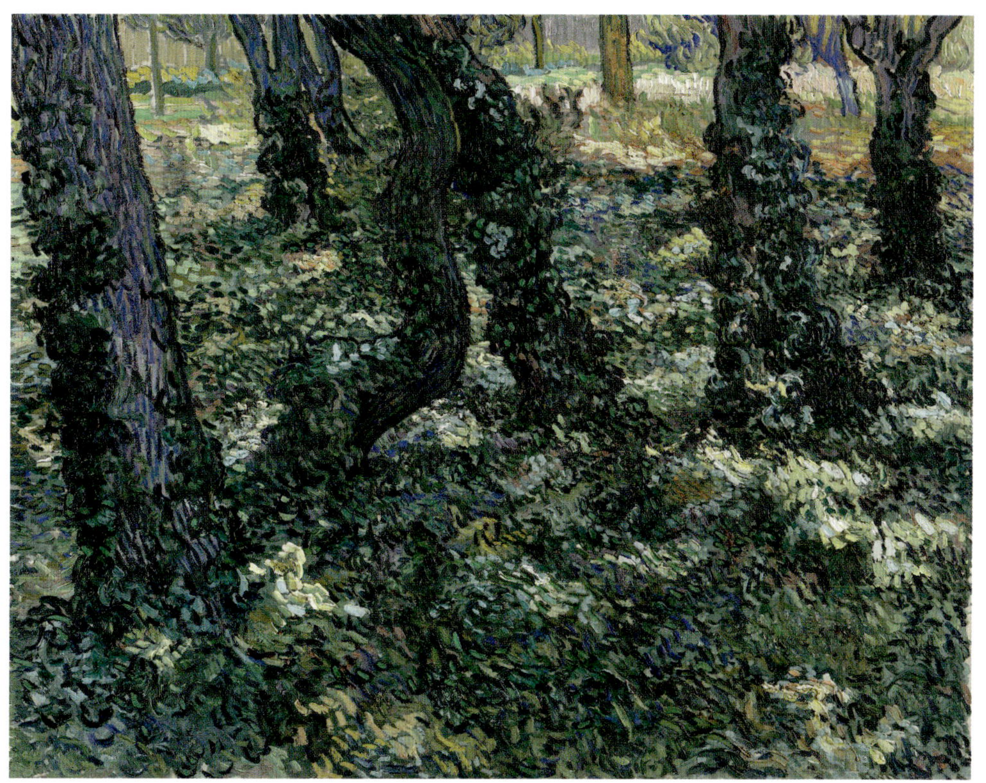

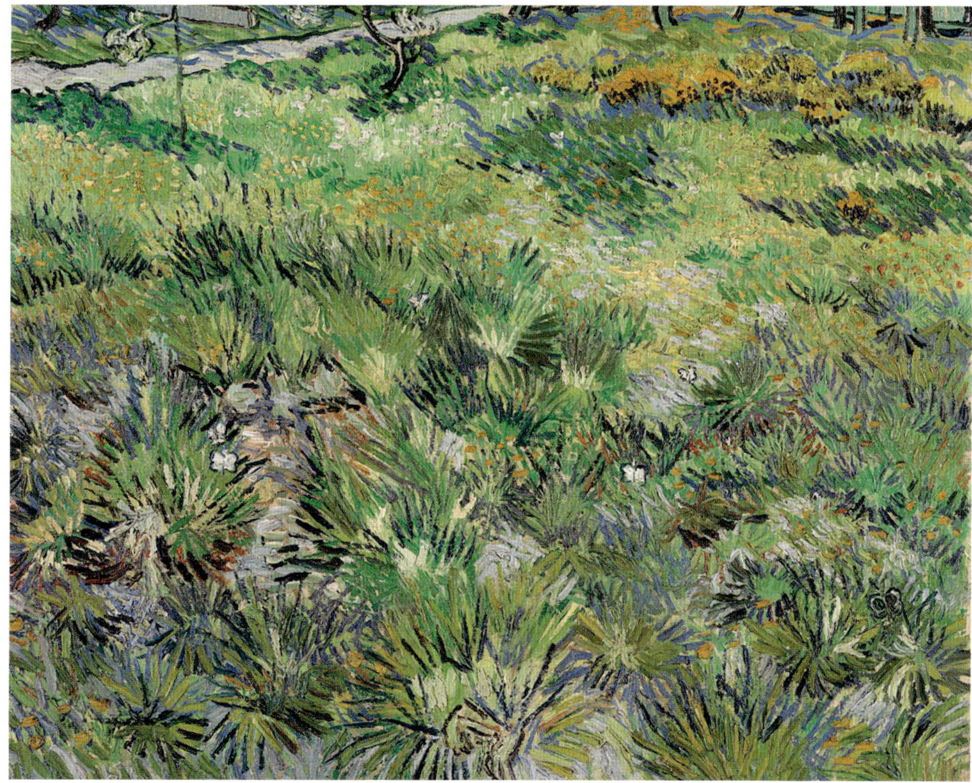

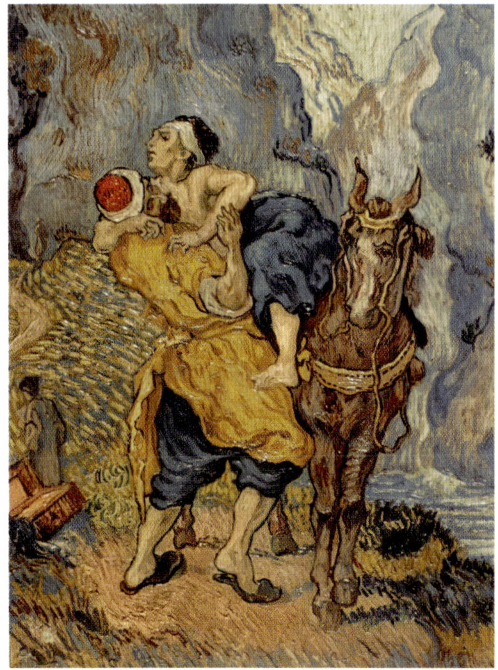

Fig. 20
The Good Samaritan (after Delacroix), May 1890, oil on canvas, 73 × 59.5 cm, Otterlo, Kröller-Müller Museum

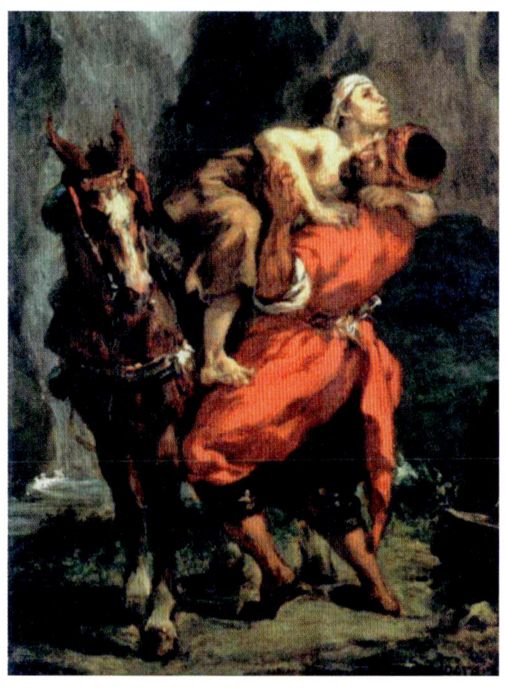

Fig. 21
Eugène Delacroix, *The Good Samaritan*, 1849, oil on canvas, 36.8 × 29.8 cm, private collection

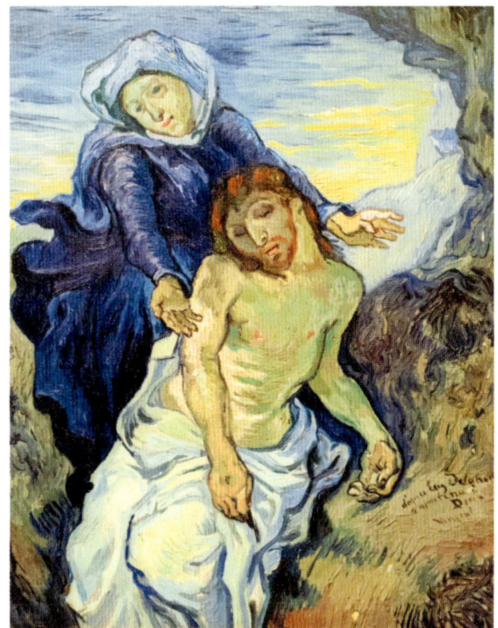

Fig. 22
Pietà, ca. 1890, oil on canvas, 41.5 × 34 cm, Vatican City, Vatican Museums, Collection of Modern and Contemporary Art

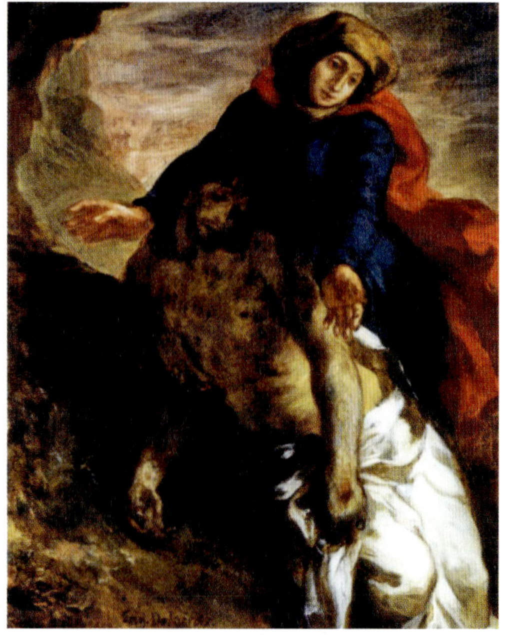

Fig. 23
Eugène Delacroix, *La Pietà*, 1850, oil on canvas, 35.6 × 27 cm, Oslo, National Museum of Art, Architecture and Design

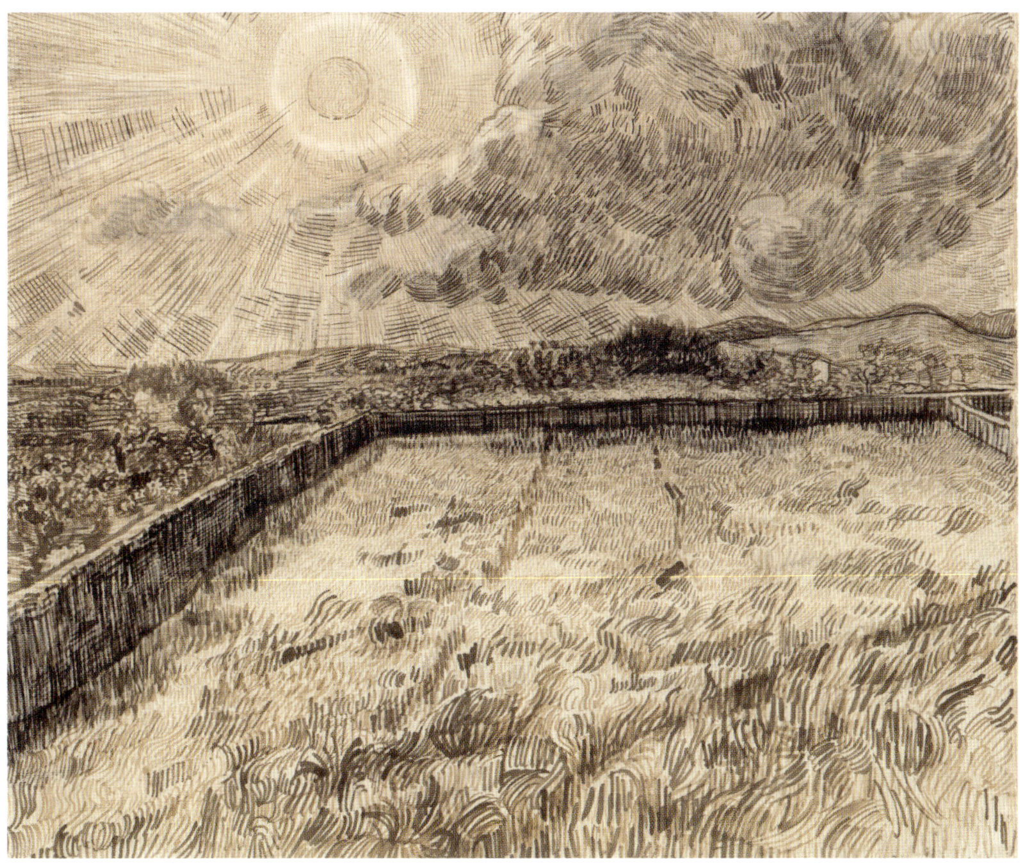

Fig. 24
Enclosed Wheat Field with Sun and Cloud, May-June 1889, black chalk and reed pen, ink and opaque white watercolour on laid paper, 47.5 × 56.6 cm, Otterlo, Kröller-Müller Museum

a tribute to Theo's unwavering support, or to Van Gogh's own desire to bring aid to others (figs. 22-23).
His work had no religious function, as it was not intended for prayer or worship. Although not classified as sacred art, it conveys a certain sacrality in the background. This spirituality would intertwine in other paintings that glorify the surrounding nature of Saint-Paul, celebrating its beauty and grandeur. Indeed, the landscapes transcend mere reality. While they still convey his emotions through twisted cypresses and swirling stars, they also suggest a profound spiritual connection between nature and human beings (figs. 29, 30, and 31).
The light emanating from *The Starry Night*, as well as from real or imagined suns, acquires a deep significance, symbolising the infinite: "Through the window with iron bars, I perceive a Van Goyen-like perspective in which I see the sun rise every morning in its glory."
Among the fourteen depictions of the wheat field that fascinated him from his room, the reaper evokes death in a biblical manner (fig. 25).

> The work is going fairly well—I am struggling with a canvas begun a few days before my indisposition, a reaper;

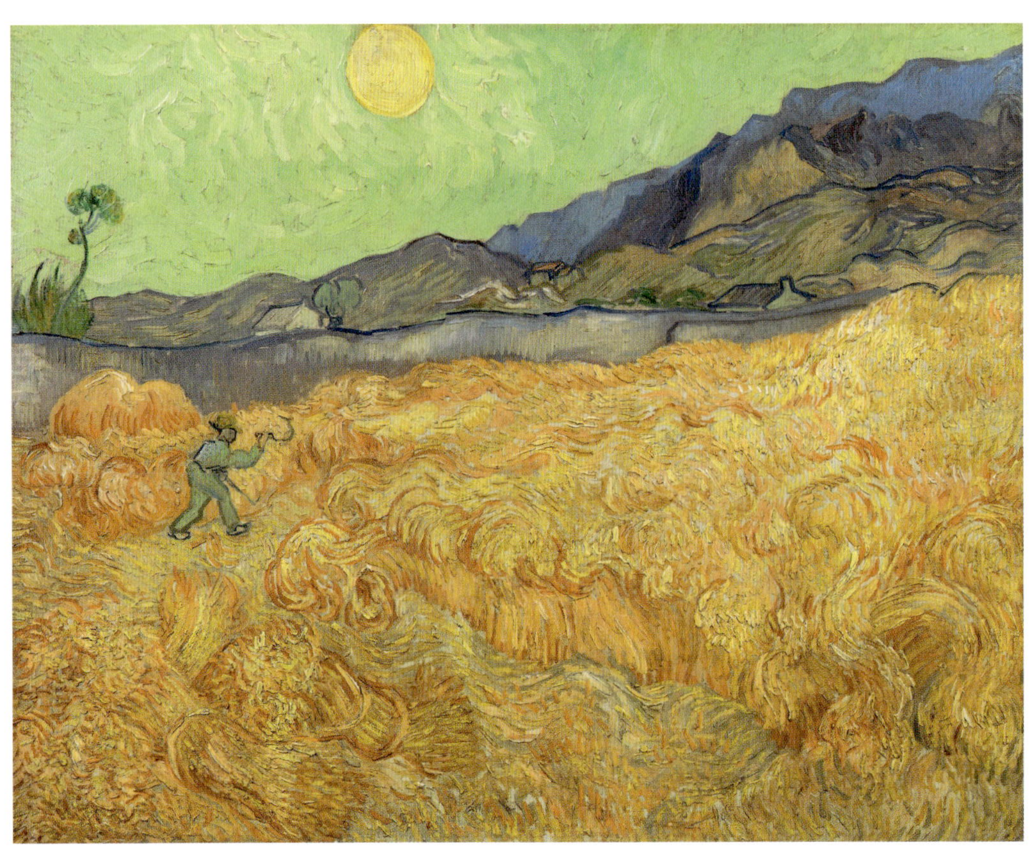

Fig. 25
Wheatfield with a Reaper, September 1889, oil on canvas, 73.2 × 92.7 cm, Amsterdam, Van Gogh Museum

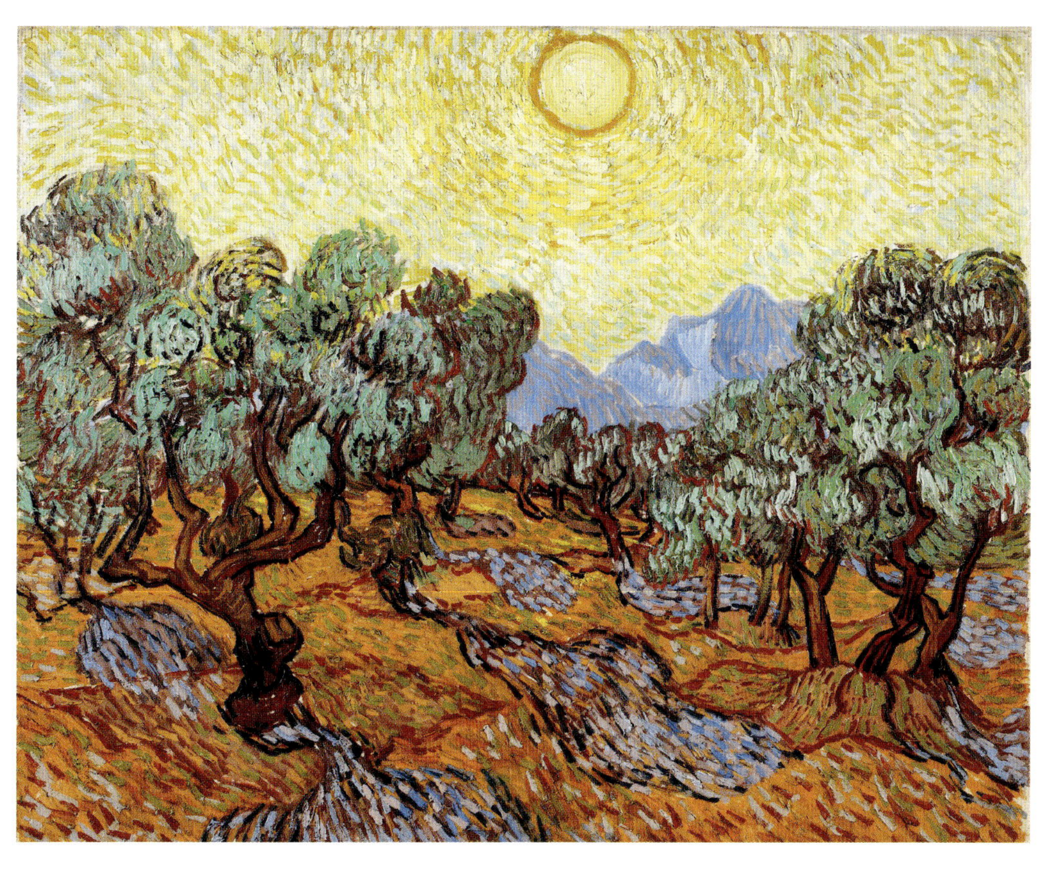

Fig. 26
Olive Trees with Yellow Sky and Sun, novembre 1889, oil on canvas, 73 × 92 cm, Minneapolis, Minneapolis Institute of Art

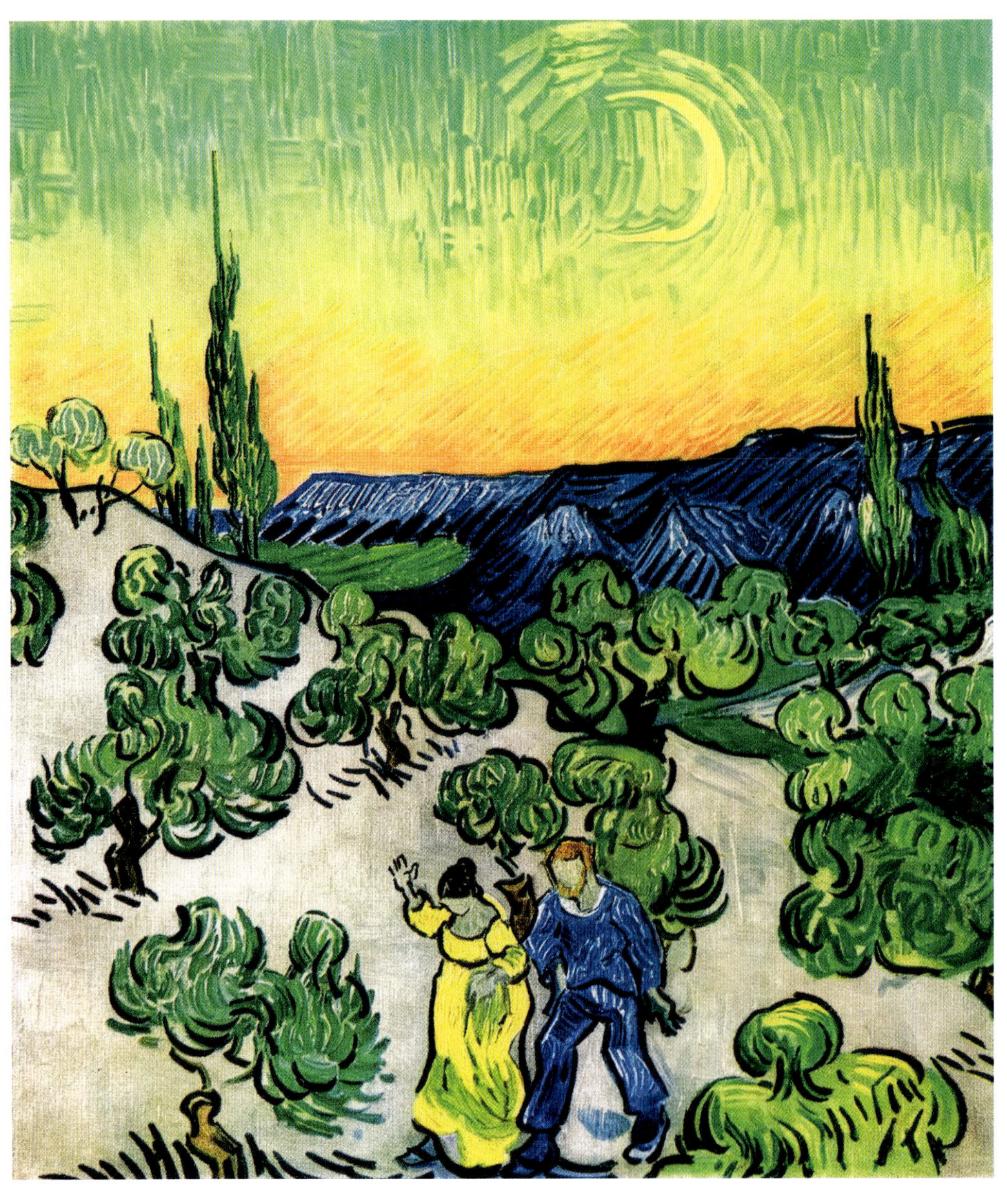

Fig. 27
Walk at Twilight, May 1890, oil on canvas, 49.5 × 46.5 cm, São Paulo, Museo de Arte de São Paulo

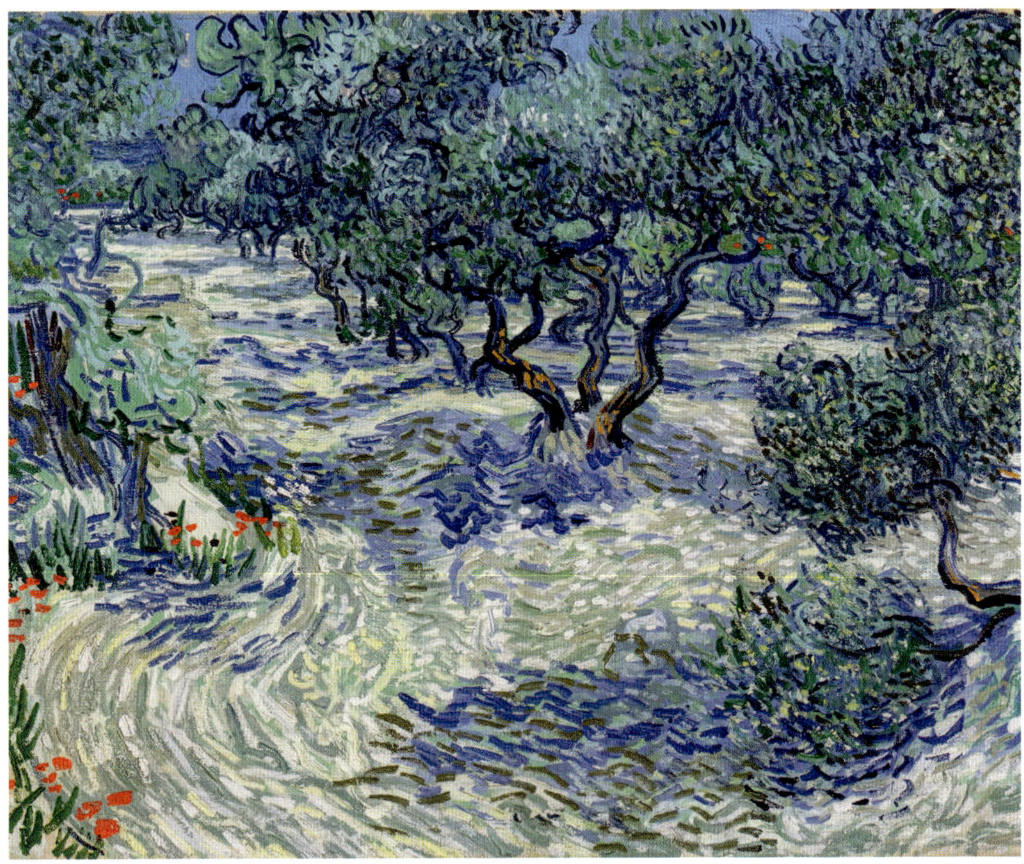

Fig. 28
Olive Trees, June 1889, oil on canvas, 73 × 93 cm, Kansas City, Nelson-Atkins Art Museum

> the study is entirely yellow, terribly thickly painted, but the motif was beautiful and simple. In this reaper—I saw a vague figure struggling like a devil in the height of summer to complete his task—I saw the image of death, in which humanity itself becomes the wheat to be reaped. It is, if you like, the opposite of the sower I had attempted previously. Yet in this death there is nothing sorrowful; it takes place in full light, with a sun flooding everything with a light of pure gold.

Later he wrote:

> The reaper is finished… it is an image of death as the great book of nature presents it to us—but what I sought was "almost smiling". It is all yellow, except for a line of violet hills, of a pale and blond yellow, which I saw thus through the iron bars of a little shed.

When he painted several olive groves surrounding the asylum without depicting Christ, he was likely aware of their connection to the Passion narrative on the Mount of Olives. Yet he visualised it in his mind and attributed to colour—particularly blue and yellow—the role of expressing his mystical emotions (figs. 26, 27, and 28). His faith evolved towards a sacred vision of the world, guiding his philosophy and actions. Rather than adhering to traditional

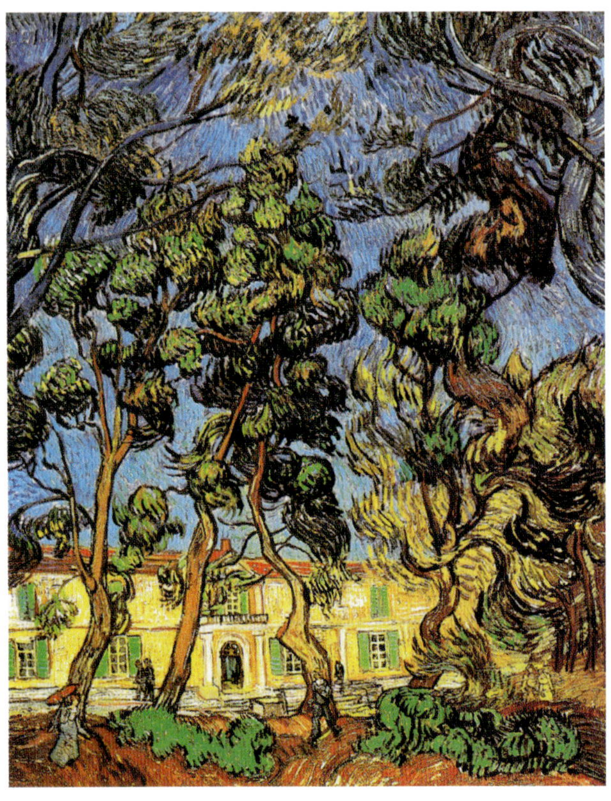

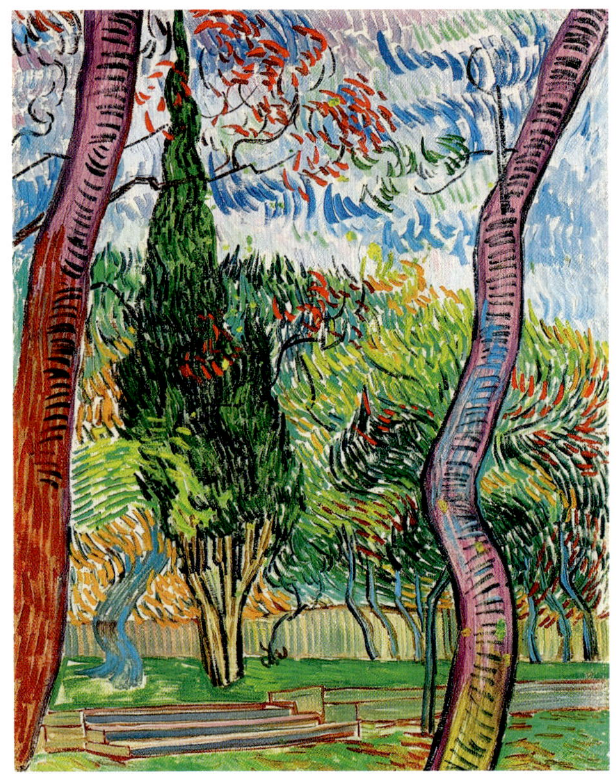

Fig. 29
Trees in the garden of the Hospital Saint-Paul, October 1889, oil on canvas, 90 × 73 cm, Los Angeles, The Armand Hammer Collection

Fig. 30
The Garden of Saint-Paul Hospital, October 1889, oil on canvas, 65 × 40 cm, Geneva, private collection

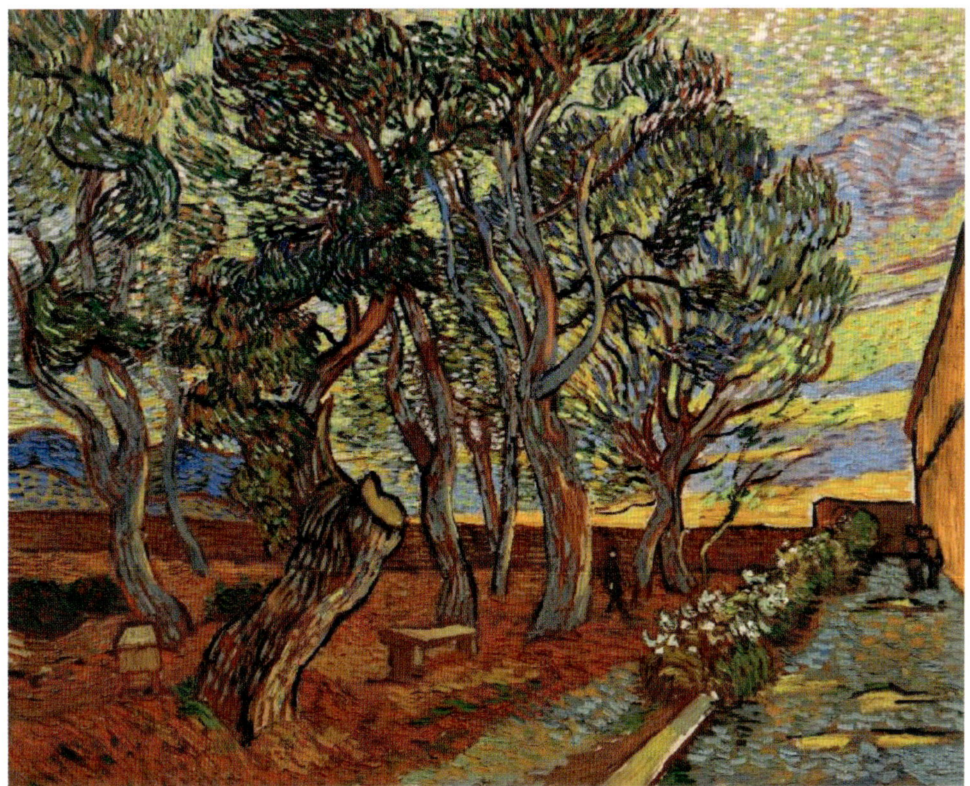

Fig. 31
Garden of the Asylum, November 1889, oil on canvas, 72 × 91 cm, Amsterdam, Van Gogh Museum

religion, his paintings and letters to Theo reveal his concern for others and for nature: "I have a terrible need of—shall I say the word—religion, so I go outside at night to paint the stars..."
In accordance with this personal need, the park of Saint-Paul served as a haven of peace, a bulwark against the inner and outer torments that haunted him (figs. 29, 30, and 31). Marcel Bonnet had identified the outdoor locations painted by Van Gogh, first accompanied by the attendant Poulet, then alone with Dr Peyron's permission, about an hour's walk from the hospital. Among these were the local farmhouses, whose old names remain dear to the people of Saint-Rémy, including the "Mas de Saint-Paul", depicted in this painting (fig. 32).
Van Gogh's painting intensely expresses his emotions through vibrant or sombre colours. Yet he never compromised the pursuit of beauty and artistic harmony. Nature, beautiful and diverse, became a profound spiritual language, offering refuge and inspiration.

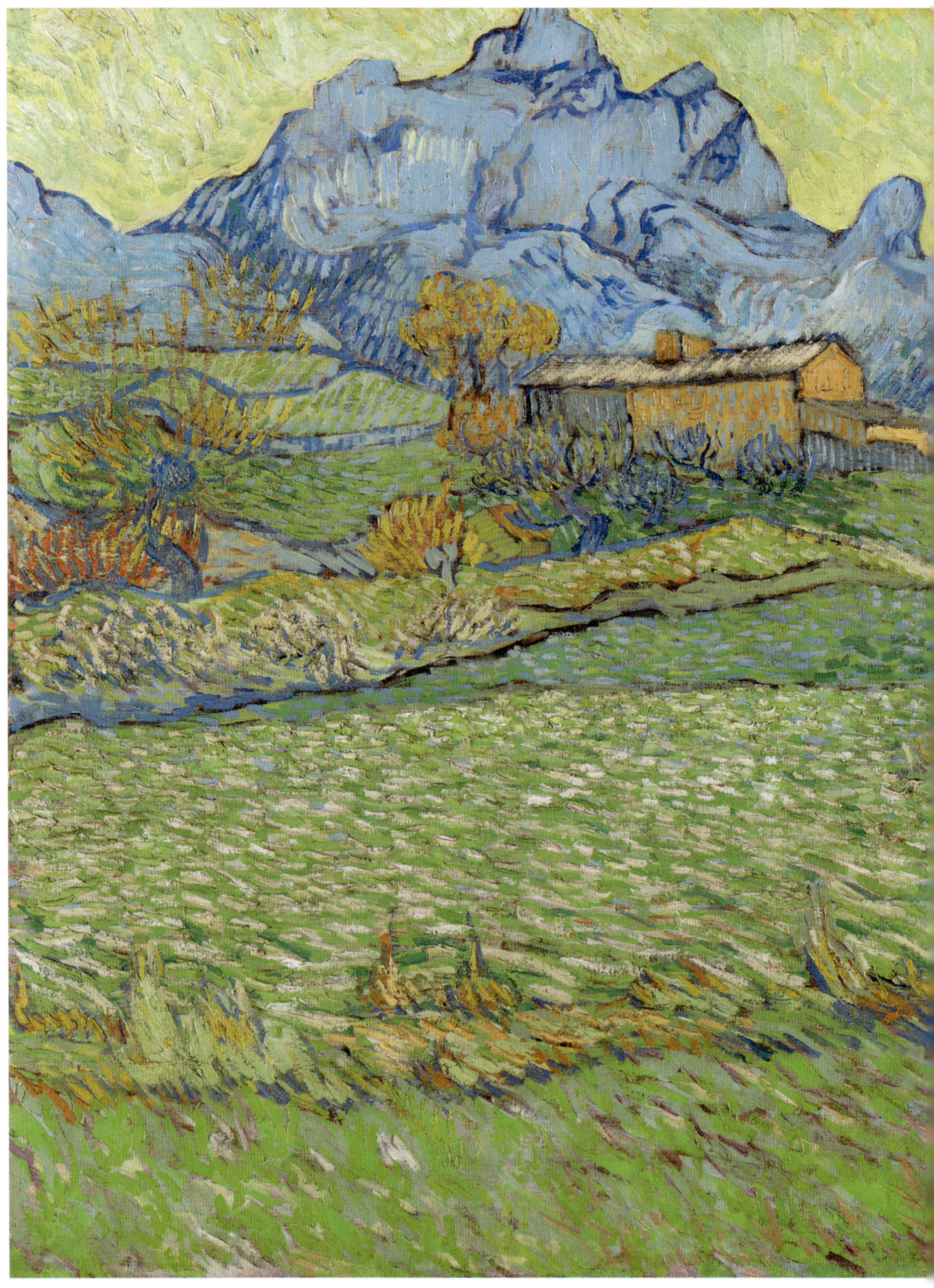

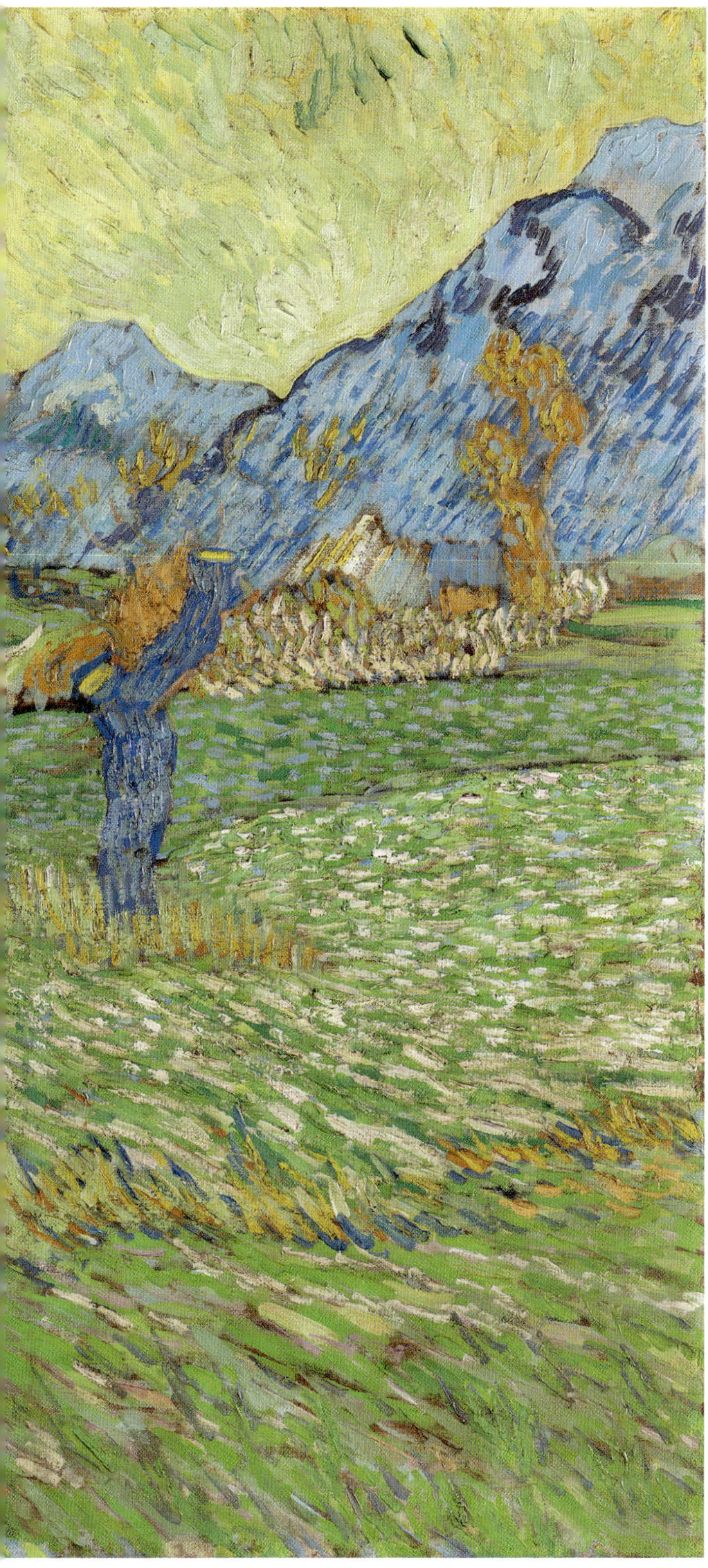

Fig. 32
A Meadow in the Mountains: Le Mas de Saint-Paul, December 1889, oil on canvas, 73 × 91.5 cm, Otterlo, Kröller-Müller Museum

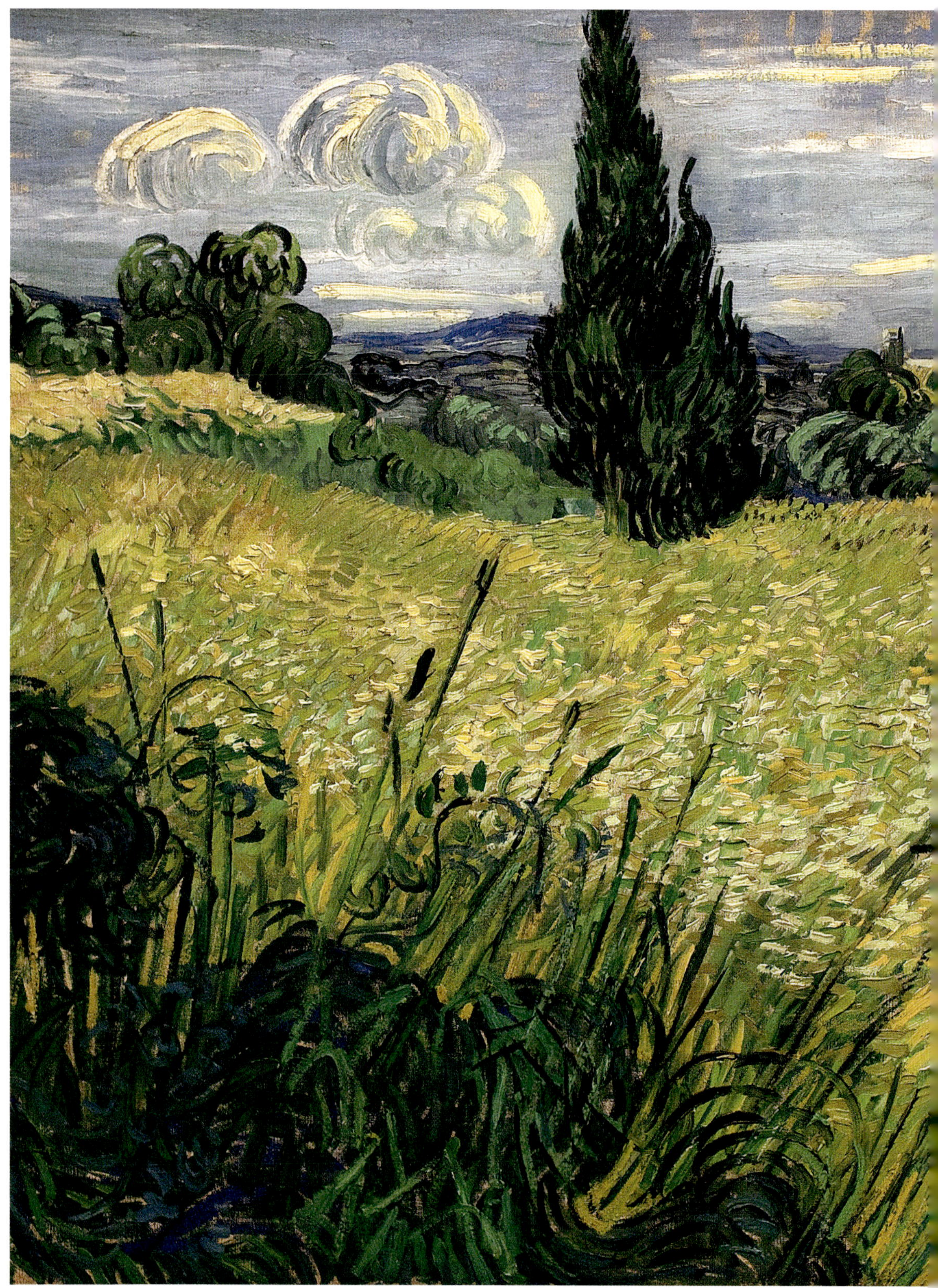

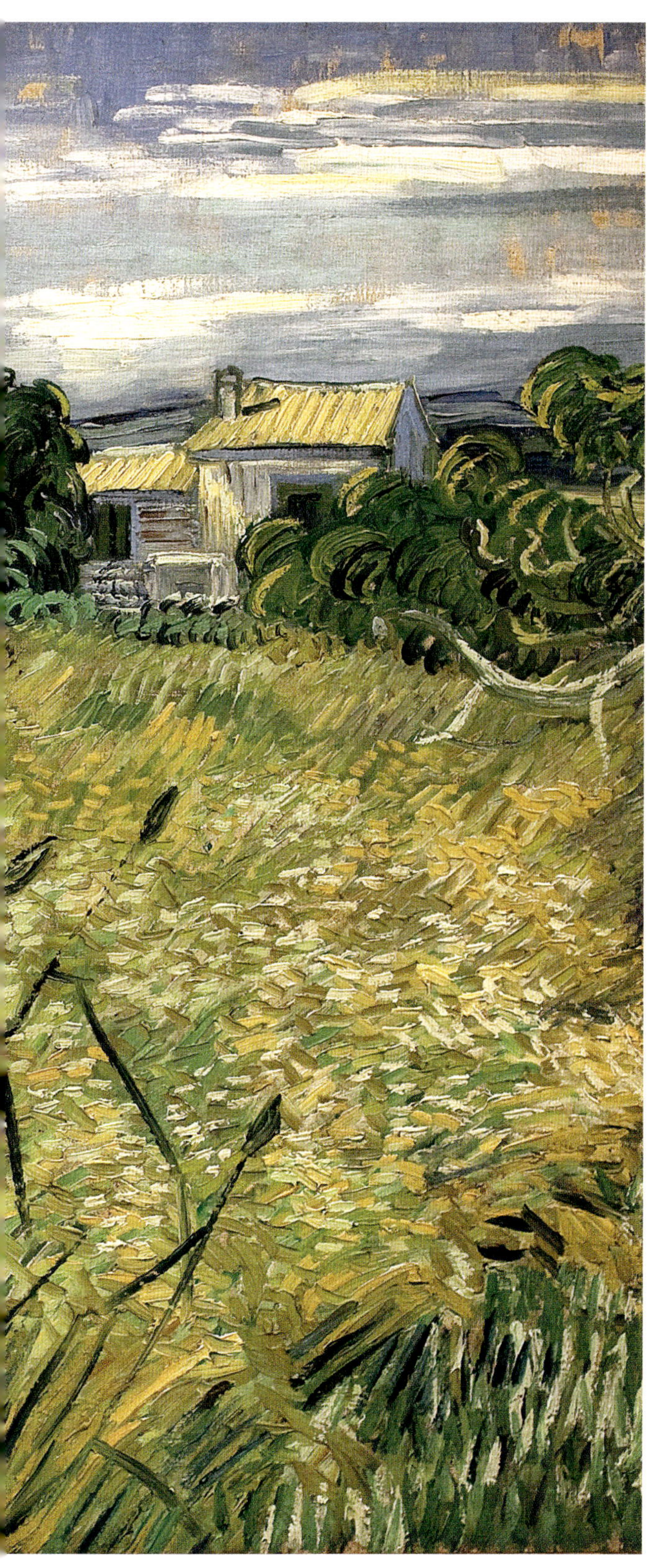

Fig. 33
Green Wheat Field with Cypress, June 1889, oil on canvas, 73.5 × 92.5 cm, Prague, Narodni Galerie

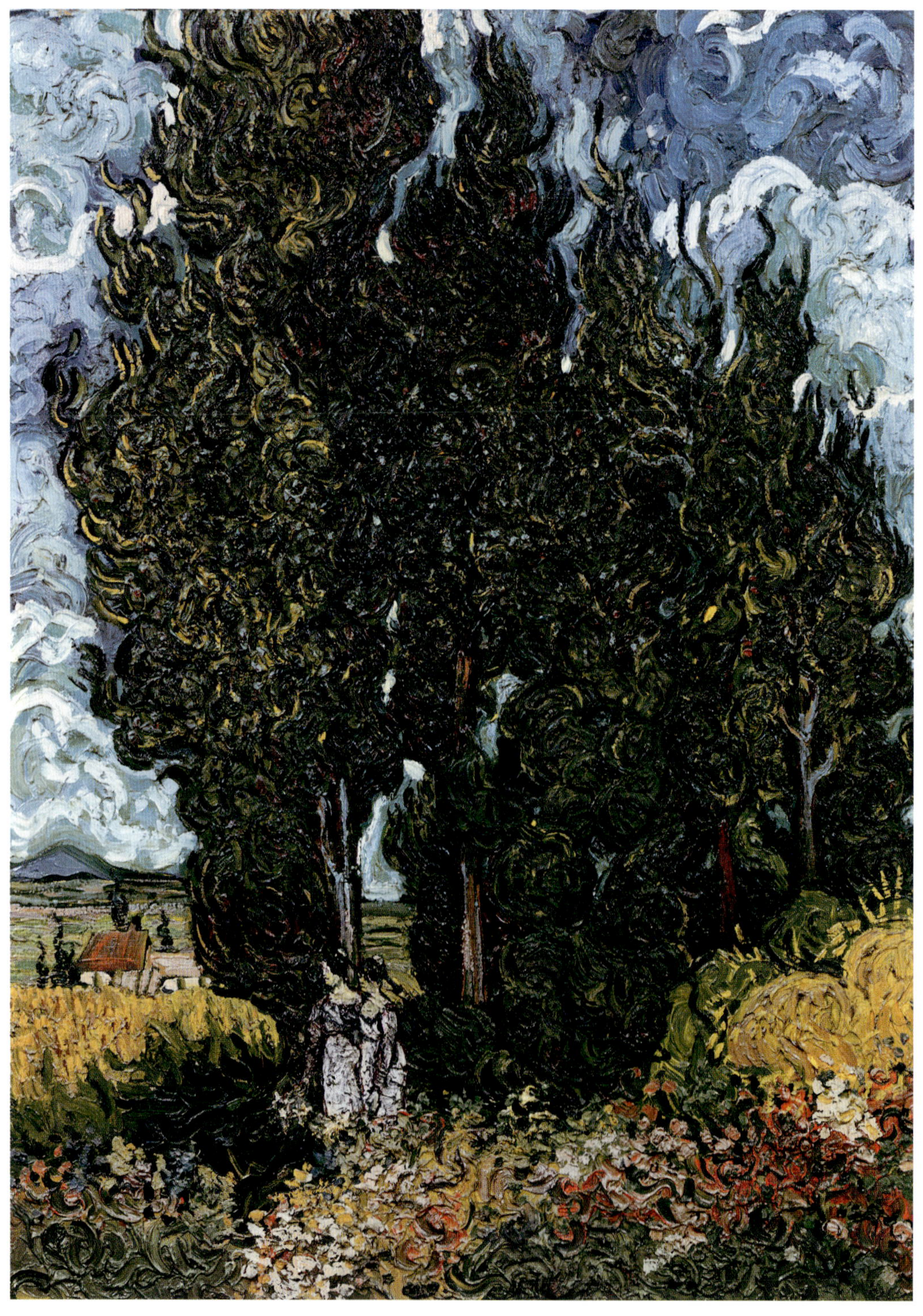

Fig. 34
Cypresses with Two Women, June 1889, oil on canvas, 92 × 73 cm, Otterlo, Kröller-Müller Museum

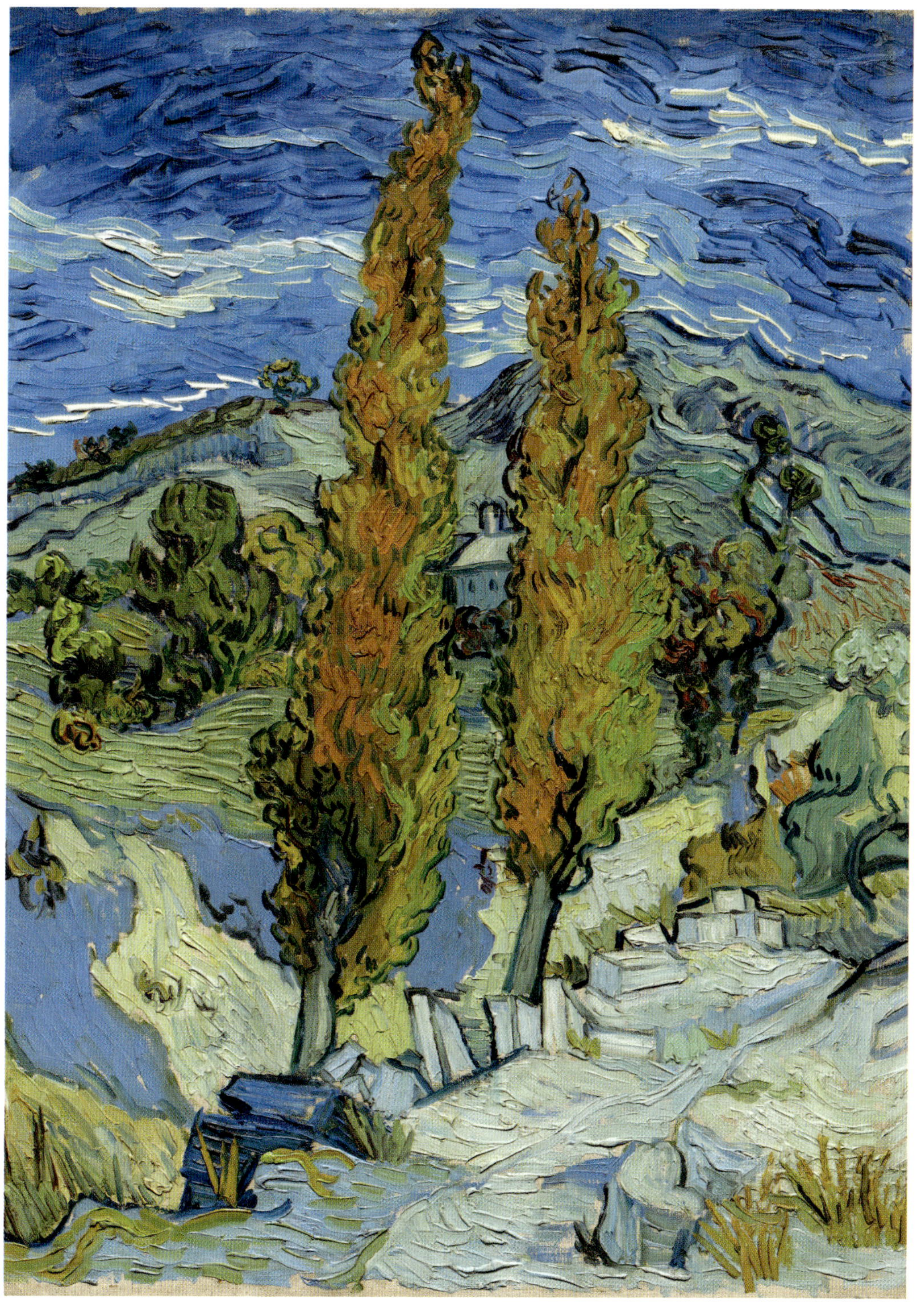

Fig. 35
Two Poplars in the Alpilles near Saint-Rémy, October 1889, oil on canvas, 61 × 45 cm, Cleveland, Cleveland Museum of Art

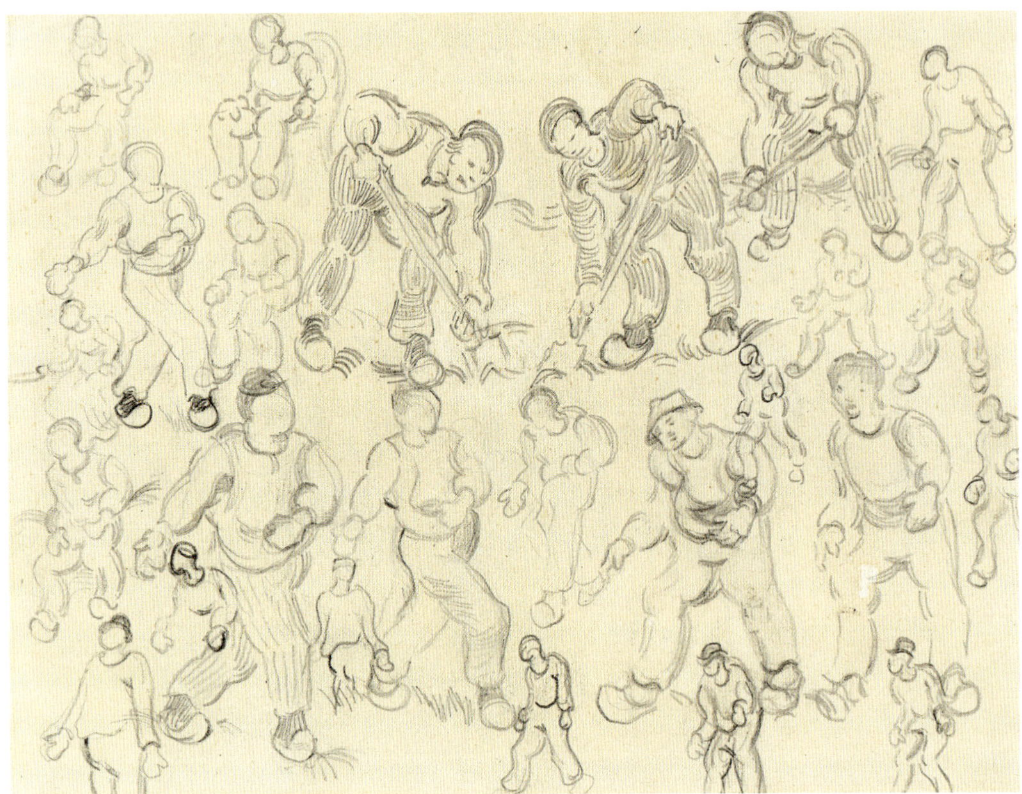

Fig. 36
Figure sketches, March-April 1890, ink on paper, private collection

The artist devoted himself to depicting with precision the lofty, majestic cypresses, the vast undulating wheat fields, the sturdy, fruit-laden olive trees, and the imposing Alpilles rising on the horizon (figs. 33, 34, and 35).

"Is it not almost a true religion, what these Japanese teach us—so simple and living in nature as if they themselves were flowers?" he wondered. And he reflected: "One cannot study Japanese art, it seems to me, without becoming much gayer and happier, and it brings us back to nature despite our education and our work in a world of convention."

Van Gogh exalted the figures, portraits, and silhouettes of simple and modest workers, often present in his landscapes. Indeed, he remained fascinated by the beauty of rural life, the humility and sincerity of the peasants. He accorded them respect and esteem through his enduring tributes. The same holds for his moving interpretations of Millet's nourishing engravings (figs. 36, 37, 38, and 39).

"The more I think about it, the more I feel that there is nothing truly more artistic than loving people," he declared. "And in a painting, I wish to convey something comforting, like music. I would like to depict men or women with that certain *je ne sais quoi* of the eternal, once symbolised by the halo, which we now seek through the very radiance and vibration of our colours."

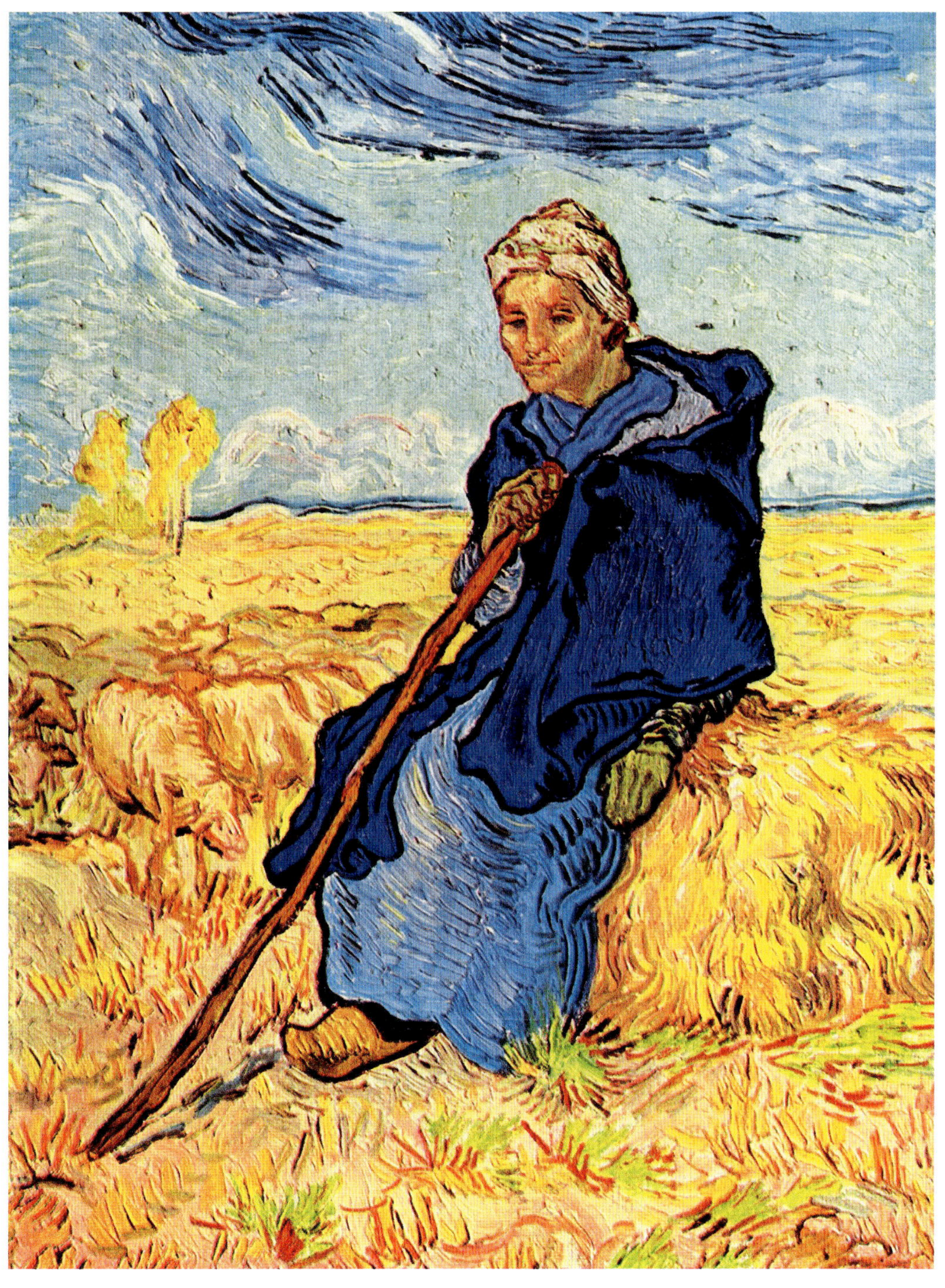

Fig. 37
The Shepherdess (after Millet), November 1889, oil on canvas, 53 × 41.5 cm, Tel Aviv, Mr and Mrs Moshe Mayer Collection on deposit at the Tel Aviv Museum

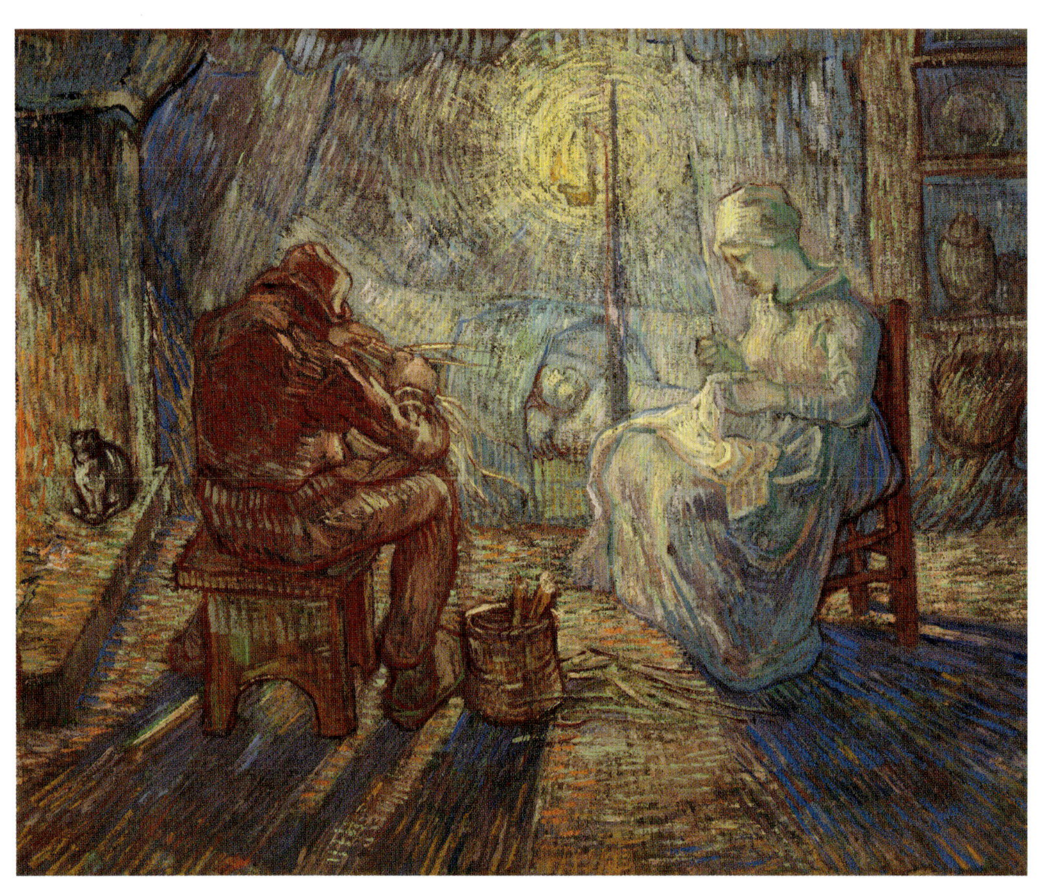

Fig. 38
Evening (after Millet), October 1889, oil on canvas, 74 × 93 cm, Amsterdam, Van Gogh Museum

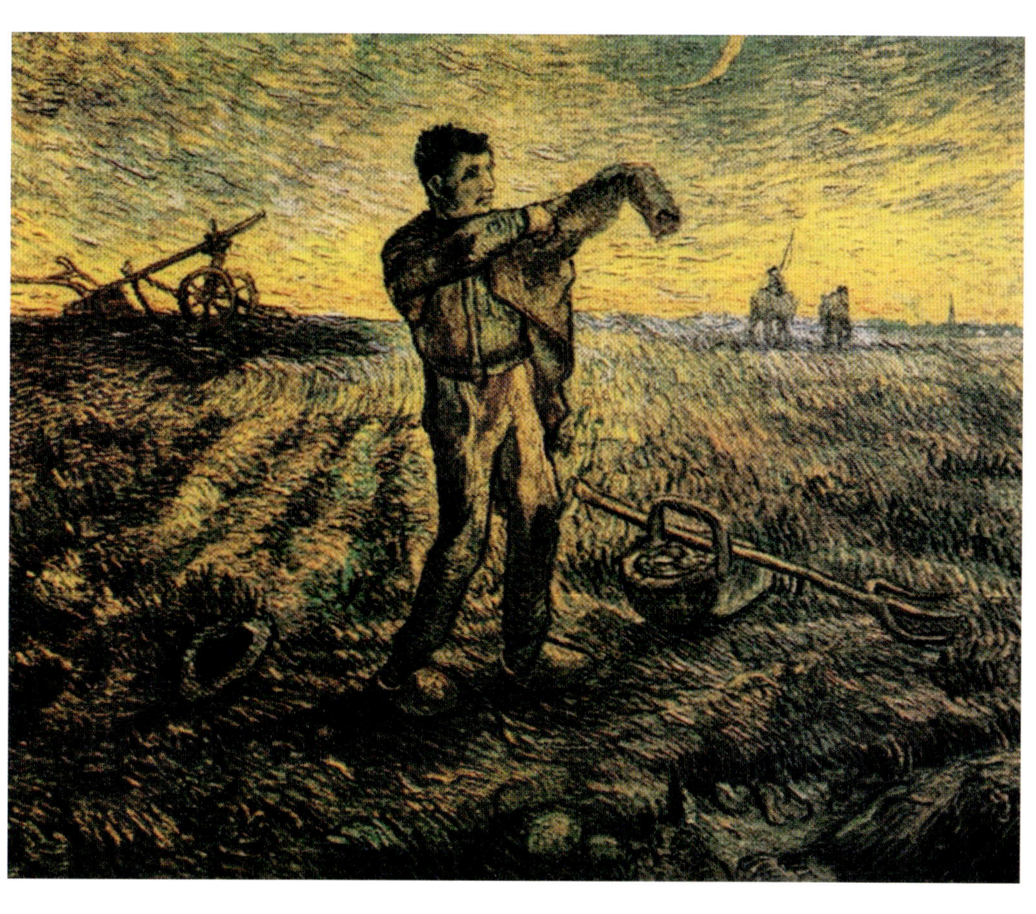

Fig. 39
The End of the Day (after Millet) November 1889, oil on canvas, 72 × 92 cm, Komaki, Ménard Art Museum

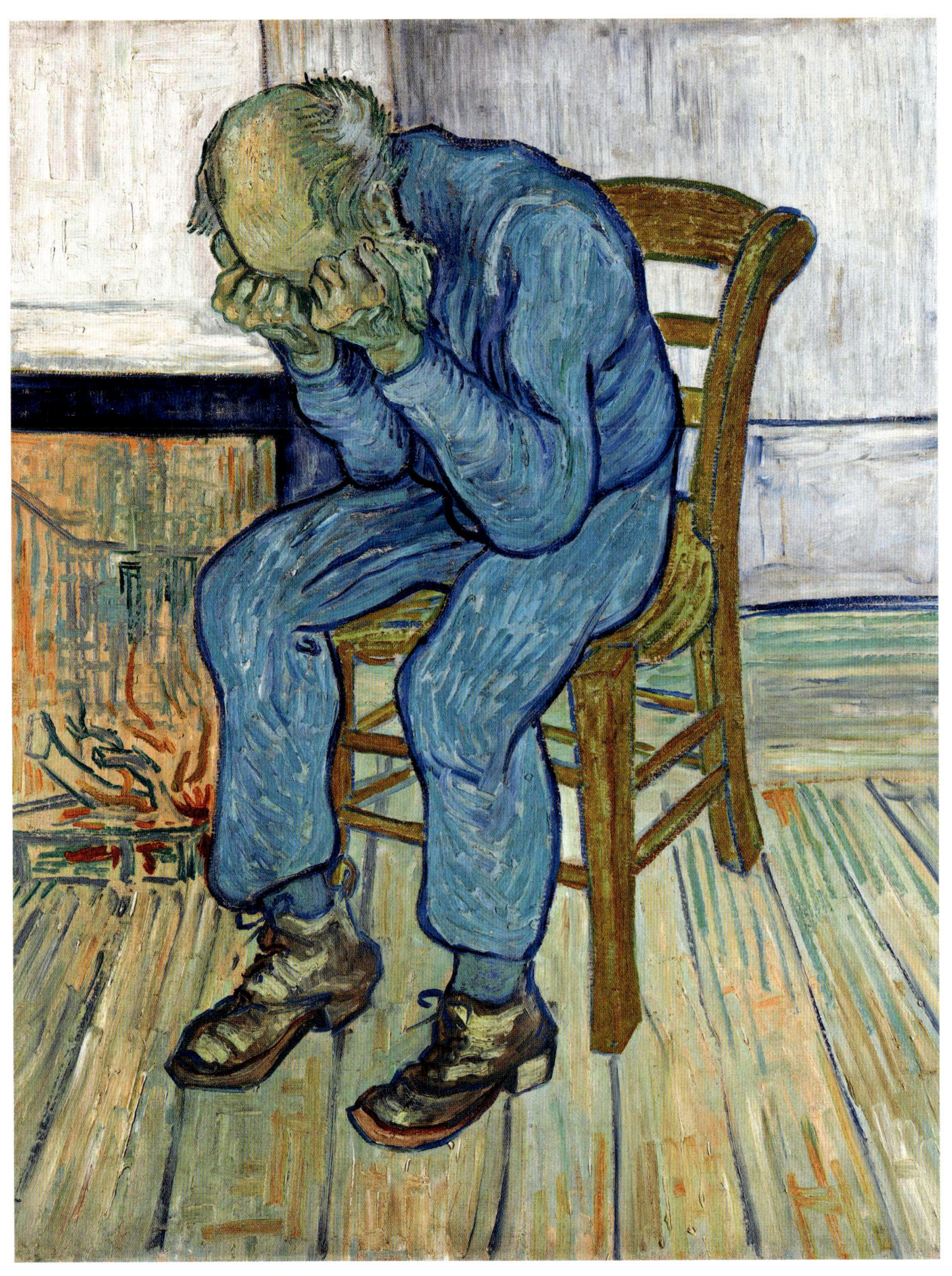

Fig. 40
At Eternity's Gate, April-May 1890, oil on canvas, 81 × 65 cm, Otterlo, Kröller-Müller Museum

Medical Approach

A psychiatrist listens, questions, rephrases, exchanges, perceives, analyses, translates, and records what he has heard and believes he has understood, in order to lead to diagnostic hypotheses and therapeutic proposals. For Van Gogh, the sources are his biography, his letters, and the medical correspondence of the time. They reveal precious clues about his personality, his knowledge, his philosophy, his mental state, and his lived experience.

Collection of Symptoms
The following were identified:

1. **From the biography:**
   Having been a "replacement child" for his elder brother of the same name, who had been stillborn one year before his own birth.
   A hypersensitivity provoking emotional crises, relational difficulties, and adaptation disorders.
   Episodes marked by confusion, absences, terrifying auras, strangeness, and automatisms.
   Overconsumption of absinthe with distressing withdrawal periods.
   A temperamental personality: irritable, sensitive, whimsical, melancholic, and excitable.
   A disappointing love life, marked by repeated and painful failures.
   Behaviours more or less maladaptive, leading to ruptures and rejections (the Goupil gallery, the Borinage, Drenthe, Arles).
   Periods of exaltation and hyperactivity.
   Periods of creative inhibition lasting from a few days to several weeks.
   Self-mutilation, suicide attempts, and ultimately his death by suicide at the age of thirty-seven.

2. **From his letters to family and close friends:**
   - Cognitive functions:
     No signs of impairment were detectable. On the contrary, he displayed dazzling intelligence.
   - Sadness to melancholy:
     "Except for much melancholy, nightmares no longer torment me";
     "At present, the melancholy is less acute";
     "At times, I am left with rather heavy inner despair".
   - Anxiety:
     "For the sufferings of anxiety are not amusing";
     "So as not to be taken by surprise by anxiety and dread";
     "It is very difficult for me to write as my mind is disturbed. I take advantage of a brief interval... it is to be expected that these crises will return".
   - Phases of exaltation and delirium, with a predominance of auditory-verbal and visual hallucinations:
     "I do not believe that my madness would be that of persecution, since my feelings in a state of exaltation...";
     "I assure you that in these strange days many things seem amusing to me because my brain is agitated";
     "The derangement has seized me once more, a rather violent attack of exaltation and delirium";
     "I observe in others that they, too, have heard in their crises strange sounds and voices, and that things likewise appear to them in a state of flux";
     "Whilst in my delirium so many beloved things are stirred";
     "There is a man who shouts and

speaks as I do for a fortnight at a time, believing he hears voices and words in the echo of the corridors"; "The intolerable hallucinations have now ceased, reduced merely to simple nightmares"; "When one suffers greatly, one sees everyone at a great distance. The voices seem to come from afar. The people I see appear different from what they are".

- Moments of delirium with post-delirious insight:
  He describes original, sometimes delusional thoughts, but they are brief. He questions his experiences of depersonalisation, aware of his disorder. He is neither psychotic nor schizophrenic.
  Some thoughts occur during phases of mood excitation or periods of alcohol withdrawal:
  "I have crises as a superstitious person might, and I am visited by confused and atrocious religious ideas";
  "During these crises, it seemed to me that all I imagined was reality".
- Crises suggestive of loss of consciousness with secondary amnesia:
  "It is astonishing to fear nothing and yet to be unable to recall anything"; "I have had four major crises in which I had no idea whatsoever of what I was saying or doing, not to mention that previously I fainted three times without plausible reason and retained not the slightest memory of what I felt".
- Phases of return to a normal state:
  "I feel entirely normal now. My health is good. I believe Dr Peyron is right when he says I am not mad, for my thoughts are perfectly normal, even clearer than before".

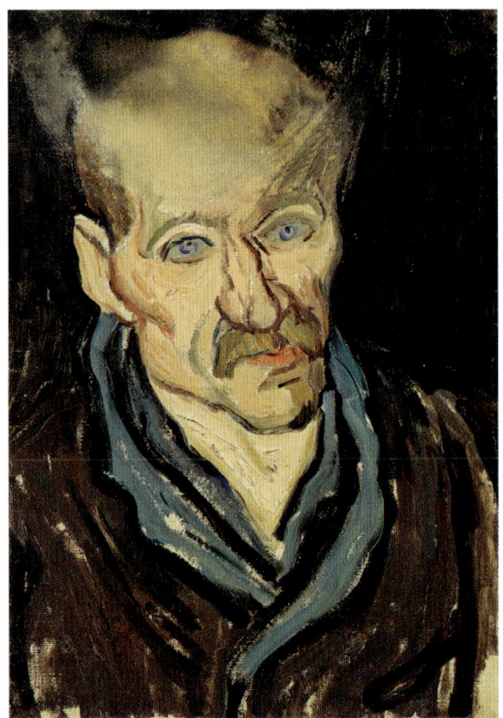

Fig. 41
Portrait of a Patient in Saint-Paul Hospital, October 1889, oil on canvas, 32 × 24 cm, Amsterdam, Van Gogh Museum

Diagnostic Hypotheses

A bipolar disorder with:

1. Family history of dysthymia;
2. Alternating phases:
   - Exaltation and excitement (warm, extroverted personality), referred to as manic states;
   - Mild hyperactivity, called hypomanic states, during which he was capable of creating these remarkable paintings and letters;
   - Intense depressions, sometimes melancholic, sometimes triggered by psychogenic events such as:
     a) the rejections he endured from the clergy in the Borinage, from women he courted,

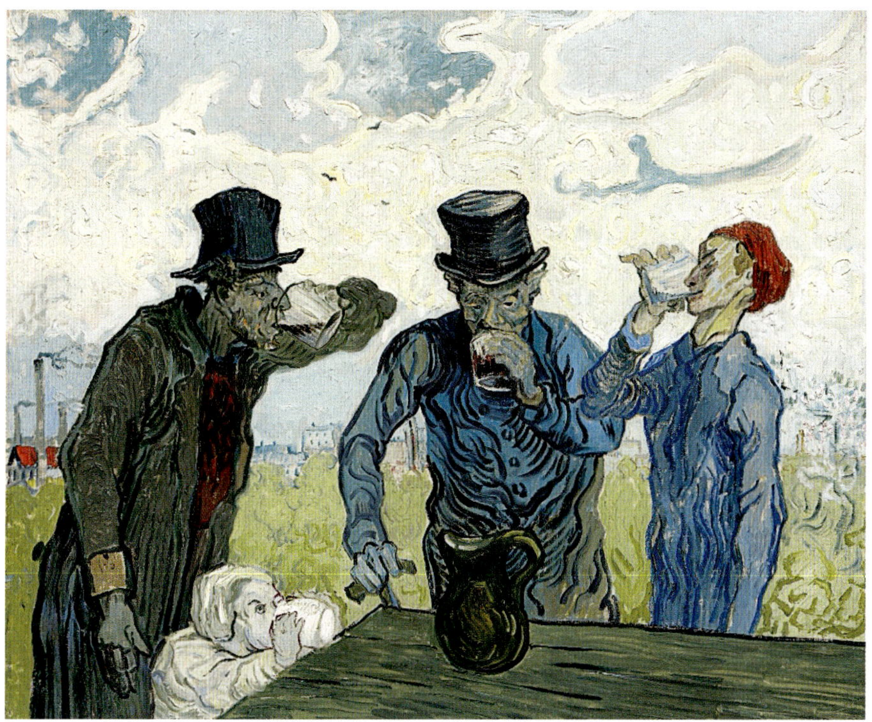

Fig. 42
The Drinkers, February 1890, oil on canvas, 59 × 73 cm, Chicago, The Art Institute of Chicago

from Gauguin, and from the people of Arles;

b) Theo's announcements regarding his gradual absence due to engagements, marriage, the birth of his child, and his return to Holland at the beginning of summer 1890;

3. Classic mood periods;
4. Two suicide attempts during his stay at Saint-Paul, followed by the fatal act at Auvers-sur-Oise.

Masked epileptic crises:
Periods of malnutrition in Arles, accompanied by excessive coffee consumption, smoking, and overindulgence in absinthe, leading to confusional states occurred during bouts of alcohol consumption, and there were two delirious crises following withdrawal. He exhibited neither Menière's vertigo nor signs of digitalis intoxication.

Van Gogh's Treatment at Saint-Paul

The treatment was humane, centred on the respect and compassion of Dr Peyron and the caregivers inspired by the Sisters of Saint Joseph. Van Gogh benefited from relaxing warm or hot baths, sometimes prolonged, but without coercion. Dr Peyron was the first physician to fully and immediately authorise and support a patient in painting with oils and turpentine. In doing so, he became a pioneer of art therapy.

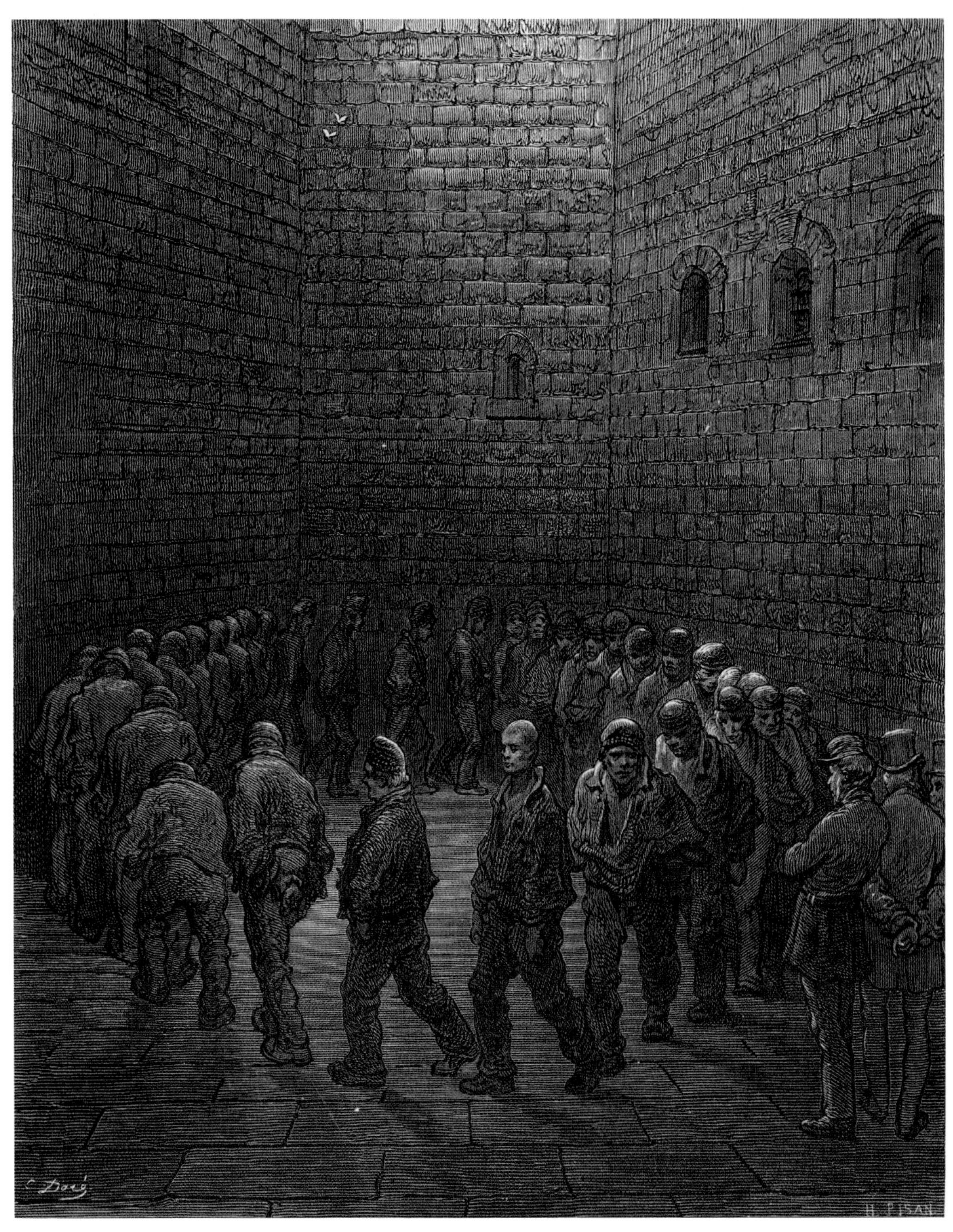

Fig. 43
Gustave Doré, *In Prison (The Prisoners' Walk)*, illustration plate published in *London, a Pilgrimage* by Gustave Doré and Blanchard Jerrold, engraving by Héliodore Pisan, Grant (London), 1872, p. 136

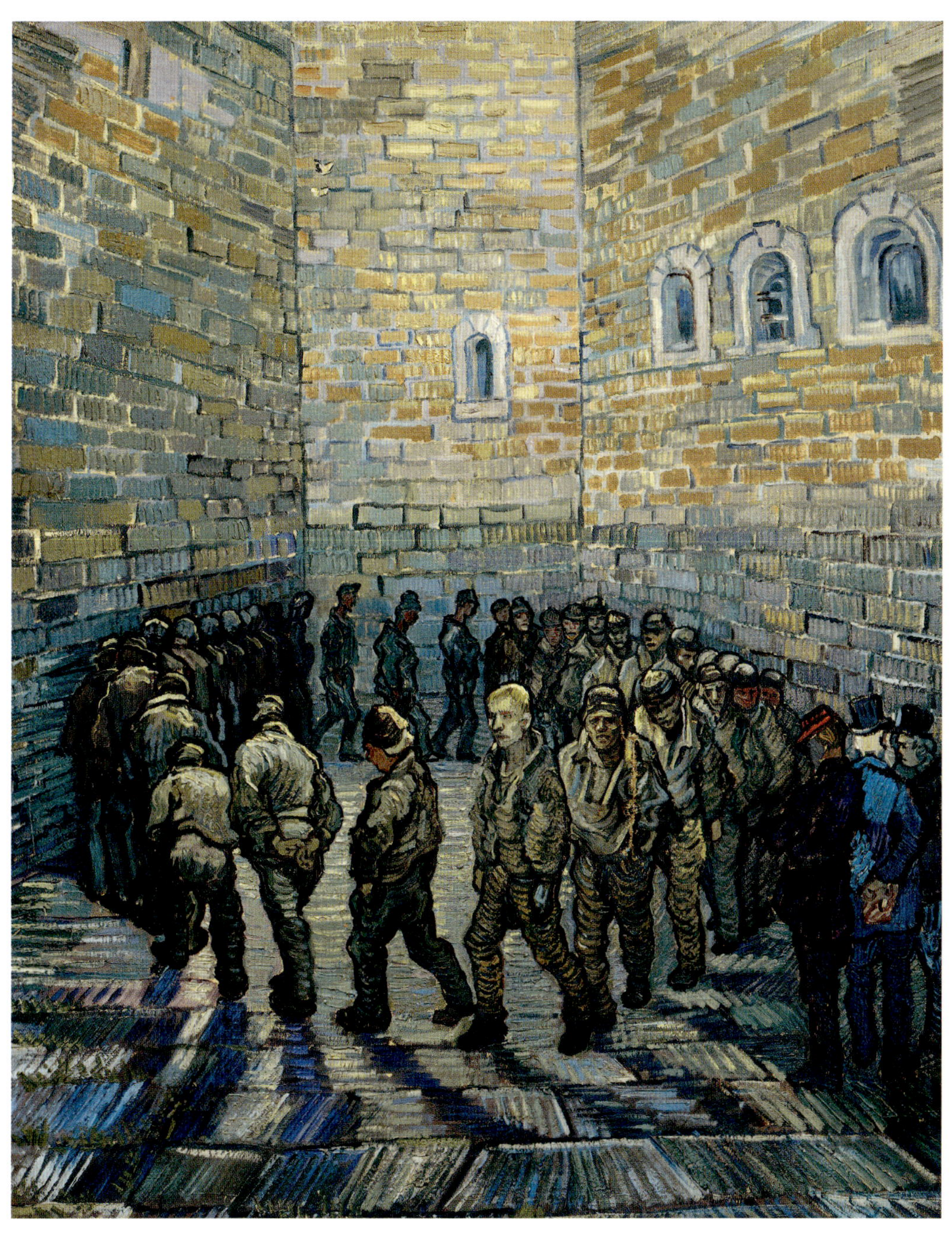

Fig. 44
Prisoners' Round (after Gustave Doré), February 1890, oil on canvas, 80 × 63 cm, Moscow, Pouchkine Museum

Influence of His Illness on His Work

Mood

Psychomotor rhythm impacts the creativity and style of artists. During manic phases, some patients paint standing, their brushes dancing precisely to a lively tempo, colours vivid and warm, their imagination strikingly fertile. Conversely, depressive individuals remain seated, their movements slow, laying down sombre colours and themes on their canvases.
At times, sadness and anxiety permeate Van Gogh's paintings. At others, his thick, dense impasto is applied vigorously in swirling motions. The brushstroke conveys vital energy and profound inner movement through its gesture and application on the canvas.
The Dutch painter intertwines what he sees with what he experiences: the traumas of his childhood and later life, rejections, sorrows, deliriums, and hopes for restoration. All of this forms the hidden backdrop of his work, as reflected in the sense of confinement he expresses in his letters or his interpretation of Doré's *The Round of Prisoners* (figs. 43 and 44).

Alcohol

Precision and creativity depend upon the quantity of alcohol consumed. Effective in moderation, absinthe became sterilising as the amounts ingested increased.

His Personality

His personality is reflected in the three dominant themes of his Saint-Rémy work: nature, spirituality, and figures, including his four self-portraits. These depict a man sometimes broken, yet standing, evoking almost a Christ-like figure beset by profound solitude. Beyond the simple visage in a mirror, they tell a story of confession, struggle, and a descent into a tormented yet lucid soul. He faithfully represents his inner truth in suffering, without seeking to please or to charm. The subject stands alone, with no background setting, immersed in a whirlwind of emotions and agitation. His gaze, vacant and distant, and his greenish complexion create a chilling atmosphere. The expression is a mixture of gravity, deep reflection, weariness, and even exhaustion. The gaze in the portrait with the palette (fig. 45), more serene, conveys a stubborn hope for better days. His state of mind is reflected in the colour palette, ranging from cold shades of blue, green, and violet to striking contrasts of exaltation with vivid touches of orange.

How Van Gogh Would Be Treated Today

Today, care would begin with a thorough clinical, psychological, and paraclinical assessment, including biological and possibly genetic tests, an electroencephalogram, a brain MRI, and projective psychological tests, supplemented if necessary at a specialised diagnostic centre. If a sole diagnosis of manic-depressive psychosis were established, Van Gogh would be treated with an antipsychotic during manic phases, a modern antidepressant during depressive phases, and subsequently stabilised with a lithium-based mood regulator.
Should the diagnosis of manic-depressive psychosis with epileptic seizures be confirmed, specialists would prescribe a mood-regulating anticonvulsant, alongside ambulatory clinical and biological monitoring, psychotherapy, and hygienic-dietary recommendations with avoidance of toxic substances. During periods of

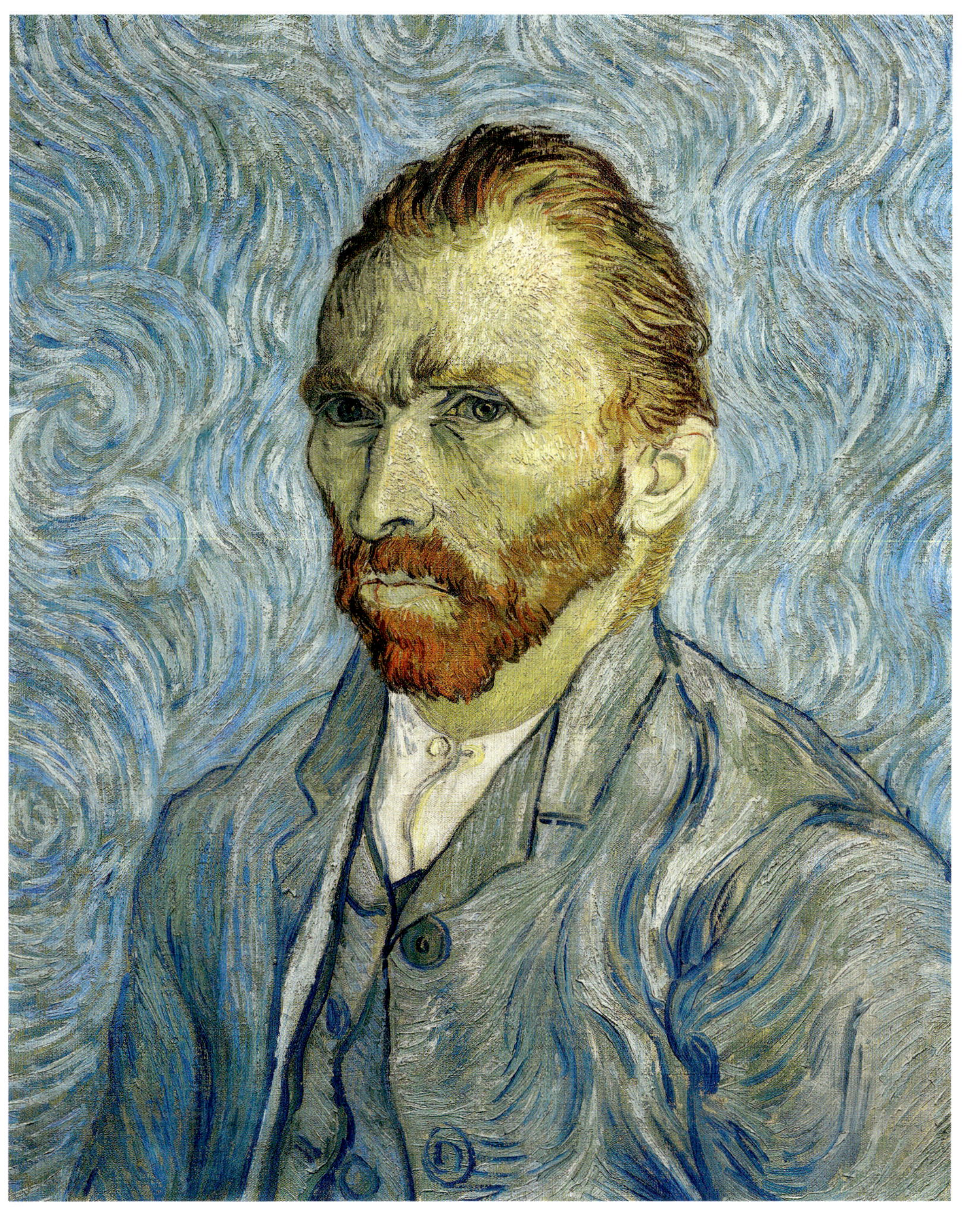

Fig. 45
Self-Portrait, September 1889, oil on canvas, 65 × 54 cm, Paris, Musée d'Orsay

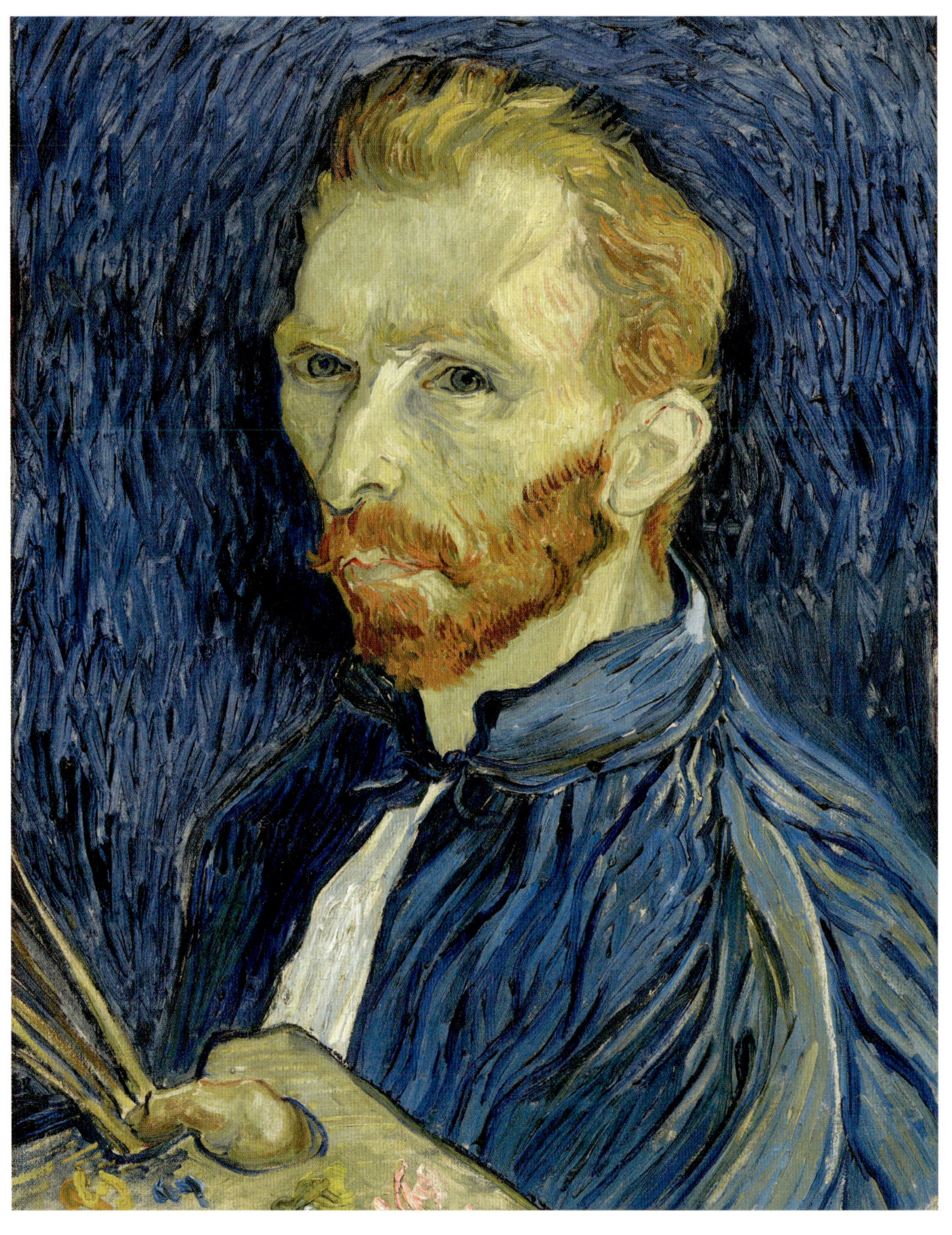

Fig. 46
Self-Portrait, August 1889, oil on canvas, 57 × 43 cm, Washington D.C., Washington National Gallery of Art

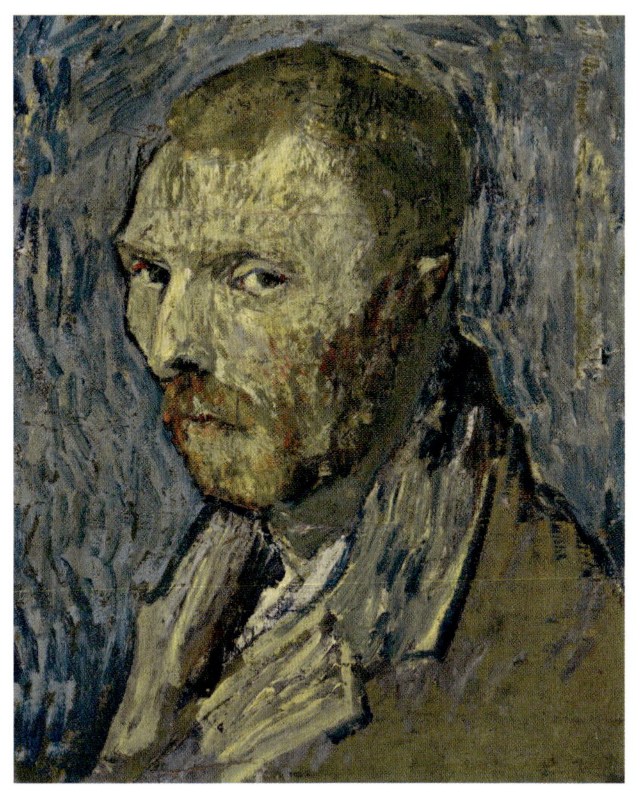

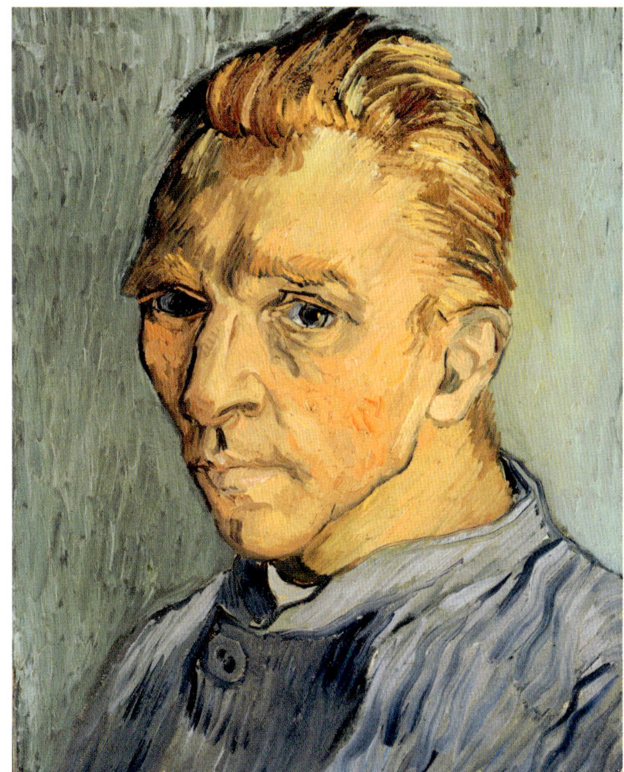

Fig. 47
Self-Portrait, July 1890, oil on canvas, 51 × 45 cm, Oslo, Nasjonalgalleriet

Fig. 48
Self-Portrait, September 1889, oil on canvas, 40 × 31 cm, private collection

decompensation, short-term inpatient or day-hospitalisation would be offered in a facility where therapeutic creativity is integrated into a structured therapeutic education programme, supported by a psychosocial rehabilitation team visiting his home. Social support measures (housing allowance, registration with the artists' association) would be provided, alongside coordinated outpatient psychotherapeutic and psychiatric follow-up supervised by the attending physician.

Conclusion

Torn by an inner struggle against mental suffering, Van Gogh finds at Saint-Paul de Mausole far more than a place of care. It is here, amid the sweetness of the Saint-Rémy landscapes, in the serenity of the buildings, and in the attentive presence of the caregivers, that he discovered a refuge, a consolation, and a form of elevation. The fifty-three weeks he spent in this exceptional institution mark one of the pinnacles of his artistic journey. Through light and nature, he transformed his pain into beauty.

The work he produced is the fruit of a rare alchemy: suffering transcended by genius, nourished by profound spirituality, a quest for inner truth, and a unique communion with nature. This Saint-Rémy chapter remains today one of the most powerful testaments to art as a path to resilience. From painting to painting, Van Gogh gradually moved away from the academic realism of his early canvases to express his emotional truth, thus becoming a precursor of Expressionism.

Sadly, the gap that had grown too wide between him and the realities of life became intolerable. Faced with the dilemma of preserving his artistic freedom or adapting in order simply to survive, the despair that overtook him three months after his arrival in Auvers-sur-Oise led him into a wheatfield on a hot day at the end of July 1890. Having resolved to bring his earthly existence to an end, he fired a fatal pistol shot into his chest, and succumbed in Theo's arms after two days of suffering. On that tragic day, his melancholy tolled the final knell of both his artistic and literary creation.

Saint-Paul de Mausole has managed to evolve while preserving its soul. Since 2017, it has been managed by the association *Vivre et Devenir – Villepinte – Saint-Michel*, which has been committed since 1920 to the reception, care, and support of society's most vulnerable individuals. The site now encompasses the Saint-Paul psychiatric clinic, composed of the Saint-Paul and Van Gogh short-stay units, dedicated to women for full hospitalisation, mixed day-hospital places, a mobile psychosocial rehabilitation team, the specialised Iris reception house both on-site and off-site, inclusive housing facilities, a space for carers, and the Vincent van Gogh Cultural Centre, open every day for eleven months of the year. Visitors can explore the Roman cloister, the chapel with its permanent nativity scene, and *the community* of the Sisters of Saint Joseph, now transformed into a "third space" where former lounges host patients, residents, their relatives, and tourists alike.

Visitors can also explore reconstructions of Van Gogh's room, his studio, the restraint cell, and the therapeutic bathhouse, as well as the asylum as he knew it – including the dormitories, the visitors' lounge, the pharmacy, the offices of Dr Peyron and the Mother Superior of the time, his own room, the corridor where the patients' wardrobes were kept, and part of the gardens he painted during his fifty-three-week stay.

The site also houses the Valetudo Gallery, a project echoing Van Gogh's dream of founding an artists' association in the South of France. This gallery exhibits and sells works by patients of the Valetudo association, created during hospitalisation or post-care, blending art, therapy, and resilience.

Classified as a historical monument, Saint-Paul has become today an essential destination in Provence, at the crossroads of memory, creation, and transmission.

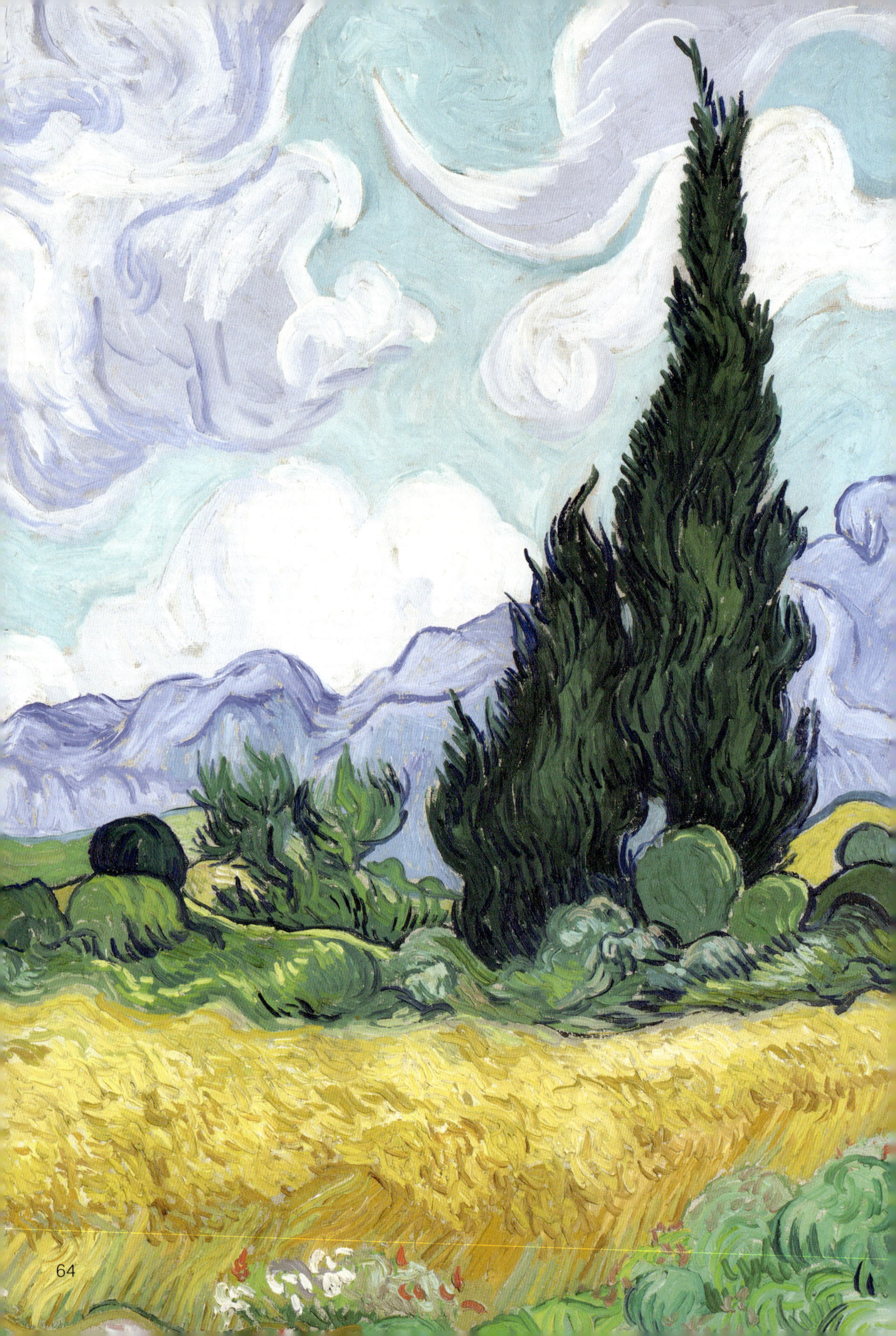

Élisa Farran

To See the Painting, to Make the Landscape

> "For me, I believe, nature, in its own simplicity, will render more benefit than any remedies could ever achieve." (L761)*

Vincent van Gogh arrived in Saint-Rémy-de-Provence on the 8th of May, 1889. For nearly a year, until the 16th of May, 1890, he resided at the Saint-Paul de Mausole asylum, nestled at the foot of the Alpilles mountains, before departing for Paris and subsequently to Auvers-sur-Oise. The year was marred by significant health crises, both in the summer and winter, which incapacitated him from working, leading him to fall into a state of profound despair. In May of 1890, he wrote to his brother, Theo: "The surroundings here are beginning to weigh upon me more than I can possibly convey, my word, I have waited patiently for more than a year now, I require fresh air; I feel broken by the monotony and sorrow." (L868)

During his time in Saint-Rémy-de-Provence, Van Gogh created one hundred and fifty works of art, several of which have since risen to the status of masterpieces, now regarded as treasures in the collections of esteemed museums around the world: *The Starry Night* and *The Olive Trees* at MoMA in New York; *Irises* at the J. Paul Getty Museum in Los Angeles; *Almond Blossom* at the Van Gogh Museum in Amsterdam; the blue *Self-Portrait* at the Musée d'Orsay in Paris; *Country Road in Provence by Night* at the Kröller-Müller Museum in Otterlo; and *A Wheatfield, with Cypresses* at the National Gallery in London, among others. This geographical dispersion, together with the complexities inherent in assembling these works for exhibition, explains in part why Van Gogh's period in Saint-Rémy is often undervalued. Nevertheless, upon closer examination of the subjects he chose, an analysis of their formal qualities, and by correlating them with the psychological state he was experiencing at the time, this phase of his artistic journey reveals itself as a critical moment in the formation of Van Gogh's oeuvre.

Upon his arrival, he penned: "You can only

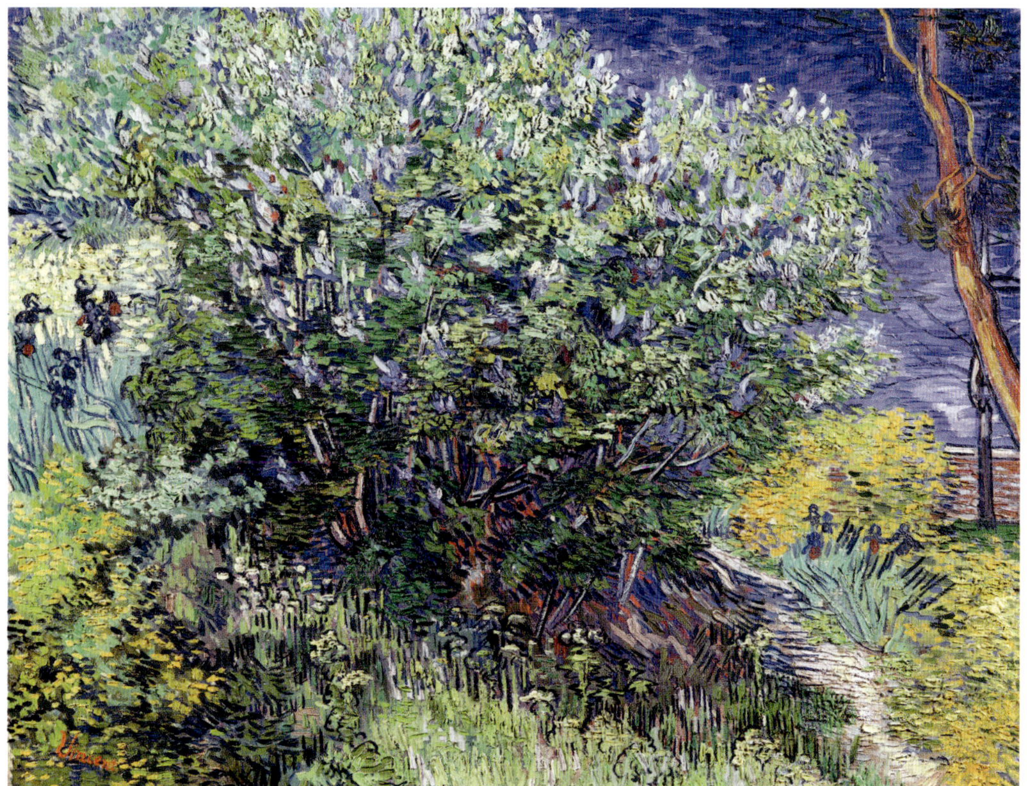

Fig. 1
Lilac Bush, May 1889, oil on canvas, 73 × 92 cm, Saint Petersburg, Hermitage Museum

rely on the fact that I am doing everything within my power to regain activity and perhaps, in time, prove myself useful once more; and in this respect, at least, I seek to create works that are more accomplished than those I have done previously." (L779)

Painting Nature, What Subjects for Art!

> "In the face of nature, it is the feeling for work that sustains me." (L779)

Saint-Paul de Mausole and Its Garden

At the outset of his voluntary stay at the Saint-Rémy hospital, Van Gogh was not permitted to leave the grounds of Saint-Paul de Mausole. However, he would wander within its confines, capturing in paint whatever caught his eye. *Lilac Bush* (fig. 1) and *Irises* (fig. 12, pp. 26-27), two oils painted during the same period, both reflect his emotional state and underscore his profound affinity for plant life.

He soon developed a keen interest in portraying the earth, the undergrowth, and the expansive fields of grass, as exemplified in *Undergrowth* (fig. 2). In a letter to Theo, he wrote: "Since my arrival, I have found ample subject matter in the neglected garden, overgrown with tall pines beneath which sprawls untended grass, interspersed with various weeds. This has provided me with enough to keep me busy, and I have yet to venture beyond

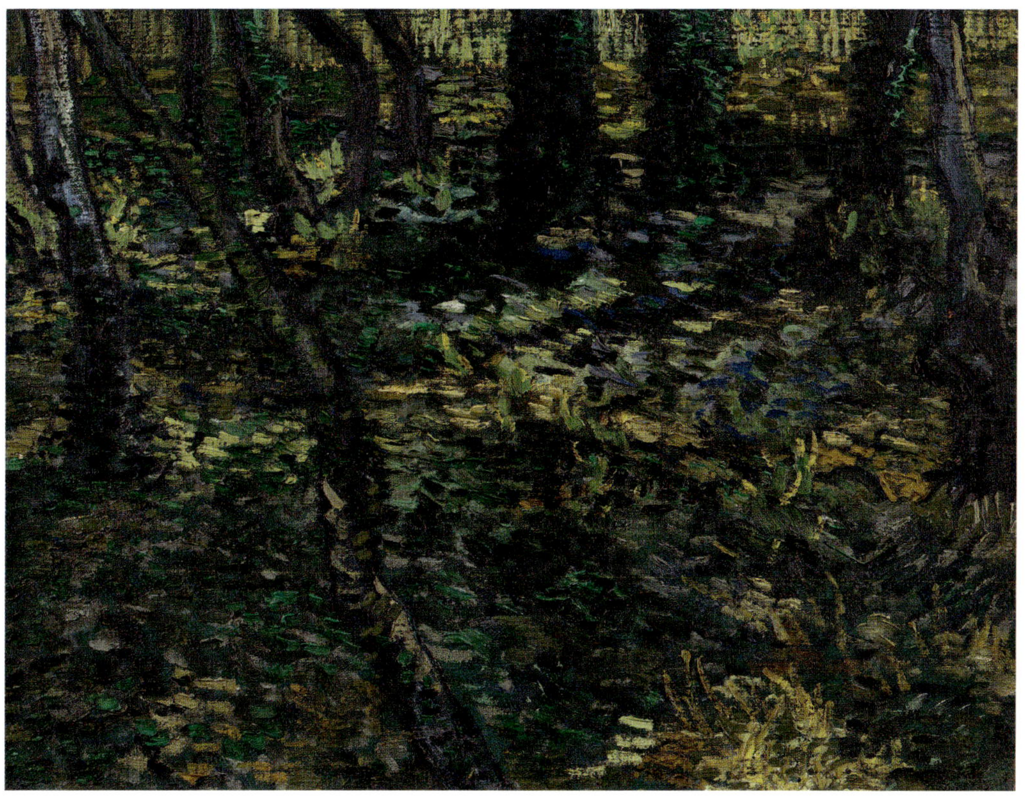

Fig. 2
Undergrowth, July 1889, oil on canvas, 49 × 64.3 cm, Amsterdam, Van Gogh Museum

it" (L776). In his early works, Van Gogh chose to centre his compositions on these wild grasses and the gnarled trunks of the pines. His approach was marked by an exploration of light playing upon the ground, resulting in dense compositions full of contrasting effects. *Tree Trunks in the Grass* (fig. 3), painted just before his departure in May 1890, represents the most refined version of this approach. To his brother, he wrote: "Work is progressing well. I have completed two canvases depicting the fresh grass in the park, one of which is strikingly simple. The trunk of a pine tree, violet-pink in hue, stands against a backdrop of grass dotted with white flowers and dandelions, a small rose bush, and further tree trunks in the distance, near the top of the canvas" (L868). A large, double tree trunk anchors the left side of the composition, while a twisted pine on the right forms a sweeping V-shape, guiding the viewer's gaze back through the meandering, flowery grass towards the path that runs along the top of the scene. The careful arrangement of space, rendered in a style of remarkable simplicity, imbues the painting with a distinctly pictorial quality that, for Van Gogh himself, would verge on what he termed "abstraction".

Van Gogh, however, would paint only a handful of views of the hospital itself. Van Gogh produced but a scant number of depictions of the hospital. *Corridor in the Asylum* (fig. 4) is constructed as

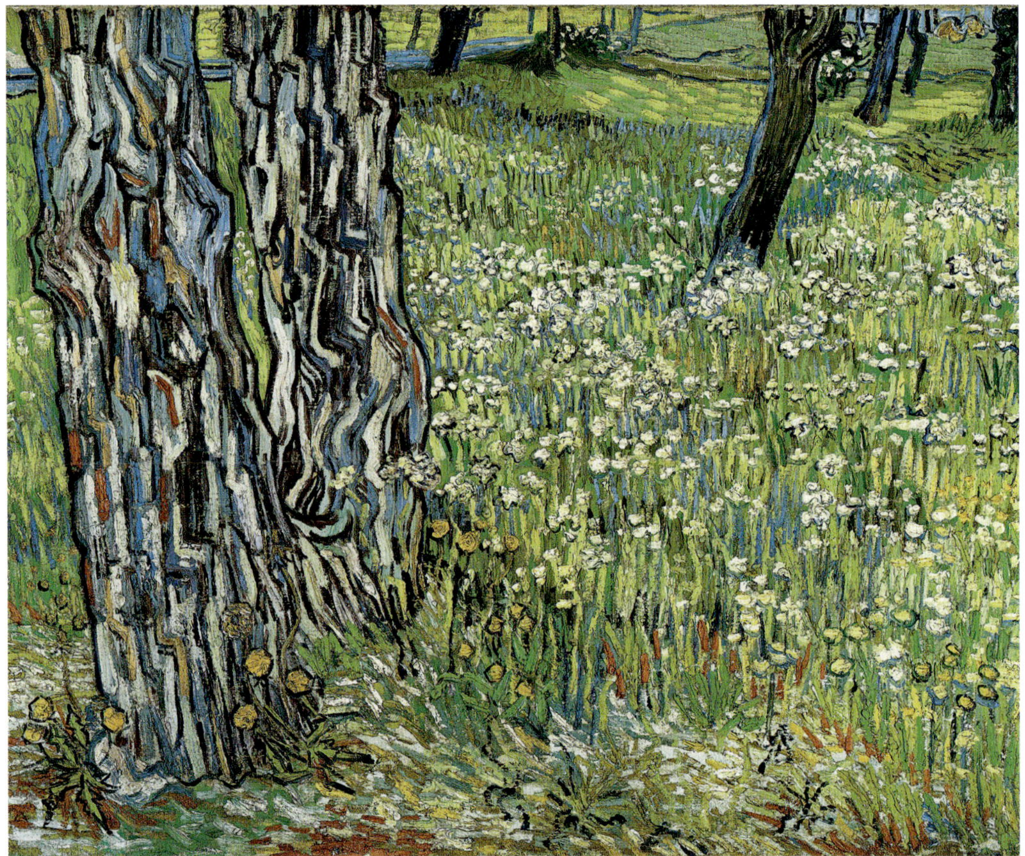

Fig. 3
Tree Trunks in the Grass, May 1890, oil on canvas, 72 × 90 cm, Otterlo, Kröller-Müller Museum

a prolonged succession of groin vaults, evocative of a Piranesian repetition extending towards infinity, imparting a sense of vertiginous enclosure. He lamented, in numerous letters to his brother, the severity of existence within this community of the insane. There can be no doubt that the garden afforded him a refuge, granting him the space in which to breathe. For this reason, he devoted all his attention to it and placed it at the very heart of his meditations on painting.
In the two versions of the *Garden of the Asylum at Saint-Rémy* (fig. 5), executed in November and December 1889, he employed the motif as a metaphorical armature. He wrote to the painter Émile Bernard: "You'll understand that the combination of red ochre, of green saddened with grey, of black lines that define the outlines, gives rise to a little of the feeling of anxiety from which some of my companions in misfortune often suffer, and which is called 'seeing red'. And what's more, the motif of the great tree struck by lightning, the sickly green and pink smile of the last flower of autumn, confirms this idea" (L822).
At this time, he was searching for a style which he described to his brother as "a more manly and more deliberate drawing" (L816). This inclination towards

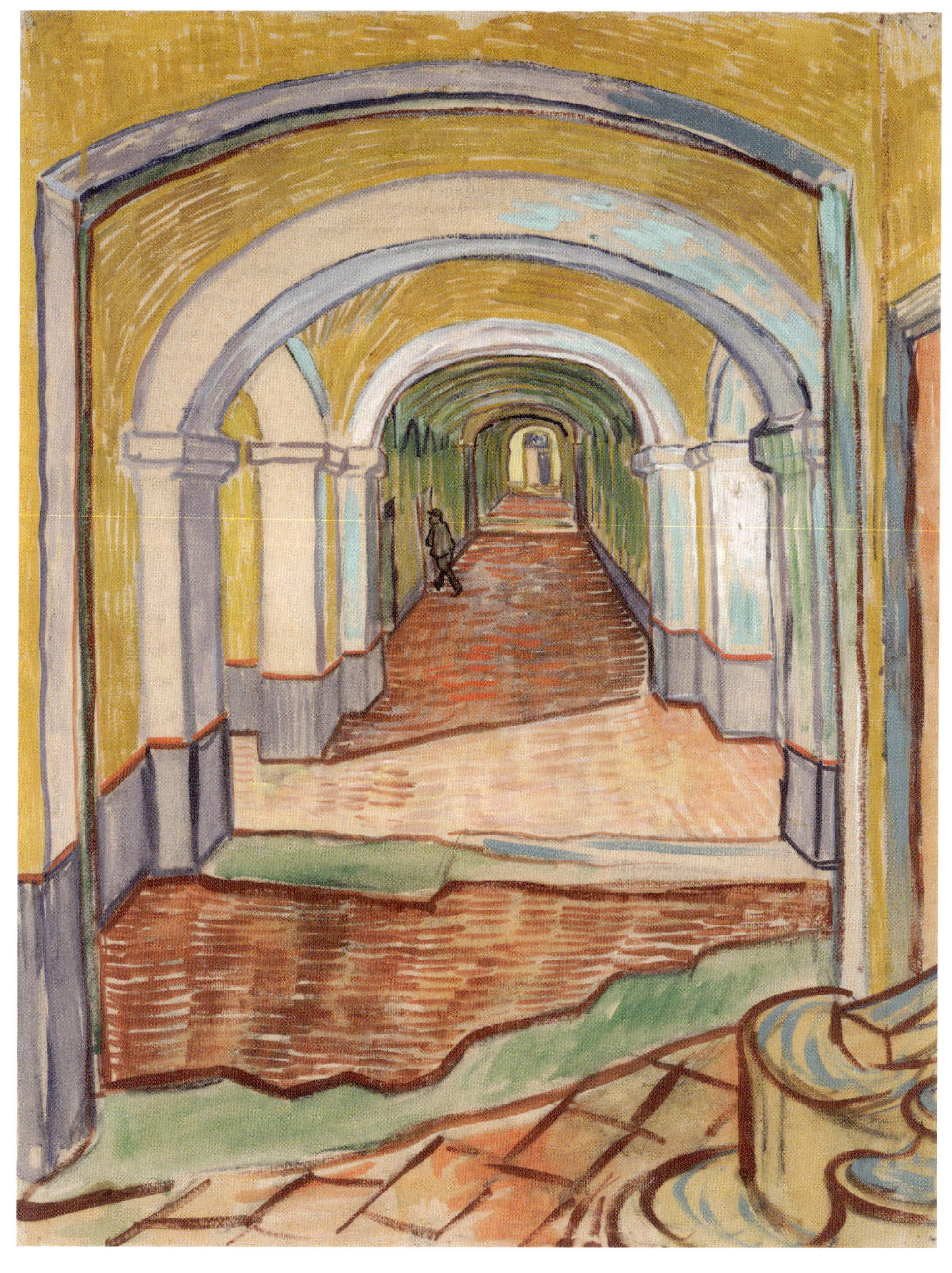

Fig. 4
Corridor in the Asylum, May-June 1889, gouache and black chalk, 65 × 49 cm, New York, Museum of Modern Art

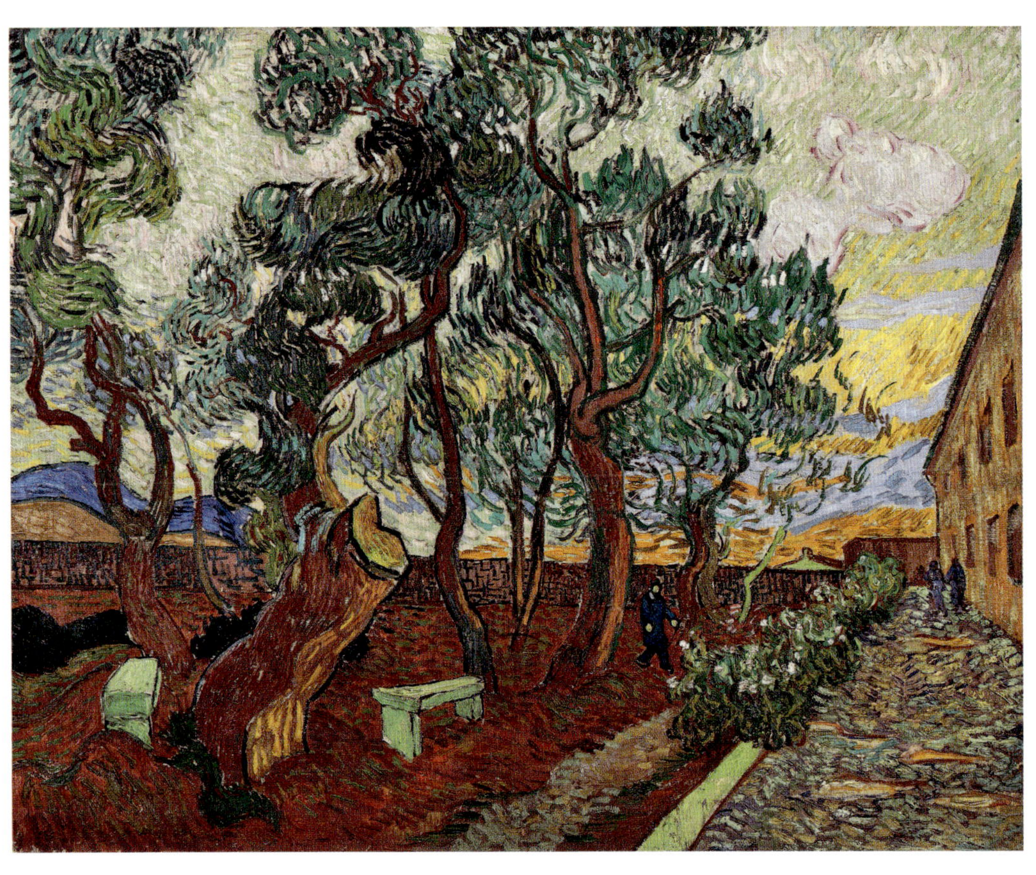

Fig. 5
Garden of the Asylum at Saint-Rémy, October-November 1889, oil on canvas, 73 × 92 cm, Essen, Museum Folkwang

abstraction resonates with the work of Paul Gauguin and Émile Bernard, as well as with their exchanges concerning the necessity, or otherwise, of representing reality within mythological painting.

For Van Gogh, the introduction of the sacred into a realistic rendering was wholly possible. Indeed, he considered it preferable to depict a wheatfield or an olive grove rather than offer yet another representation of Christ in the Garden of Gethsemane, for the simplicity of the subject heightened the emotion that emanated from it.

Wheat Field, Reaper and Ploughman

The wheat field constitutes a true *leitmotiv* within Van Gogh's oeuvre, and it resurfaced during the very first weeks of his hospitalisation. He confided to his brother: "Through the iron-barred window I can make out a square of wheat in an enclosure, a perspective in the manner of Van Goyen, above which in the morning I see the sun rise in its glory" (L776). This vista engendered a series of variations in which the human figure would occasionally appear.

In one of the earlier treatments, *Wheatfield After the Storm* (fig. 7), Van Gogh renders the prospect from his window. "In the foreground a field of wheat, ravaged and knocked to the ground after a storm. A boundary wall and beyond, grey foliage of a few olive trees, huts and hills. Finally, at the top of the painting a large white and grey cloud swamped by the azure. It's a landscape of extreme simplicity, in terms of colouring as well" (L779). The sweeping diagonal cutting through the wind-bent grass opens the space, whilst the chromatic choices communicate the palpable humidity of the air.

Van Gogh frequently complained to his family about the peasants in the South, whom he believed worked less strenuously than those in the North. He wrote to his brother: "In our country one sees men, women, children, animals at work everywhere and at all times of the year, and here not a third of that" (L779). It is therefore unsurprising that the sight of this harvester, this reaper, labouring in the hospital field should have presented itself to him as a veritable vision.

After the attack that incapacitated him from July to September, Van Gogh returned to the motif of the reaper (fig. 6). He invests it with an entirely biblical resonance, which he elucidates in a letter to his brother: "I then saw in this reaper—a vague figure struggling like a devil in the full heat of the day to reach the end of his toil, I then saw the image of death in it, in this sense that humanity would be the wheat being reaped. So if you like it's the opposite of that Sower I tried before. But in this death nothing sad, it takes place in broad daylight with a sun that floods everything with a light of fine gold. [...] It's an image of death as the great book of nature speaks to us about it, but what I sought is the 'almost smiling'" (L800).

The *Sower* (fig. 8) is thus counterbalanced by *The Reaper* (fig. 6): one who bestows life set against one who takes it away. Mirror works, diptychs, and series are recurrent features in Van Gogh's practice; he deemed it essential that certain paintings converse with one another, be viewed together, and in a particular order. As he wrote to his brother, *Wheatfield After the Storm* (fig. 7) might serve as the pendant to the damaged *Bedroom in Arles* (fig. 9), a subject he would revisit in Saint-Rémy.

Van Gogh's oeuvre should therefore be conceived as a kind of constellation, within which the paintings are interwoven to form coherent visual constellations. And finally, how can one fail to discern, in this portrait of a peasant grappling

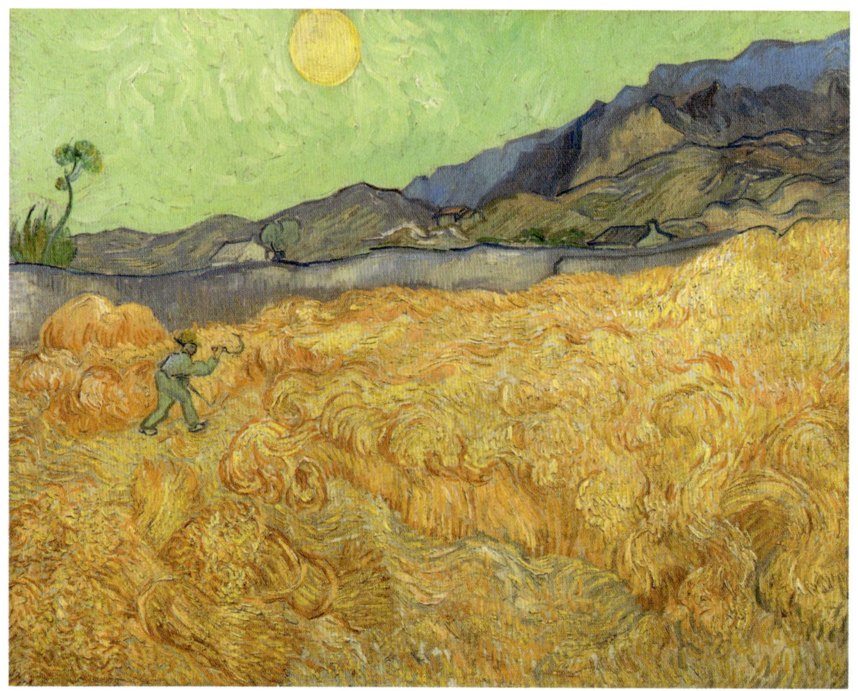

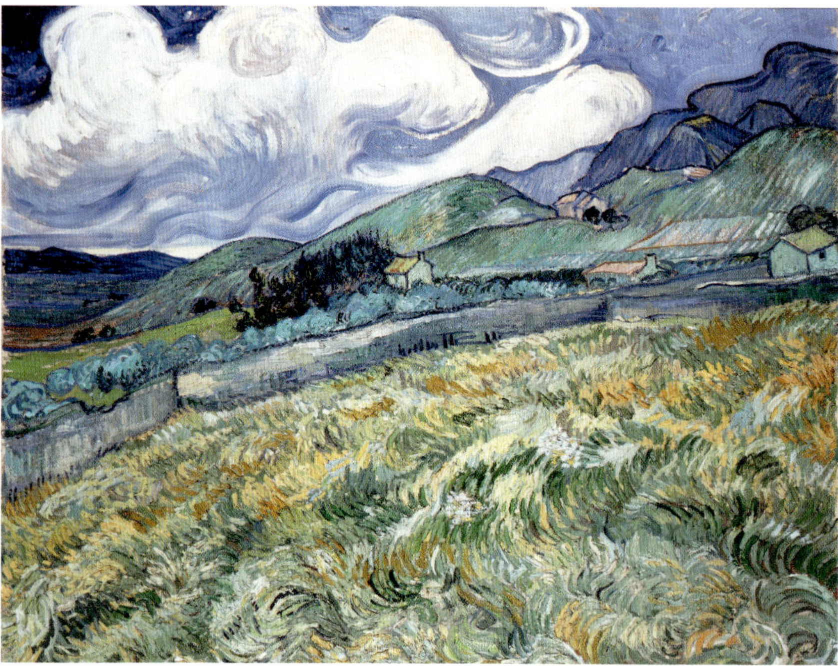

Fig. 6
Wheatfield with a Reaper, September 1889, oil on canvas, 73.2 × 92.7 cm, Amsterdam, Van Gogh Museum

Fig. 7
Wheatfield After the Storm, 1889, oil on canvas, 70 × 88.5 cm, Copenhagen, Ny Carlsberg Glyptotek

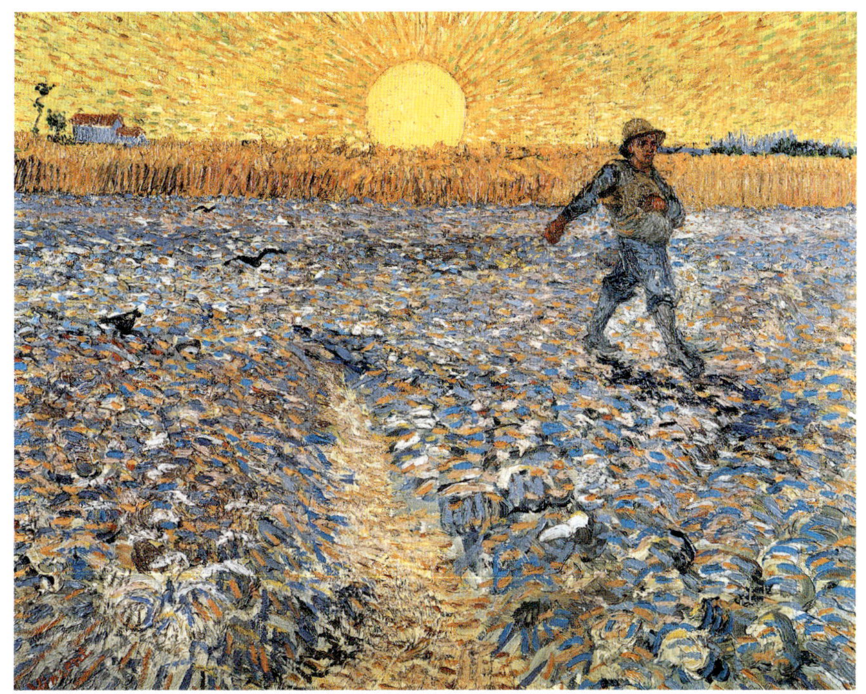

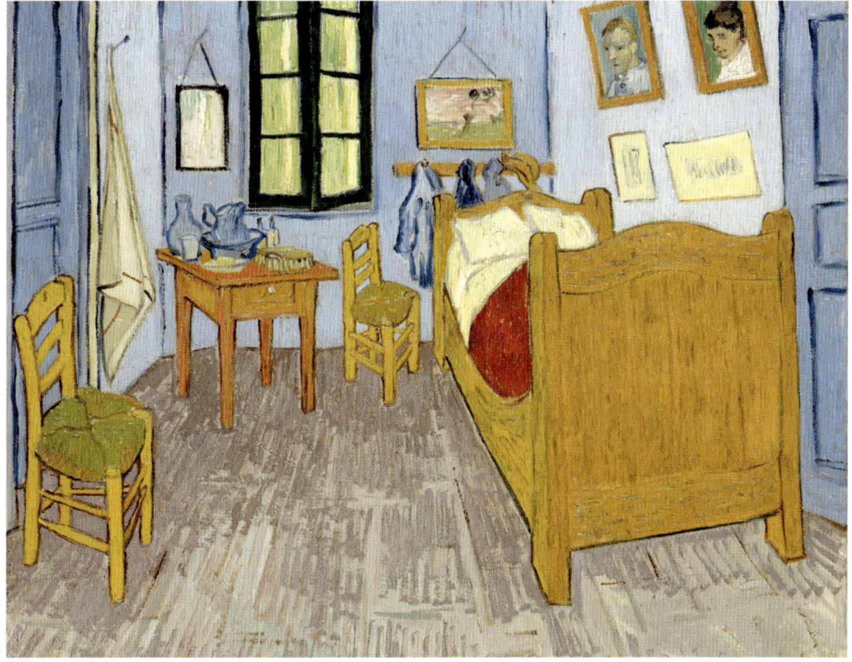

Fig. 8
The Sower, June 1888, oil on canvas, 64 × 80.5 cm, Otterlo, Kröller-Müller Museum

Fig. 9
Bedroom in Arles, September 1889, oil on canvas, 56 × 74 cm, Paris, Musée d'Orsay

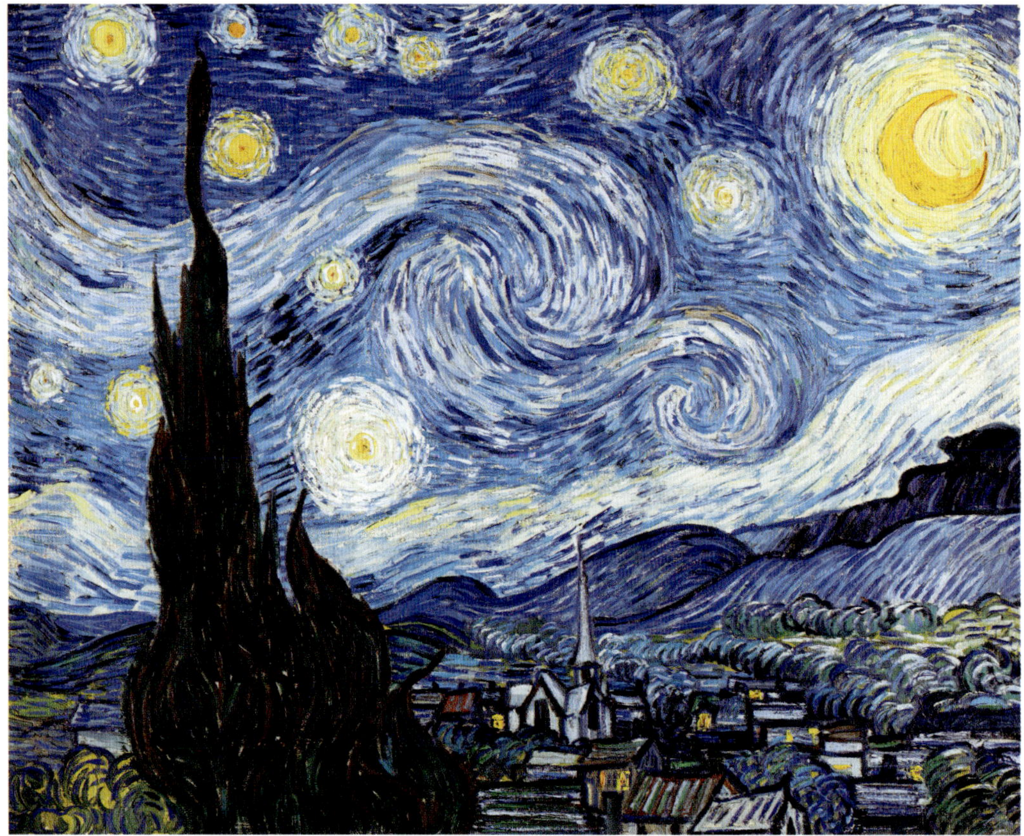

Fig. 10
The Starry Night, June 1889, oil on canvas, 74 × 92 cm, New York, Museum of Modern Art

with the elements, the image of the artist himself, caught in the throes of a profound existential crisis?

Outside, Immersed in the Landscape

Once Van Gogh was permitted to leave the hospital grounds in order to paint, he created two works that today rank among his most celebrated: *The Starry Night* (fig. 10) and *The Olive Trees* (fig. 11), each offering a glimpse into the tenor of his mind. Conceived as a diptych, one is a meditation upon the night sky, reminiscent of a composition by Millet, while the other dwells upon the earth, upon olive trees rooted in the stony mountains. Van Gogh's gaze unsettles conventional perceptions of perspective, drawing inspiration from Japanese art.

By daylight, the topography of the foothills collapses olive trees, hills, and mountains into a single plane, surmounted by a slender band of sky. By night, these same forms are engulfed by the vastness of a radiant sky. In painting these two canvases, Van Gogh articulated the very essence of what he experienced when contemplating the Alpilles: an immersion

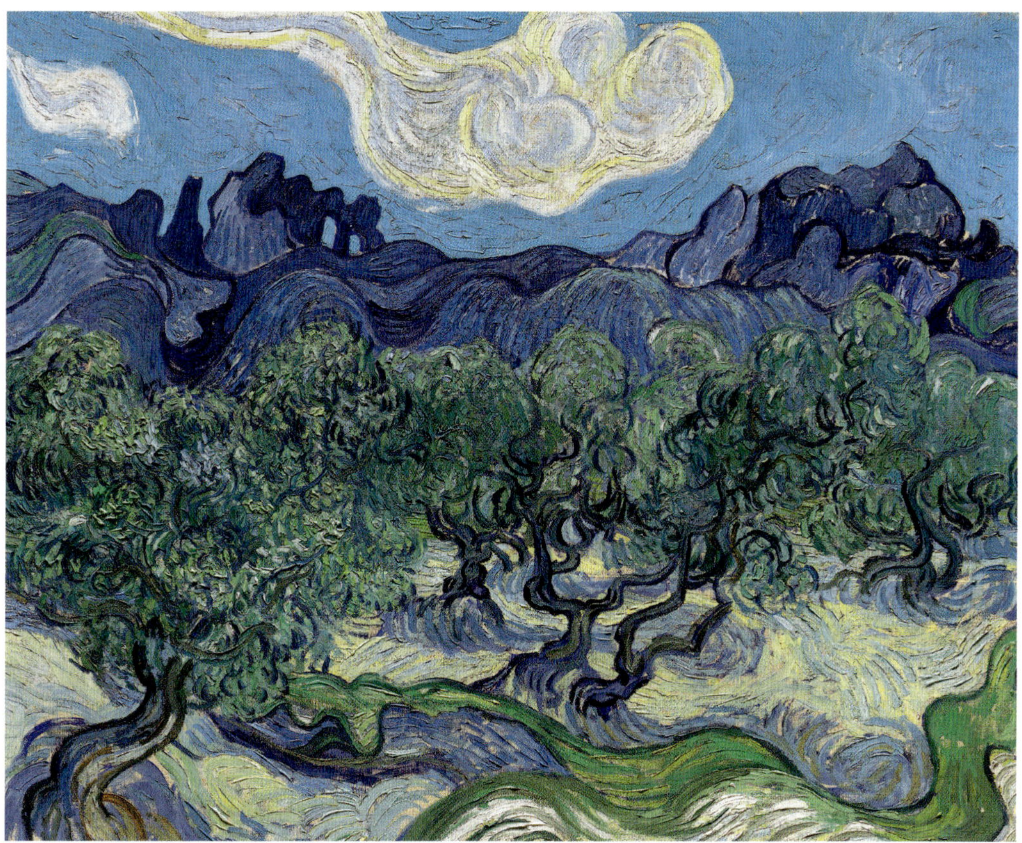

Fig. 11
The Olive Trees, June 1889, oil on canvas, 73 × 92 cm, New York, Museum of Modern Art

in nature and the boundlessness of the heavens, or, metaphorically, a grounding in the earth enveloped by the spiritual force of the sky. Their pairing constitutes a profession of faith, a vow to translate the spirituality of Nature.

From a formal standpoint, Van Gogh positioned these works in continuity with Gauguin's and Bernard's explorations of stylisation and colour. "The olive trees with white cloud and background of mountains, as well as the moonrise and the night effect, these are exaggerations from the arrangement point of view, their lines are contorted like those of the ancient woodcuts. The olive trees are more in character" (L805). The force of impact, at times associated with religious or sacred feeling, derives solely from the pictorial labour itself, reinforced by the artist's desire to display the paintings together, as indeed they still appear at MoMA in New York.

Van Gogh was always acutely attentive to the reception of his works. The greater part of the correspondence exchanged between the brothers concerned painting: the quality of the canvases he regularly sent to Theo, their framing ("For the colourings absolutely need to be set off by the white frame to judge the ensemble" [L834]), their hanging, the selection of exhibitions, potential sales, painter friends, the contemporary art scene, and the history of art. Van Gogh affirmed himself as an erudite artist, fully cognisant of the mechanisms of the art world and possessed of a profound understanding of its history, as well as of literature and science, far removed from the myth of the mad, solitary artist struck by some mystical grace.

Rock Paintings, Quarries and the Ravine

After this panorama of night-sky and day-earth, Van Gogh turned his attention to the principal motifs that define the landscape of the Alpilles, beginning with the rocky formations near the hospital in *Hut in the Alpilles* (fig. 35), the two versions of *Entrance to a Quarry* (figs. 12 and 36), and *The Ravine* (fig. 37). Of the latter he wrote to Theo: "And it was precisely a more sober attempt, matt in colour without looking impressive, broken greens, reds and rusty ochre yellows, as I told you that from time to time I felt a desire to begin again with a palette like the one in the North" (L797).

In these works, Van Gogh sought to paint the volume and texture of stone, to reveal the inner structure of the landscape itself. These paintings constitute compositional digressions in which the interplay of frontal perspectives evokes the unseen, buttressing architecture of the terrain. He also offers expansive variations on the motif of the rock, so beloved in Japanese art, which he treats with remarkable virtuosity. As he wrote to Theo: "Then this week I've done the entrance to a quarry, which is like a Japanese thing, you'll well remember that there are Japanese drawings of rocks where grass and little trees grow here and there" (L810). And again: "Two bases of extremely solid rocks, between which flows a trickle of water, a third mountain that closes off the ravine. These motifs certainly have a beautiful melancholy, and it's enjoyable to work in really wild sites where you have to bury your easel in the stones so that the wind doesn't send everything flying to the ground" (L809).

The Ravine exists in two versions, one of which was exhibited at the Salon des Indépendants in March 1890, where it received unanimous acclaim. Gauguin wrote to Van Gogh about it: "The one I'm talking about is a mountain landscape. Two tiny travellers seem to be climbing up there in search of the unknown. It contains an emotion *à la* Delacroix, with a very evocative colour. Here and there red notes like lights, the whole in a violet note. It's beautiful and imposing" (L859). Theo added: "Gauguin said that your paintings are key to the exhibition" (L858), and Monet declared that "they were the best paintings in the exhibition" (L862).

The Cypress Tree

Van Gogh discovered another of the great motifs of the Provençal landscape in the cypress tree. In June 1889, he wrote to Theo: "The cypresses still preoccupy me [...]. It's beautiful as regards lines and proportions, like an Egyptian obelisk. And the green has such a distinguished quality" (L783). The reference is significant: at the 1889 Exposition Universelle in Paris, a faithful reconstruction of an Egyptian house was displayed, and its art captivated Van Gogh. He reminded Theo: "Egyptian artists thus have faith, working from feeling and instinct, they express all these intangible things: goodness, infinite patience, wisdom, serenity, with a few masterly curves and marvellous proportions. That's to say once more,

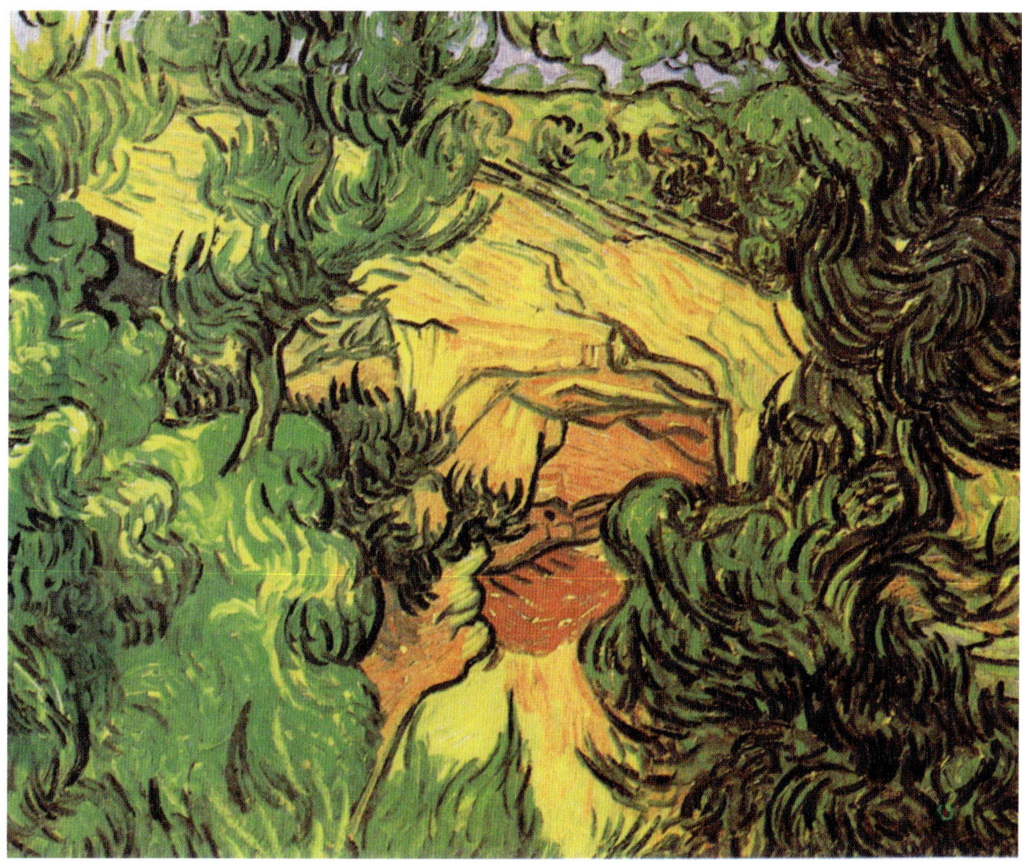

Fig. 12
Entrance to a Quarry, June 1889, oil on canvas, 60 × 74.5 cm, Amsterdam, Van Gogh Museum

when the depicted thing and the manner of depicting it are in accord, the thing has style and quality" (L779). The intention is clear: to discover a simple mode of representation capable of conveying the sacred force of Nature.

The bottle-green hue of the cypress appeared to him as "the dark patch in a sun-drenched landscape" (L783). The tree commands the gaze, compelling Van Gogh to labour over his drawing and compositions in order to express its full power. Numerous works on paper (figs. 13 and 14) and canvas (fig. 15) play with this broad "dark patch". In the drawings, the cypresses stand at the heart of the composition, their swelling curves and exuberant counter-curves unfurling upwards. In the paintings, they sometimes assume the role of an architectural element, almost a column, as in *A Wheatfield, with Cypresses* (fig. 16), and at other times become a veritable icon of Provençal nature. In the celebrated *Country Road in Provence by Night* (fig. 7, p. 105), the cypress is the central subject around which path and sky twist and coil. Ever mindful of the reception of his works, Van Gogh was particularly struck by critic Albert Aurier's analysis, who interpreted

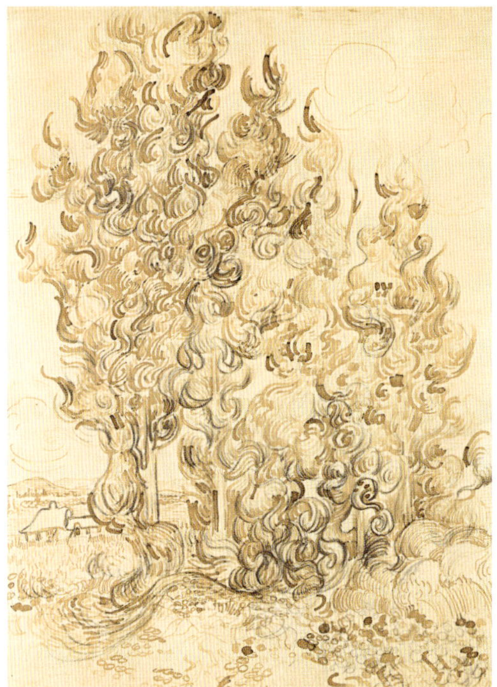

Fig. 13
Cypresses, 1889, ink on paper, New York, Brooklyn Museum

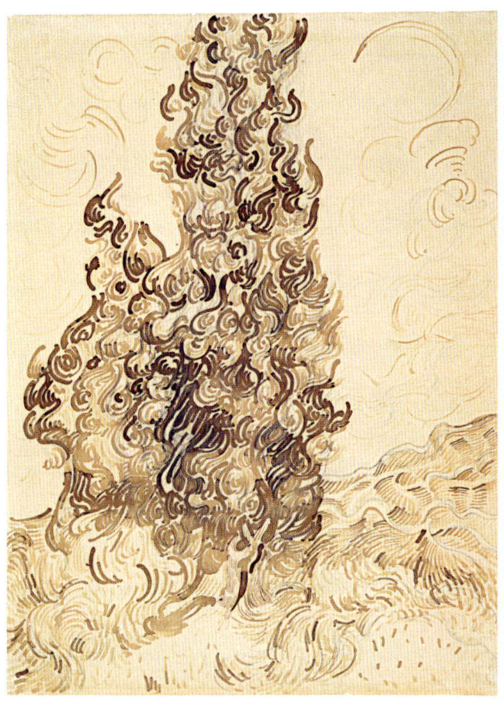

Fig. 14
Cypresses, 1889, ink on paper, Chicago, The Art Museum of Chicago

these cypresses as "nightmarish silhouettes of black flames".[1] Granting dark tones such prominence was daring indeed, signalling a new vision. In response to this enthusiastic review, Van Gogh told his brother that he had always viewed the cypress paintings as pendants to his *Sunflowers*: "I'd like to do something with them like the canvases of the sunflowers because it astonishes me that no one has yet done them as I see them" (L783). The final cypress was painted in Saint-Rémy in 1890. *Country Road in Provence by Night* (fig. 7, p. 105) is a major work, which Van Gogh described as a last attempt to align himself with Gauguin's ideas. Yet the painting also offers an unprecedented formal synthesis, in which the artist seems to oscillate between the codes of Impressionism, abstraction, and figuration.

Olive Trees and Olive Harvesters

The second great Provençal tree is the olive tree, which Van Gogh admired for its tonal subtleties and gnarled form. He dedicated a dozen canvases to it (figs. 17,

1 Albert Aurier, "Les isolés : Vincent van Gogh", Mercure de France, January 1890, pp. 24-29.

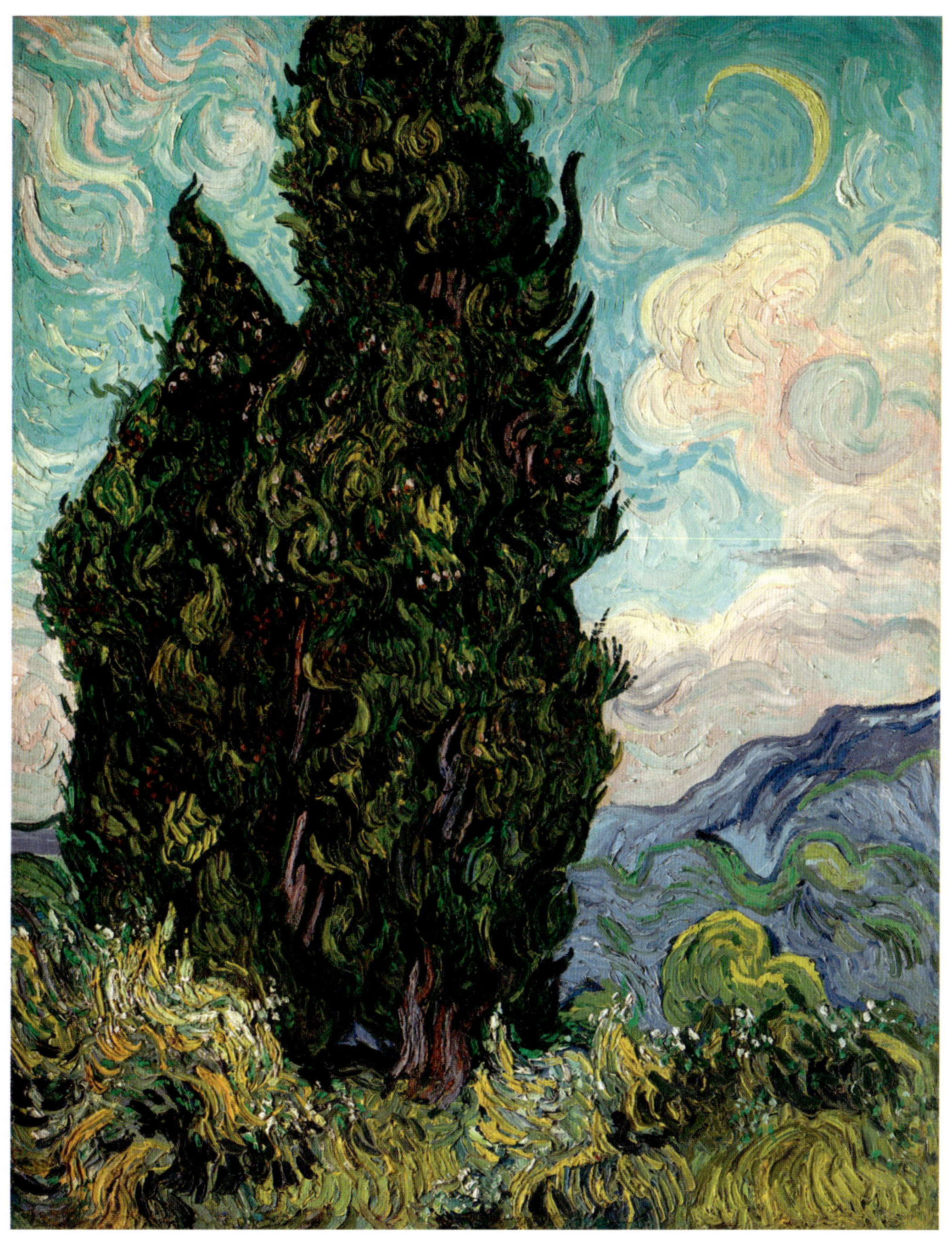

Fig. 15
Cypresses, June 1889, oil on canvas, 93.5 × 74 cm, New York, The Metropolitan Museum of Art

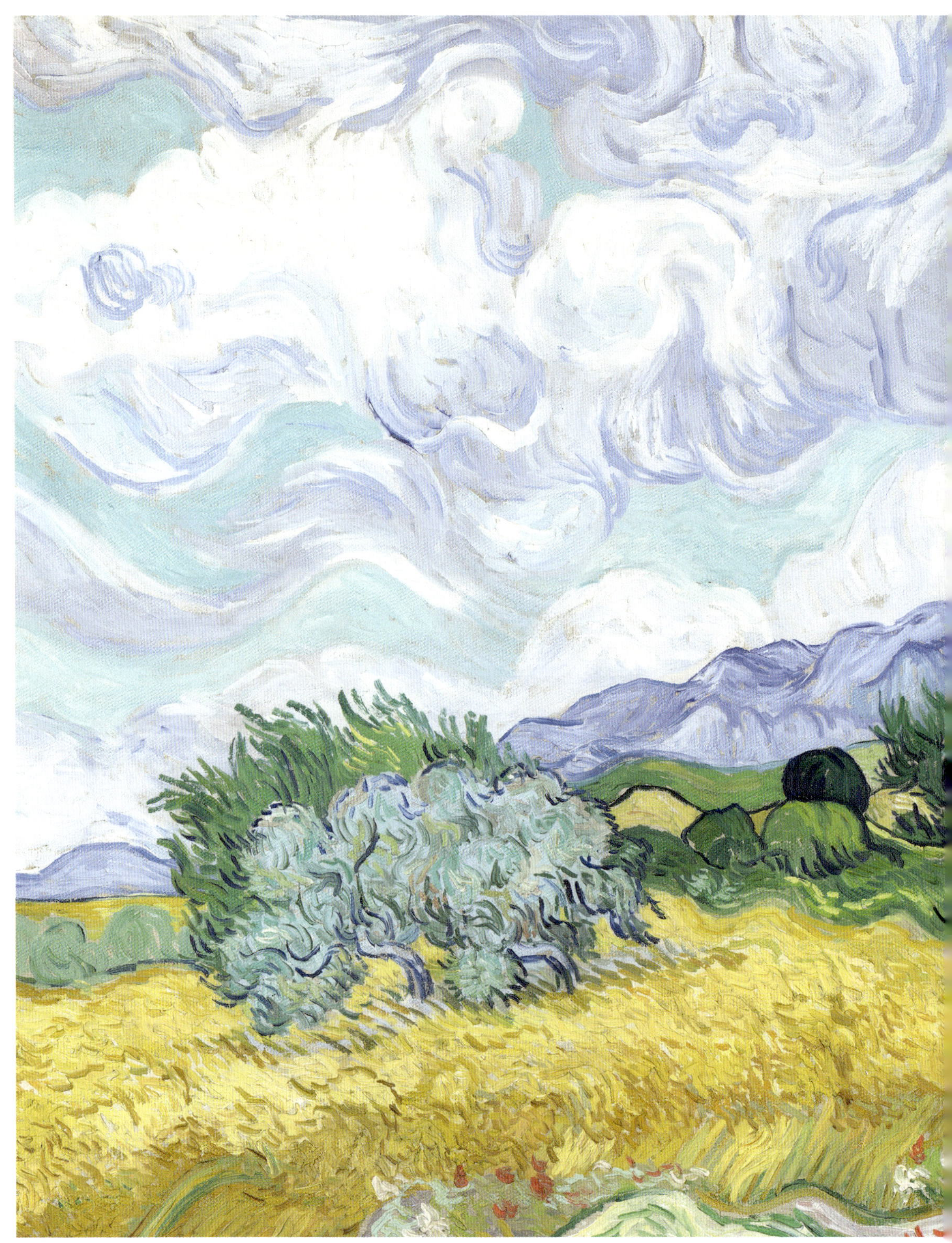

Fig. 16
A Wheatfield, with Cypresses, June 1889, oil on canvas, 72.1 × 90.9 cm, London, National Gallery

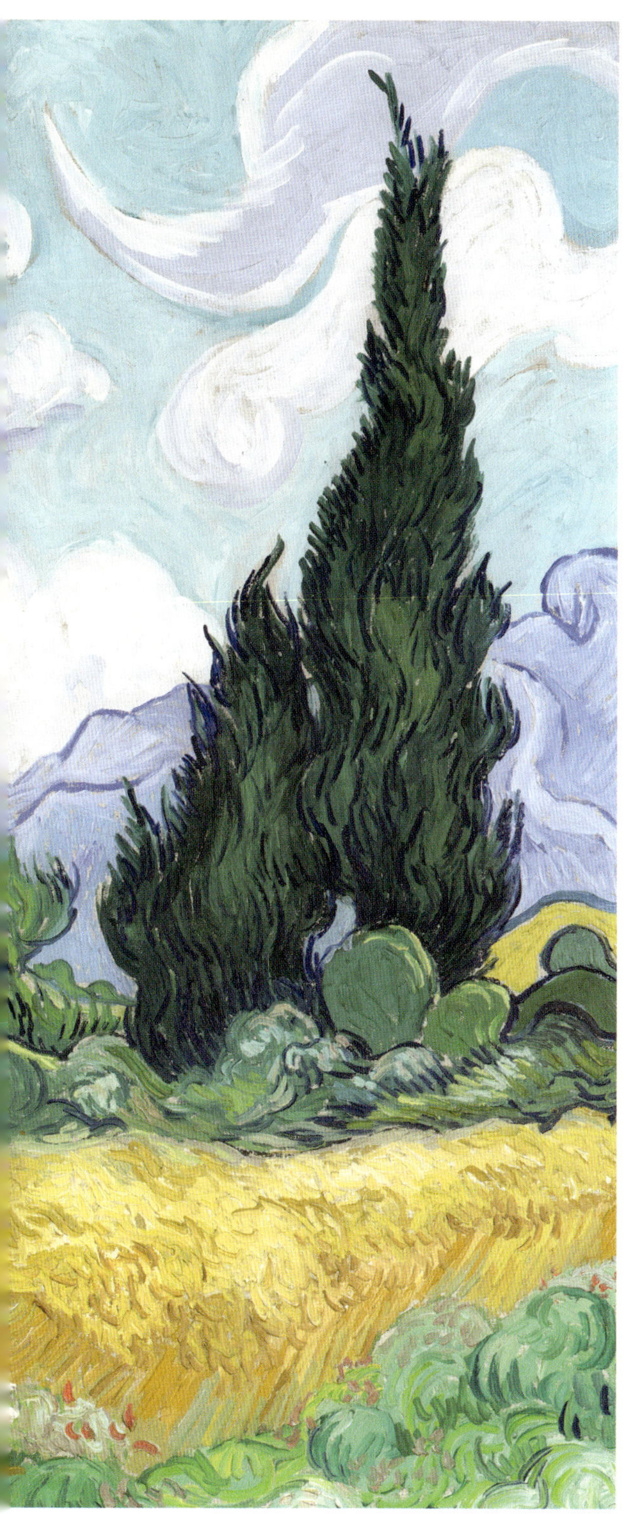

18, 19, 20 and 21). "It's silver, sometimes bluer, sometimes greenish, bronzed, whitening on ground that is yellow, pink, purplish or orangish to dull red ochre. But very difficult, very difficult" (L806). He endeavoured to capture it through a series of studies in which he experimented with synthesising several styles, abstraction, Impressionism, and Neo-Impressionism (figs. 18 and 19).

The olive-tree series appears in Van Gogh's oeuvre shortly after he received from Gauguin and Bernard photographs of their respective *Christ in the Garden of Gethsemane*. Still sceptical about the choice of biblical subject, Van Gogh decided to distance himself from it, favouring instead the pure emotion elicited by the simple spectacle of peasant life. "If I remain here I wouldn't try to paint a Christ in the Garden of Olives, but in fact the olive picking as it's still seen today, and then giving the correct proportions of the human figure in it, that would perhaps make people think of it all the same" (L820) (figs. 20 and 21).

Copying Millet

The vision of the wheat field and the reaper reintroduced into Van Gogh's art the figure of the labouring peasant, a subject to which he had always been deeply attached. From the autumn onwards, he devoted himself to the pictorial reinterpretation of works by Millet, *Les Travaux des Champs*, *The Diggers*, *The Siesta* (fig. 23). This series of copies coincided with a period of introspection, during which he returned to his sources by revisiting his great masters: Millet, Rembrandt, and Delacroix. Upon arriving in Saint-Rémy, Van Gogh wrote: "The more I think about it the more I find that there's justification for trying to reproduce things by Millet" (L493). Since his first encounter with the Barbizon painter's art, Van Gogh

Fig. 17
Olive Trees, June 1889,
oil on canvas, 72 × 92 cm,
Otterlo, Kröller-Müller Museum

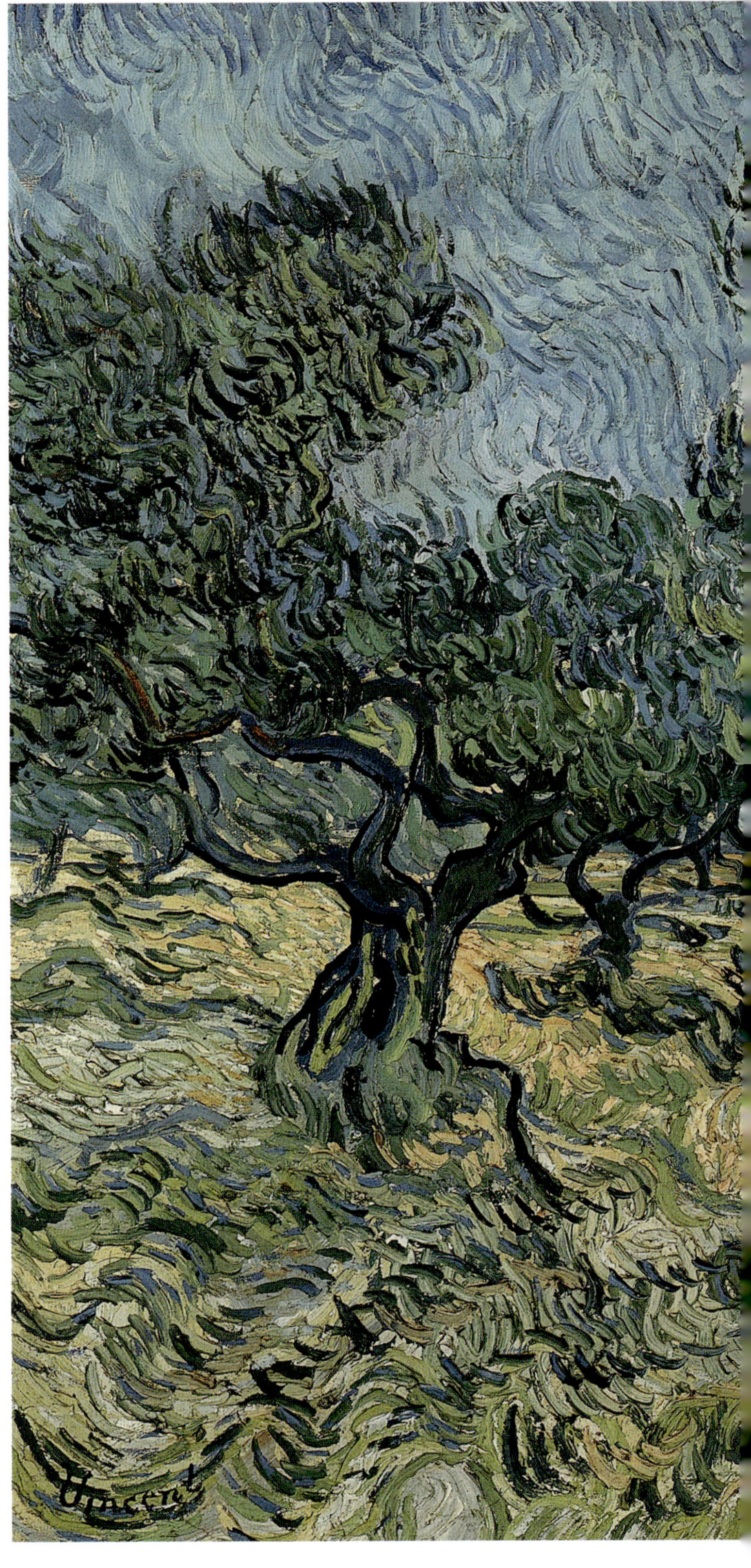

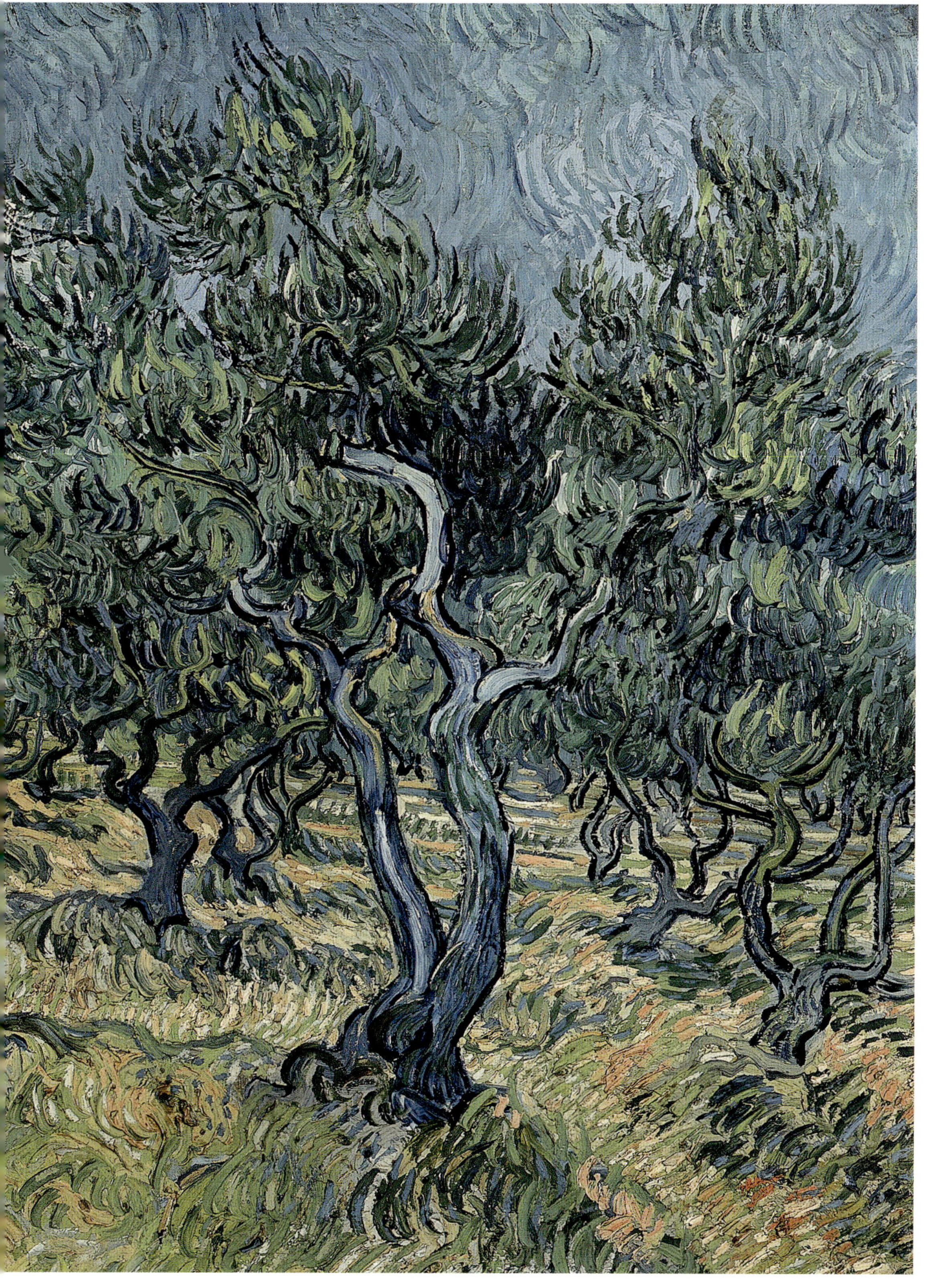

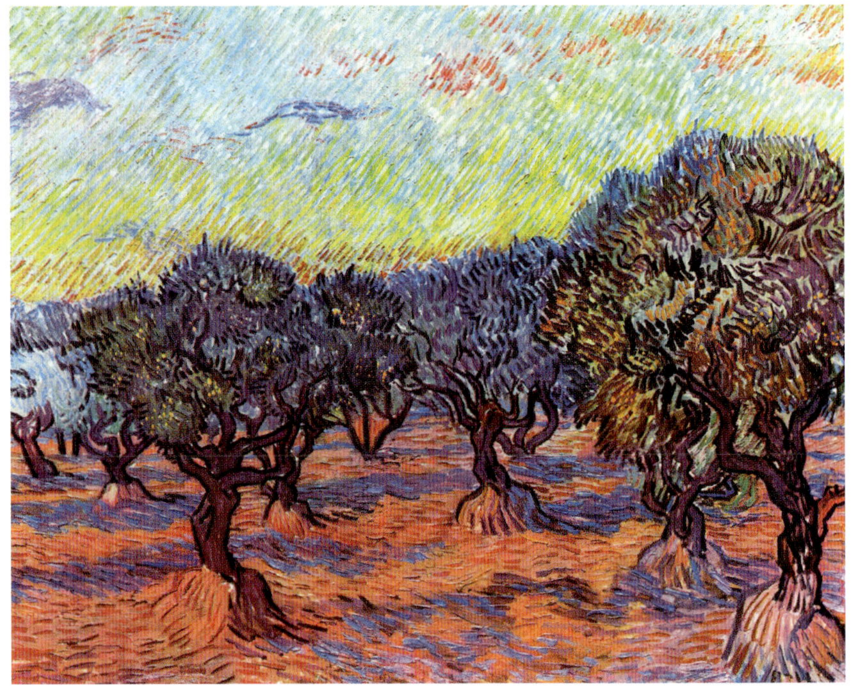

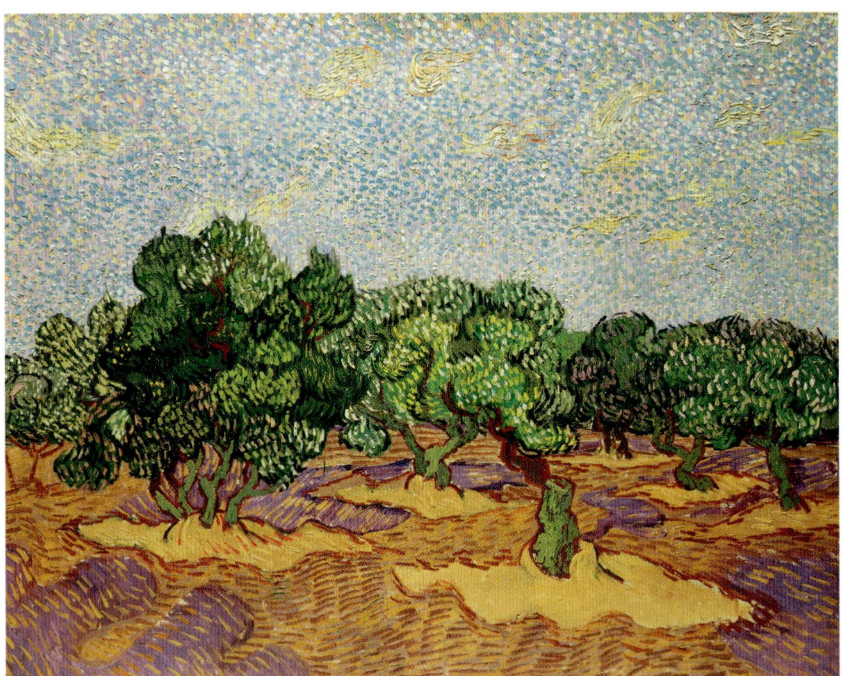

Fig. 18
Olive Grove – Orange Sky, November 1889, oil on canvas, 74 x 93 cm, Gothenburg, Kunstmuseum

Fig. 19
Olive Trees, November 1889, oil on canvas, 73.5 × 91.5 cm, Rancho Mirage, Collection W.H. Annenberg

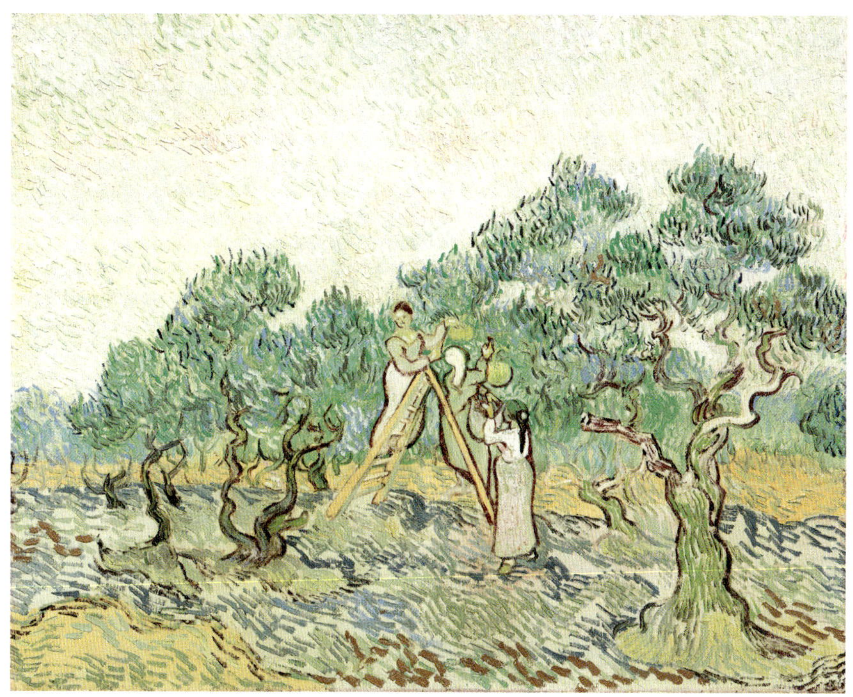

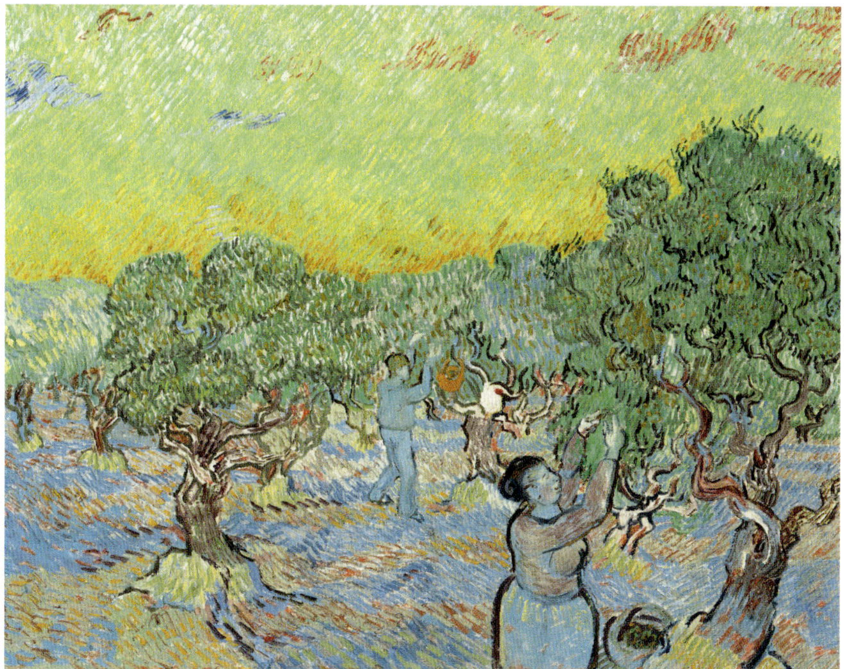

Fig. 20
Women Picking Olives, December 1889, oil on canvas, 73 × 92 cm, Washington D.C., National Gallery of Art

Fig. 21
Olive Grove with Two Olive Pickers, November 1889, oil on canvas, 73 × 92 cm, Otterlo, Kröller-Müller Museum

had regarded Millet as a model to emulate, a spiritual father, a guide.
Millet had invented the figure of the peasant-painter, one who worked outside cities, beyond the modern world, in harmony with the rhythms of nature, like a peasant himself. Van Gogh thus wrote: "So in my own estimation I definitely reckon myself below the peasants. Anyway, I plough on my canvases as they do in their fields" (L811). Millet's painting, combined with his moral authority, made him a guide for an entire generation of artists, from the Impressionists to the Symbolists: "Millet is PÈRE Millet, that is, counsellor and guide in everything, for the younger painters. [...] As to me, I think the same, and entirely believe what he says" (L493). His rejection of modernity and his faith in Nature were to transform art, for rigorous labour and an austere life were the necessary ingredients of this metamorphosis.
Van Gogh saw in Millet a prophet capable of interpreting the sacred dimension of Nature, of projecting "something on high" or "the existence of a god or eternity" (L856) into it. Yet, although Van Gogh believed the future of painting lay in the experiments of Gauguin, Bernard and others, he realised at Saint-Rémy that he could not wholly embrace their path: "I can see from a distance the possibility of a new painting, but it is too much for me. [...] And I'll always regret that in our times people believe in the incompatibility of the generation of, say, 1848 and the present one. I myself believe that the two hold their own all the same, though I can't prove it" (L878).
Van Gogh could not entirely detach himself from observing the world. Saint-Rémy became the place where this recognition, an indicator of his artistic maturity, emerged. He believed that "ten years were needed to learn the profession" (L811) and thus to gain the freedom to transcend it. A decade was precisely the span he had already dedicated to painting by the time of his arrival in Saint-Rémy. He was therefore able to distance himself from the avant-garde race at all costs and reaffirm his affiliation with Millet and with a conception of painting profoundly rooted in Nature.
His religious sensibility, stirred anew by his stays in religious houses in Arles and Saint-Rémy, troubled him. He confessed to Theo: "I being such an ardent admirer of Zola, of De Goncourt and of artistic things which I feel so much, I have crises like a superstitious person would have, and that mixed-up, atrocious religious ideas come to me such as I never had in my head in the North" (L805). Quite naturally, he transposed this faith into a form of pantheism in which Nature was the divine force. God was no longer above humanity, as in monotheistic religions, but omnipresent in the natural world. Henceforth, his dialogues with natural elements and with peasants acquired a new dimension.
This initiation, if one may call it such, was manifested in the care with which he copied Rembrandt, Delacroix, and especially Millet. Though Van Gogh was convinced that modernity could be asserted through landscape painting, he did not forget the central place of the human figure in the history of art. "I can assure you that making copies interests me enormously, and since I have no models for the moment, it ensures me that I don't lose sight of the figure" (L805).
Van Gogh responded to the ten engravings produced by Jacques Adrien Lavieille (fig. 22) after Millet's works with nine paintings which he reinterpreted in the sun-drenched environment of the Mediterranean South (figs. 24 to 31). He completed this series with versions of *The Diggers*, *First Steps*, *The End of the Day*, and *Snow-Covered Field with a Harrow*.

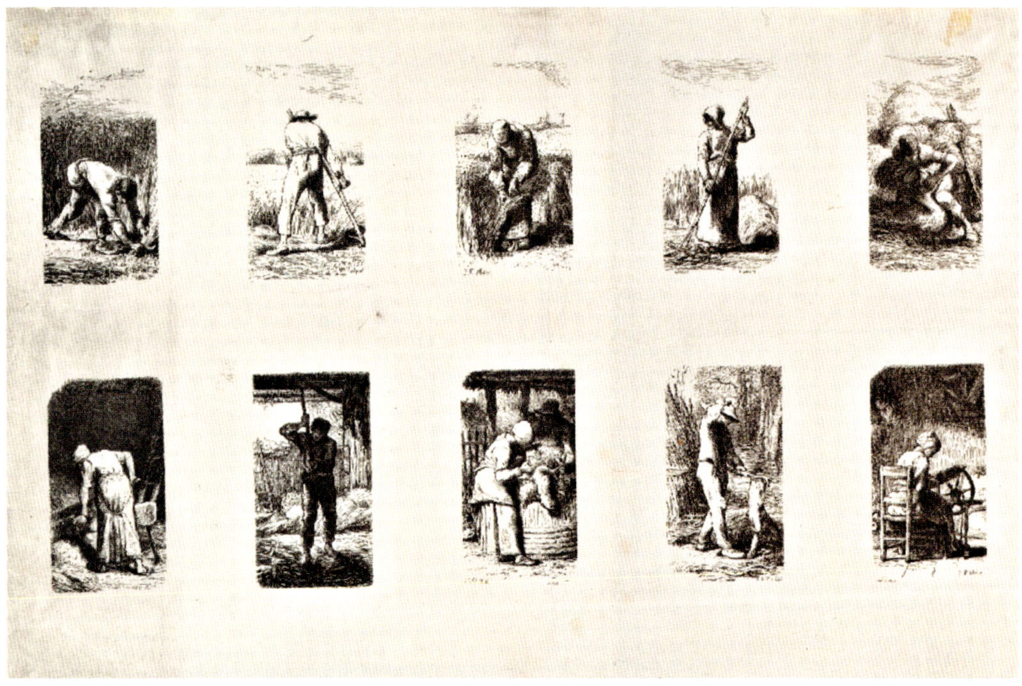

Fig. 22
Jacques Adrien Lavieille, engraving after *Les travaux des champs* by Millet

In his rendering of *The Siesta* (fig. 23), he preserved, and inverted, the composition, employing instead a style and palette derived from his meticulous study of the Provençal South.

He wrote again to Theo: "You'll be surprised what effect the *Travaux des champs* take on in colour, it's a very intimate series of his. [...] What I'm seeking in it, and why it seems good to me to copy them, I'm going to try to tell you. We painters are always asked to compose ourselves and to be nothing but composers. Very well, but in music it isn't so, and if such a person plays some Beethoven he'll add his personal interpretation to it [...]. Good, since I'm above all ill at present, I'm trying to do something to console myself, for my own pleasure. [...] And then I improvise colour on it but, being me, not completely of course, but seeking memories of their paintings—but the memory, the vague consonance of colours that are in the same sentiment, if not right—that's my own interpretation" (L805).

Mulberry Tree, Almond Blossom, and Vineyards

Mulberry Tree (fig. 33), painted in the autumn of 1889, and *Almond Blossom* (fig. 32), executed in the spring of 1890 to mark the birth of his nephew, Theo's son, constitute two portraits of trees in the strictest sense, rendered in an unmistakably Japanese manner (fig. 32bis). The composition takes the motif as its point of departure without recourse to perspective, allowing it to occupy the entire pictorial surface in unmediated primary colours.

As he reiterated in several letters to his family, Van Gogh lamented the absence of vines at the foot of the Alpilles. "The

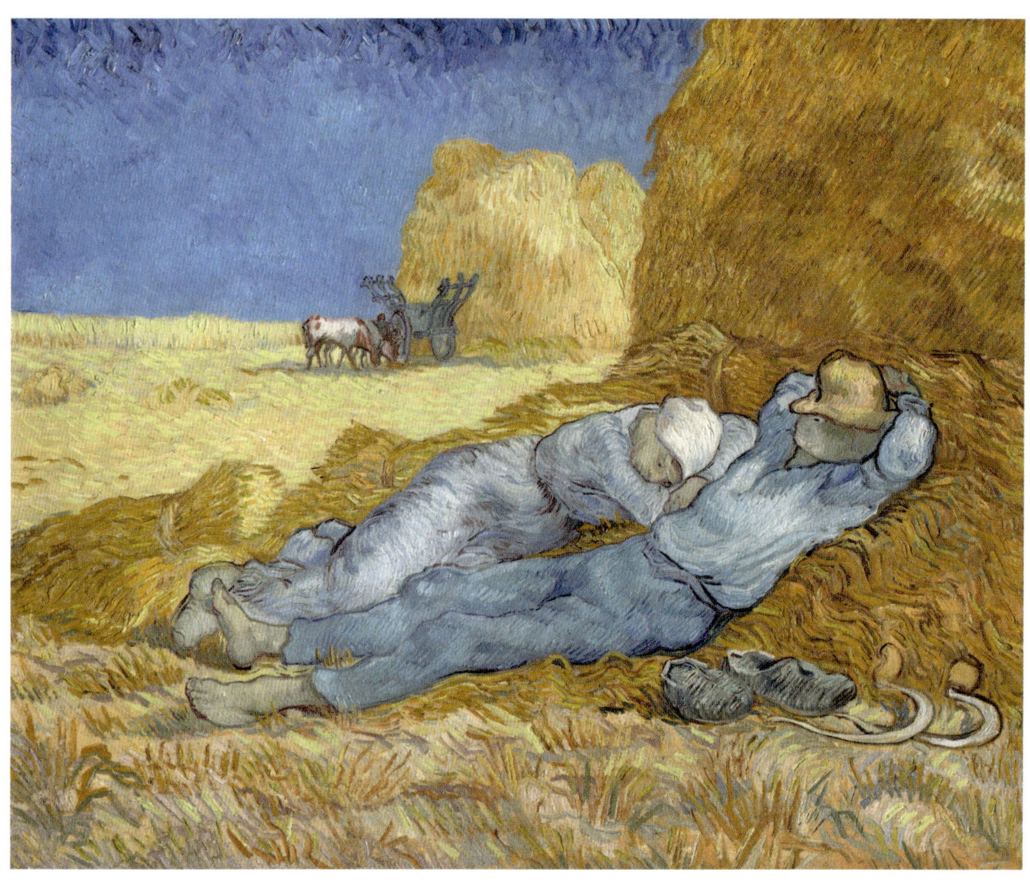

Fig. 23
The Siesta (after Millet), November 1889, oil on canvas, 73 × 91 cm, Paris, Musée d'Orsay

Fig. 24-31
Thresher (after Millet), September 1889, oil on canvas, 44 × 33 cm, Amsterdam, Van Gogh Museum

The Sower, October 1889, oil on canvas, 80 × 64 cm, New York, private collection

The Woodcutter (after Millet), September 1889, oil on canvas, 44 × 26.2 cm, Amsterdam, Van Gogh Museum

The Reaper (after Millet), September 1889, oil on canvas, 44 × 33 cm, Amsterdam, Van Gogh Museum

Peasant Woman Bruising Flax (after Millet), September 1889, oil on canvas, 40 × 26 cm, Amsterdam, Van Gogh Museum

The Sheepshearer (after Millet), September 1889, oil on canvas, 43.6 × 29.5 cm, Amsterdam, Van Gogh Museum

The Sheaf-Binder (after Millet), September 1889, oil on canvas, 44.5 × 33.1 cm, Amsterdam Van Gogh Museum

Peasant Woman Binding Sheaves (after Millet), September 1889, oil on canvas on cardboard, 43.2 × 33.2 cm, Amsterdam, Van Gogh Museum

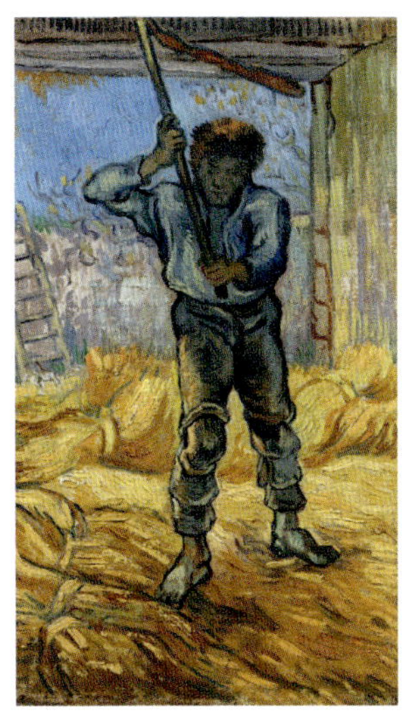
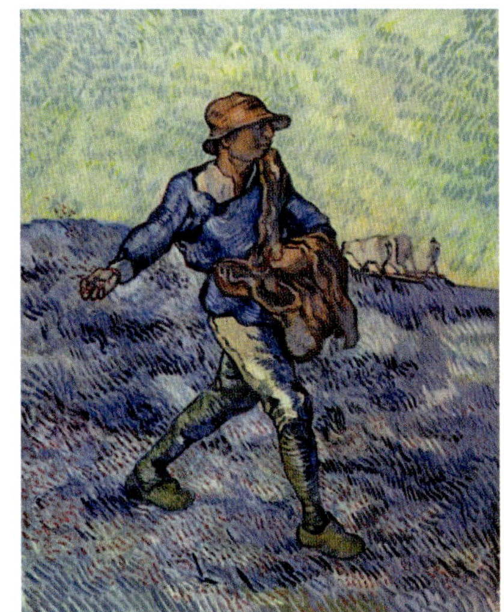
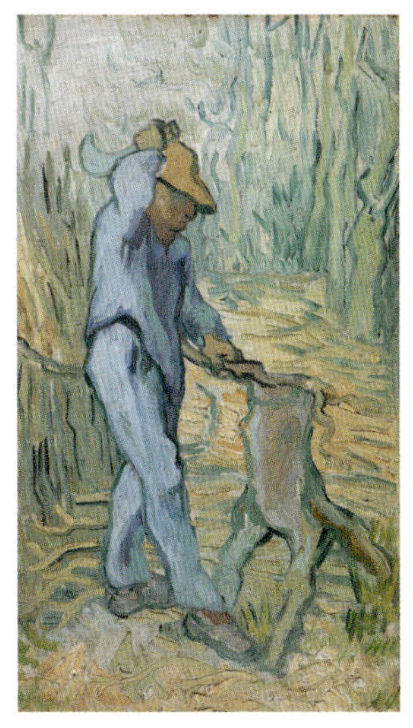
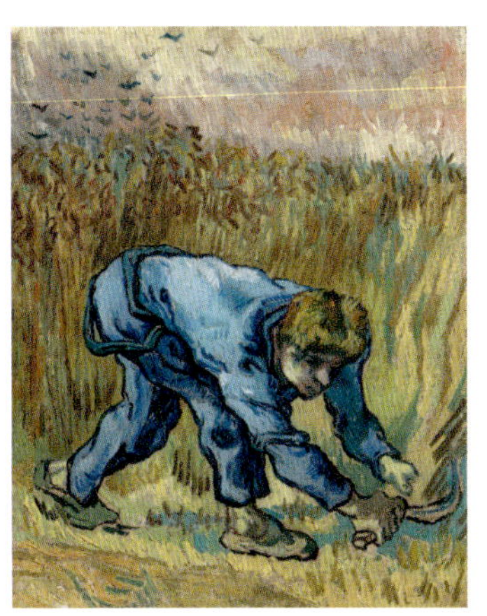
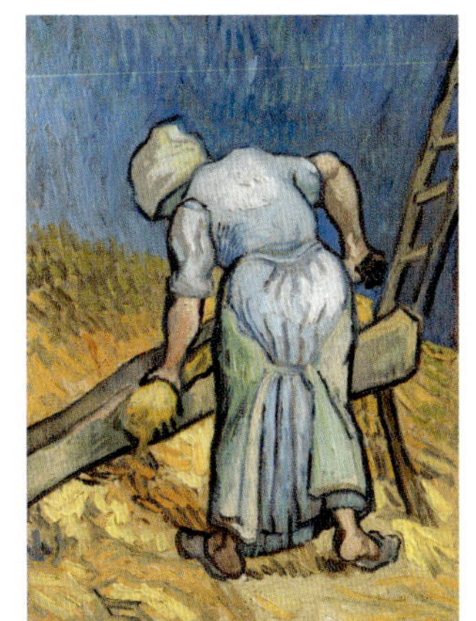
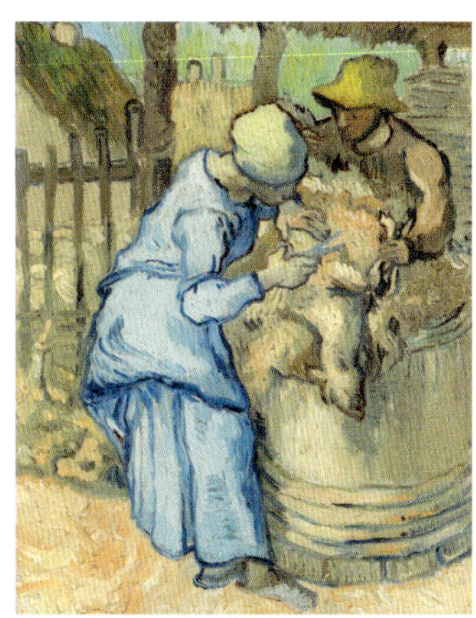
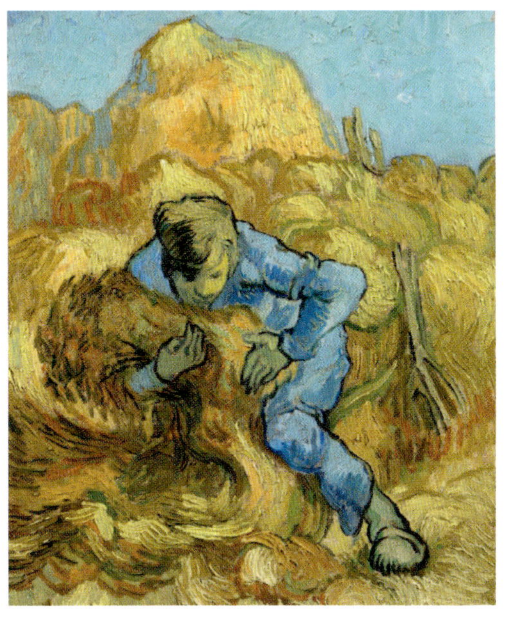
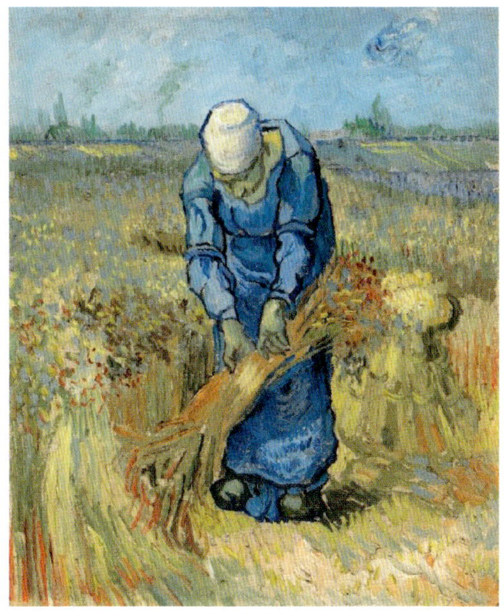

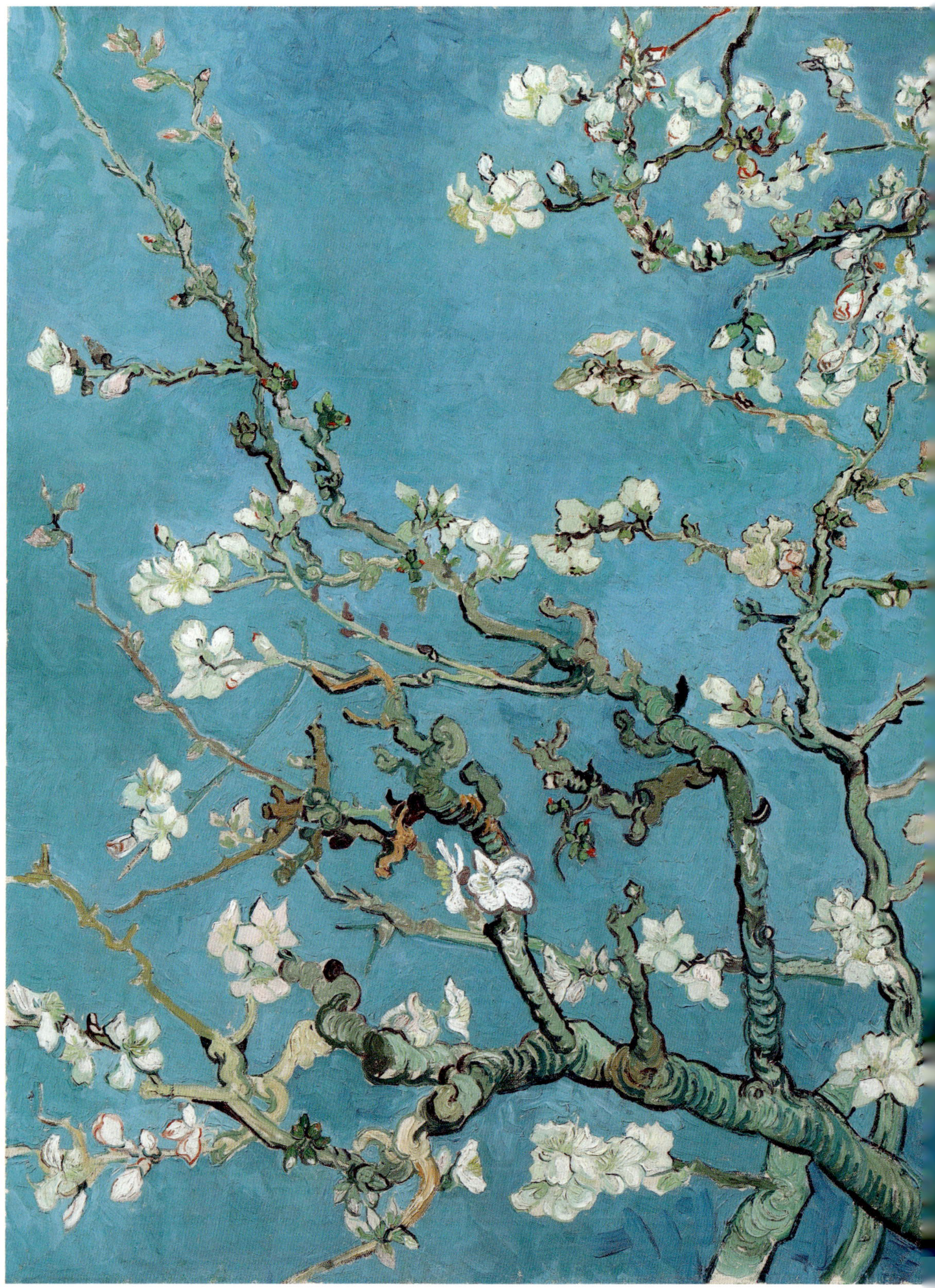

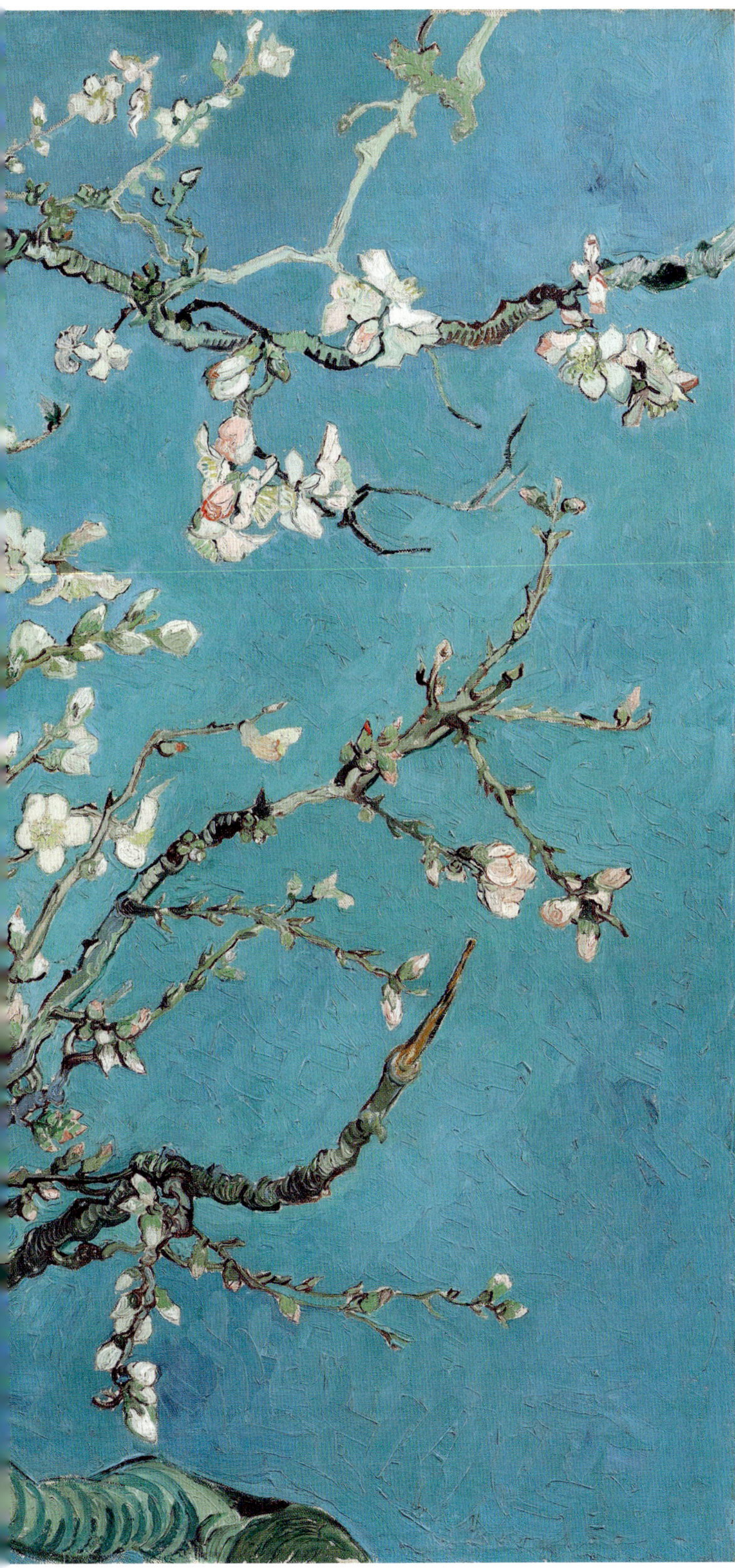

Fig. 32
Almond Blossom, February 1890, oil on canvas, 73.3 × 92.4 cm, Amsterdam, Van Gogh Museum

countryside here is very beautiful in the autumn, and the yellow leaves. I'm just sorry there aren't more vineyards here" (L811). He would ideally have pursued the series of vines he had begun in Arles, which included *The Red Vineyard* (fig. 34). Exhibited at the Salon des XX in Brussels in March 1890, this was the only canvas sold during Van Gogh's lifetime, for 400 francs. This sale, accompanied by the favourable reviews of the Salon des Indépendants and the text by Albert Aurier, prompted Van Gogh to observe, not without irony, that "it's almost always the case that success is the worst thing that can happen in a painter's life" (L864).

Portrait-Self-Portrait

The personification of Nature through arboreal motifs or scenes of peasant life serves as a reminder of the role portraiture held within the Dutch master's oeuvre. While he considered landscape to be the prerogative of modernity, he nonetheless acknowledged the significance of the human figure in the history of art and was eager to devote himself to it more fully. Unfortunately, Vincent van Gogh lacked models in Saint-Rémy, a fact about which he complained to his family.
He painted very few portraits: a *Peasant, Mr Trabuc* (fig. 9, p 23), his attendant at the hospital; his wife, *Madame Trabuc*;

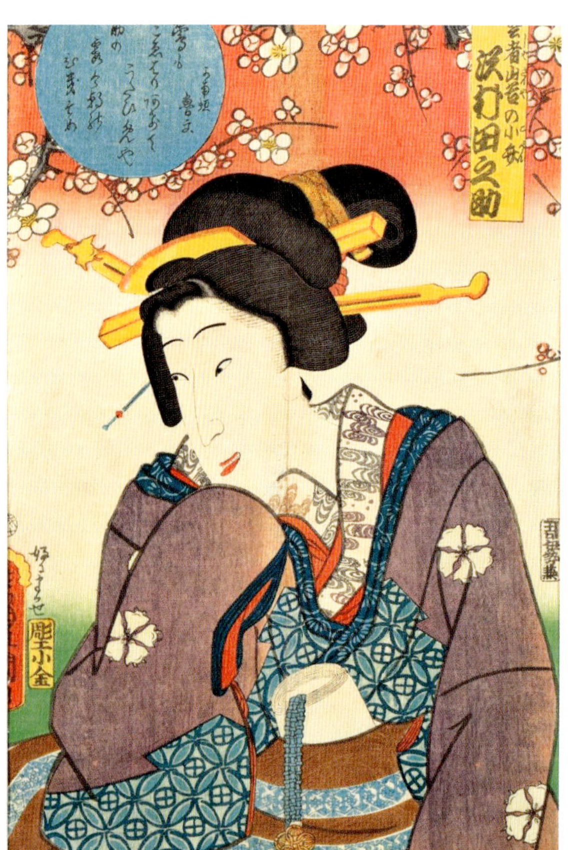

Fig. 32bis
Utagawa Kunisada (1786–1865), *Portrait of a Woman*, ca. 1840, print

Fig. 33
Mulberry Tree, October 1889, oil on canvas, 54 × 65 cm, Pasadena, Norton Simon Museum

Fig. 34
The Red Vineyard, November 1888, oil on canvas, 75 × 93 cm, Moscow, Pushkin Museum

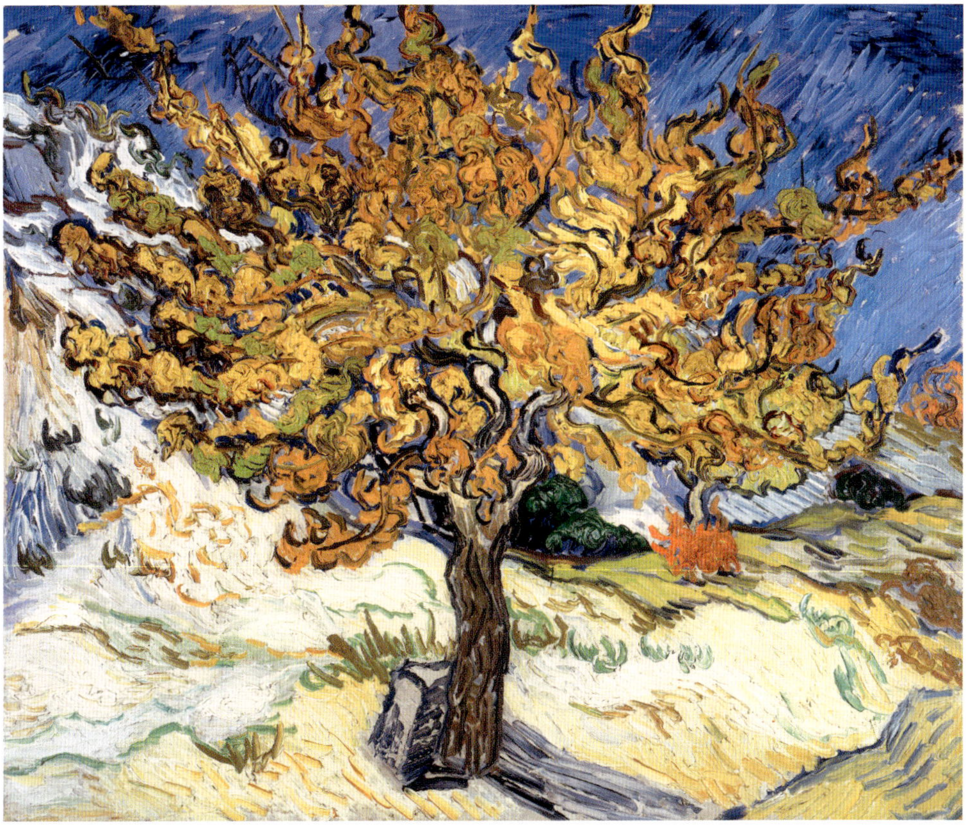

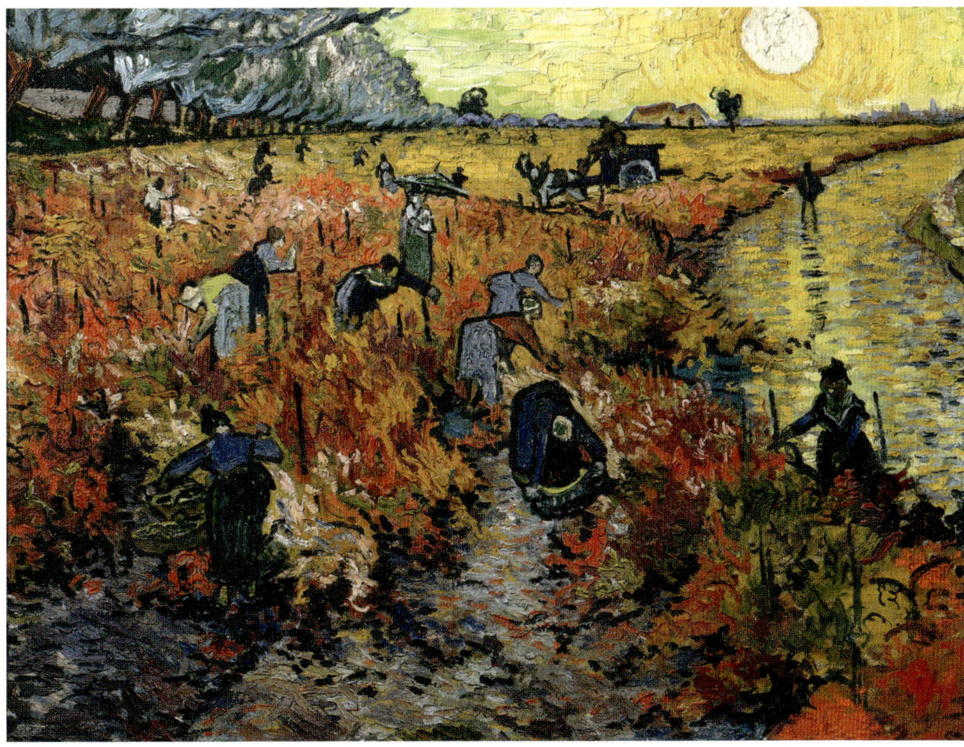

a patient; and, on several occasions, *Madame Ginoux* (figs. 10 and 11, p. 120), in increasingly stylised variations. He did not, however, abandon the self-portrait, and his *Blue Self-Portrait* (fig. 45, p. 59), painted in the summer of 1889, is now regarded as a masterpiece of the genre. He depicts himself in a three-quarter bust view, his gaze unwavering, clad in blue against a pulsating background of the same hue. This portrait is neither that of a painter nor an invalid, but that of a resolute and self-assured man. As Van Gogh wrote to his brother Theo: "People say and I'm quite willing to believe it, that it's difficult to know oneself, but it's not easy to paint oneself either. [...] You will also perceive this when you put the portrait with the light background, which I've just finished, beside those I did of myself in Paris, that at present I look healthier than then, and even a great deal more so" (L800).

All the subjects Van Gogh addressed in Saint-Rémy are rooted in Nature; they offer clear evidence of the strategic place it held in his painting, as well as in his relationship with the world. The translation of these subjects into art, and the formal decisions made by the painter in Saint-Rémy, tell us much about the role painting occupied within society and how profoundly Van Gogh wished his work to participate in it. The simplicity he evoked on numerous occasions must be regarded as the guiding thread he sought to follow. The simplicity of the motifs drawn from Nature, combined with the simplicity of their representation, was intended to reveal the full emotional and "consoling" power, his word, of painting. To Theo, he wrote: "If I continue, certainly I'm in agreement with you that perhaps it's better to attack things with simplicity than to seek abstractions" (L820).

Saint-Rémy or How to Create a Style

Upon his arrival in Arles in March 1888, Van Gogh described Provence as his "Provençal Japan". He dreamt of discovering a new land that would allow him to see differently and provide the foundations for a new plastic language. The Provençal landscape confronted him with new perceptions of nature, markedly distinct from those he had experienced in the Netherlands, Belgium, and Paris. Devoid of humidity, the southern light possesses an unparalleled clarity, conferring infinite sharpness. It brings the background forward and unsettles the classical hierarchy of linear perspective. For the painter, this justified the choice of staged compositions in which planes overlap one another. Van Gogh was already familiar with new principles of construction thanks to Japanese prints, which he had copied and collected with his brother Theo. Observing the reality of the Provençal landscape and other perceptual principles afforded him the opportunity to devise new perspectives and new relationships to the natural motifs he elected to depict. "Perhaps my journey into the South will bear fruit however, because the difference of the stronger light, the blue sky, that teaches one to see, and then above all and even only when one sees that for a long time" (L800). He wrote to Theo: "You know that I came to the South and threw myself into work for a thousand reasons. Wanting to see another light, believing that looking at Nature under a brighter sky can give us a more accurate idea of the Japanese way of feeling and drawing. Wanting, finally, to see this stronger sun, because one feels that without knowing it one couldn't understand Delacroix paintings from the point of view of execution, technique, and because one feels that the colours of

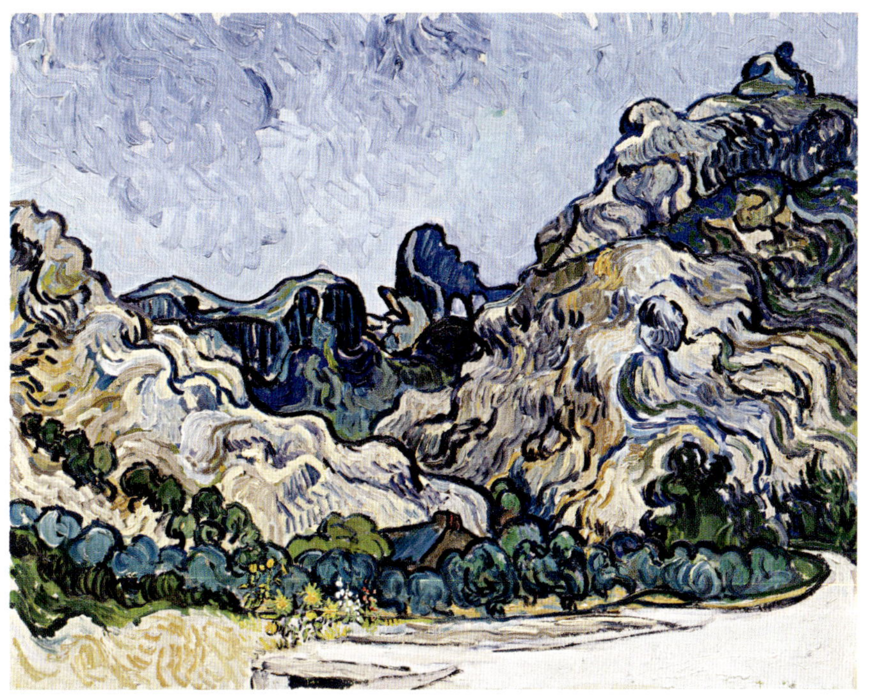

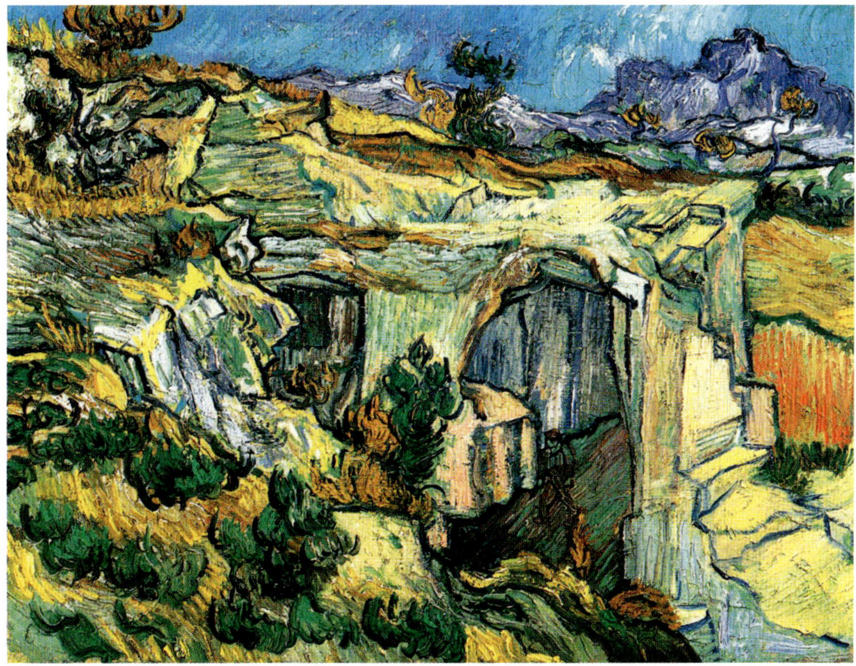

Fig. 35
Mountains at Saint-Rémy, July 1889, oil on canvas, 71 × 90 cm, New York, Guggenheim Museum

Fig. 36
Entrance to a Quarry, October 1889, oil on canvas 52 × 64 cm, private collection

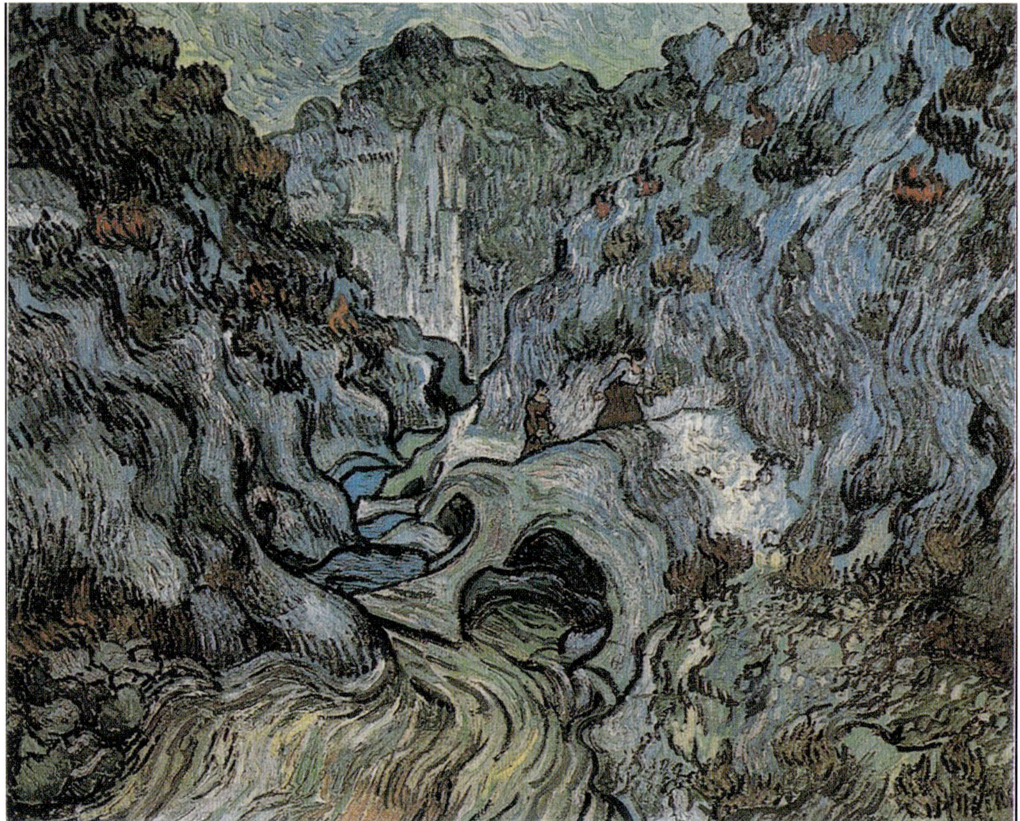

Fig. 37
The Ravine of the Peyroulets, December 1889, oil on canvas, 72 × 92 cm, Otterlo, Kröller-Müller Museum

the prism are veiled in mist in the North" (L801).

The other great virtue of this Provençal light is the variety and brilliance of the colours it reveals. Pure colours employed in the full force of their complementarity provided a response to the duller tones of the North. Van Gogh's palette embraced yellows, blues, reds, and violets in their utmost vitality, with more transitions, more modulated gradations than broken tones, in short, fewer compromises. The colours are juxtaposed in subtle combinations to express all the nuances observed in nature. Finally, after composition and colour, it was line that Van Gogh placed at the heart of his work in Saint-Rémy. "We must return to line" he wrote to his brother; to move beyond the impressionistic touch and to labour towards the development of a new formal grammar.

Composing with Nature as He Saw It

The structural components of the Alpilles landscape, its atmospheric clarity, rocks, Mediterranean vegetation, the frontal character of the mountains, and its light, nourished the painter's reflections on the representation of nature. Van Gogh had always painted landscapes, but it was perhaps in Saint-Rémy that he first brought to them the clearest and most personal plastic solutions.

His deeply immersive position within the hospital grounds and at the foot of the Alpilles offered him an entirely new experience of landscape. Privately, he was passing through a decisive stage in accepting his illness and the care it demanded. He sought complete refuge in nature in order to heal, to draw inspiration, and, above all, to find in it a breath of life that would sustain his belief in a sacred power. This pantheistic faith can be felt in the paintings, which propose far more immersive viewpoints, drawing the gaze in through high-angle framings, low-angle shots, and striking effects that capture the energy of reality. To reinforce the pantheistic immanence already present in Japanese art, Van Gogh employed arabesque lines even in the organisation of pictorial space. Lines, movements, and motifs combine in myriad circular and concentric rhythms. It is the vital force of the natural elements that is celebrated, as in the sky of *The Starry Night* (fig. 10) or *The Olive Trees* (fig. 11), its companion piece. In the wheatfield series, the movements of the mistral in the grasses take up again the metaphor of life's breath. Finally, in *The Ravine* (fig. 37), the composition structured around the arabesque expresses the full telluric density of the rocks.

The Arabesque, Ridge Line of the Alpilles

"It took me all the time to observe the character of the pines, cypresses, etc. in the pure air here, the lines that don't change and which one finds again at every step" (L836).

One need only look at the ridge line of the Alpilles, the hills, the fields, and Mont Gaussier to understand that the entire Saint-Rémy landscape is an arabesque. This motif appears vividly and unmistakably to anyone who observes it, and Van Gogh was born an observer. From the stone of the Alpilles to the knots of the olive tree and the foliage of the cypress, this sinuosity of curves and counter-curves is omnipresent in Provençal nature. The mistral, a frequent visitor, moves through the landscape like a wave, an undertow instilling a vibration, a pulse, in the perception of the whole.

Van Gogh seized upon line to embody this reality and convey its deeply religious sacredness. His line was long and doubled, inherited from his ink drawings made with a cut reed. The reed or Provençal cane he used in Arles split into two points when pressed onto the paper. He transposed this experience to the canvas, combining this form of drawing with a touch that is at times light, at others very thick. For the first time, he embraced the idea of synthesising all the processes with which he had experimented and, in so doing, freed himself from an aesthetic ideology that had become somewhat constraining. By liberating himself from it, he achieved a sensitive rendering of the motif, privileging his immediate feeling over the cold idea of pure representation.

A particularly revealing example of his state of mind upon his arrival at Saint-Paul can be found in two paintings executed at the same time, *Lilac Bush* and *Irises*. The former displays impressionistic virtuosity, lightness of touch, and an evanescent rendering of texture; the latter, entirely Japanese in influence, is presented frontally as if detached from its environment, with a strong line and drawing that suggest Gauguin's "abstraction". The year spent in Saint-Rémy tended to narrow this gap through a process of synthesis, rationalisation, and emancipation of his style. Just as he accepted his illness, Van Gogh accepted being the painter he was, positioned at the crossroads of his learning and ideals. From *Almond Blossom* to *The Cypresses*, he selected from all his influences those that best expressed his aspirations. It was undoubtedly Japan that was evoked and

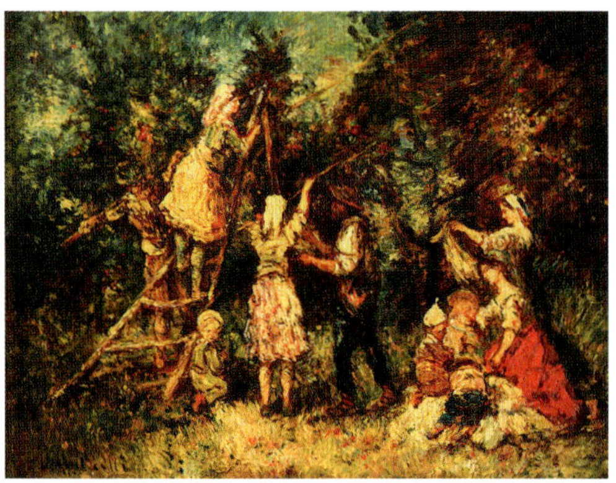

Fig. 38
Adolphe Monticelli (1824–1886), *The Olive Harvest*, ca. 1875, oil on wood, 37.5 × 48.5 cm, Saint-Rémy-de-Provence, Musée Estrine

reinterpreted in *Almond Blossom* (figs. 32 and 32bis). Whereas in *The Cypresses* and *Wheatfields*, Van Gogh produced a veritable synthesis—a fusion of arabesque lines with a sometimes deliberately heavy impressionistic touch. He wrote to Theo: "I have a canvas of cypresses with a few ears of wheat, poppies, a blue sky, which is like a multicoloured Scottish plaid, *Cypress with Two Women*. This one, which is impasted like the Monticellis, and *The Wheatfield* with the sun that represents extreme heat, also thickly impasted" (L784).
He combined this diversity of styles with a sinuous perspective articulated around a large diagonal that reinforces the pulsating dynamic. Speed of execution, in order to retain the truth of the moment, was also essential: "What a funny thing the touch is, the brushstroke. Outdoors, exposed to the wind, the sun, people's curiosity, one works as one can, one fills one's canvas regardless. Yet then one catches the true and the essential, that's the most difficult thing" (L801).
Van Gogh saw in this intensity something primitive, referring to the primary essence of sensation and emotion. He mentioned "descriptions of landscape with colour notes of accuracy, feeling and primitiveness of the first order" (L798). Theo replied: "You'll perhaps tell me that any work of art must be the result of a quantity of complicated combinations, that's right, but with the painter also there must be moments when he's so inspired by his motif or his subject that he renders it as one might grasp it, or at least feel it like a thing one finds oneself in front of. I have this feeling in front of several of your canvases" (L819).

Colours, Alpilles Music

One experience that anyone can replicate is that of the colours. Observing those of the Saint-Rémy landscape at different times of year and of day, and comparing them with the hues Van Gogh employed in his paintings, it becomes immediately apparent that there was no exaggeration. Everything is true: the violet and blue, the orange on the pine trunks, the pink upon the olive trees, the solar blue of the sky, the black-green of the cypresses. The power of the Provençal light is such that it naturally produces these iridescences and saturations. The painter, as a consummate observer, merely perceived them as they were and employed them to evoke the emotional force of his compositions.
Van Gogh articulated his choice of colours in representing Nature at an early stage in a letter to his brother Theo in 1884: "The spring is tender green (young wheat) and pink (apple blossom). The autumn is the contrast of the yellow leaves against violet tones. The winter is the snow with the little black silhouettes. But if the summer is the opposition of blues against an element of orange in the golden bronze of the wheat, this way one could paint a painting in each of the contrasts of the complementary colours (red and green, blue and orange, yellow and violet, white

and black) that really expressed the mood of the seasons." For *Entrance to a Quarry* (fig. 36), Van Gogh wrote: "And it was precisely a more sober attempt, matt in colour without looking impressive, broken greens, reds and rusty ochre yellows, as I told you that from time to time I felt a desire to begin again with a palette like the one in the North" (L797).
Nothing changed at Saint-Rémy: these defined colours, these associations, remained the bedrock of his painting, unlike in Arles, where he experimented with the electrical violence of complementary colours to instil tension. In Saint-Rémy, a certain repose and flexibility emerged. The painter mastered them, shaping their use with consummate skill. The duo of high-note yellow and its blue pendant, together with the deep green-black of the cypresses, constitute the key chromatic elements of his work in Saint-Rémy. No colour is applied merely to offset a drawing or to seduce easily; each reinforces a structure that is itself profoundly renewed. Theo wrote to him: "All of them have a power of colour which you hadn't attained before, which in itself is a rare quality, but you have gone further, and if there are people who occupy themselves seeking the symbol by dint of torturing the form, I find it in many of your canvases through the expression of the summary of your thoughts on nature and living beings, which you feel are so strongly attached to it" (L781).

Through the affirmation of a new plastic style at the crossroads of all these experiences and his own conceptions of painting, Van Gogh entered in Saint-Rémy a new stage of artistic maturity, during which he reconciled both his psychological fragilities and his pictorial choices.

To discover Saint-Rémy-de-Provence is to encounter an exceptional natural landscape and, still today, to traverse Vincent van Gogh's art. Few places in the world can claim such a confluence. The emotion aroused by the spectacle of Nature, coupled with that elicited by the paintings, constitutes a rare and accessible experience. In Saint-Rémy-de-Provence, Nature and painting appear inextricably bound; just as painting will always create the landscape, so too will the landscape shape the painting.
Many painters and sculptors have come to engage with the Dutch master's experience, making Saint-Rémy an artists' village in which Van Gogh's story continues to unfold. From the Roche-Gleizes and Hepworth-Nicholson couples in the 1930s to more recent sojourns by the sculptor Richard Long and the painter Marine Wallon, and including the art of Mario Prassinos and Lucio Fanti (permanent residents), they have all felt compelled to enter into dialogue with this pictorial landscape. The majority are represented in the collection at the Musée Estrine, founded in 1989 in homage to Van Gogh, who dreamed of a house for painters, a large *atelier du Midi* in the South.
Even today, as one strolls around Saint-Paul de Mausole or journeys from Noves to Saint-Rémy, the landscapes recall Van Gogh's genius for painting wheat fields, cypress trees, the Alpilles, and olive groves. It is impossible not to feel the love emanating from his paintings, a love that renders them so beautiful, so truthful, and so potent. As Van Gogh reminded his brother: "It's difficult to leave a land before proving what we have felt and loved" (L808). One can be certain that he has left us proof of this for all eternity.

* Letters from the correspondence of Vincent van Gogh, according to the numbering established by the Van Gogh Museum in Amsterdam in 2009.

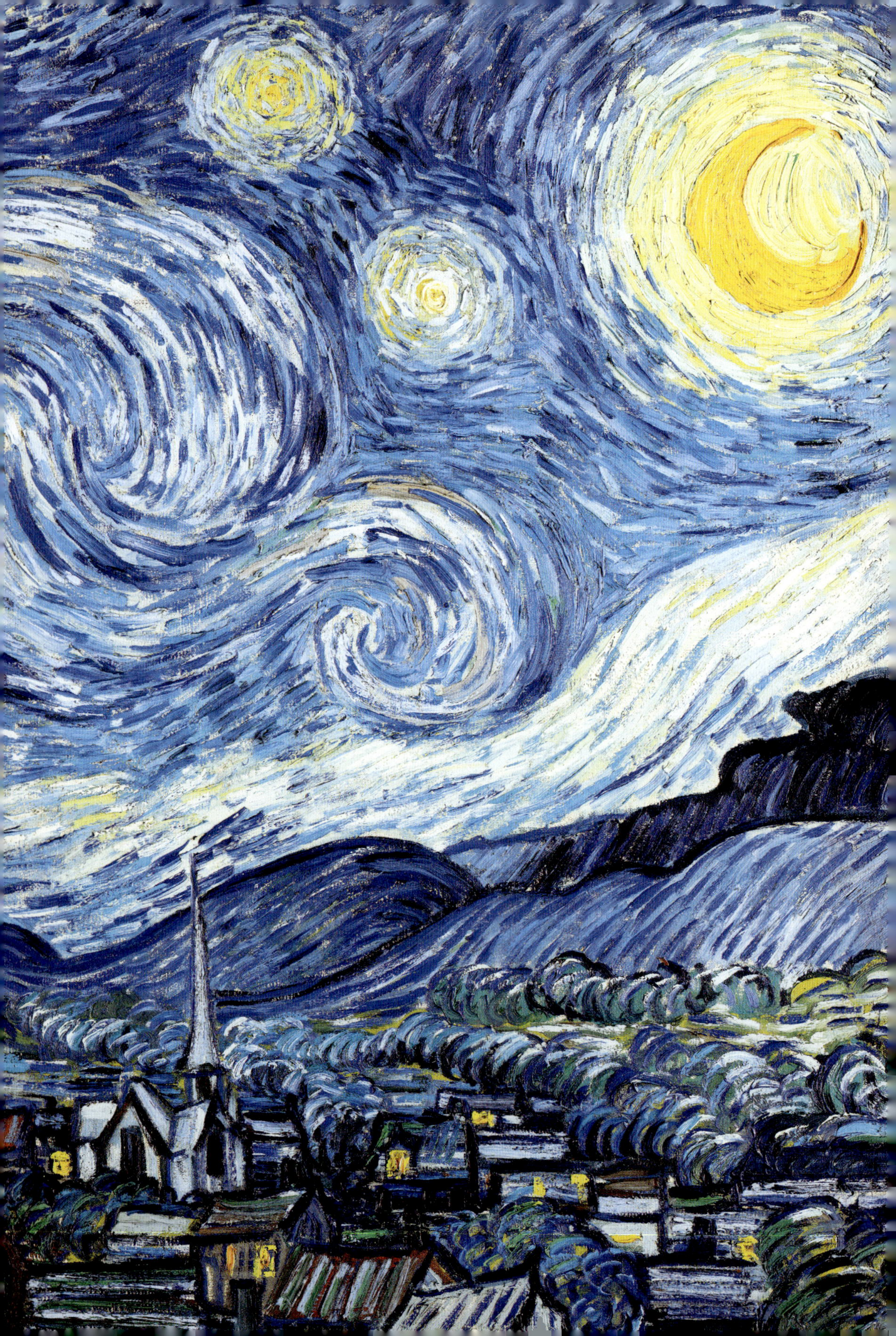

Jean-Pierre Luminet

The Starry Night

Introduction: A Masterpiece in Search of Interpretation

Vincent van Gogh stands among the most celebrated painters of the 19th century, renowned for his expressive style and his vibrant colours. Among his most emblematic works is *The Starry Night*, painted in 1889 while he was confined in the Saint-Paul de Mausole asylum in Saint-Rémy-de-Provence. Now housed in the MoMA in New York, this canvas, depicting a tormented nocturnal sky, streaked with dynamic whorls and studded with dazzling stars, has long raised questions about the manner in which Van Gogh represented the night.

For decades, art historians have wondered: is this depiction realistic, or purely the fruit of imagination? Did Van Gogh paint an actual celestial and terrestrial landscape observed from his room, or is it a mental creation, a symbolic construction in which his troubled state of mind finds expression?

The approach I have undertaken, combining astronomy, a study of Van Gogh's letters, and pictorial analysis, offers new elements of response.[1]

A Sky Observed or Imagined?

The sky in *The Starry Night* is particularly spectacular: it is dominated by immense swirling forms, oversized stars, a radiant moon, and a whirling dynamism that seems in perpetual motion. At first glance, the work conveys a dramatic intensity, heightened by the chromatic contrast between the luminous yellows of the celestial bodies and the deep blues of the sky.

An astronomical analysis allows certain precise elements to be identified. The orientation of the crescent moon and its illumination from below indicate an

1 Jean-Pierre Luminet, *Les Nuits étoilées de Vincent van Gogh*, Paris: Seghers, 2023.

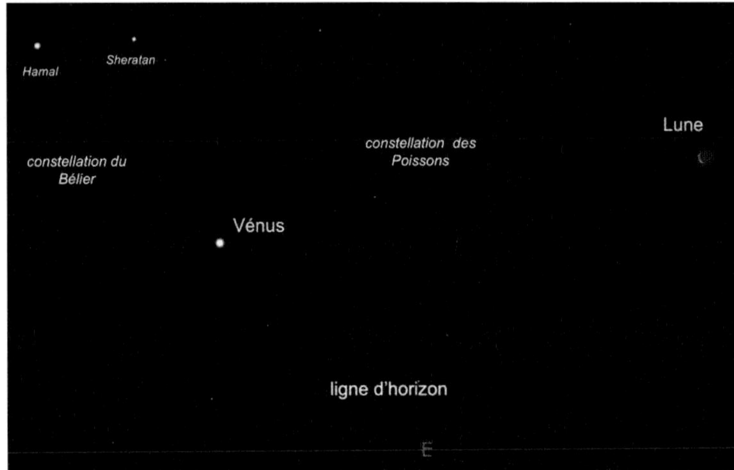

Fig. 1
The sky on 25 May at 04:40 a.m. seen from Van Gogh's bedroom window at Saint-Paul de Mausole. Stars are shown up to magnitude 5, that is, visible to the naked eye

observation made shortly before dawn, when the sun still lies beneath the horizon. The brightest body, situated slightly above the horizon, corresponds to the planet Venus, often visible before sunrise.
The other stars depicted belong to the constellation Aries, notably Hamal and Sheratan, visible near the large cypress, and others of lesser brightness to the constellation Pisces. These observations correspond to the description Van Gogh gives in his letters to his brother Theo.
In a correspondence dated May–June 1889, he mentions having observed, from the east-facing window of his room, the Provençal countryside at dawn, his gaze drawn to Venus, the "morning star", particularly brilliant.
In 1995, the American art historian Albert Boime proposed an astronomical reconstruction in order to date the depicted scene precisely. According to his calculations, on 19 June 1889, at dawn, Venus was visible in the position indicated by Van Gogh. However, using a more sophisticated astronomical reconstruction software, I observed, on the one hand, that the Moon on 19 June had the shape of a rugby ball rather than the thin crescent painted by Van Gogh, and on the other, that the position of Venus in relation to the stars of the constellation Aries was not accurate.
It also seemed improbable to me that Van Gogh painted his canvas in a single day, the 19th of June, on which he writes to his brother that he has "several canvases on the go", including a "night study".
By pursuing my investigation further, I eventually discovered that a sky far more faithful to the painting would have been visible on 25 May 1889 at 4:40 a.m. This suggests that Van Gogh may have taken visual notes or made a sketch on that date, when he was still confined to his room, before beginning the painting a few weeks later.

The Terrestrial Landscape: Between Reality and Recomposition

If the analysis of the sky demonstrates a certain faithfulness to real astronomical configurations, the terrestrial landscape raises more questions. Indeed, from Van Gogh's room at the asylum, with its window facing east, it would have been impossible to see such a panorama of the land. The most intriguing element is the village depicted in the middle ground.

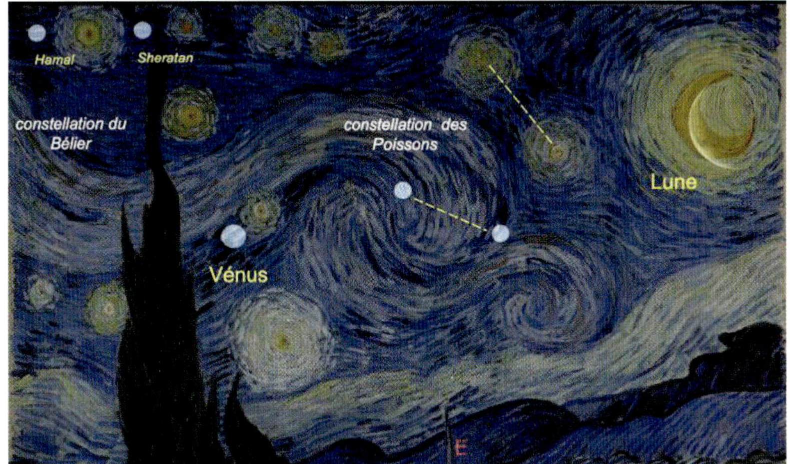

Fig. 2
The agreement between Van Gogh's painting and the actual configuration on 25 May is much more satisfactory than for the date of 19 June

Many commentators have "logically" assumed that it was Saint-Rémy-de-Provence.
Yet, from any viewpoint near the asylum, the village, located to the north, cannot be seen set against the backdrop of the Alpilles hills.
The topographical study carried out on site shows that:

1. The Alpilles mountain range, depicted with reasonable fidelity, could only have been painted from the enclosure adjoining the asylum—an area where Van Gogh was permitted to walk in early June. The same profile of the hills is also found in daytime paintings from that same month, in which Van Gogh painted the wheat field occupying the

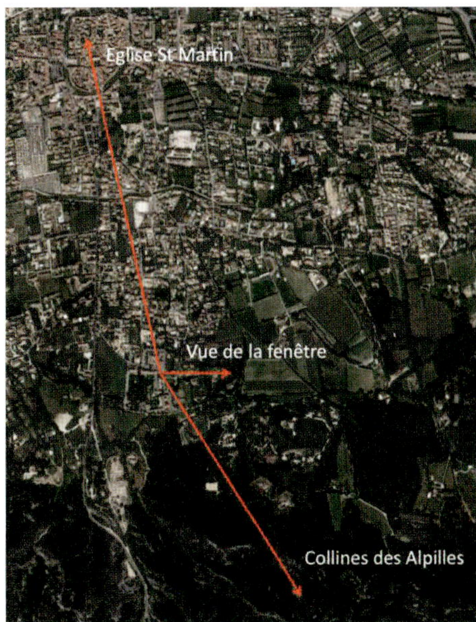

Fig. 3
Orientations

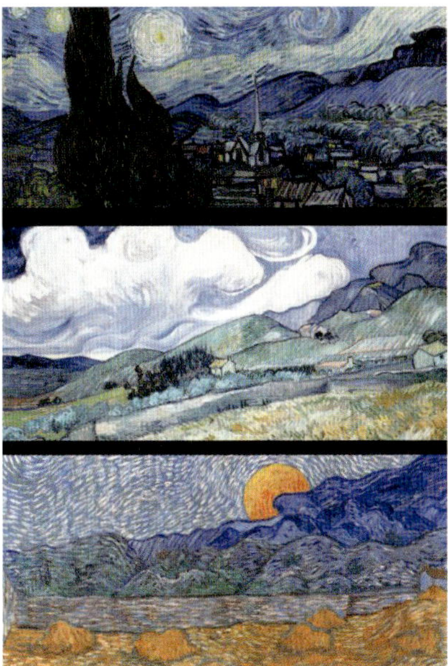

Fig. 4
Identical profiles of the hills in *The Starry Night*, *Mountainous Landscape behind Saint-Paul Hospital* (detail) and *Rising Moon: Haycocks* (detail)

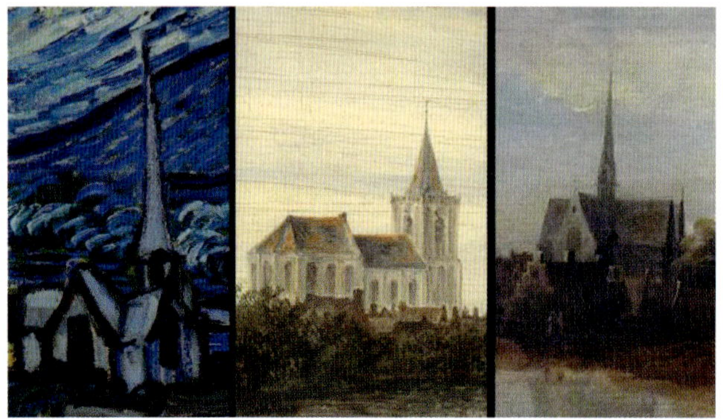

Fig. 5
Comparison of church steeples.
Centre: Salomon van Ruysdael, *River Landscape with Ferry*, 1649 (detail), National Gallery of Art, Washington.
Right: Jan van Goyen, *View of a Village Bordering a River*, ca. 1650 (detail), Musée des Beaux-Arts de Quimper

enclosure, surrounded by a wall.

2. The church steeple in the centre of the village does not resemble the church of Saint-Martin in Saint-Rémy, but rather the typical steeples of Dutch villages.

This pictorial choice may be explained by several reasons. Despite his stay in Provence, Van Gogh remained deeply attached to his native country, and his memories of Dutch architecture may well have mingled with his imagination. It is also possible that he wished to lend his village a more universal character, creating a scene that is timeless and evocative.
I was able to identify the same type of pointed church spires in the classical Dutch paintings of Van Goyen and Van Ruysdael, landscape masters whom Van Gogh admired and often mentioned in his correspondence.
Thus, *The Starry Night* combines observed elements with recomposed ones, confirming an artistic approach in which memory and imagination intertwine with reality.

The Whirling Forms in the Sky: A Scientific Influence?

One of the most fascinating features of the painting is the presence of dynamic spirals in the sky, which seem to give tangible form to the wind or to cosmic forces. Albert Boime put forward the hypothesis that these shapes might have been inspired by scientific representations.
In 1845, the astronomer William Parsons, also known as Lord Rosse, produced a drawing of the nebula M51, the so-called "Whirlpool" nebula, observed through one of the largest telescopes of the period. This image, widely circulated in works of popular astronomy, could well have been known to Van Gogh. Moreover, Camille Flammarion, the famous French science populariser, published *L'Astronomie populaire* in 1881, a richly illustrated

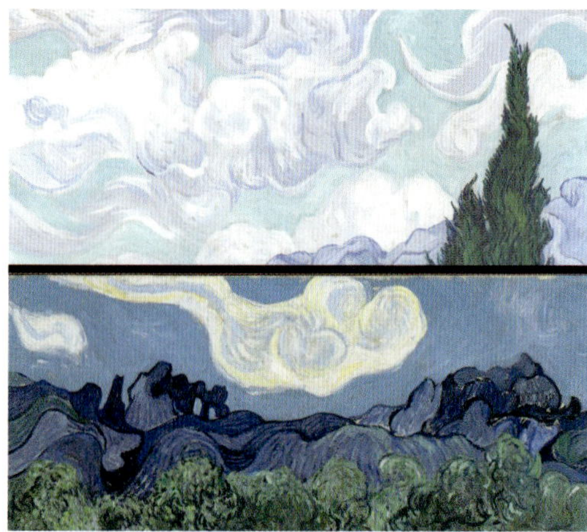

Fig. 6
Depictions of clouds in *Wheatfield with Cypresses* (detail) and *Olive Trees with the Alpilles in the Background* (detail), both dating from June 1889

volume reproducing Lord Rosse's drawings.
However, in examining the entirety of Van Gogh's correspondence (902 letters), I found no mention of any direct interest in astronomy as a science. He speaks often of the stars, but always within an aesthetic or emotional framework, never a scientific one. The very word *astronomy* is never used, nor is Flammarion's name ever cited, even though Vincent did not hesitate to inform his brother of his many readings and favourite authors. It is therefore far more likely that the whirling forms of the sky in *The Starry Night* were inspired by cloud formations—indeed, such forms appear in other daytime landscapes painted during the same period, such as *Wheatfield after the Storm* or *Olive Trees with the Alpilles in the Background*.
As for the cypress, a central element of the work, it plays a strongly symbolic role.

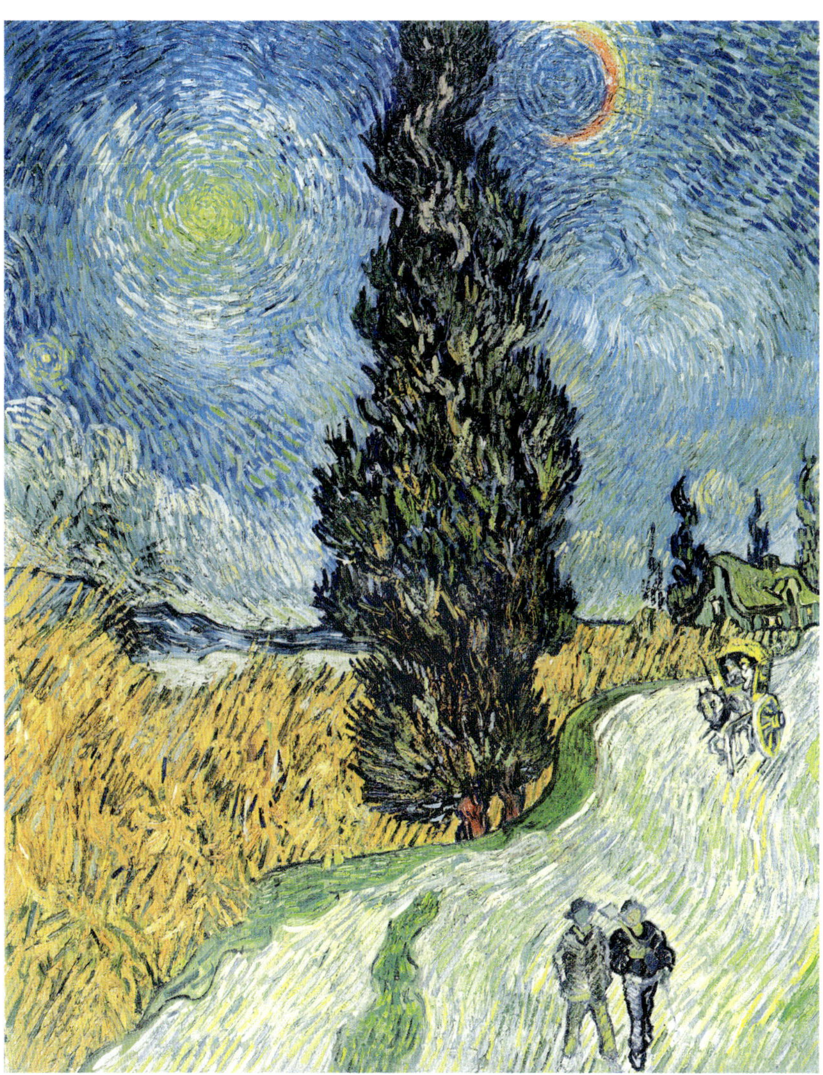

Fig. 7
Road with Cypress and Star (sometimes called *Country Road in Provence by Night*), Otterlo, Kröller-Müller Museum

Present in several canvases, it is often interpreted as a metaphor for the link between earth and sky, a passage towards the infinite. Its verticality, contrasted with the swirling movements of the sky, heightens the dramatic effect of the painting.

***Road with Stars and Cypress*: A Similar Recomposition**

In February and March 1890, Vincent van Gogh went through a period of intense crisis marked by violent outbursts and phases of depression. It was only in April that he regained a certain clarity and took up painting again.
Road with Stars and Cypress, painted in April 1890, follows a logic similar to that of *The Starry Night*. It depicts a winding road bordered by an imposing cypress beneath a sky where a crescent moon and two bright celestial bodies shine.
Astronomical analysis reveals that the scene corresponds very precisely to a rare alignment of Mercury, Venus, and the crescent Moon observed on 20 April 1890 at sunset. Although Van Gogh does not mention this event in his correspondence, it is likely that he was informed of it by a newspaper article. However, as with *The Starry Night*, Van Gogh altered their arrangement for pictorial reasons. In particular, the crescent Moon is illuminated on the wrong side, suggesting a complex compositional assembly on the part of the artist. The cypress, the central element of the painting, symbolises the link between earth and sky. Van Gogh reversed the positions of the celestial bodies to satisfy the aesthetic imperatives of his

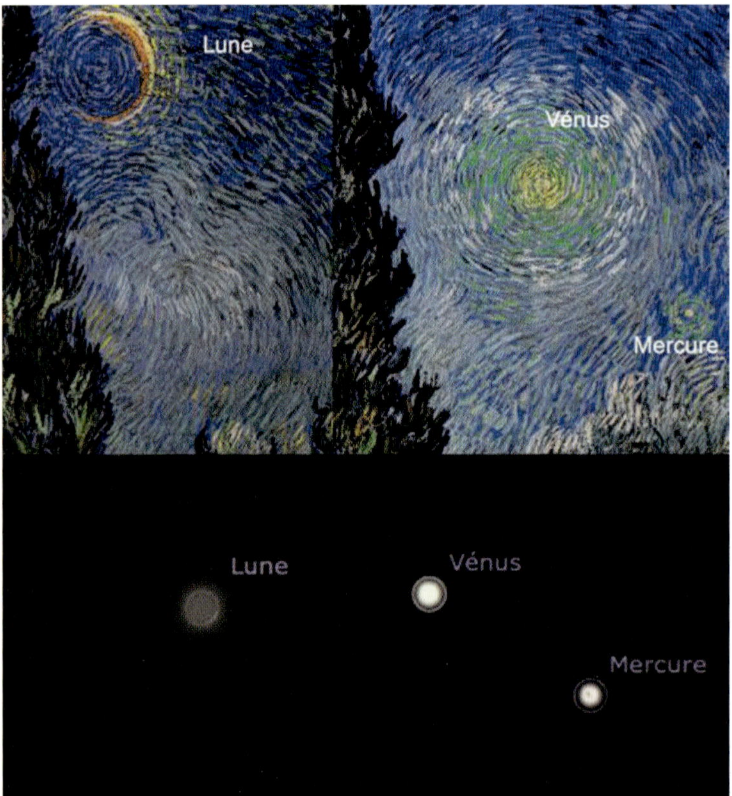

Fig. 8
Correspondence with the real sky

composition. This subtle and deliberate process demonstrates the painter's mastery, who, while drawing inspiration from reality, did not hesitate to depart from it in order to achieve the formal balance and expressiveness he sought.
Thus, his painting perfectly illustrates Delacroix's definition: "A painting is a machine whose systems are all intelligible to a trained eye."

Conclusion: Between Observation and Imagination

Far from being mere realistic representations or purely invented visions, Van Gogh's starry nights are composite works in which observation, memory, and imagination coexist. They testify to the manner in which Van Gogh apprehended the world: he observed attentively, retained the striking elements, then transformed them so as to adapt them artistically to his own sensibility.
These paintings do not seek to reproduce an exact moment, but rather to convey the emotion of a starry night—its light, its atmosphere, and its mystery. Thus, this study confirms that Van Gogh, though influenced by what he saw, favoured above all the expression of his inner response, creating vibrant canvases in which the boundary between reality and imagination fades in favour of a unique and timeless artistic vision.

Legend for Fig. 1, 2, 3 and 8

Ligne d'horizon = Horizon
Lune = Moon
Vénus = Venus
Constellation du Bélier = Constellation of Aries
Constellation des Poissons = Constellation of Pisces
Église St Martin = Church of St Martin
Vue de la fenêtre = View from the window
Collines des Alpilles = Alpilles hills
Mercure = Mercury

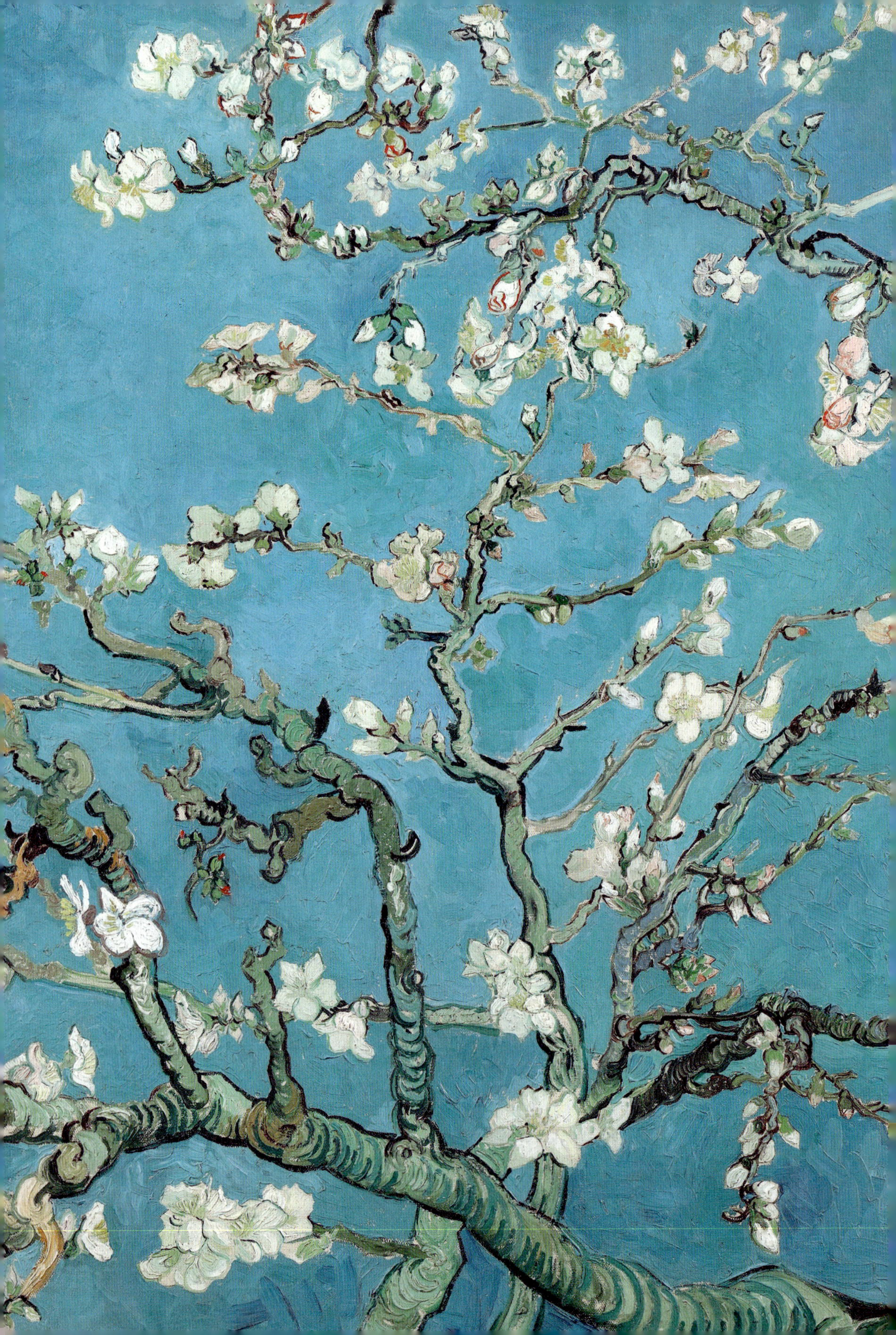

Adrien Bosc

Almond Blossom

> "[...] some canvases, which even in the midst of collapse retain their calm."

I grew up in Saint-Rémy, precisely in that neighbourhood between the Alpines Canal and the Antiques, at the corner of Avenue Joseph d'Arbaud and Avenue Vincent van Gogh. In the painter's time, there were two fields on either side of a road that did not yet bear his name. For a long while, and like many locals, his paintings struck me with a disquieting familiarity. Not that I understood them better; rather, they seemed to me to be set within a childhood landscape. The hospice enclosure at the foot of the hills, Glanum beneath the mown wheat, the path leading to the Deux Trous, the old quarry, its tortuous track winding around the roots of the pines one crosses, and from the window, in the distance, Mont Gaussier. Winters are less harsh now, the trees blossom earlier, yet it is always the same landscape; in places, the same stones, the same trees. Besides, how long can an almond tree live? A hundred years, they say. Among the almond trees in the fields surrounding Saint-Paul, did one of them offer to painting three of its branches?

These are branches cut from a dead tree upon which flowers have regrown. It resembles a sky seen from below, turquoise, the image of an inverted world, floating. A deceptive lull. Painted during the same period as *The Cypresses* and *Prisoners' Round*, *Almond Blossom* resembles none of the painter's other canvases and conveys—or, one might say, betrays—a form of unusual tranquility. "The work went well, the last painting of the flowering branches, you'll see, it was perhaps what I had done most patiently and best, painted with calm and greater assurance", Vincent writes to Theo on 17 March 1890, yet immediately adds: "And the next day, done for, like a brute." The paradox—or rather the misunderstanding—is already there. Just as *The Water Lilies* conceal the war's charnel houses, *Almond Blossom*, however beautiful, however perfect, comes to embrace a fissure.

It was two years earlier, in the vicinity of Arles, that Van Gogh began his study of the almond trees: "Here, it is freezing hard, and in the countryside there is still snow. I have a study of the countryside whitened, with the town in the background. Then two small studies of a branch of almond tree already in blossom nevertheless" (2 March 1888). What is he seeking to capture in the motif? He sketches it out in his letters. Unlike cherry trees in blossom, almond trees do not herald the spring; they bloom in the very heart of winter, symbolising a resistance to adversity.

Van Gogh goes through several crises during his stay at the hospice of Saint-Paul de Mausole in Saint-Rémy. The most acute comes at the end of 1889, when in a desperate gesture he attempts to swallow his paint tubes and a flask of turpentine. Its origin lies in the month of July, while he is painting in the open fields on a windy day. It is shortly after receiving Jo's letter announcing the imminent arrival of a child. The "very big news" moves him as much as it unsettles him—being named godfather frightens him—and the idea that his brother intends to give his son the same accursed first name terrifies him. He, who learned to read his own name, Vincent, on the tombstone of his elder brother, sees in it a sign that he will soon be forgotten, that he is approaching his own end. He anticipates a distance, the disintegration of that foundational and vital bond which links him to Theo: "I often think of you and Jo, but with a feeling as if there were an enormous distance between here and Paris, and as if it were years since I had seen you."
He congratulates the couple even as he warns them—about Theo's health, the child's, and also his own: "As for being godfather to a son of yours, when firstly it might be a girl, true, in the circumstances I would prefer to wait until I am no longer here [Saint-Paul]. And as for the mother, she would certainly care somewhat that he be named after our father; I, for my part, would find that more fitting under the circumstances."
He would insist on this first name: "Now, for the little one, why on earth do you not call him Theo in memory of our father; it would certainly give me so much pleasure." And addressing his mother after the birth, he evokes those branches suspended, without roots, much as he seems himself to be, properly uprooted: "I would far have preferred that Theo give his son the name of Pa, to whom I have been thinking so often these days, rather than mine; but as it is, I immediately set to work on a painting for him, so that they might hang it in their bedroom. Large branches of almond blossoms against a blue sky."

The fragility of the branches, the joints marked in black like the fingers of old men imploring the heavens. This painting, which he dedicates and reserves for his nephew Vincent Willem, is a Japanese print. It is well known that he found another Japan in Provence. From the Langlois Bridge, or from La Vigne Rouge at Montmajour, one believes one can detect the inspiration of Utagawa Hiroshige (fig. 1). In the south, "one sees with a more Japanese eye, one feels the colour differently". In a letter of September 1888 to Theo, he confides this desire for simplicity: "I envy the Japanese the extreme clarity with which all things are rendered among them; their work is as simple as breathing, and they depict a figure with a few sure strokes." Later, he writes: "Their work is as simple as breathing, and they depict a figure with a few sure strokes with the same ease, as if it were as simple as buttoning one's waistcoat."
This is precisely what Van Gogh achieves in *Almond Blossom*: an unprecedented

simplicity and a new breath. And yet, how could one imagine that the suspended universe of the *ukiyo-e* ("image of the floating world" in Japanese) that the painter transposes originates in a paradox? It is a farewell painting, and yet it is a promise made for the morrow.

In Maurice Pialat's film, there is a scene in which Van Gogh's *Almond Blossom* can be seen above the cradle. Jo, Theo's wife, says to the critic Aurier: "He painted it when the little one was born… I put it there because I adore it. Like this, as it faces the bed, I see it every morning when I wake…" I remember, as a child, the garden of an uncle's house at the end of Avenue Edgar Leroy, below the hospice, a bountiful harvest, in the early evening, sitting with my cousin cracking, with the help of a large stone, hundreds of almond shells. I like to believe that this almond tree with its enormous trunk was the same one that, a century earlier, in February 1890, had supplied Vincent with his flowering branches.

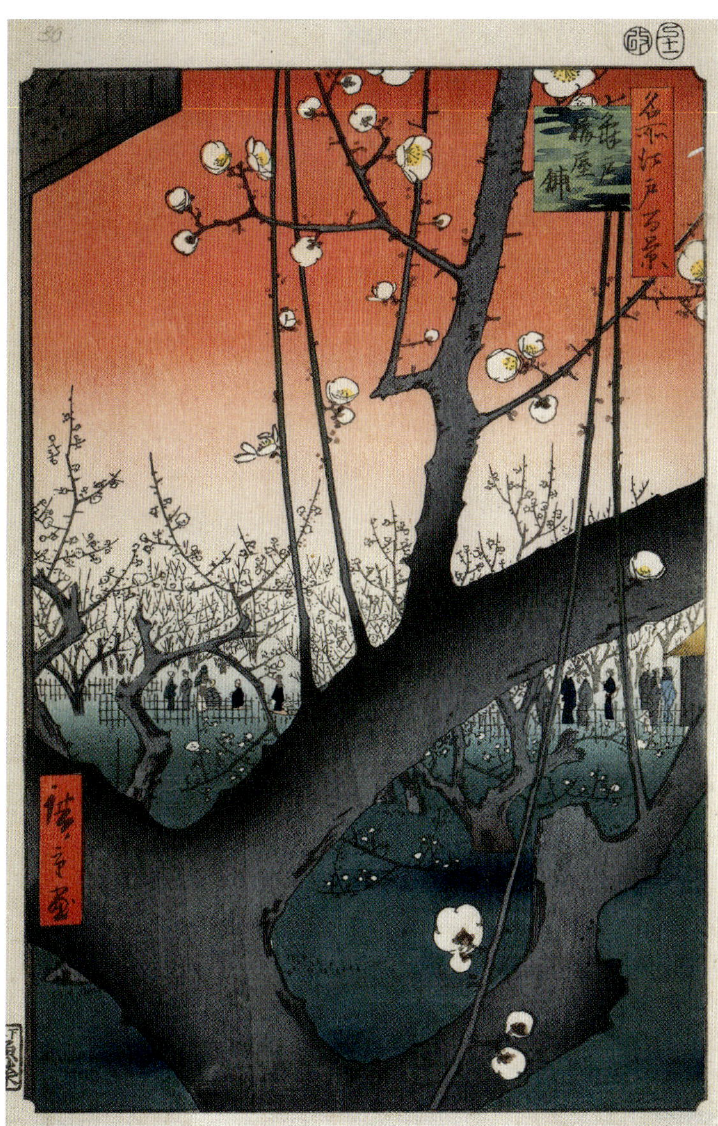

Fig. 1
Utagawa Hiroshige,
The Plum Garden at Kameido, 1857

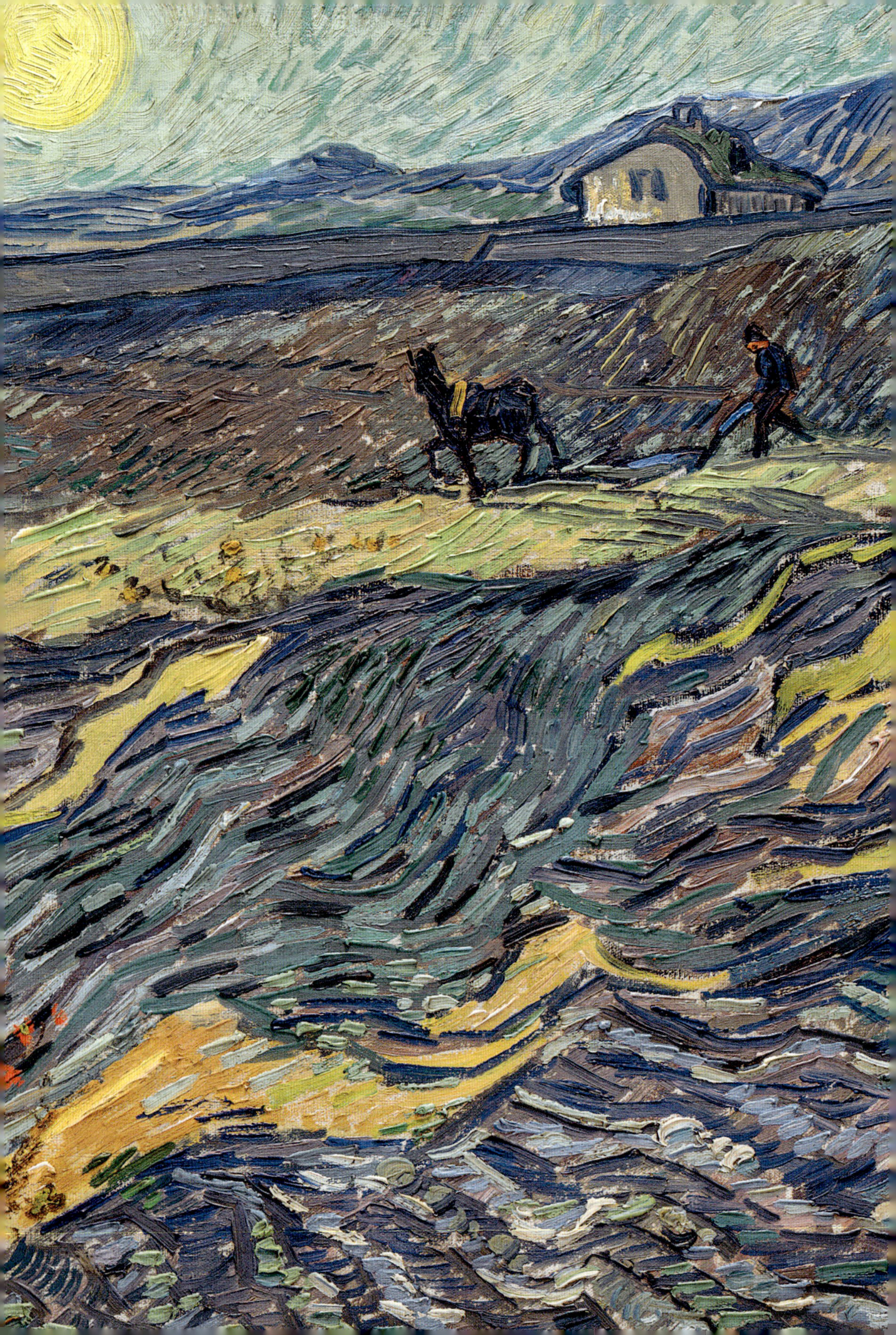

Alexandra Roche-Tramier

Saint-Rémy in the Time of Vincent van Gogh

When Vincent van Gogh stayed in Saint-Rémy (from May 1889 to May 1890), the small Provençal town was still governed by slow rural rhythms, with its olive groves, the tenacious Mistral winds and its peaceful daily life, but it was also opening up to commercial and industrial developments. It was in this harsh yet luminous setting that the painter, self-admitted at the Saint-Paul de Mausole asylum, would find new creative inspiration. The nature, light and silence of the Alpilles offered him a space conducive to introspection and creativity. Arlesian agitation and hostility were now far away, even if, a month after his arrival here, he indicated that he felt highly anxious about frequenting the centre of Saint-Rémy and engaging in its social life: "Once, and again accompanied, I went to the village, just the sight of people and things made me feel as if I was going to faint, and I felt dreadful. In the face of nature, it is the feeling of work that grasps me."[1] Thereafter, individual and always limited meetings would give rise to more positive reactions.[2]
This chapter attempts to portray the main features of Saint-Rémy at the end of the 19th century, based on the town archives and the documentary resources of the Musée des Alpilles, in order to recreate local life as Vincent would have seen it.

Social and Political Life

At that time, the town's mayor was Émile Daillan (1836–1892) (fig. 1), who led the municipality from 1878 until his death in 1892. This radical republican, who was also departmental councillor of Bouches-du-Rhône from 1880 to 1892, was known for his integrity and human qualities, characteristics which earned him the great esteem of his fellow citizens. In particular, he founded the secular school in Saint-Rémy, where education was free from 1850 onwards, but where he asked, in 1872

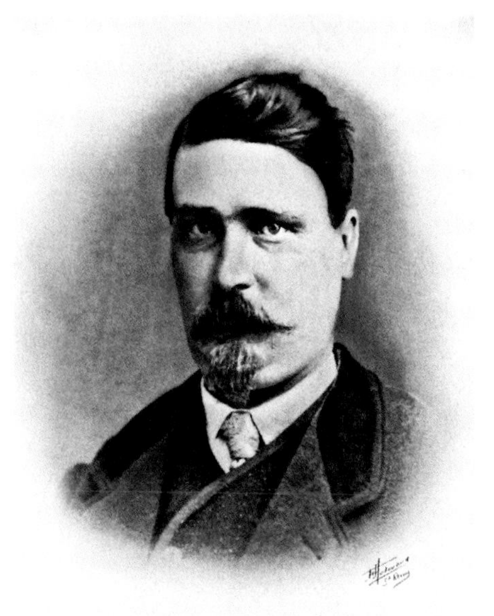

Fig. 1
Official portrait of Émile Daillan (1836–1892), Municipal Archives of Saint-Rémy-de-Provence

(well before the Ferry laws) for a secular teacher's post to be created, and where he first established the school of the Republic, "the boys' school", then "the girls' school", in a building located in the hamlet of Bras d'Or, in the district of Orgon.[3] Referred to as "the Jules Ferry of Saint-Rémy", he decided to finance the teachers' salaries (before the 1889 law gave this responsibility to the State), to create a school fund to help the poorest students, and to award scholarships to students from the municipality. He was also responsible for expanding the cemetery, building a police barracks, building the Peiroou dam, inaugurated on 7 October 1891, and founding a public library, whose regulations were passed during Van Gogh's stay in Saint-Rémy, at a meeting of the municipal council on 12 August 1889: the collection was to consist of works acquired through grants, donations and individual bequests: "The volumes will be lent, without guarantee, to all persons domiciled in Saint-Rémy presenting sufficient moral character. They can be taken home, provided they are returned within a maximum of twenty days."[4]

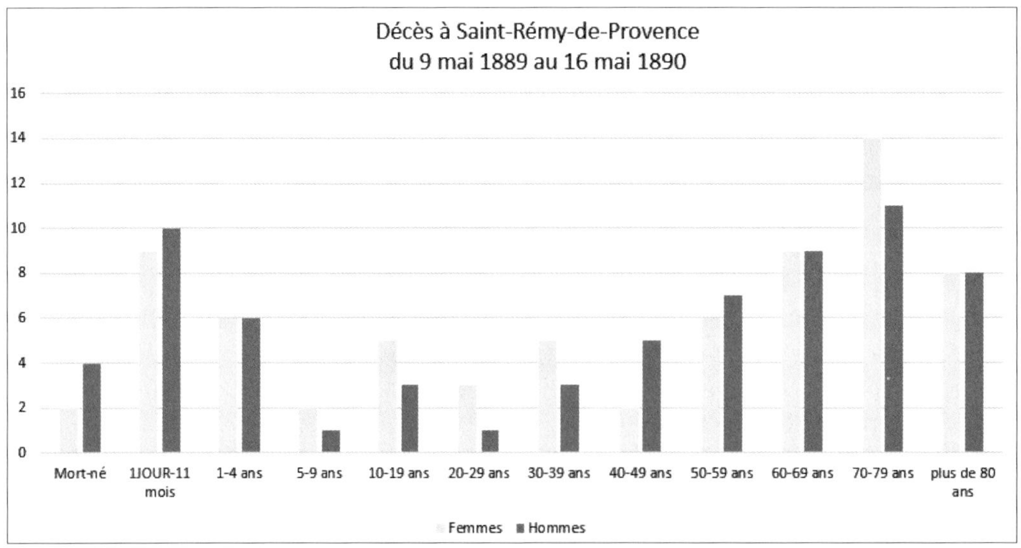

Fig. 2
Chart of deaths in Saint-Rémy from 9 May 1889 to 16 May 1890, compiled from civil registration records

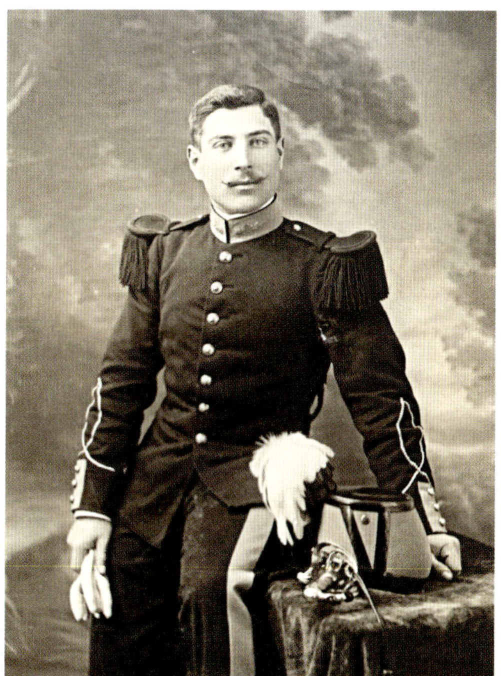

Fig. 3
Picture of Jean Joseph Aurran (1889–1914), private collection

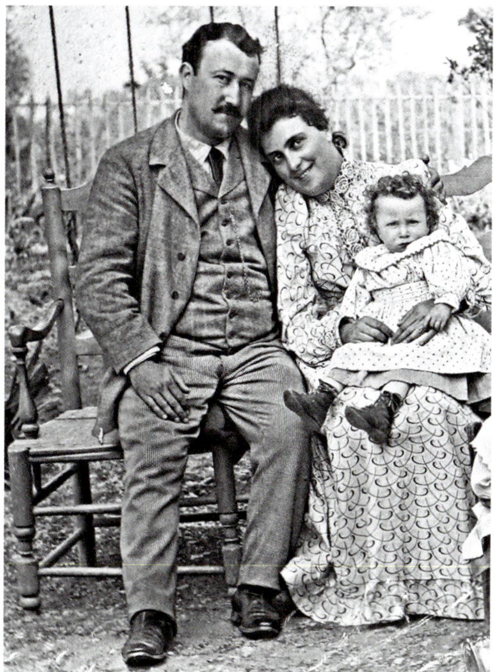

Fig. 4
Picture of Antoine Blain and Louise Daillan, private collection

The People of Saint-Rémy

At the end of the 19th century, Saint-Rémy had between 5,700 and 5,800 inhabitants.[5] During the Dutch painter's stay in Saint-Rémy, there were 139 deaths and 130 births. The distribution of deaths by age group reveals that infant mortality was still high: 6 children were still born, 18 died before their first birthday and 12 died before the beginning of their fifth year (fig. 2).[6]
It should be noted that at this time deliveries took place exclusively at home: although major developments in hygiene date back to the end of the 19th century, it was not until the early 20th century that deliveries would begin to take place in hospitals. Moreover, because vaccination was not widespread, children were vulnerable to childhood epidemics and diseases.

The boys born at the end of the 19th century were the generation that would be called up during World War I. 1889 was the birth year of many sons of Saint-Rémy who "died for France". For example, Jean-Joseph Aurran (fig. 3): a gifted pupil, he enrolled at the Saint-Cyr military school in 1909, joining the Fès year, alongside Alphonse Juin and Charles de Gaulle, and would probably also have enjoyed a great career in the army had he not died in the very first days of the war, on 20 August 1914. During Van Gogh's year in Saint-Rémy, there were 31 weddings. The last of them, on 14 May 1890 (two days before the painter's departure), was that of the mayor's daughter, Louise Daillan (1868–1946) to Antoine Blain (1863–1921) (fig. 4): son of André Blain (1836–1918), the pioneer of seed trading in Saint-Rémy, Antoine Blain settled in the

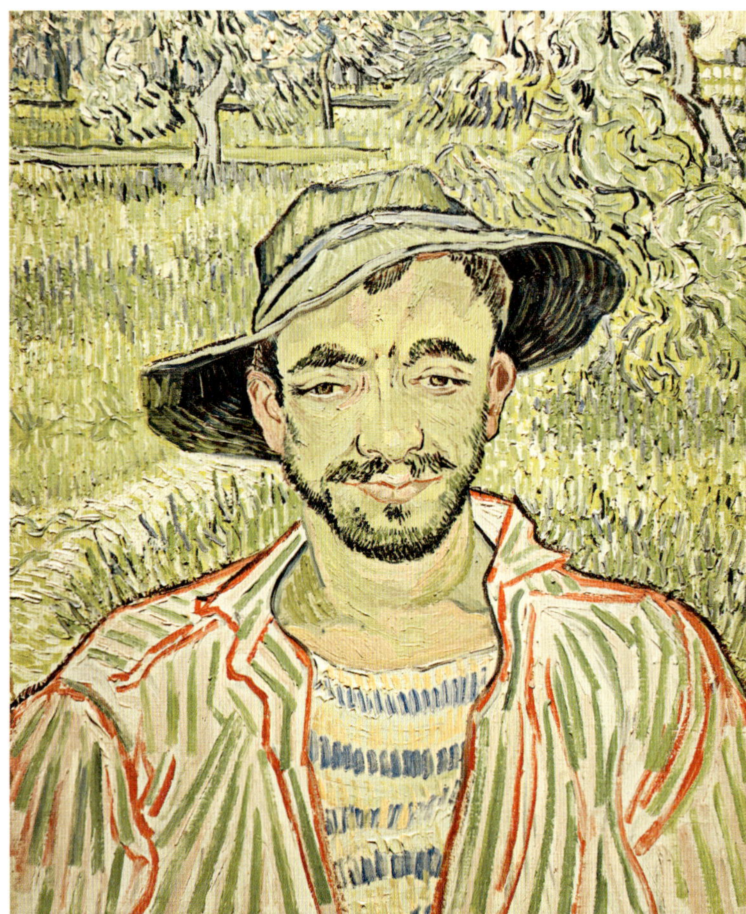

Fig. 5
The Gardener,
September 1889,
oil on canvas,
61 × 51 cm, Milan,
Galleria Nazionale
d'Arte moderna

imposing Villa Louise, which he built after his marriage and named after his wife. He became a leader of sorts to all Saint-Rémy seed merchants and would organise the industrial, commercial and agricultural exhibition of 1910.
Since he visited the centre of Saint-Rémy so rarely, Van Gogh never came to know most of its key figures. Nevertheless, he painted the portrait of various Saint-Rémy residents, of modest condition, most of whom worked in or around Saint-Paul. We can first mention the portrait of the "Gardener" (fig. 5). Van Gogh does not mention this painting in his letters. It was first attributed to his Arles period, and then to that of Saint-Rémy. This gardener appears to be a certain Jean Barral,[7] born on 21 January 1861 in the nearby village of Eyragues, in the Arignès district, in his father's cart. His parents were *vanniers*,[8] an itinerant craft, comprising the making and selling of wicker objects, which Frédéric Mistral attributed to the family of Vincent in his poem *Mirèio* (1859).[9]
At the time of his marriage to Marie Brun on 28 December 1887, Jean Barral's profession was recorded as "a farmer residing and domiciled in Saint-Rémy". Indeed, he appears, with his wife and his two-year-old daughter, in the 1891 census, listed on Rue Notre-Dame.[10] He therefore did not live in the Saint-Paul

area, but came to work the land there. At the time Van Gogh is thought to have painted him, he was twenty-eight years old, which corresponds to the age of the person in the portrait. In a twist of fate, his daughter Adeline died at the age of five days, the day before Van Gogh's departure.[11] At the age of eighty-one, Jean Barral died in the municipal hospital of Saint-Rémy in 1942, as his wife had done twelve years earlier. His portrait was identified thanks to a note kept in the archives of the Musée Estrine, where the Saint-Rémy local Louis Poulet (1928–2007) recounts that, according to his grandfather François Poulet (1863–

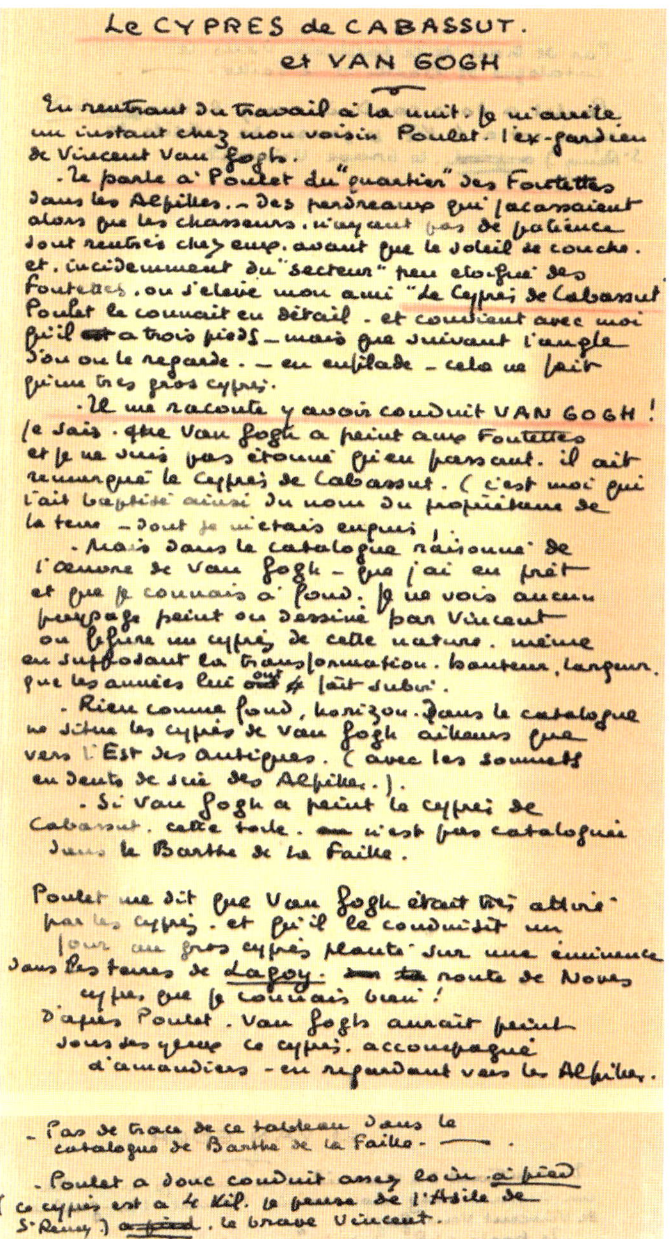

LE CYPRES de CABASSUT.
et VAN GOGH

En rentrant du travail à la nuit. je m'arrête un instant chez mon voisin Poulet. l'ex-gardien de Vincent Van Gogh.
- Je parle à Poulet du "quartier" des Fontettes dans les Alpilles. - Des perdreaux qui jacassaient alors que les chasseurs. n'ayant pas de patience sont rentrés chez eux. avant que le soleil se couche. et. incidemment du "secteur" peu étoffé des Fontettes. où s'élève mon ami "le Cyprès de Cabassut". Poulet le connait en détail. et convient avec moi qu'il a trois pieds - mais que suivant l'angle d'où on le regarde. - en enfilade - cela ne fait qu'un très gros cyprès.
- Il me raconte y avoir conduit VAN GOGH ! Je sais. que Van Gogh a peint aux Fontettes et je ne suis pas étonné qu'en passant. il ait remarqué le Cyprès de Cabassut. (c'est moi qui l'ait baptisé ainsi du nom du propriétaire de la terre - dont je m'étais enquis).
- Mais dans le catalogue raisonné de l'oeuvre de Van Gogh - que j'ai eu prêt et que je connais à fond. je ne vois aucun paysage peint ou dessiné par Vincent où figure un cyprès de cette nature. même en supposant la transformation. hauteur, largeur. que les années lui ont fait subir.
- Rien comme fond, horizon. Dans le catalogue ne situe les cyprès de Van Gogh ailleurs que vers l'Est des Antiques. (avec les sommets en dents de scie des Alpilles.).
- Si Van Gogh a peint le cyprès de Cabassut. cette toile. n'est pas cataloguée dans le Barthe de la Faille.

Poulet me dit que Van Gogh était très attiré par les cyprès. et qu'il le conduisit un jour au gros cyprès planté sur une éminence dans les terres de Lagoy. route de Noves cyprès que je connais bien !
D'après Poulet. Van Gogh aurait peint sous ses yeux ce cyprès. accompagné d'amandiers - en regardant vers les Alpilles.

- Pas de trace de ce tableau dans le catalogue de Barthe de la Faille - .

- Poulet a donc conduit assez loin à pied (ce cyprès est à 4 Kil. ou pense de l'Asile de S-Remy.) . le brave Vincent.

Fig. 6
Page from Jean Baltus's agenda dated 22 September 1936, collection of the Friends of Jean Baltus, with the agreement of France de la Rocque and Jacqueline Leroy

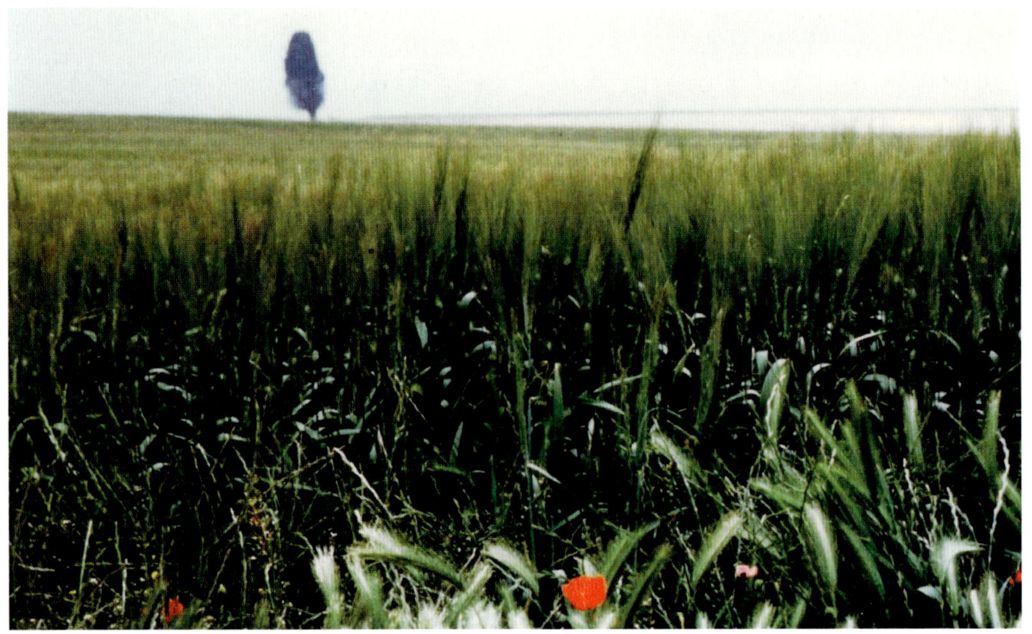

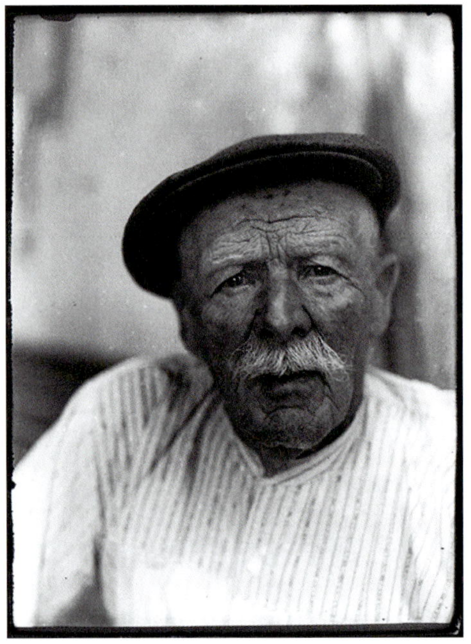

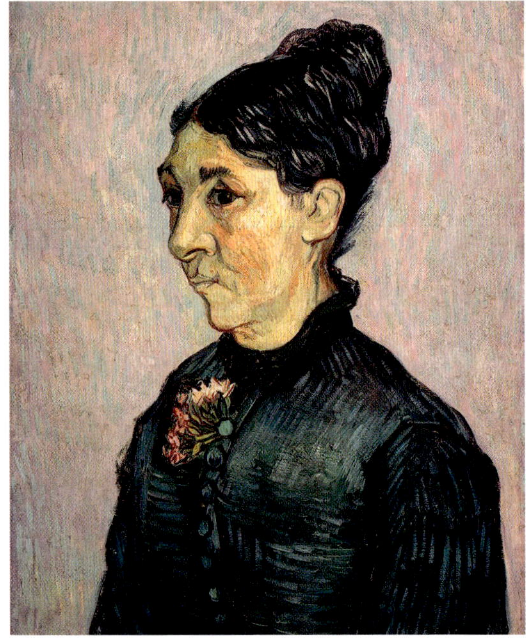

Fig. 7
Picture of the cypress at Mas Rou, private collection

Fig. 8
Picture of François Poulet, Claudette and Roger Olivier Collection, gift of Roger Guillot, Municipal Archives of Saint-Rémy-de-Provence

Fig. 9
Portrait of Jeanne Trabuc, September 1889, oil on canvas, 64 × 49 cm, Saint Petersburg, Hermitage Museum

1954), this young gardener was Jean Barral.

François Poulet was a caretaker and a coach driver at the hospice when Van Gogh was being treated. He often accompanied the Dutch painter on his trips through the local countryside. The painter Jean Baltus (1880–1946) wrote in his notebooks[12] of an exchange with François Poulet, who was his neighbour (fig. 6), who told him that he had brought Van Gogh to paint a cypress "on the road to Noves, on a hill in the Lagoy estates". Indeed, for several centuries, there was a cypress in one of the Mas Rou estates,[13] on the slope of the Petite Crau plateau. Almost a hundred years later, this tree was still standing, falling only on a day of strong Mistral winds in the 1990s (fig. 7). Unfortunately, the painting has never emerged, and although Van Gogh mentions cypress trees several times in his letters,[14] they never seem to be the one in Lagoy. What we do at least learn is that Vincent's exploration of the Saint-Rémy countryside extended much further than the surroundings of Saint-Paul or central Saint-Rémy. This is confirmed by a letter in which, in the autumn of 1889, he "regrets that there are no more vineyards", saying: "I went to paint one, but it was a few hours away from here."[15] The municipal iconographic archive contains photographs of M. Poulet, probably taken by Jean Baltus during their meetings (fig. 8).

Van Gogh also painted the portrait of a Saint-Rémy couple, Charles Elzéard Trabuc (1830–1896) and his wife Jeanne, née Lafaye (1834–1903) (fig. 9). A native of Manosque, Charles Trabuc was the chief supervisor of the men's division in Saint-Paul de Mausole. The 1891 census mentions the couple in this neighbourhood, and M. Trabuc's 1896 death certificate states: "Died in his house in the Antiquities district."[16]

In a letter to his brother Theo dated 5 September 1889, Vincent said: "Yesterday, I started the portrait of the chief supervisor and may also paint his wife, because he is married and lives in a small farmhouse a stone's throw from the establishment." Van Gogh gave the couple the two paintings (which were since lost), having made copies of them which he sent to his brother. In his letter to Theo dated 10 September 1889, he said of Mme Trabuc: "She is a withered woman, a poor, resigned soul, and so insignificant, like a straggly blade of grass, that I felt a strong urge to paint her. I sometimes talked with her when I was painting the olive trees behind their little farmhouse. She told me that she didn't think I was ill..."[17]

Jeanne Trabuc was fifty-five years old when she posed for the painter. She was originally from Châteauneuf in Maine et Loire, which explains why she was not wearing the traditional Arles costume, unlike Mme Ginoux.

The Traditional Dress of Saint-Rémy

Marie Ginoux (1848–1911) was the owner, with her husband, of the Café de la Gare in Place Lamartine in Arles, where Vincent stayed a few months before moving to "the yellow house". He made several paintings of her in Arles (fig. 10) and several others in Saint-Rémy, working from memory (fig. 11). At the time Van Gogh painted her, this famous costume was everyday dress.

Until the beginning of the reign of Louis XIV, the costumes worn in the provinces of the kingdom all followed the same fashion, that of the court, without regional differences: the shapes

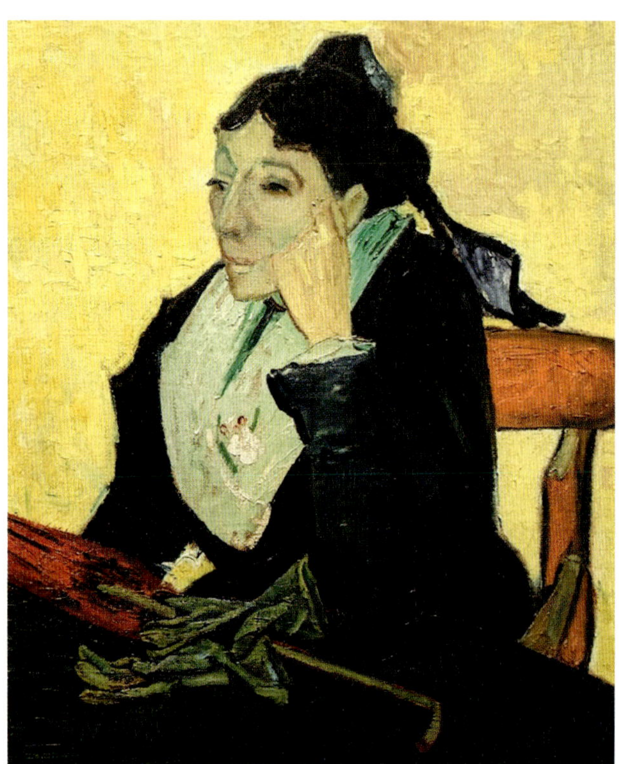

Fig. 10
Madame Ginoux with Gloves and Umbrella, November 1888, oil on canvas (on gauze canvas), 92.5 × 73.5 cm, Paris, Musée d'Orsay

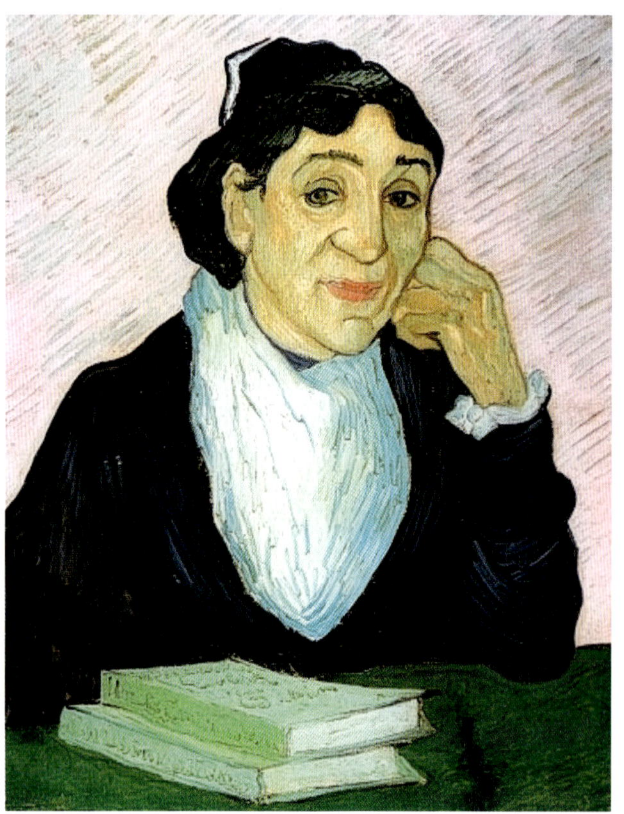

Fig. 11
L'Arlésienne (Portrait of Madame Ginoux), February 1890, oil on canvas, 65 × 49 cm, Otterlo, Kröller-Müller Museum

were identical, only the materials varied according to income. The early 18th century saw the appearance of the first regional costumes. The establishment of a strong regionalist sentiment in France is a process that goes back to the provinces and their parliaments, and which continued, at the beginning of the French Revolution, with the emergence of the "Girondin" spirit. From then on, fashion would change every twenty years, corresponding roughly to a generation.
The characteristics of the costume worn in Provence is that women followed the fashion, especially that of Paris. So, in the middle of the 19th century, during the Second Empire and under the influence of Empress Eugénie, wife of Napoleon III (who came to Provence after the great flood of the Rhone in 1856), Arles women wore crinolines. They were discreet when they travelled by train, but it was a different story if they were receiving distinguished guests. The visit of the Emperor and Empress would serve as a pretext for costumes of unprecedented luxury. The influence of Parisian fashion continued under the Third Republic with the bustle.[18]
At the end of the 19th century, the costume consisted of a black bodice with large pieces of lace adorning the sleeves (fig. 12). The skirt matches the top headscarf, which is worn rounded in front, revealing the white headscarf underneath. The costume of this era is characterised mainly by the velvet head ribbon,[19] which extends down the back or onto the shoulders. We can see these details in Vincent van Gogh's paintings. Family photos from the time show that only women wore the Arles costume (fig. 13). The men and children followed French fashion, while the mother and eldest daughter, who had to

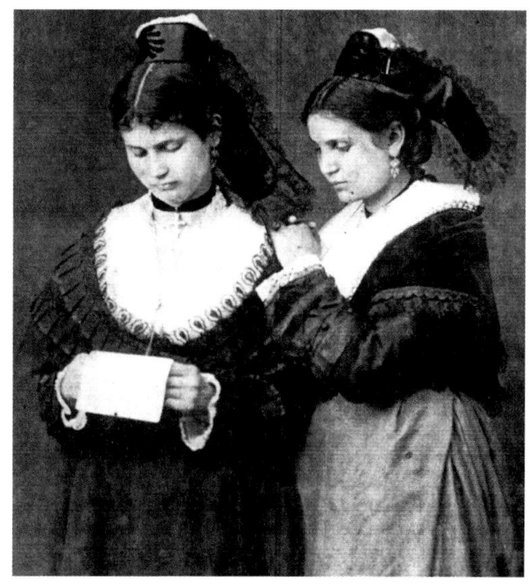

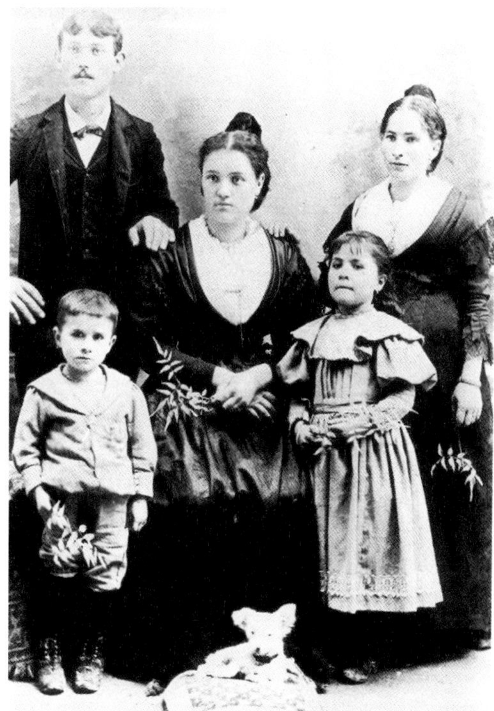

Fig. 12
The Saint-Rémy women Magdeleine and Louise Mauron, ca. 1889–1890, private collection

Fig. 13
Saint-Rémy family in 1890, private collection

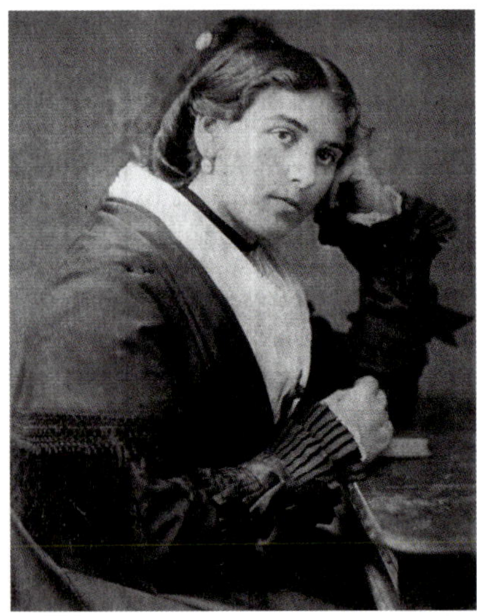

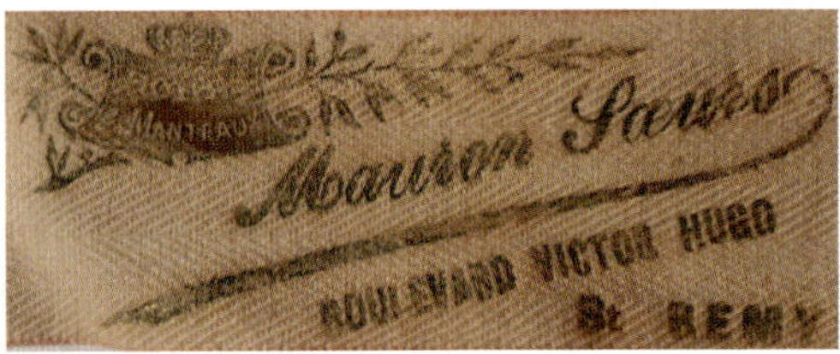

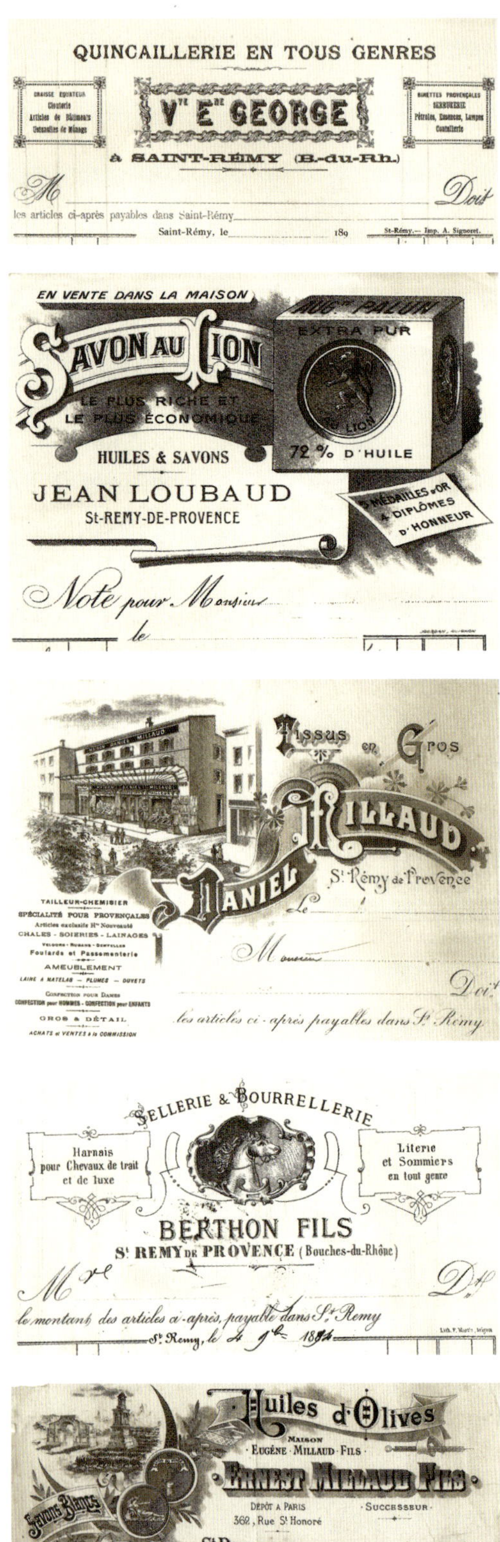
QUINCAILLERIE EN TOUS GENRES

Vve E. GEORGE

à SAINT-RÉMY (B.-du-Rh.)

M Doit

les articles ci-après payables dans Saint-Rémy

Saint-Rémy, le 189

St-Rémy. – Imp. A. Signoret.

EN VENTE DANS LA MAISON

SAVON AU LION

LE PLUS RICHE ET LE PLUS ÉCONOMIQUE

EXTRA PUR

72 % D'HUILE

5 MÉDAILLES D'OR & DIPLÔMES D'HONNEUR

HUILES & SAVONS

JEAN LOUBAUD

St-REMY-DE-PROVENCE

Note pour Monsieur

le

Tissus en Gros

DANIEL MILLAUD

St Rémy de Provence

TAILLEUR-CHEMISIER

SPÉCIALITÉ POUR PROVENÇALES

CHALES - SOIERIES - LAINAGES

Foulards et Passementerie

AMEUBLEMENT

GROS & DÉTAIL

Le

Monsieur

Doit

les articles ci-après payables dans St Rémy

SELLERIE & BOURRELLERIE

Harnais pour Chevaux de trait et de luxe

Literie et Sommiers en tout genre

BERTHON FILS

St REMY DE PROVENCE (Bouches-du-Rhône)

Mr D

le montant des articles ci-après, payable dans St Remy

St Remy, le

Huiles d'Olives

Savons Blancs

MAISON EUGÈNE MILLAUD FILS

ERNEST MILLAUD FILS

DÉPÔT A PARIS 362, Rue St Honoré

SUCCESSEUR

St REMY-DE-PROVENCE le 189

Fig. 14
One of the four Mauron sisters in 1890, private collection

Fig. 15
Stamp of the Mauron Sisters' shop preserved on a bodice, Respelido Prouvençalo collection

Fig. 16
Letterhead of Mme George's hardware store, M245, Municipal Archives of Saint-Rémy-de-Provence

Fig. 17
Letterhead of Jean Loubaud's oil and soap shop, M245, Municipal Archives of Saint-Rémy-de-Provence

Fig. 18
Letterhead of Daniel Millaud's fabric shop, located on the main street of Saint-Rémy, M245, Municipal Archives of Saint-Rémy-de-Provence

Fig. 19
Letterhead of Berthon et fils saddlery and harness shop, M245, Municipal Archives of Saint-Rémy-de-Provence

Fig. 20
Letterhead of Ernest Millaud's oil and soap shop, M245, Municipal Archives of Saint-Rémy-de-Provence

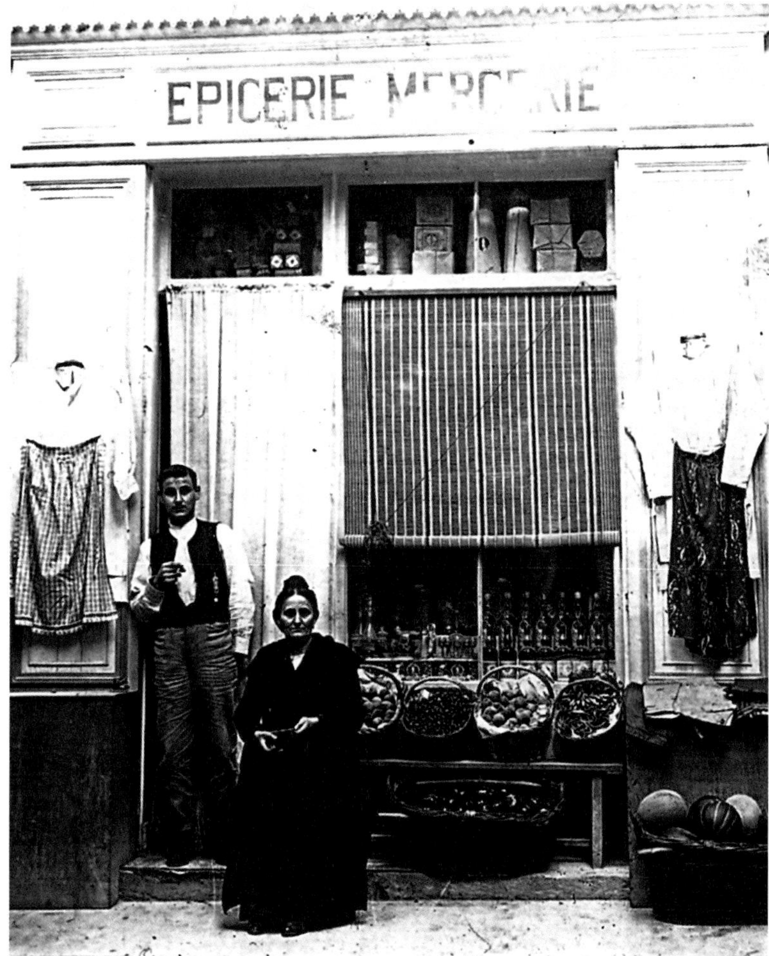

Fig. 21
Picture of a Saint-Rémy grocery store in the early 20th century, Marcel-Bonnet Collection, Municipal Archives of Saint-Rémy-de-Provence

be over fifteen years old, wore the Arles costume.
At the time of Van Gogh's stay, four unmarried sisters Mauron, Magdeleine (1829–1910), Marie (1834–1918), Antoinette (1844–1911), and Louise (1846–1943), lived in the Saint-Paul district, more precisely in a farmhouse in the Tor-Blanc between Saint-Clerg and Valrugues (figs. 12 and 14), which has retained the name of "Mas des Maurouneto" ("Maurouneto Farmhouse"), deriving from the feminisation[20] of their family name. For a long time, the two eldest had a shop on Boulevard Victor-Hugo, a large Provençal fashion boutique manufacturing Provençal clothes for their fellow Saint-Rémy women. A bodice bearing their brand is preserved in the collections of the Respelido prouvençalo, Saint-Rémy's folk arts and traditions group (fig. 15). This shop is an example of those found in the town centre, a lively shopping hub at the time. Various letterheads, kept in the town archives, shows the great diversity of these businesses (figs. 16 to 20). Old photos of shops are also a valuable visual record of the commercial architecture and lifestyles of the early 20th century (fig. 21). They reveal how the shop fronts and signs looked, as well as the

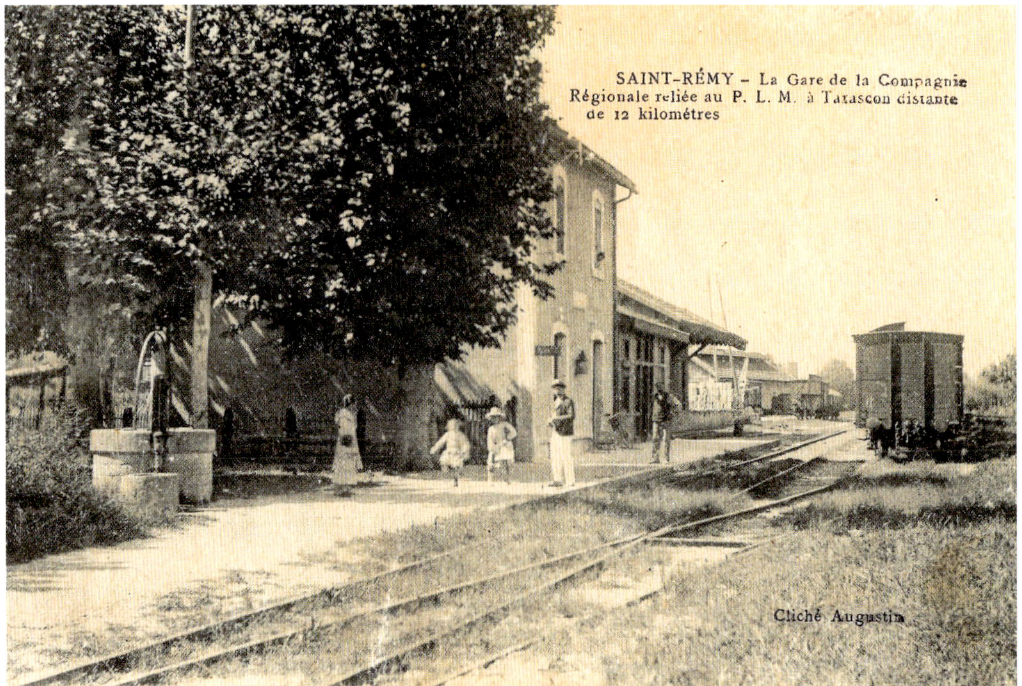

Fig. 22
Saint-Rémy train station, Marcel-Bonnet Collection, Municipal Archives of Saint-Rémy-de-Provence

highlighted products. For this Saint-Rémy grocery store, for example, the owner posing in front of her shop works in traditional Arles costume every day.

The Railway and the Seed Trade

Along with the completion of the Canal des Alpines, the railway was the other major development in mid-19th-century Saint-Rémy. In 1852, the South-East was traversed by two main lines that intersected: the first one connected Sète to Avignon via Nimes, Beaucaire and Tarascon, while the second connected the Grand-Combe coal mines to Marseille via Alès, Nîmes, Beaucaire and Tarascon. Several secondary lines would be completed, whose construction was favoured by the law of 1865, becoming part of the vast railway development that spread across France during the Second Empire and the Third Republic, with the goal of opening up rural territories and stimulating local economies. The railway line linking Saint-Rémy and Tarascon, a station in the P.-L.-M. network, opened in 1872. Trade and agriculture had much to gain from these connections, which facilitated shipments and greatly promoted human relations (fig. 22). Saint-Rémy station was therefore very busy, with three regular services per day in both directions and additional services during markets and fairs.

It was this line, on Wednesday 8 May 1889, that brought Vincent van Gogh to Saint-Rémy station, accompanied by the Arlesian pastor Frédéric Salles. In Arles, the two men took a train of the

PLM Company to Tarascon, where they caught the slow shuttle service to Orgon via Saint-Rémy.[21] It was also this train that the artist used to send his paintings to his brother Theo in Paris—and to leave Saint-Rémy. In the years 1889–1890, the station played an essential role in the economic development and modernisation of the town, facilitating trade and strengthening the links between the municipality and major urban centres. For Saint-Rémy, whose agricultural activity was flourishing—particularly vegetable seeds, early produce, olive oil and wine—the railway became an indispensable means of rapid and reliable export to regional markets (such as Arles, Beaucaire, and Avignon) but also national markets and beyond, all throughout Europe. This allowed local producers to sell their goods more efficiently, which strengthened the town's competitiveness in the food industry. Moreover, this accessibility promoted the arrival of visitors, traders and new ideas, contributing to the cultural expansion and modernisation of the municipality. Even if Van Gogh, hidden away in the Saint-Paul de Mausole asylum, remained on the sidelines of this railway life, he likely perceived the indirect effects of this infrastructure in the seasonal activity of the countryside and the rapid evolution of the Provençal landscape. The station therefore became the symbol of a future-oriented Saint-Rémy, where agricultural tradition met technical progress.

The railway's arrival allowed the town's urban fabric to expand beyond its medieval ramparts. Emerging companies would indeed come to understand the importance for their business of the railway's proximity. It was during this time that the seed trade grew and diversified. Along with Anjou, Provence (and Saint-Rémy in particular) was one of the two most important French centres for seed production at this time. Bona fide dynasties of trader-producers, almost all from agricultural backgrounds,

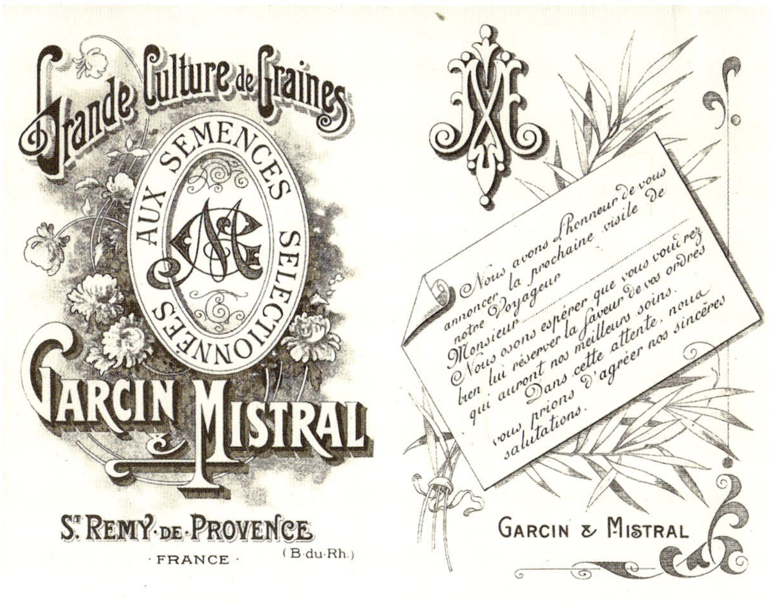
Grande Culture de Graines
Aux Semences Sélectionnées
Garcin Mistral
St Remy de Provence
France
(B du Rh.)

Nous avons l'honneur de vous annoncer la prochaine visite de notre Voyageur Monsieur .... Nous osons espérer que vous voudrez bien lui réserver la faveur de vos ordres qui auront nos meilleurs soins. Dans cette attente, nous vous prions d'agréer nos sincères salutations.

Garcin & Mistral

Fig. 23
Letterhead of Garcin-Mistral seed company, M245, Municipal Archives of Saint-Rémy-de-Provence

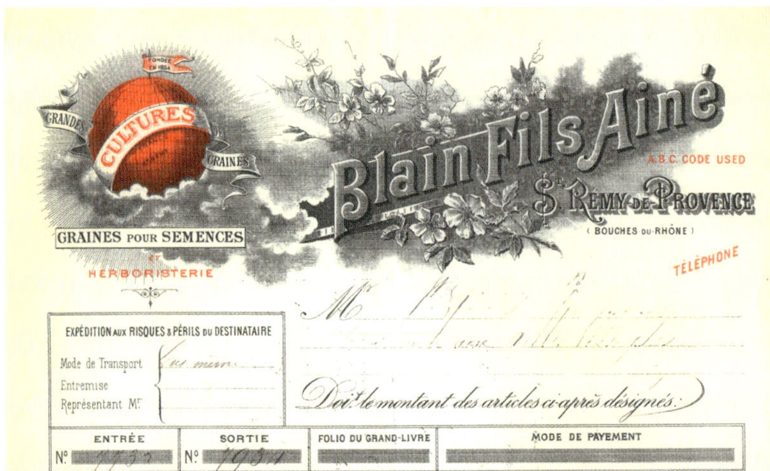

Fig. 24
Letterhead of Blain seed company, M245, Municipal Archives of Saint-Rémy-de-Provence

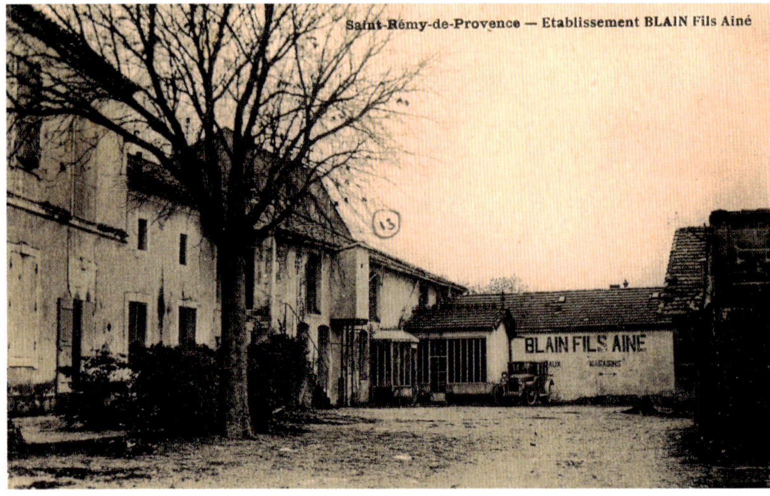

Fig. 25
Blain seed company factory next to the train station, Marcel-Bonnet Collection, Municipal Archives of Saint-Rémy-de-Provence

sprang up one after the other and, with the help of experienced brokers and qualified personnel, firmly established their specific trades. By the end of the 19th century, over 2,600 tons of seeds of all kinds were being shipped from Saint-Rémy station. After the Blain company, created around 1855, came the Roumanille, the Garcin-Mistral and the Mauron companies, which settled permanently in the trade (figs. 23, 24 and 25). The Saint-Jean mill was built at the same time, and was one of the largest and most modern in the region.
To conclude, the railway indirectly allowed the growth of the cultivation and international trade of seeds (flowers, vegetables, and fodder), which brought fame and prosperity to Saint-Rémy for almost two centuries. This period was also one of notable modernisation. Efforts were being made to improve communication routes (roads and nearby railways), facilitating trade. The town experienced a noticeable economic boom in the development of its urban infrastructure: the improvement of public buildings, beautification of the town centre, construction of bourgeois residences and appearance of new shops.

Industrial Modernity: Works on the Boulevards, the Wash House, Urban Lighting and the Dam

At the end of the 19th century, urbanisation and modernisation profoundly transformed Saint-Rémy, particularly the development of boulevards that redesigned the urban landscape (figs. 26 and 27). These new, wide and tree-lined streets reflected the will of the local authorities to open up the town, facilitate its traffic flows and beautify it. The boulevards became places of passage but also of social and commercial life, with cafés, shops and bourgeois residences springing up along them. They helped to refresh the ancient urban fabric, with its narrow alleyways, and create a more accessible town centre. This new urbanism reflected the economic growth of Saint-Rémy and the desire to bring the town into the modern age. Although Van Gogh, interned outside of the centre, did not directly describe these transformations in his letters or artworks, he nevertheless evolved within a rapidly changing urban environment.

In November 1889, Vincent came to set up his easel on the avenue of Saint-Rémy, or more precisely on the Cours Est, now known as the Gambetta and Mirabeau boulevards respectively (fig. 28). He described this study to his brother Theo: "The last study I did is a street in the village, where people were in the process—beneath huge plane

Fig. 26
Vincent van Gogh, *Saint-Rémy-de-Provence*, May-June 1889, pencil on paper, 23.8 × 63.8 cm, Amsterdam, Van Gogh Museum

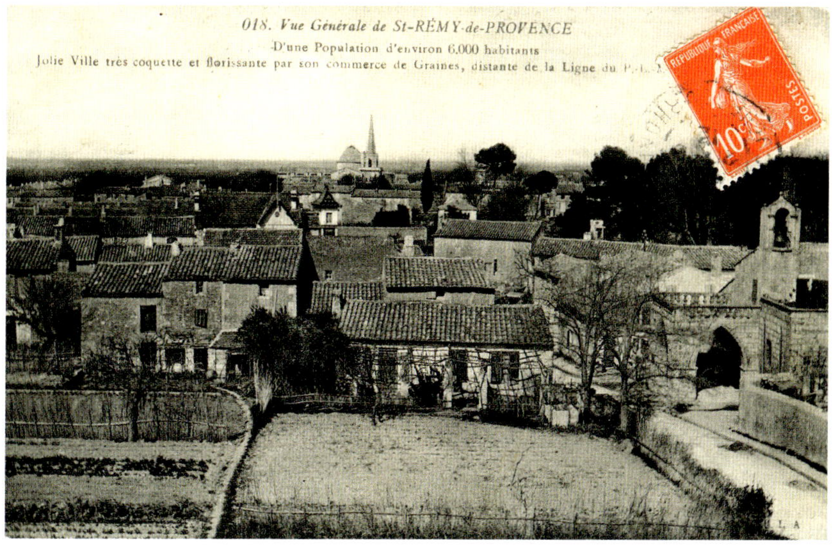

Fig. 27
General view of Saint-Rémy, Musée des Alpilles Collection, 997-1-6

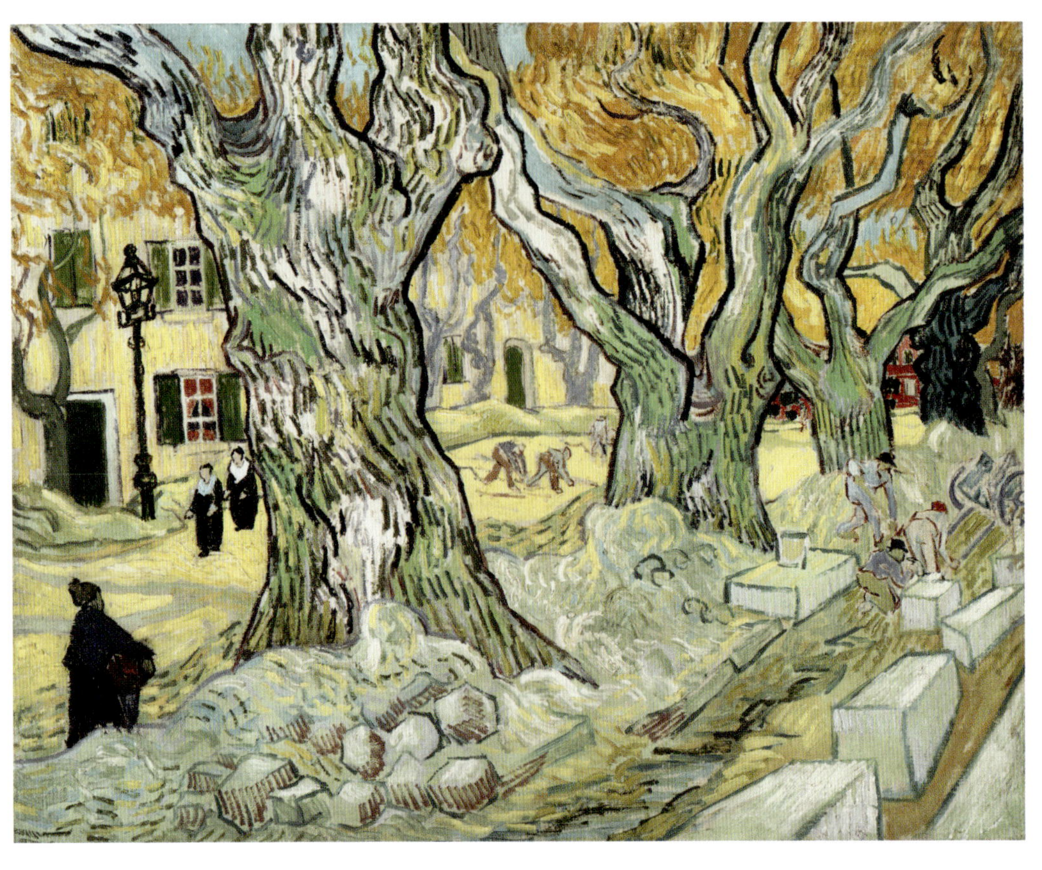

Fig. 28
The Large Plane Trees (Road Menders at Saint-Rémy), November 1889, oil on canvas, 73.5 × 92.5 cm, Washington D.C., The Phillips Collection

trees—of repairing the pavements. So there are piles of sand, stones and gigantic tree trunks."[22] The archives tell us that these works were repairing and redesigning the boulevard's stone curb and paved gutter.[23] The subtitle of the painting is *Les Grands Platanes* ("The Great Plane Trees") but we know, thanks to a photograph taken by the local Frédéric George (1868–1933) (fig. 29) a few years later, that they were in fact elm trees. At the end of the 19th century, in Provence, elms were often planted along roads and village squares for one very practical reason in particular: to provide shade during walks or cart journeys.[24] The aim of these works was to improve the lives of Saint-Rémy's residents. This is also the case for the ruling of 31 May 1889, only a few days after Van Gogh's arrival in Saint-Rémy. On that day, the town council decided to expand the municipal wash house with the "creation of an area to hang the laundry".[25] The old wash house (fig. 30), a meeting place of the *bugadiero*[26] and social hub for the local women, was built at the end of the 18th century on

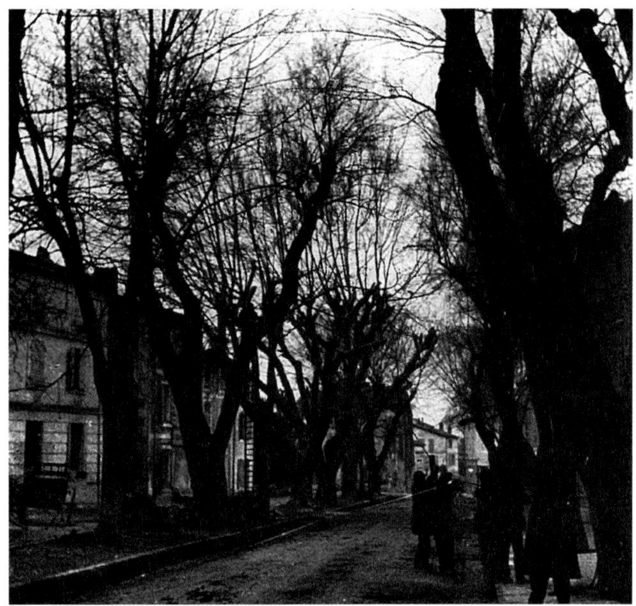

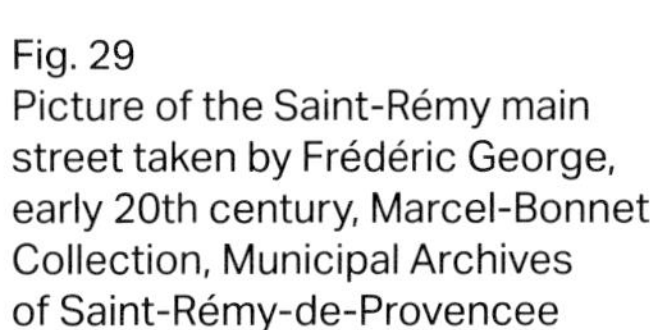

Fig. 29
Picture of the Saint-Rémy main street taken by Frédéric George, early 20th century, Marcel-Bonnet Collection, Municipal Archives of Saint-Rémy-de-Provencee

Fig. 30
Picture of the Saint-Rémy washhouse, Marcel-Bonnet Collection, Municipal Archives of Saint-Rémy-de-Provence

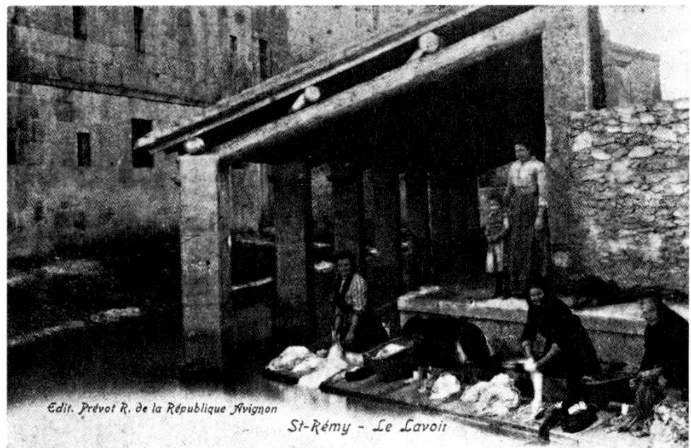

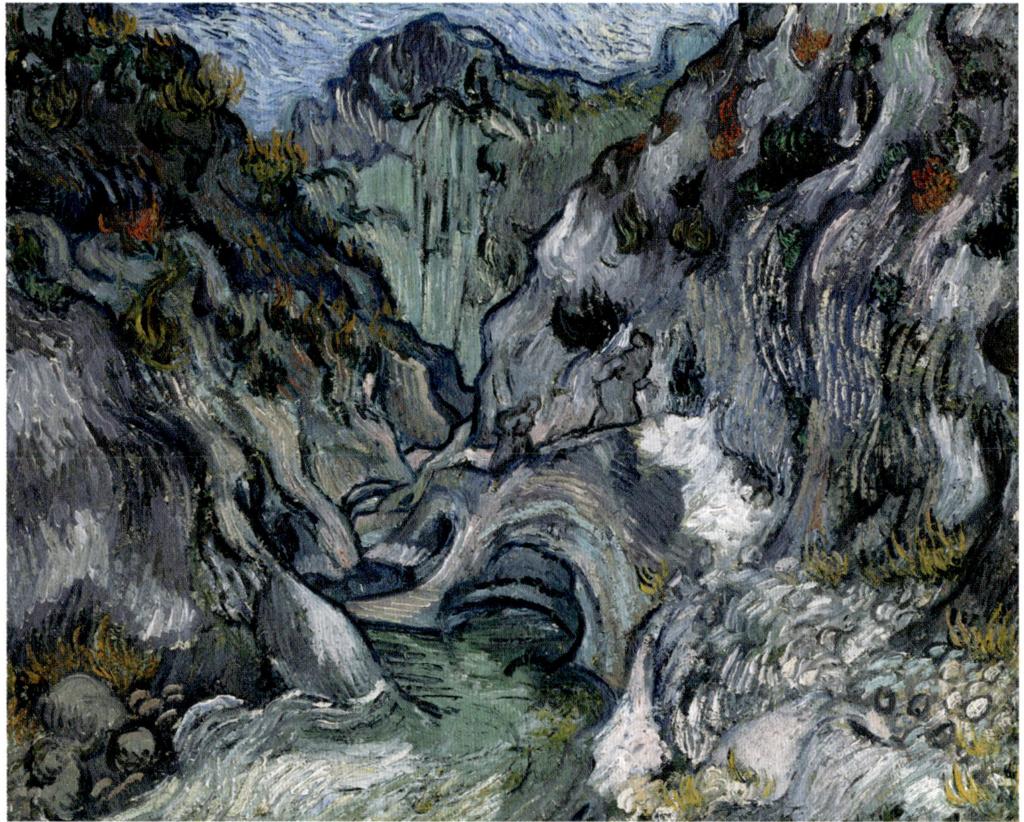

Fig. 31
The Ravine of the Peyroulets, October 1889, oil on canvas, 73 × 92 cm, Boston, Museum of Fine Arts

the banks of the Réal, Saint-Rémy's only river at that time, originating in the Paluds district. It was located near today's Jan-Léger Stadium, on the site of the former municipal swimming pool. In 1883, the municipal council voted to renovate it and later, in 1889, to roof it. In this configuration, the wash house remained in use until the mid-20th century.
At the next meeting, on 12 August 1889, another ruling to modernise the town was made: this one approved a treaty by mutual agreement, concluded on 10 August 1889, with Auguste Noailles, a mineral oil merchant, to light the town for three years, from 1 September 1889 to 31 August 1892. This lighting took the form of 65 street lights equipped with lamps, wicks, glass tubes, reflectors and appliances designed to stop the mineral oil freezing.
However, the most important development of the late 19th century in Saint-Rémy was undoubtedly the Peiroou[27] dam project, which the council had been considering since 1883. It was indeed necessary to build an artificial lake to retain rainwater for irrigation and especially for supplying the town's fountains, which played a crucial role in supplying water to the population at that time.[28] In May 1889, the town obtained subsidies for the dam project in the Peiroou gorge. The operation required the acquisition of

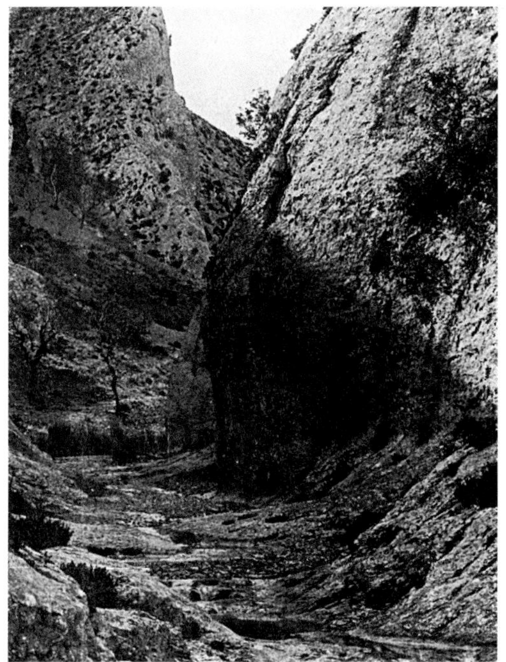

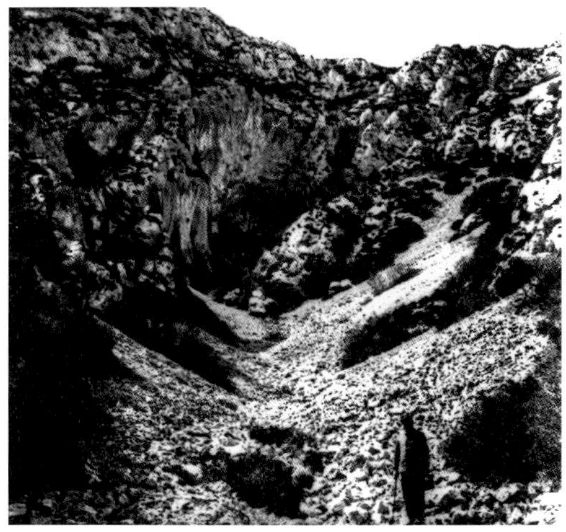

Fig. 32
Future site of the dam by Frédéric George, 1889, Marcel-Bonnet Collection, Municipal Archives of Saint-Rémy-de-Provence

Fig. 33
The ravine, 1889, Musée des Alpilles Collection, 88.19.30

land or rocks belonging to the widow Gros, née Deville: "This lady did not think she had to accept the town's offer to her, despite it being a very reasonable one", and therefore the municipal council noted that it was necessary to proceed with expropriating the land. After having attempted one last time to acquire the land from Mme Gros amicably, on 12 August 1889, the mayor declared the dam to be of public utility so that the project could proceed. Works were completed in 1891, replacing an older system in the valley of the Gros farmhouse that dated back to Roman times.

This is most likely the ravine that Van Gogh painted twice at the end of 1889 (fig. 31). The painter wrote about it in his letters: "I am working on a large canvas of a ravine [...] two bases of excessively solid rocks between which a trickle of water flows,[29] a third mountain that closes the ravine."[30]

At the same time, Frédéric George, owner of Café Moscou in Saint-Rémy, began learning photography with professional photographer Henri Brouchican (1872–1946). He would create about 3,000 glass-print images, which would later be deposited at the Musée des Alpilles.[31] Frédéric George photographed the valley upstream of the Gros farmhouse (figs. 32 and 33) before the construction of the dam, and, in his book on this photographic collection published in the early 1990s.[32] Marcel Bonnet made a comparative study to highlight the places painted by Van Gogh and photographed by Frédéric George.

During Vincent's stay in Saint-Rémy, the olive was his favourite tree: there were numerous groves near Saint-Paul de Mausole (fig. 34), to which he devoted about fifteen canvases.[33] He was impressed by the shapes and colours of the olive trees, which he deliberately exaggerated in the hope of creating more intense and timeless views. Again,

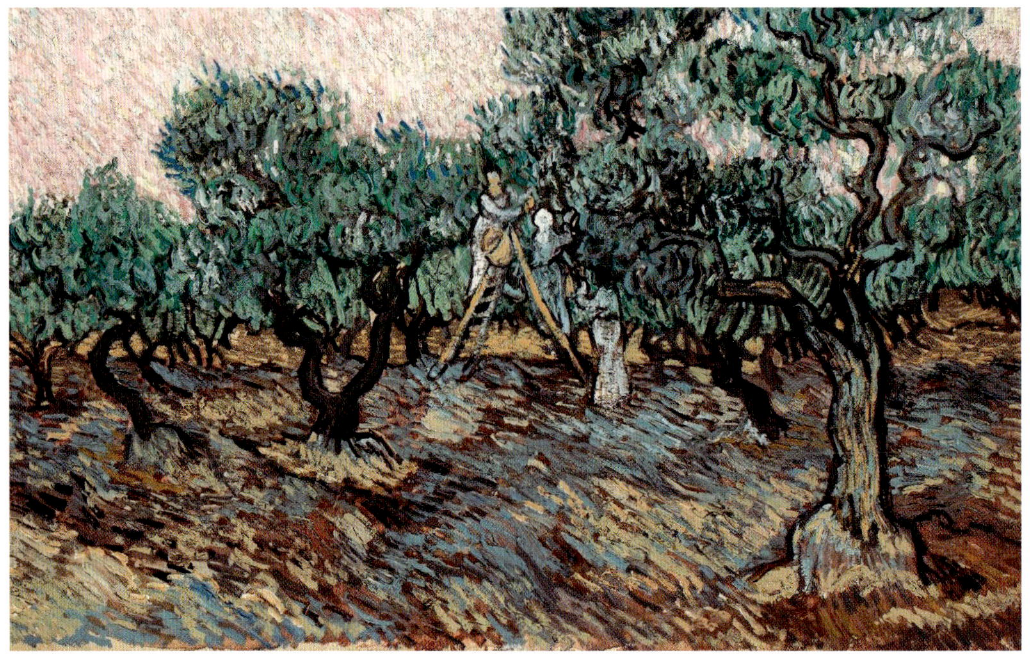

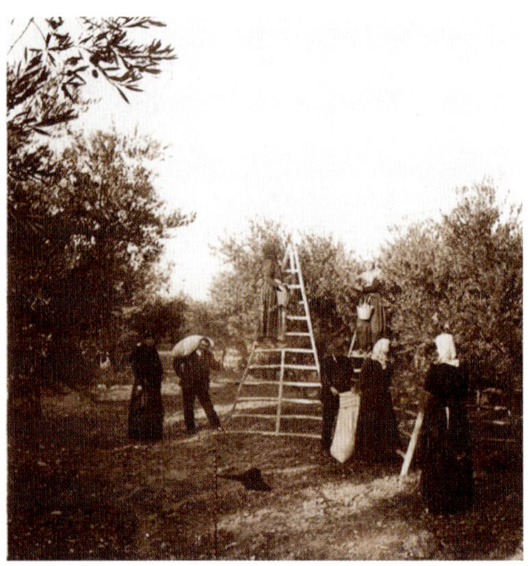

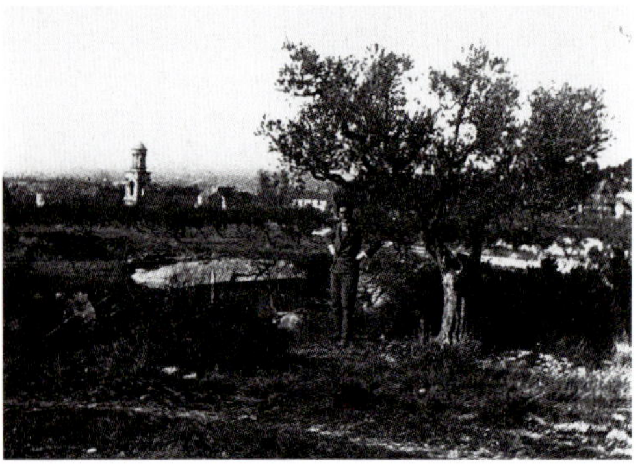

Fig. 34
Olive Picking, 1889, oil on canvas, 73 × 92 cm, Washington D.C., National Gallery of Art

Fig. 35
Picture of the olive harvest by Frédéric George, Musée des Alpilles, num2012-2009-1-46

Fig. 36
Picture of the olive trees of Saint-Paul by Frédéric George, early 20th century, Marcel-Bonnet Collection, Municipal Archives of Saint-Rémy-de-Provence

Frédéric George also photographed the olive season from early November to late December.[34] Olive picking was the main activity in the Saint-Rémy countryside in autumn (fig. 35). Both in the painting and photographs, we see the use of the traditional step ladders made from willow wood. At the end of the 19th century, the hand-picked olives were placed in a basket attached to the waist of the pickers. Another photograph by Frédéric George (fig. 36) was taken before 1921, when the Glanum excavations began, at what is

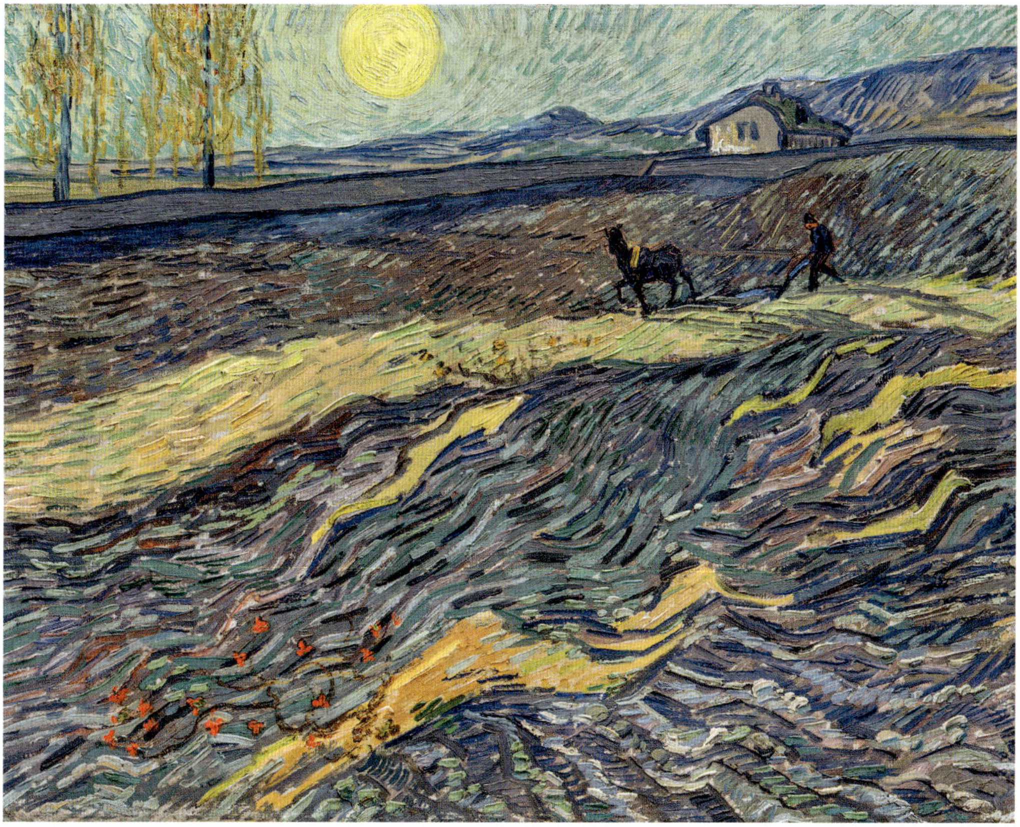

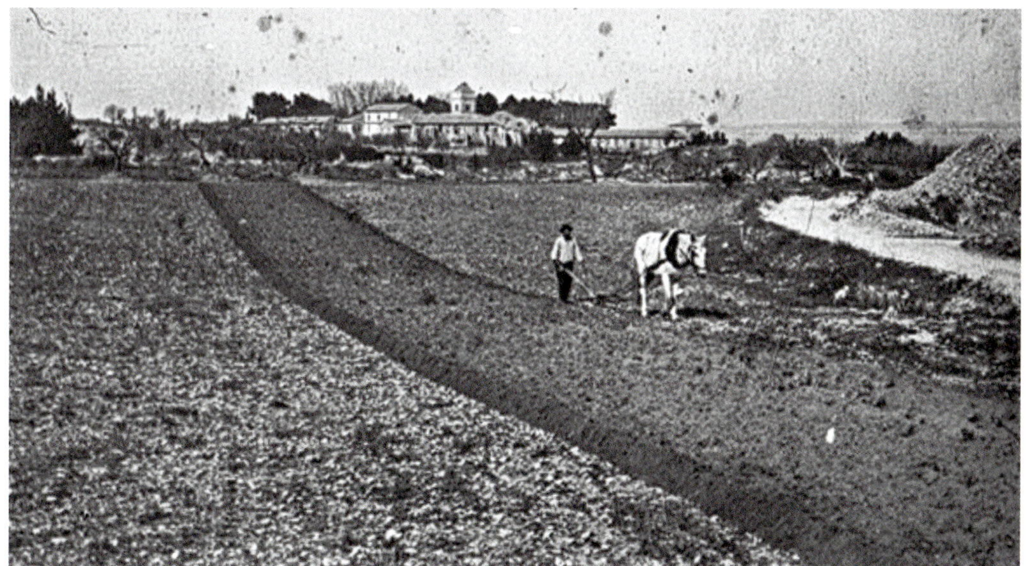

Fig. 37
Enclosed Field with Ploughman, August 1889, oil on canvas, 49 × 62 cm, private collection

Fig. 38
Picture of a ploughman in the countryside around Saint-Paul de Mausole by Frédéric George, Musée des Alpilles, num2012-2009-1-485

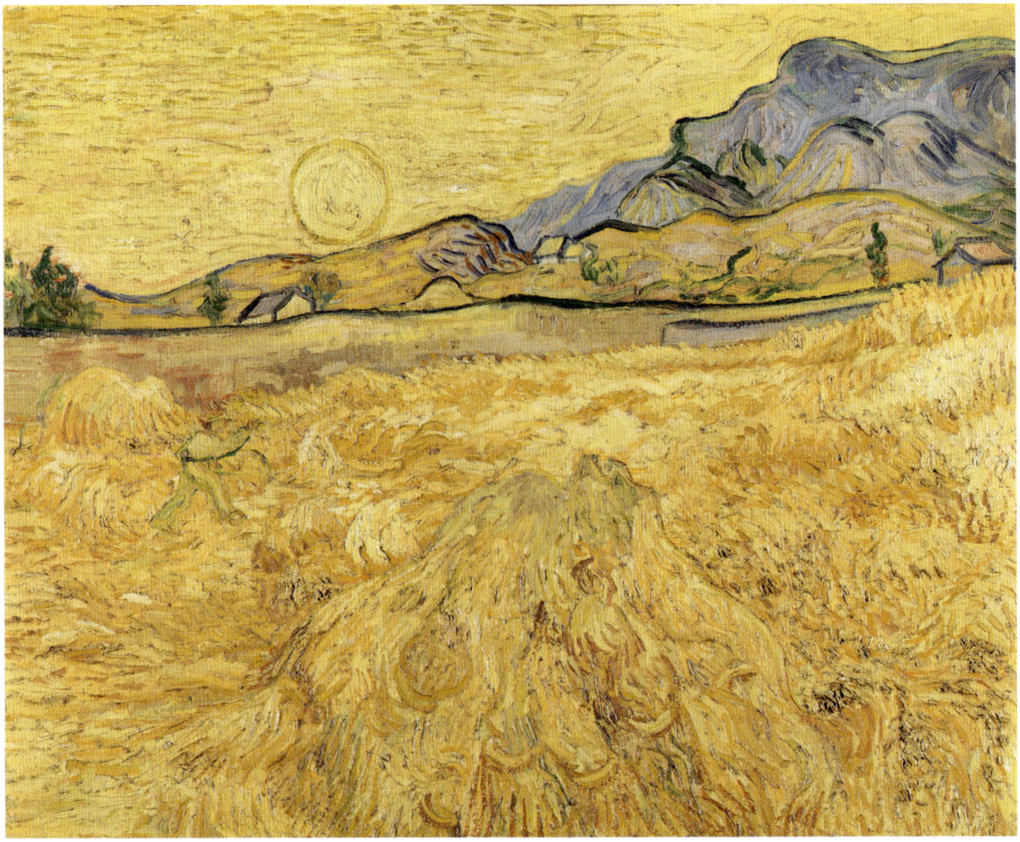

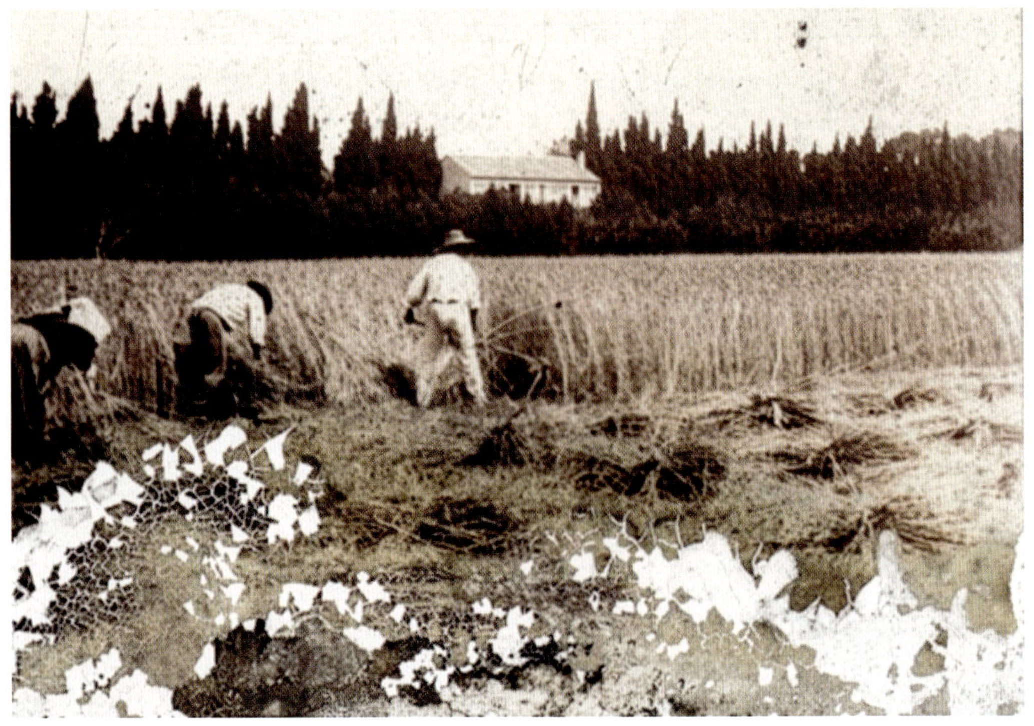

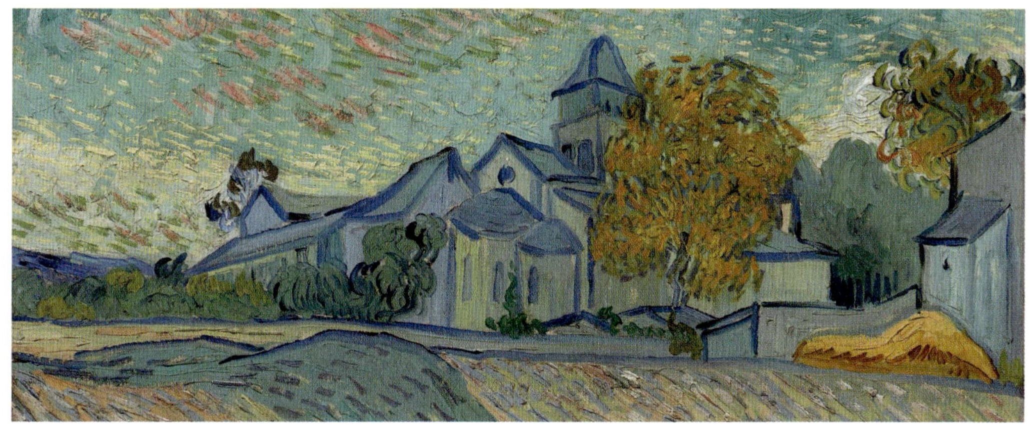

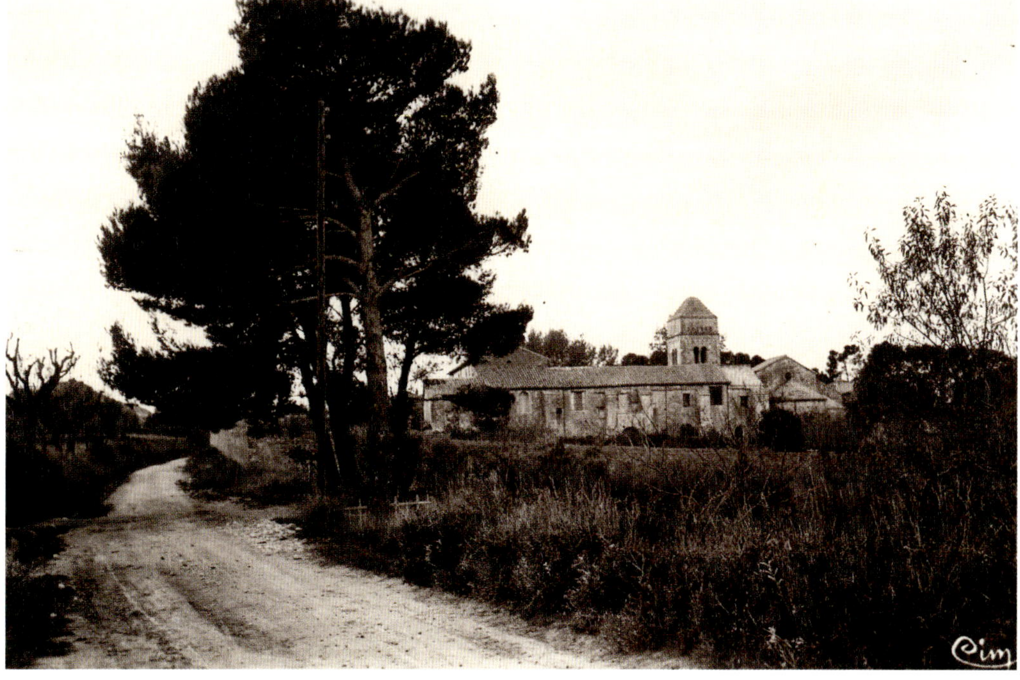

Fig. 39
Reaper, June 1889, oil on canvas, 72 × 92 cm, Otterlo, Kröller-Müller Museum

Fig. 40
Picture of a mower in the Saint-Rémy countryside by Frédéric George, Musée des Alpilles, num2012-2009-1-479

Fig. 41
View of the Church of Saint-Paul de Mausole, autumn 1889, oil on canvas, 44 × 60 cm, private collection

Fig. 42
The eastern part of the buildings of Saint-Paul de Mausole by Frédéric George, Musée des Alpilles, 997-1-577

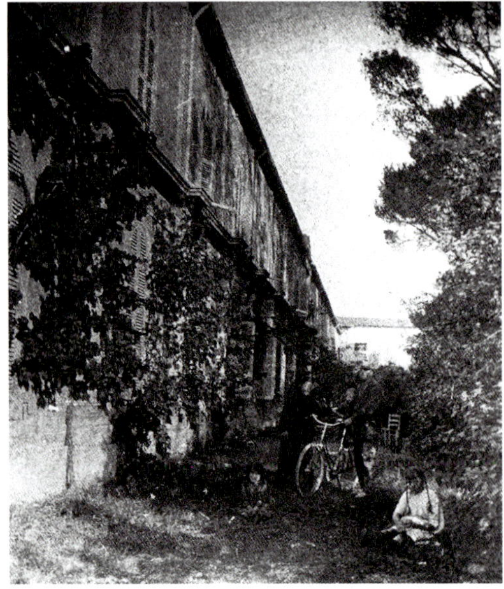

Fig. 43
Picture of the former garden or the courtyard of the men's ward by Frédéric George, early 20th century, Marcel-Bonnet Collection, Municipal Archives of Saint-Rémy-de-Provence

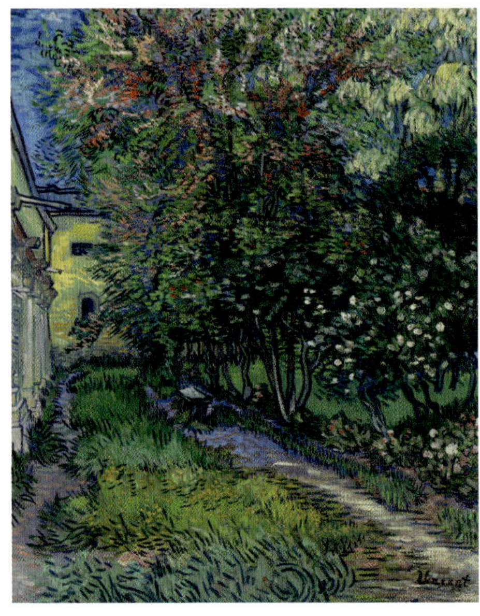

Fig. 44
The Garden of Saint-Paul Hospital, May-June 1889, oil on canvas, 95 × 75 cm, Otterlo, Kröller-Müller Museum

now the entrance to the archaeological site. In the background, we can see the Antiques and the olive trees of Saint-Paul that Van Gogh painted. Some were dug up in the 1950s during the expansion of the archaeological site and the diversion of the road.

Van Gogh produced other paintings of agricultural labour such as *Farmer in a Field* (fig. 37): "Yesterday I started working a little again—something I see from my window—a yellow field of stubble being ploughed, the contrast between the blue-purple ploughed land and the yellow stubble, a background of hills."[35] This is another subject that Frédéric George also immortalised (fig. 38). During the summer of 1889, Vincent observed a reaper in the wheat field: "The last one I started was the wheat field, with a small reaper and a big sun. The canvas is all yellow except for the wall and the background of blue-purple hills"[36] (fig. 39); similarly, Frédéric George's photographs also captured labourers harvesting crops (fig. 40). These last two paintings feature the field in the eastern part of Saint-Paul, often depicted in Van Gogh's paintings (fig. 41). Frédéric George took numerous photographs in Saint-Paul (fig. 42), and particularly in the garden (fig. 43) that Van Gogh painted so often during his stay (fig. 44). When he was in his room painting the wheat field, he always depicted the roof of this building, which he had to pass frequently (figs. 45 and 47). This was Michel L'Huissier's cabin, located east of Saint-Paul de Mausole. A few years later, Frédéric George also photographed it. It is known as the *cabano de Michèu l'Ussié* in Provençal (fig. 46).

After this cabin, to the north, the olive fields became numerous and almost continuous until they met the Alpines Canal. This is an area that has

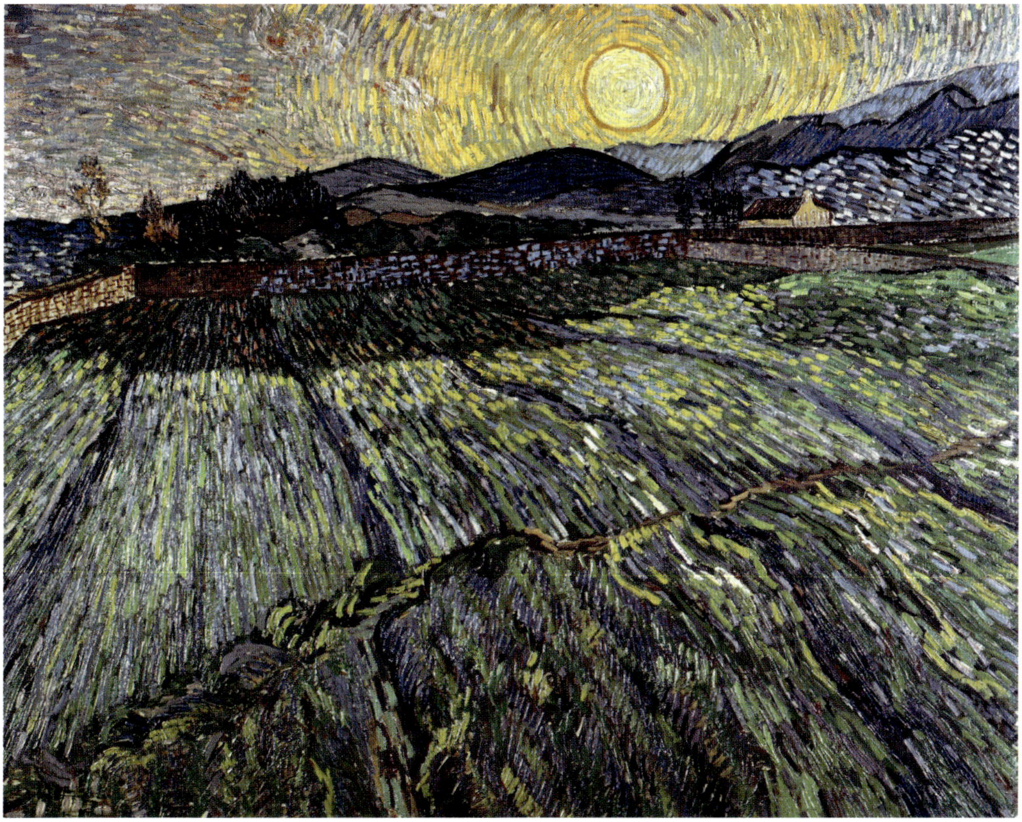

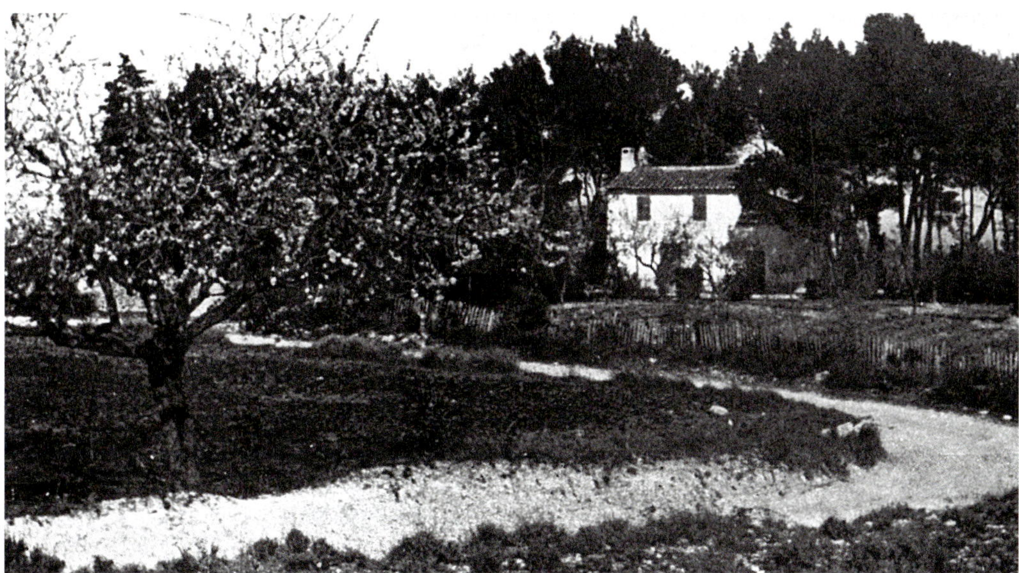

Fig. 45
Enclosed Field with Rising Sun, November 1889, oil on canvas, 71 × 90 cm, private collection

Fig. 46
Picture of Michel L'Huissier's cabin by Frédéric George, early 20th century, Marcel-Bonnet Collection, Municipal Archives of Saint-Rémy-de-Provence

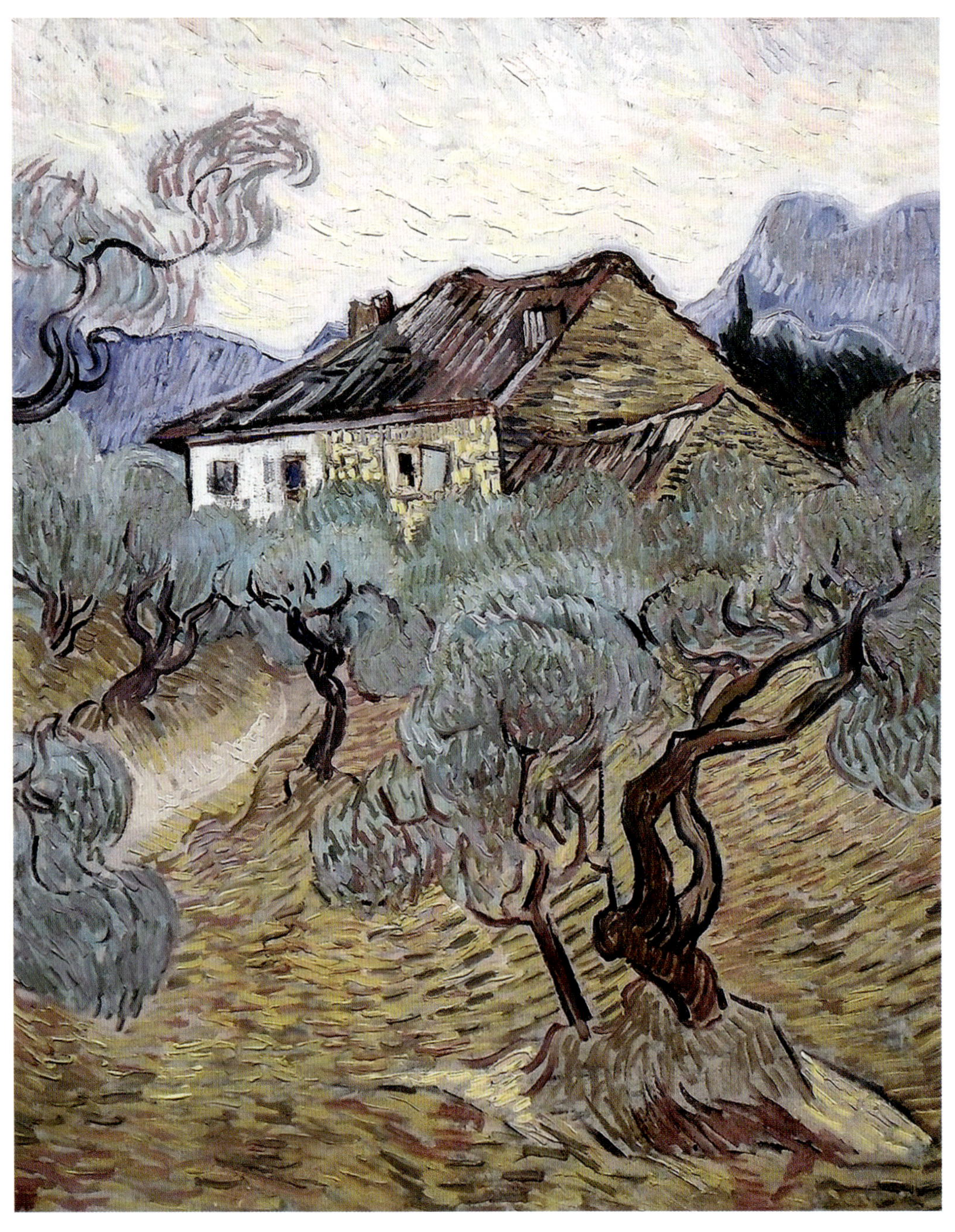

Fig. 47
The White Cottage among the Olive Trees, December 1889, oil on canvas, 70 × 60 cm, private collection

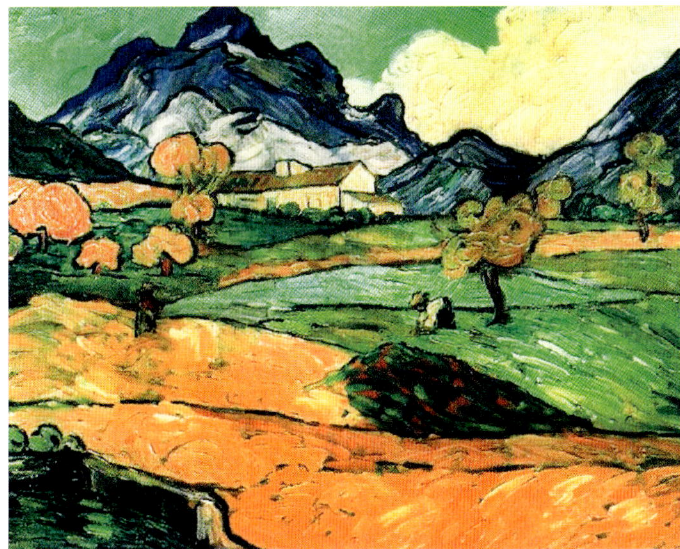

Fig. 48
View to the Mont Gaussier, May 1890, oil on canvas, 53 × 70 cm, private collection

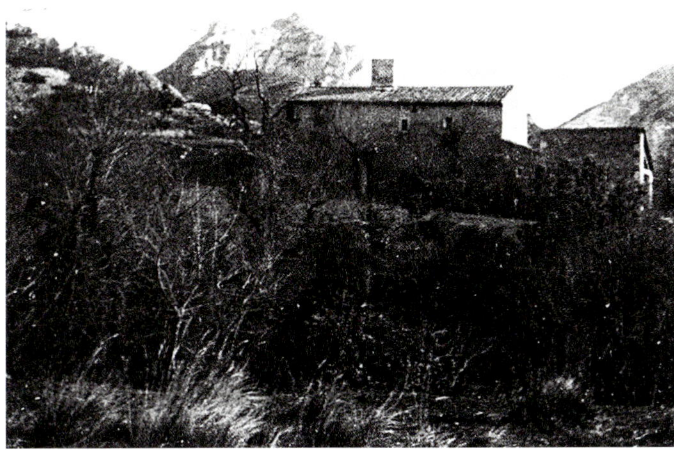

Fig. 49
Le mas de George at the end of the 19th century by Frédéric George, early 20th century, Marcel-Bonnet Collection, Municipal Archives of Saint-Rémy-de-Provence

become highly urbanised since the days of Van Gogh and Frédéric George. During the month of December 1889, Van Gogh chose to paint a farmhouse just behind Saint-Paul, well known to the locals (fig. 48). It is now called the "Mas de Saint-Paul" ("the Saint-Paul Farmhouse") but was long recorded on the cadastre as the "Mas de George" ("the George Farmhouse"). This farmhouse—one of the oldest and most characteristic of the Saint-Rémy Alpilles—belonged to Frédéric's own grandfather, Joseph George, a master dyer and town prosecutor in 1793. The George farmhouse was then bought, in the early 19th century, by Doctor Louis Mercurin who, in 1807, converted the Saint-Paul de Mausole monastery into the insane asylum where Van Gogh was later interned. It was built around the mid-17th century, and was the property of Dominique de Mistral de Mondragon, Sieur de Crozes. This farmhouse, which was also called "the farmhouse of the Pissarote", is recognisable by the pigeon house on top of the roof that we can see in a painting by Van Gogh (fig. 49).

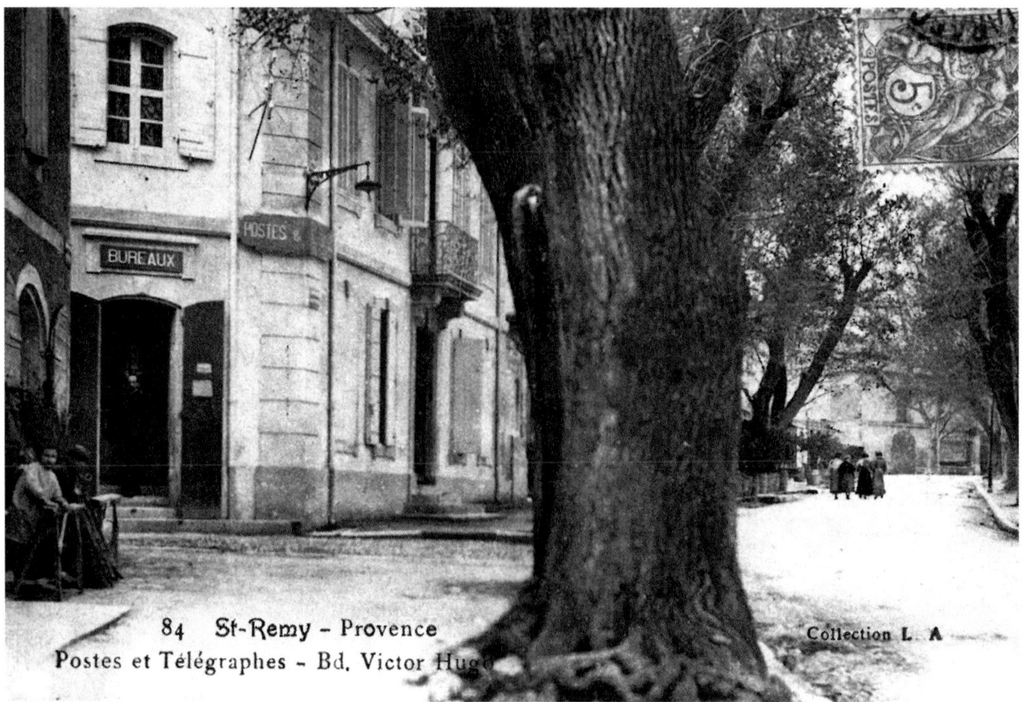

Fig. 50
Post office, Boulevard Victor-Hugo, early 20th-century postcard, Marcel-Bonnet Collection, Municipal Archives of Saint-Rémy-de-Provence

Conversely, Van Gogh made abundant comments about his time in Saint-Paul in his letters, but never mentioned the religious buildings of the hospice: "Would Degas want me to go to the cloisters or churches, I'm the one who's afraid."[37] The same goes for the Roman monuments, the Antiques, despite their close proximity. On the other hand, he painted "the entrance of a quarry", very close to the southern boundary of Saint-Paul, which proves that he was in contact with the activity of Saint-Rémy's quarries, which were still operational at the time.

The Delivery of Mail

Just as the Saint-Rémy railway served to transport Vincent van Gogh's paintings to his brother in Paris, the town post office enabled the painter's numerous epistolary exchanges during his year in Saint-Rémy. He wrote and received about a hundred letters, exchanged with members of his family (Theo van Gogh, his brother, Jo van Gogh Bonger, his sister-in-law, his sister Wilhemine van Gogh, and his mother Anna van Gogh Carbentus), but also with friends such as the painters Paul Gauguin and Émile Bernard. From 1888, the post office was housed in the former hotel of the Blain family, known as the Hôtel Château (fig. 50).
The 1889 municipal registry of proceedings indicates that mail delivery, including its modernisation, was one of the municipality's concerns at the time.[38] During its meeting of 31 May 1889, the municipal council discussed a solution to reduce the delay between the arrival of

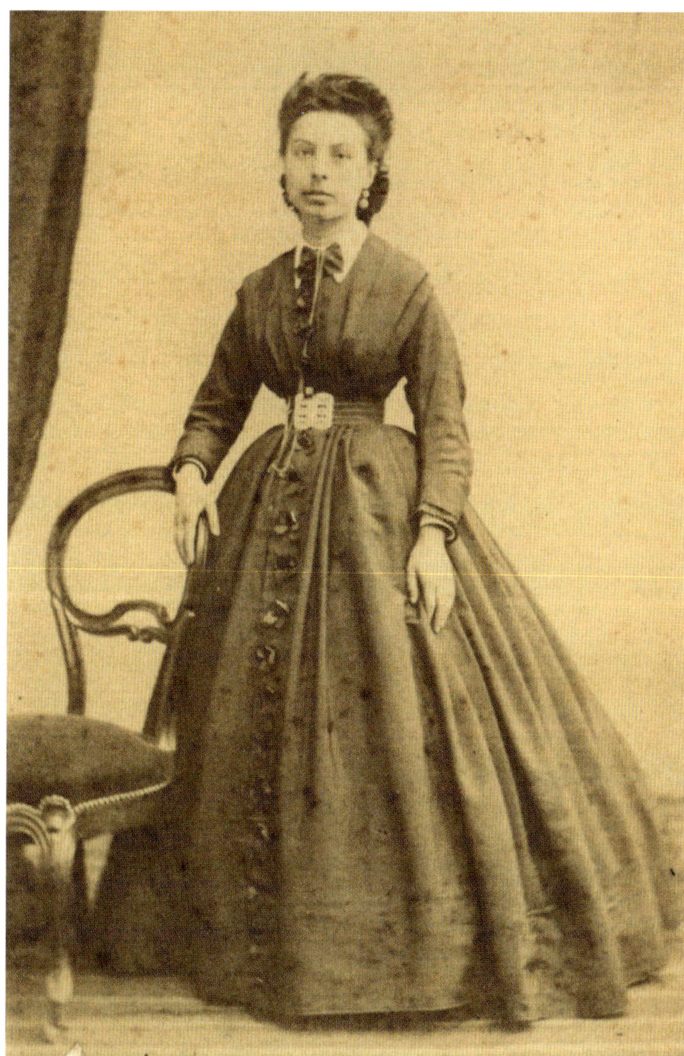

Fig. 51
Portrait of Marie Suzanne Lecacheux, wife of Girard, ca. 1860–1870, Archives *Escolo dis Aupiho*

the mail and its delivery by the postmen. The importance of the shipment of fruits and vegetables required connections with Paris and other major cities in France and even abroad to be as rapid as possible.

At that time, the postmistress was Marie Suzanne Lecacheux (1836–1919), wife of Marius Girard (fig. 51), who we know had practised this profession for decades, as it was mentioned on her marriage certificate in 1868.[39] It is also noted on the census register of 1886[40] and that of 1891,[41] where Mme Girard is recorded as having two postal employees, Lucie Lamoureux and Baptistine Bonnifay, and only one subordinate, Charlotte Belli, in 1896. When her daughter Marie Girard married Joachim Gasquet in 1896, she was still qualified as such. Then, on her husband's death certificate in 1906, her profession was recorded as "ex-postmistress". She must have worked in this role between the ages of thirty-two and sixty-five, and had fourteen postmen under her

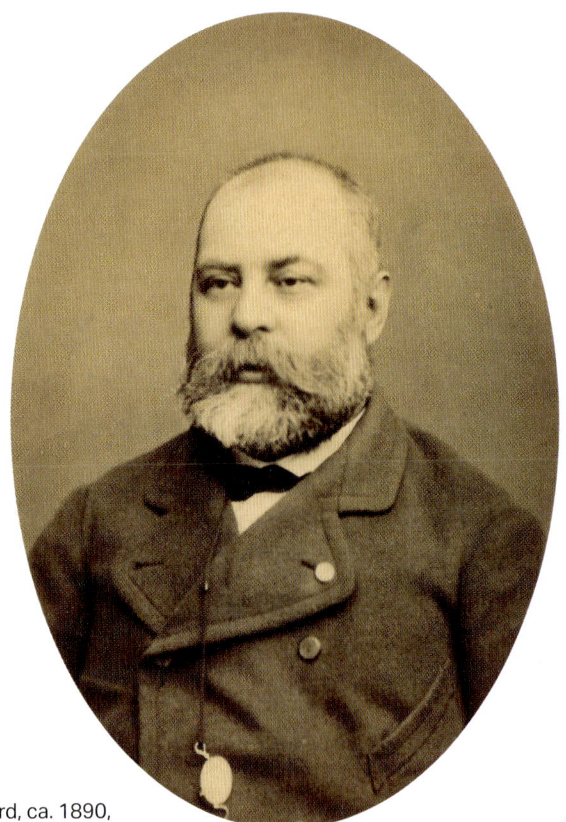

Fig. 52
Portrait of Marius Girard, ca. 1890, Archives *Escolo dis Aupiho*

direction in Saint-Rémy, which reflects the importance of her responsibilities. Such a career in administration was rare for a woman of this social class, belonging to the petty bourgeoisie and having a cook. It was certainly this job that enabled her husband, Marius Girard, to devote himself to a literary career.

Literary Life in Saint-Rémy at the End of the 19th Century

Naturally, we cannot overlook the local works of literature in French, such as the book of verse *Saint-Rémy et la vallée des Baux*, published in 1875 by Abbé Eugène de Tamisier (1823–1894), chaplain of Saint-Paul with whom Vincent inevitably rubbed shoulders.[42] But the most striking component was the works in Provençal, in the homeland of the "father of the Félibrige" Joseph Roumanille (1818–1891), which corresponded to the language spoken at the time: indeed, from 30 March to 21 April 1889, Father Xavier de Fourvière (1853–1912), of the Prémontrés de Frigolet, filled his church with sermons in Provençal, which were later published.[43] A few years later, *la lengo nostro* was used in Mayor Pierre Barbier's speeches (1841–1908) and those of district councillor Joseph Coste (1847–1902).

Marius Girard (1838–1906) was the son of the Saint-Rémy architect Joseph Girard (1803–1875) (fig. 52). Very soon, he became a close friend of Frédéric Mistral (1830–1914)[44] (fig. 53) and, in 1868, he was the efficient organiser of the international literary festivals that brought Catalans and Provençals together in Saint-Rémy. In 1870, he was appointed secretary general of the town, under the mandate of Jules Pellissier,[45] but in 1874, because of his republican convictions, he was dismissed by the royalist mayor Bouchaud de Bussy. He was later reinstated thanks to the return of the republicans, led by Émile Daillan. In 1877, his first collection of poems and rhyming legends, *Lis Aupiho*, was published in the Librairie Roumanille; the second, *La Crau*, appeared in 1894. He also produced *Aneto*, a long poem that remains unpublished, whose action takes place in the farmhouses of the quarrymen of Saint-Rémy and features the mythical Golden Goat that haunts the Alpilles. In 1881, he was named Majoral du Félibrige, the first holder of the *Cigalo dis Aupiho.*[46]

We know that Van Gogh became aware of this Provençal literary context as soon as he arrived in Arles.[47] On 1 September 1888, he wrote to Theo: "It hurts me

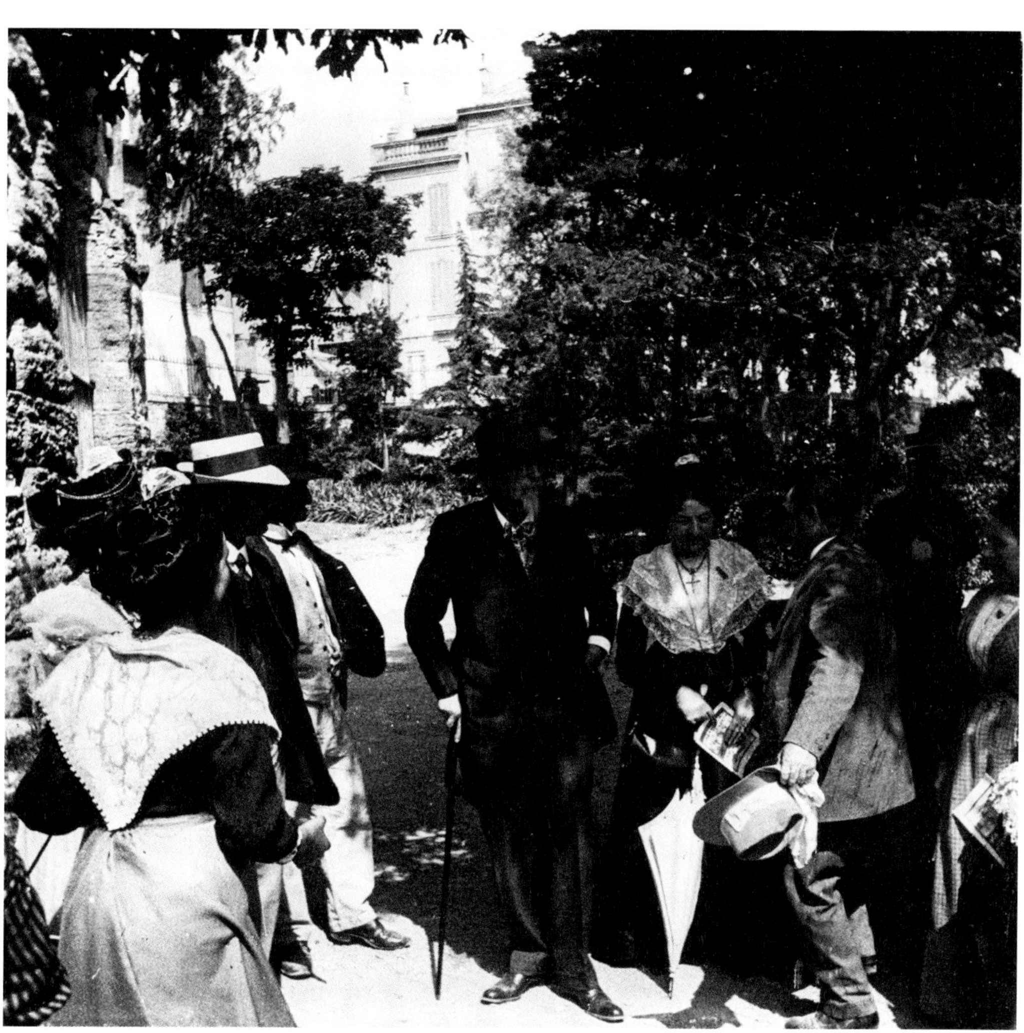

Fig. 53
Picture of Frédéric Mistral by Frédéric George, Musée des Alpilles, 2009.1.709

enormously that I do not speak the Provençal patois", and, on 15 October 1888: "I'm sending you the article on Provence, which seemed well written to me. These félibres are a literary and artistic group, Clovis Hugues, Mistral, others, who write sonnets in Provençal and sometimes in French, quite well, even very well sometimes. If the fellows ever stop ignoring my existence, they will all be welcome at the little house. I'd rather this did not happen before I finish decorating. But loving Provence as frankly as they do, I may have the right to their attention." And again, on 3 February 1889: "You ask me if I have read Mistral's *Mireille*, I am like you, I can only read it in fragments of the translation. But you've heard it before, because maybe you know that Gounod put it to music, at least I think he did. Naturally, I ignore this music, and even when I hear it I would

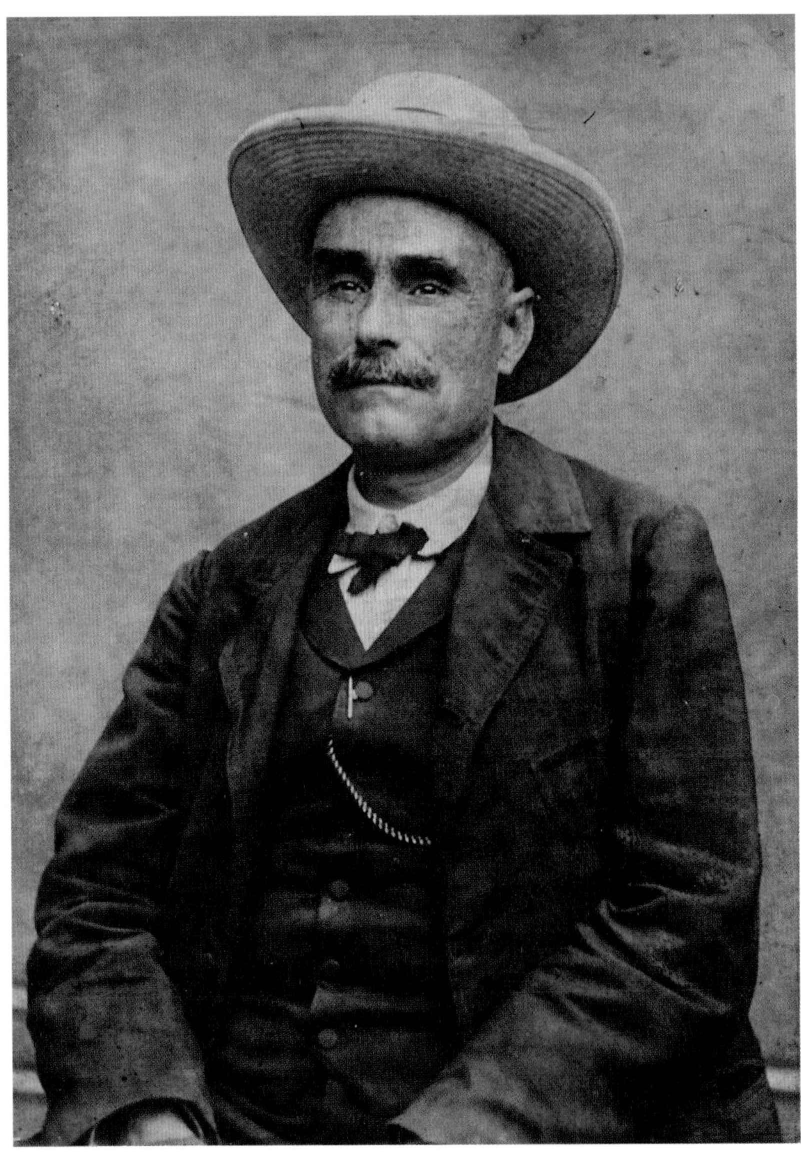

Fig. 54
Picture of Édouard Marrel, Archives *Escolo dis Aupiho*

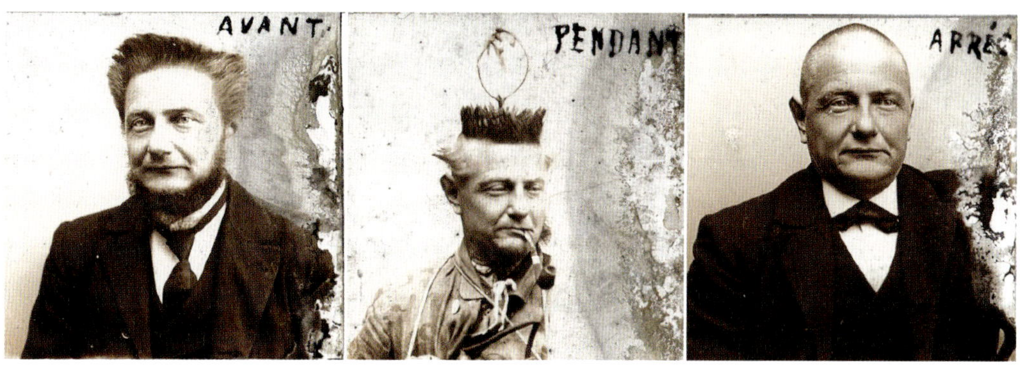

Fig. 55
Pictures of Paul Blanchet, "Le Sauvage", Marcel-Bonnet Collection, Municipal Archives of Saint-Rémy-de-Provence

rather watch the musicians than listen. But I can tell you this, that the original language written here as lyrics becomes music in the mouth of the women of Arles!"[48] Marcel Bonnet suggests that Van Gogh's letters contain hints that he read *La Revue félibréenne*[49] magazine in which all the Provençal writers of the time were published. At the beginning of 1889,[50] Vincent told Theo about the importance of Provençal customs at Christmas time: "Yesterday I went to the Folies Arlésiennes, an emerging theatre here [...]. They performed (it was a Provençal literary society) what is called a Noël ["Christmas"] or Pastourale ["Pastoral"], a reminiscence of Christian medieval theatre. It was very carefully done and it must have cost them some money. Naturally, this represented the birth of Christ, intertwined with the burlesque story of a family of astounded Provençal peasants." Van Gogh was aware of this Provençal cultural context in Arles, which was substantially the same as that in Saint-Rémy, but here the Saint-Paul de Mausole establishment was detached from the town, and with Van Gogh residing there under a regime of internment, no similar testimony exists.

Similarly, the painter never visited the municipal library that had recently been created and was entrusted to the council secretary Édouard Marrel (1851–1922) (fig. 54). A Saint-Rémy native, he was initially clerk of the telegraph office, then, in 1878, succeeded Marius Girard in the town administration, remaining there until his death. He worked under twelve different mayors, with whom his republican and secular political convictions aligned. Marrel was also a Provençal-speaking writer,[51] who kept regular correspondence with Mistral[52] between February 1881 and October 1913.

To complete this picture of Saint-Rémy's cultural life at the end of the 19th century, we must mention a prominent figure of the Alpilles area, whom Van Gogh could have met in the countryside around Saint-Paul: Paul Blanchet (1865–1947), known as "The Savage" (fig. 55). Born into a rural bourgeois family in Saint-Rémy, he received a solid education, but fell victim to bad luck and had to perform military service for several years among the colonial troops of Africa. He returned with deeply-held sentiments of antimilitarism and social revolt which, along with family setbacks, caused him to choose a free and poor life as a farmworker, working hard in the fields or oil mills of the Baux Valley, and occasionally manufacturing sundials. Fundamentally anti-conformist, he refused to wear a hat (so as not to have to greet anyone), refrained from killing any animal, and installed dozens of bells on his bicycle as a warning device.[53] He multiplied his eccentricities, especially during the carnival period, when he recited his picturesque *Nouvello dóu Carnava,* printed in Provençal on loose sheets of paper. An admirer of Mistral and his friend and neighbour Charloun Rieu, and endowed with a solid literary technique, he composed poems in French and Provençal.[54]

This is the Saint-Rémy that Van Gogh knew for a year, and which seems to have brought him some peace: a small town in Provence, rooted in its agricultural traditions, but already on the march toward modernity. He discovered a spirited community here, with its boulevard developments, bustling wash house, improved lighting, dam, railway and flourishing seed trade. Here, he found a place of mooring, a peaceful and yet animated reflection of his own inner universe.

He turned a deeply admiring and tender gaze upon Provençal society, which he expressed sincerely in his letters to his brother Theo. He often evoked the dignity of the people of the South, their intimate connection to the land, their simplicity and their courage. In a letter dated September 1889, he wrote: "Here, we feel something patriarchal, almost biblical, in everyday life."[55] He was fascinated by the labourers at work, the peasants whom he met in the fields and painted with respect and emotion. He also noted in the same letter: "I see in this southern race something strong, stable, a rustic beauty."

This human, working class and hard-working Provence became a source of deep, almost spiritual inspiration for him. Van Gogh expressed his feelings about everyday life in Saint-Rémy-de-Provence, highlighting an atmosphere marked by ancient traditions and simplicity, characteristic of Provençal society at the time.

1 Letter 779 of 9 June 1889, to his brother Theo. The numbering of the letters is based on the book *Vincent van Gogh. Les Lettres*, édition *critique, complète et illustrée,* edited by Léon Jansen, Hans Luijten and Nienke Bakke, Paris: Actes Sud, 2009.

2 "I must not simply make paintings, but must also see people, and from time to time, by frequenting others, also remake my temperament" (letter 801, of 10 September 1889, to Theo).

3 Currently the "School of the Liberation", named after the road along which the soldiers who liberated the town arrived on 24 August 1944.

4 Record of proceedings 1889, AMSRDP, 1D20.

5 Inhabitants were exactly 5,813 in the 1886

census and 5,649 in the 1891 census (AMSRDP 1F10 and 1F11).

6 In the chart shown in fig. 2, deaths are grouped by age in ascending order from left to right. Light grey indicates female individuals, while dark grey indicates male individuals.

7 Bailey Martin, *Starry Night: Van Gogh at the Asylum*, London: Frances Lincoln, 2018, p. 63.

8 Act no. 9 of the year 1861, register of births 1861, town of Eyragues (Bouches-du-Rhône).

9 Because of his poverty, Vincent could not marry Mireille, the only daughter of wealthy landowners.

10 The eastern end of today's Rue Carnot.

11 Act no. 52 of the year 1890, AMSRDP 1E31d.

12 Conserved and indexed by the "Les Amis de Jean Baltus" Association.

13 One of the Provençal farmhouses on the road to Noves, on the Lagoy estate.

14 Particularly letters 783 and 784.

15 Letter no. 811, to his mother.

16 Death register of 1896 and census register of 1891 (AMSRDP 1E33d and 1F11).

17 Letter 801, dated 10 September 1889, to Theo.

18 An essential fashion accessory and item of women's lingerie, designed to modify the silhouette by accentuating the shape of the posterior.

19 Made using the Jacquard weaving technique in Germany.

20 Very common in Provençal.

21 Marcel Bonnet, "Avec Vincent Van Gogh autour de Saint-Paul", votive festival program for the centenary of the painter's stay in Saint-Rémy, 1989, A3078, old collection, Bibliothèque Joseph-Roumanille.

22 Letter 824, dated 7 December 1889, to Theo.

23 AMSRDP, 1O10.

24 At the beginning of the 20th century, elms came under attack by the devastating fungal disease known as "Dutch elm disease": once infected, a tree died within a few months, sometimes even weeks. To replace the missing elms, local authorities and road managers often chose plane trees, which were quite resistant at the time.

25 AMSRDP, 1D20.

26 The Provençal word for 'washerwomen'.

27 This word means 'cauldrons' in Provençal. The name comes from natural excavations caused by soil erosion, which the ancient residents of Saint-Rémy called "devil's cauldrons".

28 The supply of drinking water to homes would only begin much later in the 1920 and 1930s (AMSRDP, 1O16/1-2) and only spread gradually, not becoming widely available until the 1950s.

29 The Gavon *gaudre* ('stream') passed through there, as well as an almost permanent flow from an upper spring.

30 Letter 809 of 8 October 1889 and letter 831 of 23 December 1889.

31 Thanks to the George family and Saint-Rémy historian and scholar Marcel Bonnet (1922–2007), whose sister, Marthe, had married Étienne George (1911–2003), one of Frédéric George's sons.

32 Bonnet Marcel, *Saint-Rémy-de-Provence – Chronique photographique de Frédéric George*, Saint-Rémy-de-Provence: Éditions de l'Équinoxe, 1992.

33 He also noted the high number of mulberry trees (letter 827 to his sister, dated December 1889), whose leaves were used to feed silkworms, and which were vestiges of a sericulture industry by then in decline.

34 See Félix Laffé's recent work, *L'oléiculture en terre des Baux*, Aix-en-Provence: Presses Universitaires de Provence, 2025.

35 Letter 798 dated 2 September 1889, to Theo van Gogh.

36 Letter 784 dated 2 July 1889, to Theo van Gogh.

37 Letter 801 dated 10 September 1889, to Theo van Gogh.

38 Record of proceedings, AMSRDP, 1D20.

39 Marriage register 1868, AMSRDP, 1E22m.

40 Census of 1886, AMSRDP, 1F10.

41 Census of 1891, AMSRDP, 1F11.

42 Claude Mauron, "Histoire littéraire de Saint-Rémy" in the collective volume *Saint-Rémy-de-Provence : son histoire*, Saint-Rémy-de-Provence: Société d'histoire et d'archéologie de Saint-Rémy-de-Provence, 2014, pp. 446-455.

43 Under the title of *Espigueto evangelico* (Avignon: Aubanel frères, 1889).

44 See *F. Mistral et Saint-Rémy*, exhibition catalogue, Saint-Rémy-de-Provence: Musée des Alpilles, 2025, pp. 34-37.

45 Jules Pellissier was a witness at Marius Girard's wedding, as was Frédéric Mistral, AMSRDP, marriage registry, 1868.

46 Marcel Bonnet, *Marius Girard, la Cigalo dis Aupiho, notes et documents*, Saint-Rémy-de-Provence: Les Amis du Vieux Saint-Rémy, 1961.

47 See Marcel Bonnet, "Vincent Van Gogh et les Félibres", *Bulletin des Amis du Vieil Arles*, no. 70, March 1990.

48 Lettres 672, 704 and 745 of 1 September 1888.

49 Franco-Provençal literary publication founded in 1885 by Paul Mariéton (1862–1911), a writer close to Frédéric Mistral.

50 Letter 743 of 28 January 1889.

51 His works were published by l'Escolo dis Aupiho, under the title of *Li raconte dóu Chivau-Blanc*, in the collection of the Lou Prouvençau à l'Escolo association (nos. 38-39, 2015, for the prose texts, and no. 46, 2019, for the verse).

52 Conserved in the Mistral Museum of Maillane.

53 Conserved at the Musée des Alpilles.

54 Compiled under the title *Li sounaio dóu Sóuvage* in a collection of the Lou Prouvençau à l'Escolo association, no. 48, 2020.

55 Letter 801 of 10 September 1889.

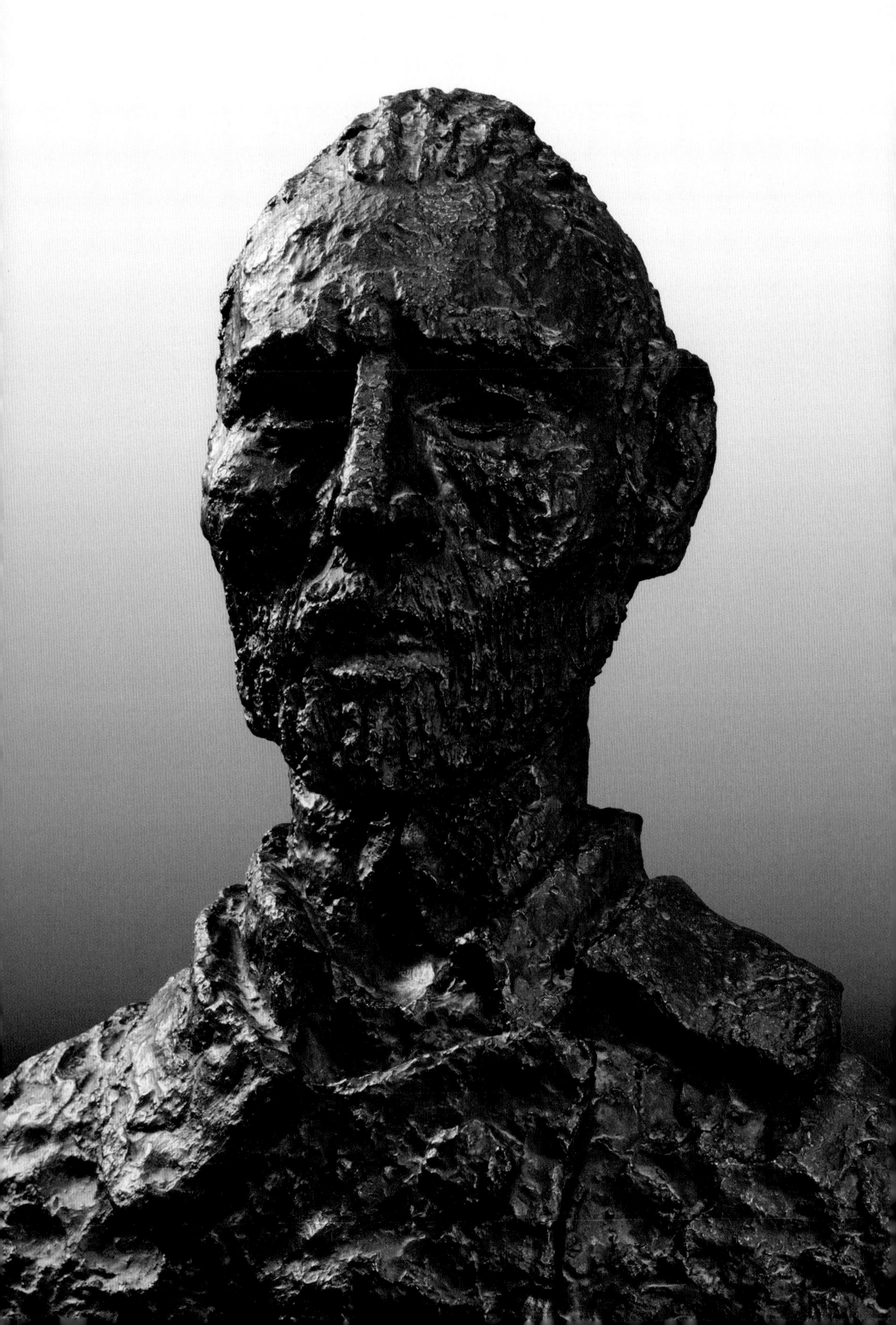

Virginie Olier

The Memory of Vincent van Gogh Rooted in Saint-Rémy-de-Provence

And What if Only a Single Painting Had Remained in Saint-Rémy...

Committed to the Saint-Paul hospital, and despite his disorders and long periods of crisis, Vincent van Gogh scarcely ever stopped painting during the year he spent in Saint-Rémy-de-Provence. Around one hundred and fifty canvases, as well as a large number of drawings, were produced during this stay. Yet none of these works was sold at the time, nor did any remain in the region.

Their commercial ascent began only several years after his death. On 11 April 1905, one could read in the newspaper *Le Sémaphore de Marseille*, in connection with the retrospective exhibition devoted to Georges Seurat and Vincent van Gogh, that the works of these two artists, much debated during their lifetimes, were then sought after by collectors.[1]

In *Le Petit Provençal* of 20 June 1926, the critic Léo Larguier wrote: "A Van Gogh painted at the time when that poor wretch lived on a crust dipped in a little coffee now fetches 500,000 francs [...]. Unforeseen revenge, sublime irony!"

One can then imagine how many inhabitants of Saint-Rémy allowed themselves to dream of discovering a canvas hanging on the wall of their kitchen, or a few sketches forgotten in an old chest up in the attic. People spoke of drawings offered as payment for tobacco to the tobacconist at the *Bar du marché*.

> As we know, Vincent van Gogh was an inveterate pipe-smoker, and unfortunately he often lacked tobacco. Moreover, we also know that he was by no means well-off. This is why he was obliged to resort to various devices in order to satisfy his craving and his passion for tobacco. When Vincent, whom some called "the Madman", arrived at the tobacconist's, they knew that, as so often, it would be difficult for him to settle his purchase. Then, in such circumstances, Vincent would offer a drawing or a simple sketch, all executed in pencil or charcoal, which he would hand over to the tobacconist.

Fig. 1
Saint-Paul Hospital in Saint-Rémy-de-Provence, 1889, oil on canvas, 63.4 × 49 cm. Donation from Max and Rosy Kaganovitch, 1973 © Musée d'Orsay, Dist. RMN-Grand Palais / Patrice Schmidt. Artwork caption copied

Fig. 2
Marie Girard at her Crowning, photographer Henri Vanel, 1892 © Musée des Alpilles – Ville de Saint-Rémy-de-Provence / Fabrice Lepeltier, *L'Œil et la Mémoire*

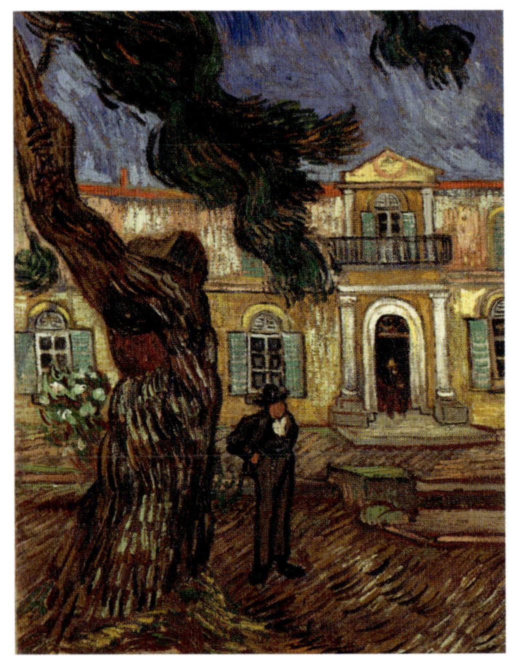

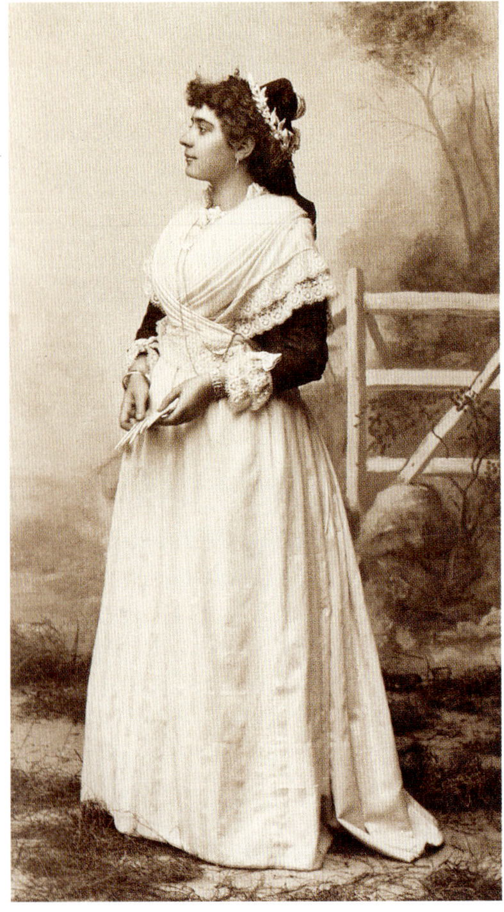

However, while the painter was able to move about freely in Arles and would occasionally settle his accounts with some Arlesian shopkeepers by means of drawings, it was not the same in Saint-Rémy, where he came down into the town only rarely.[2]
A single fact seems attested regarding the sad fate of the canvases left in Saint-Rémy. According to the local historian M. Bonnet, "all the canvases left with Dr Peyron were used as targets for the rifle of his twenty-year-old son". Only one work, whose journey is well known today, is said to have escaped this destruction: it was given to a friend of the family, Marie Girard.[3]
Vincent mentions it in a letter to his brother on 2 November 1889. The canvas depicting Dr Théophile Peyron (1827–1895) in front of the hospital was offered by the artist to the physician as a token of gratitude. Later, and it is not precisely known on what occasion, Joseph Peyron, the doctor's son, handed this work to Marie Girard (1872–1960), daughter of the Saint-Rémy *félibre* Marius Girard, renowned for her culture and her beauty. In 1896, she married the poet Joachim Gasquet from Aix (1873–1921), a close friend of Paul Cézanne. The couple settled

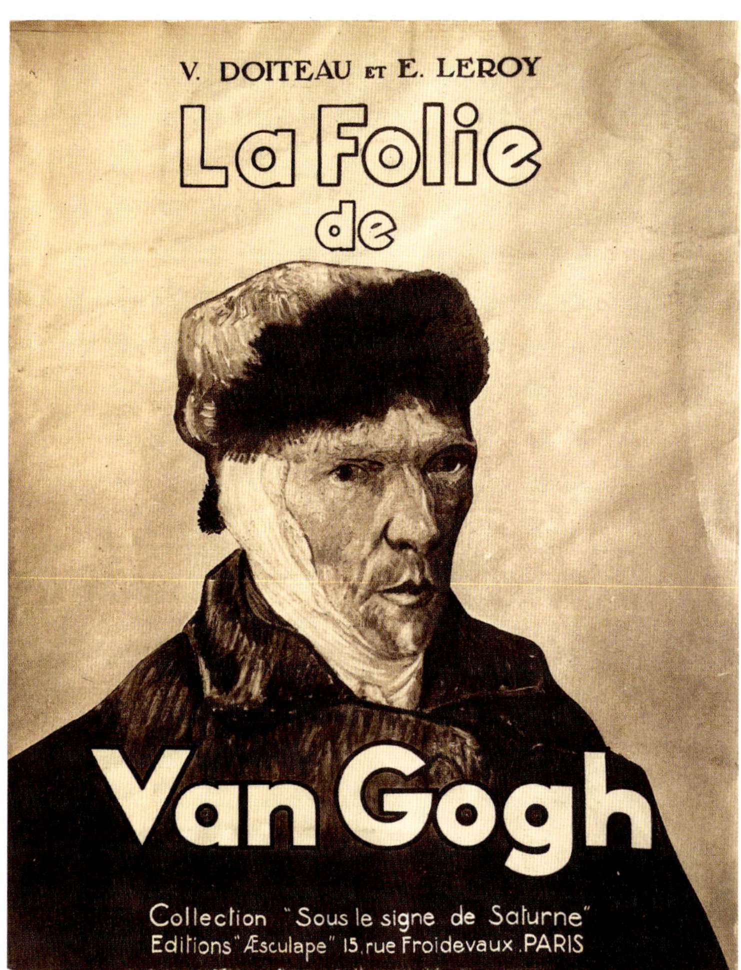

Fig. 3
Cover of the book *La Folie de Van Gogh* by Dr V. Doiteau and Dr E. Leroy, Paris: Éditions Æsculape, 1928

in Éguilles, on their Fontlaure estate, and later in Paris.

It was for the very first exhibition of Vincent van Gogh in Paris in 1901 that the Bernheim-Jeune gallery, one of the first to dedicate itself to Impressionist artists, probably acquired it. The work then passed into the hands of several collectors and art dealers before joining the prestigious collection of Max and Rosy Kaganovitch. In 1973, the canvas was accepted by the French State as a donation for the Musée du Jeu de Paume. It was then assigned to the Musée du Louvre, where it remained until 1986, when it was transferred to the Musée d'Orsay.

Van Gogh Slowly Takes His Place in the Memory of Saint-Rémy

The earliest mentions of Vincent van Gogh in the press date from his own lifetime. On September 30, 1889, the Arles newspaper *L'Homme de bronze* reported: "Mr Vincent, an Impressionist painter, is working at night, so we are told, by the light of gas lanterns on one of our public squares." However, it was chiefly in January 1890 that *Le Mercure de France* published one of the first major articles devoted to the painter, written by the art critic Albert Aurier. Entitled "Les Isolés. Vincent van Gogh", this enthusiastic essay played a

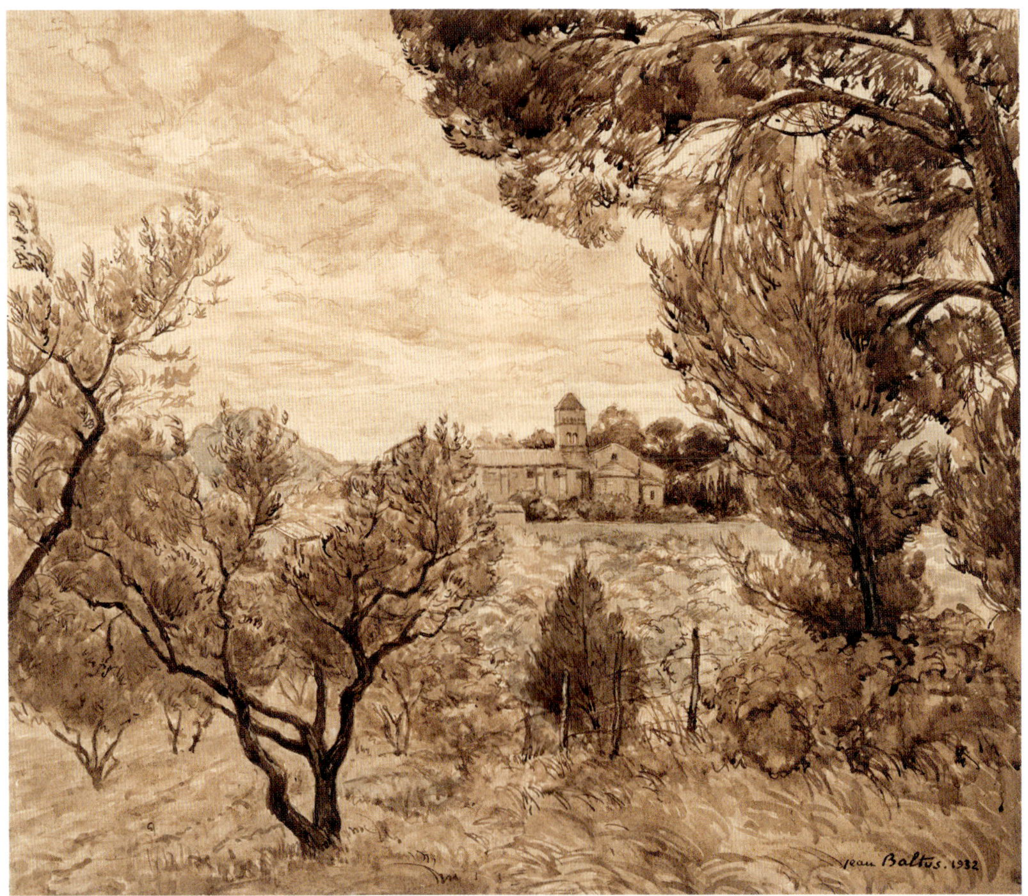

Fig. 4
Jean Baltus, *Saint-Rémy, l'asile de Van Gogh*, 1932 © Musée des Alpilles – Ville de Saint-Rémy-de-Provence / Fabrice Lepeltier, *L'Œil et la Mémoire*

decisive role in the artist's recognition. The following year, the critic Octave Mirbeau further reinforced this nascent renown with an article simply entitled "Vincent van Gogh".

It remains, however, difficult to know whether these writings ever circulated as far as Saint-Rémy-de-Provence. No one can say with certainty at what moment the people of Saint-Rémy became aware that the celebrated artist had walked the same paths as they did.

It was, without any doubt, Dr Edgar Leroy (1883–1965), physician at Saint-Paul from 1919 to 1964, who revealed the painter to the inhabitants of Saint-Rémy. Living where the artist had once stayed, he had access to unpublished files and was able to speak with people who had known the painter, such as Sister Épiphanie, who directed the institution, and Dr Rey, who had treated the painter in Arles. In 1928, he published *La Folie de Van Gogh* together with Dr Doiteau, the first posthumous analysis of the artist's madness and death. The painter from Lille, Jean Baltus, whose reproduction of the view of Saint-Paul appears in the publication, wrote in June 1928 in his journal that the book, printed in 1,650 copies, was already selling very well.

VINCENT VAN GOGH AT SAINT-PAUL DE MAUSOLE

Jacqueline Leroy

When Dr Leroy arrived in Saint-Rémy-de-Provence on 9 May 1919 to take up his role as physician and psychiatrist at the Saint-Paul de Mausole asylum for the mentally ill (men no longer being admitted since the end of the war), he was aware that the Dutch painter Vincent van Gogh had been a resident of this institution for a year, exactly thirty years prior to his arrival, from 9 May 1889 to 16 May 1890.

Dr Leroy quickly became interested in Van Gogh's fate, having admired reproductions gathered by Jacob Baart de la Faille, a Dutch expert compiling the *Catalogue raisonné* of Van Gogh, with whom he struck up a friendship. He also met several times with Dr Rey, a young intern at the Arles hospital during Van Gogh's stay, who provided him with precise and valuable information.

Therefore, Dr Leroy followed Vincent's journey closely and published in 1926, in the journal *Æsculape* across three issues, a very detailed study titled "Vincent van Gogh's Stay at the Saint-Rémy-de-Provence Asylum".

This was also the time when Jacob Baart de la Faille's *Catalogue raisonné* was about to be published, and when Dr Doiteau, a friend of Dr Gachet, began gathering materials for a biography of Van Gogh. His reading of *Æsculape* convinced him to meet his colleague Leroy, and they decided to collaborate on the work that would be published in 1928 under the title *La Folie de Van Gogh*, the first French book on the Dutch artist.

However, Dr Leroy was not content to stop there. How could he reveal the power and magnificence of Van Gogh's paintings? And how could he convince the people of Saint-Rémy, who only knew him as the figure associated with the "mad house", that he was a truly great artist, utterly unrecognised, if not despised? (Dr Peyron once gave his son the paintings offered by Van Gogh, and the boy used them as targets for his rifle!)

The wing where Vincent had stayed, his cell and his "studio", were now unoccupied in that part of the building that was no longer in use. Thus, the perfect spot was found, and the cell was already being shown… empty!

But with what budget could these reproductions be made in an era when copying a document was a significant investment? Dr Leroy would once again turn to Jacob Baart de la Faille, who would have the copies of the 146 paintings Van Gogh had created during his stay sent from the Netherlands. This shipment would include ten large colour reproductions (70 × 80 cm), including *The Irises*, *The Garden of the Saint-Paul Asylum*, *The Wheat Field with Cypresses*, *The Starry Night*, sixty-six reproductions sized 28 × 38 cm, and seventy smaller reproductions of works done in Saint-Rémy. And thus, the first Van Gogh museum was born, which, of course, would be inaugurated.

> On 30 June 1929, at 10 in the morning, a museum of reproductions was inaugurated at the Saint-Paul de Mausole asylum in Saint-Rémy-de-Provence, featuring works by Vincent van Gogh, offered by Mr J.B. de la Faille from Bloemendal, Holland, and created during his stay at the asylum from May 1889 to May 1890. The ceremony was attended by Mr Delfini, the prefect of the Bouches-du-Rhône, Mr Van der Waarden, the Dutch consul in Marseille, Mr Daniel Millaud, the general councillor of Saint-Rémy, Mr Antoine Mauron, the mayor of Saint-Rémy, Dr Paul Raimusat, president of the medical association of the Arles district, Mr J.B. de la Faille, Mr Jean Baltus, Dr Edgar Leroy*, physician at the asylum, and many admirers of Vincent van Gogh's art.
>
> At the start of the ceremony, a telegram arrived with congratulations from the Dutch government: "Touched by your kind gesture in commemoration of my great and tragic

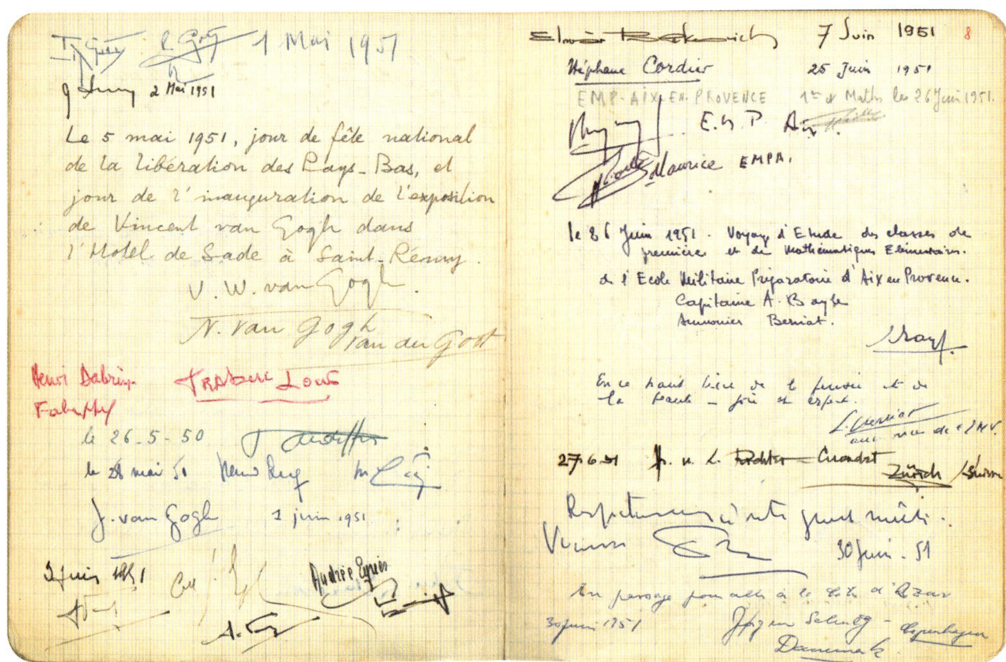

1 Mai 1951

Le 5 mai 1951, jour de fête national de la Libération des Pays-Bas, et jour de l'inauguration de l'exposition de Vincent van Gogh dans l'Hôtel de Sade à Saint-Rémy.
V. W. van Gogh.

7 Juin 1951

Stéphane Cordier 25 Juin 1951

Le 26 Juin 1951. Voyage d'Etude des classes de première et de Mathématiques Elémentaires de l'Ecole Militaire Préparatoire d'Aix en Provence.
Capitaine A. Bayle
Aumonier Berniat.

Fig. a
Pages from the guestbook of the first Van Gogh museum

> compatriot Van Gogh, I express the feelings of sympathy and gratitude of the Dutch government. Signed: Minister of Education, Fine Arts, and Sciences, Waszink."
>
> The ceremony concluded with a lecture by Mr de la Faille on Van Gogh's work, followed by a visit to the museum set up in one of the rooms that had once been occupied by the unfortunate painter.

Dr Leroy placed a register in the cell, serving as a guest book. It quickly filled up until the year 1942. After the war, the cell was reopened to visitors from June 1946 until April 1952. Considering the 3,900 signatures in the two existing registers, and the fact that many groups signed only once, it is estimated that over 13,000 people visited the museum—a significant number at the time, given the complete lack of advertising and the discreet nature of the location. Unsurprisingly, the majority of visitors were French: in 1938, there were 1,896 visitors, 1,676 of whom were French, coming from diverse backgrounds: tourists visiting the region, doctors (often attending a conference), art students, painters, teachers, school groups, and, of course, art enthusiasts—still quite few in number—discovering Vincent's work.

When the museum first opened, the foreign audience was mainly Swiss, Belgian, German, and American. By 1947, visitors came from nearly twenty countries: England, the United States, Switzerland, Belgium, the Netherlands, Norway, as well as Germany, Italy, Luxembourg, Austria, Denmark, Sweden, Poland, Argentina, Mexico, Greece, Tunisia, Egypt, South Africa, Japan, and so forth. As Van Gogh's renown grew, and his works were exhibited and his story became well-known, the public's desire to visit the place where he had lived increased.

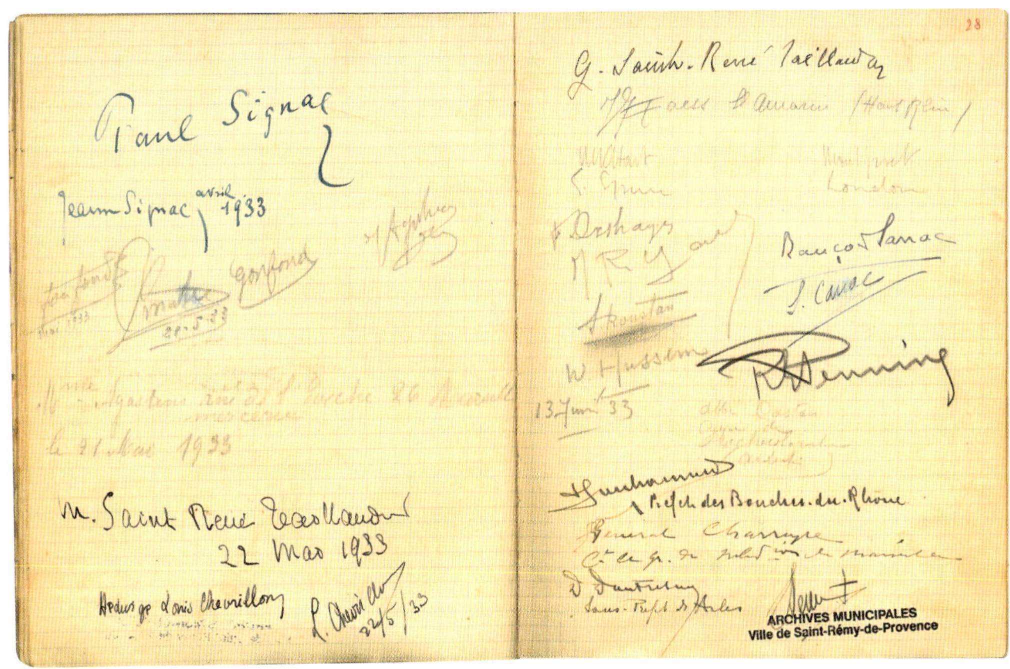

Fig. b
Pages from the guestbook of the first Van Gogh museum

Flipping through the registers, one can see the diverse range of visitors. Here are two random examples. On 5 March 1948, the records show: 4 Belgians, 1 English woman, 11 Americans from various cities, 2 Swiss, 2 Norwegians, 15 students with their teachers from a Belgian normal school, and 10 French... On the next page, we find: 4 English, 3 Americans, 3 Swiss, 3 Swedes, 1 Dane, 1 Dutch person, 2 Europeans expatriated in China and Japan, and 15 French, including the sub-prefect of Arles. And on the last page, alongside 3 Americans and 3 English people, we discover a Japanese and a Vietnamese visitor.

There are many signatures, sometimes hard to read, very few texts, and a few famous names scattered throughout the pages... I will mention first Vincent Willem van Gogh, who came on 5 May 1951 to inaugurate his uncle's exhibition at the Hôtel de Sade. Also, Léo Lelée, Jacob Baart de la Faille, Victor Doiteau, Henri Rolland, Gabriel Saint-René Taillandier, Léo Lagrange, the Minister of Leisure and Sports during an official visit in 1937, Jean Baltus, Roland de Margerie, Irving Stone, Alphonse de Châteaubriant, Michel Leiris, Jean Vilar, Jeanne Moreau, Alain Cuny, Jean-Louis Barrault, Sacha Pitoeff, Yves Brayer, André Bizette, Roger Chapelain-Midy, Juliette Roche, Torao Ataka, Tadashi Yamaha, Masato Kaguchi, and so on. The last signature in the register is, unfortunately, illegible; it dates back to 1953. Additionally, there is a card from 1955 from a psychiatrist, Dr Pereyra Käfer of the Regional University of Buenos Aires, president of the Society of Neurology, Psychiatry, and Neurosurgery, who came to meet Dr Leroy and visit Van Gogh's cell. The registers were then closed, but visitors still occasionally come to discover this modest cell, and some even return to pay their respects.

The small museum disappeared during the renovation works at Saint-Paul. It has long been that Vincent van Gogh achieved the recognition that had eluded him during his short life, but one can certainly believe that this first small museum helped bring to light one of the most famous painters in the world, who lived through suffering only to convey the beauty he held within.

*Later on, Dr Leroy was made a Knight in the Royal Order of Orange-Nassau.

A PROPOS D'UNE INAUGURATION

VAN GOGH A SAINT-REMY

Saint-Rémy-de-Provence, qui offre à l'admiration des visteurs ses « Antiquités » en ruines, les richesses de son musée lapidaire, le clocher de son église, que bâtit le pape Jean-XII, les colonnes corinthiennes de son mausolée, les archivoltes de son Arc de Triomphe et le cloître roman de l'ancien prieuré de Saint-Paul-de-Mausole, conservera désormais en ce dernier monument, transformé depuis longtemps en asile, et dans la chambre même qui lui fut réservée, le souvenir d'un peintre maudit entre tous, le Hollandais Vincent van Gogh, « l'homme à l'oreille coupée », fantastique voyageur de la folie.

On sait en effet que M. J.-B. de la Faille, de Bloemendaal, a fait don à l'asile de Saint-Paul d'une riche série de reproductions des œuvres de van Gogh, dites « de la période de Saint-Rémy », et que l'inauguration de ce petit musée documentaire — plus intéressant que bien d'autres, certes — aura lieu demain dimanche, sous la présidence du consul général des Pays-Bas à Marseille, et de M. Delfini, préfet des Bouches-du-Rhône, en qui la cause de l'art trouve toujours un défenseur éclairé.

Van Gogh arrivait à Arles en février 1888. Il a été en proie à des crises de mysticisme; il est ombrageux et fantasque. La chaude splendeur de la campagne provençale l'exalte; il peint avec fièvre toute une suite de paysages où domine le chrome, « la couleur aimée de Dieu ». Survient un peintre presque aussi étrange que lui : Gauguin. Des discussions d'ordre artistique naissent; van Gogh est exaspéré; l'intempérance achève de l'égarer; il tente de frapper Gauguin avec un rasoir, puis il se coupe l'oreille; on le conduit à l'hôpital d'Arles; il n'en sort que pour y être bientôt réintégré de force; en mai 1889, il entre dans la maison de santé du docteur Peyron, à Saint-Rémy-de-Provence; il y reste jusqu'en février 1890, où une nouvelle crise le terrasse. Il partira, et mourra en juillet, à Auvers-sur-Oise.

Or, pendant la « période de Saint-Rémy », qui se déroule entre deux accès de folie, le génie de van Gogh atteint toute sa plénitude. « Jamais il n'a tant produit — écrit le critique Florent Fels, qui a consacré au peintre des études sobres et clairvoyantes —. Jamais il ne donna plus décisivement la marque de son identité. De lumière, la couleur se fait flamme. Les arbres se tordent et jaillissent de terre lyriquement; les oliviers, les tournesols, les mûriers grésillent, la terre se creuse comme un ventre, et le soleil, pourpre et implacable, exacerbe l'horizon en gloire. »

Il a peint déjà des copies libres d'après Rembrandt, Daumier, Delacroix, Millet. Il a peint le jardin de l'asile, le bassin au milieu des plates-bandes et des arbres nus, les religieuses passant sous les arcades du préau, la maison blanche à travers les feuillages torturés, et aussi le portrait des jardiniers et celui du « gardien des fous » : tête aux dures bosses, aux yeux fixes, un peu à son image, et enfin son propre portrait : face hâve sous le pansement et le bonnet de fourrure.

A mesure qu'approche l'issue fatale, remarque M. Waldemar George, les œuvres du peintre sont plus accomplies. Ce n'est point à dire que nous admirons van Gogh *parce qu'il était fou* (les œuvres des aliénés n'ont en général de valeur que pour les psychiâtres), mais

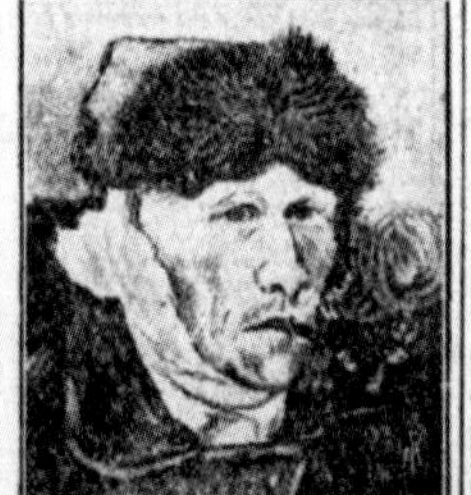

Van Gogh, peint par lui-même, pendant son séjour en Provence. Ce tableau est connu sous le nom de L'homme à l'oreille coupée.

(Photo Mougins)

parce que, quoique fou, s'il l'était, il fut un artiste; parce que son exaltation même lui permit d'éprouver des émotions plus profondes et de les exprimer plus intensément; parce que, sans qu'il possédât une technique rigoureusement parfaite, au sens académique, il sut créer un monde puissant de formes et de couleurs.

LUCIEN VALAT.

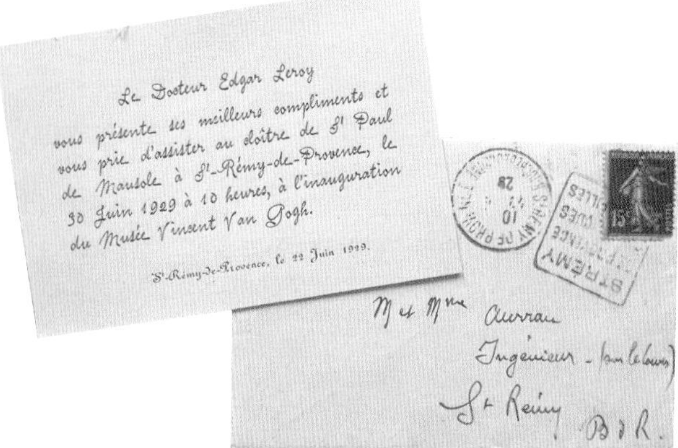

Le Docteur Edgar Leroy
vous présente ses meilleurs compliments et
vous prie d'assister au cloître de St Paul
de Mausole à St-Rémy-de-Provence, le
30 Juin 1929 à 10 heures, à l'inauguration
du Musée Vincent Van Gogh.

St-Rémy-de-Provence, le 22 Juin 1929.

M et Mme Aurran
Ingénieur
St Rémy B d R.

Fig. 5
Lucien Vallat, "À propos d'une inauguration: Van Gogh à Saint-Rémy", *Le Petit Marseillais*, 29 June 1929

Fig. 6
Dr Leroy's invitation to the opening of the Van Gogh Museum

The First Municipal Tributes

It took about fifty years for the town to officially honour the painter. On 24 April 1942, a municipal council resolution decided to rename certain streets and pay tribute to the painter by naming the road from the Mirabeau Boulevard to the Argelier district as "Avenue Van Gogh".[4] However, in 1960, the prefecture and the postal services requested a reconsideration of these street names, and in November 1962, a new resolution was passed to make some changes, as certain private property owners had raised objections. Consequently, the "Allée Vincent van Gogh" remained "Allée de Saint-Paul," and the "Route des Antiques" was renamed "Avenue Vincent van Gogh".[5]

THE 1951 VAN GOGH EXHBITION

Claude Mauron

It is significant that, shortly after the Second World War, this initiative was conceived precisely at the very place where Van Gogh had once stayed, by two distinguished figures of Saint-Rémy : Dr Edgar Leroy (1883–1965), who was the resident doctor at the Saint-Paul de Mausole asylum, and Charles Mauron (1899–1966), who lived nearby, at the top of the "chemin des Antiques", the future Avenue Vincent van Gogh. Then, Dr Leroy had already published a significant work, *La Folie de Vincent van Gogh*,[6] along with a study entitled "Van Gogh et le drame de l'oreille coupée",[7] while Charles Mauron had written an introduction for Jean de Beucken's book "Un Portrait de Van Gogh"[8] and had also published a Provençal poem titled *Vincènt Van Gogh à Sant-Roumié*.[9] Their long friendship was marked, after 1945, by continuous collaboration within the town hall, where Charles Mauron was mayor and Dr Leroy his deputy.[10]

Directed by the town hall of Saint-Rémy—and, from a legal standpoint, by the local tourist board[11]—the project was unable to come about during the years 1948–1949. The situation was finally resolved when, in December 1950, the engineer Vincent Willem van Gogh (1890–1978) (fig. a), son of Theo and thus the painter's nephew, and owner of the impressive family collection, proposed a dual exhibition in the spring of 1951, associating Saint-Rémy and Arles, following two previous exhibitions in Lyon and Grenoble, thereby reducing logistical challenges and transportation costs.

Beyond the immense artistic and cultural significance, two often-overlooked aspects deserve mention in this project. On the one hand, it was crucial to finally erase any lingering traces of hostility or disdain that still existed locally towards Vincent and his works:[12] hence the phrase in the catalogue by Dr Leroy, stating that the exhibition "brings Van Gogh triumphantly back" to the museums of both towns. Moreover, undeniably, profound human sympathies played a significant role in the project's development: Charles Mauron and Edgar Leroy had both taken part in the Saint-Remy Resistance; the young and newly appointed curator of the Musée Réattu in Arles was Jacques Latour, who, as a head of English intelligence in the Southeast, had been deported to Dachau in 1944;[13] and finally, the eldest son (born in 1920) of the engineer Van Gogh, Theodoor, member of the Dutch Resistance, had been executed by the Nazis in Amsterdam in March 1945...

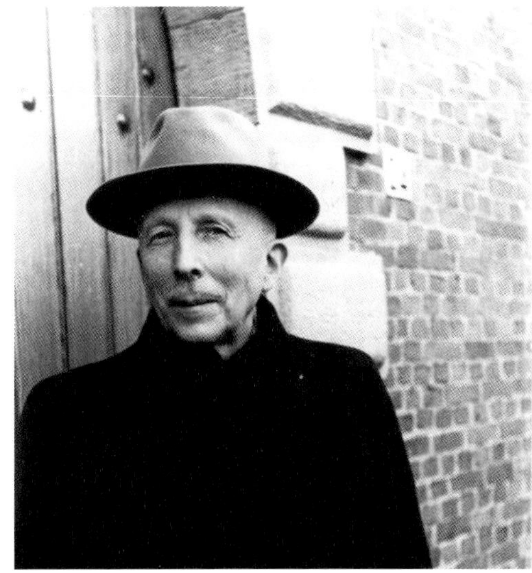

Fig. a
Photo of Vincent Willem Van Gogh, the painter's nephew, Zundert, 1953, Mauron Archives

The exhibition took place at the Hôtel de Sade, under the commission of Henri Rolland, the director of Antiquities and excavations at Glanum. Urgent repairs to the woodwork had been carried out, and, for security purposes, a telephone line was installed connecting the building to the local gendarmerie.[14] The inauguration took place on 5 May, in the presence of Gaston Defferre, then Merchant Navy Minister (fig. b and c). In the early afternoon, a reception was held at the town hall, where speeches were delivered by Dr Leroy, Charles Mauron and the Van Gogh's

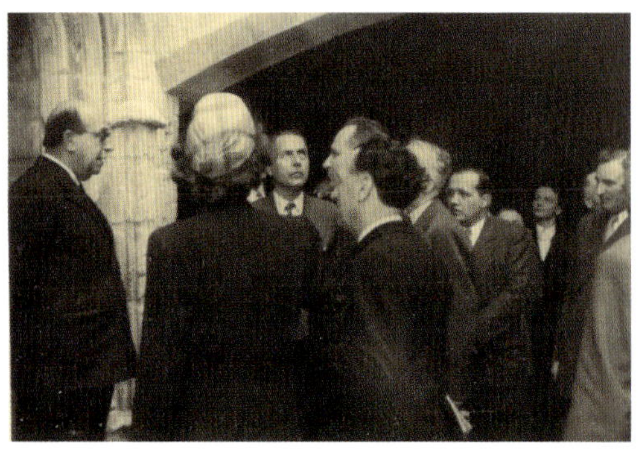

Fig. b
Inauguration on 5 May 1951: reception at the Hôtel de Sade by Henri Rolland (left); then, seen from the back, Alice Mauron; in profile, Charles Mauron and Gaston Defferre; in the background, Charles Privat, mayor of Arles, and Casimir Mathieu, first deputy, Mauron Archives

Fig. c
Inauguration on 5 May 1951. From left to right: Mr. Daudé, Director of Technical Services of the Department; Charles Mauron and his wife, Alice; Gaston Defferre; Roger Carcassonne, President of the General Council of the Bouches-du-Rhône; Engineer Van Gogh—and the self-portrait known as "Vincent with Hat", *Le Provençal,* 6 May 1951

La double et remarquable exposition des œuvres de Vincent Van GOGH a été inaugurée hier à l'hôtel de Sade, à St-Remy et au Musée Réattu d'Arles

M. Gaston DEFFERRE MINISTRE DE LA MARINE MARCHANDE
a présidé ces deux manifestations

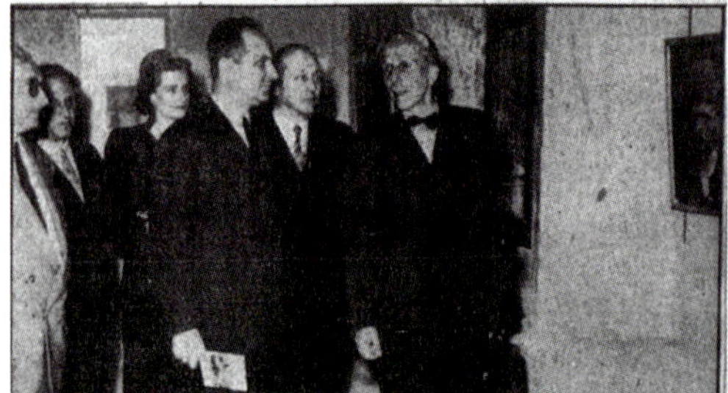

nephew, after which the guests proceeded to the Hôtel de Sade, and, later in that afternoon, the Arles inauguration took place, followed by a lecture from the engineer Van Gogh in the evening (fig. d). Between the two museums (and in the catalogue) were displayed 83 paintings and 18 drawings, spanning the entirety of the painter's life, of which 24 paintings and 6 drawings from his time in Saint-Rémy. As Marielle Latour, who assisted her husband, noted, "the success of the dual exhibition was immense":[15] originally scheduled from 5 to 27 May, it was extended until 3 June and attracted 8,818 visitors in Saint-Rémy,[16] resulting in a significant positive financial outcome, bolstered by catalogue sales (fig. e and f).[17]

Beyond its exceptional nature, in terms of the number of works exhibited, the Saint-Rémy/Arles event can truly be considered as a foundational milestone. It started a dynamic that continued into the summer of 1954, with four Van Gogh paintings featured in the exhibition *La Provence et les peintres* at the Musée Réattu in

Fig. d
Invitation card with the day's program, Mauron Archives

SAINT-RÉMY

14 h. 45: Réception à l'Hôtel-de-Ville.

15 h. Inauguration de l'Exposition à l'Hôtel de Sade (place Favier).

ARLES

17 h. Inauguration de l'Exposition au Musée Réattu (rue du Grand-Prieuré)

18 h. 30, Réception à l'Hôtel-de-Ville.

21 h. 30, Dans la Grande Salle de l'Hôtel-de-Ville, Conférence par Monsieur l'Ingénieur W.-V. VAN GOGH.

Le Maire de la Ville d'Arles,
Conseiller Général des Bouches-du-Rhône
Le Maire de la Ville de Saint-Rémy-de-Provence,

Vous prient de bien vouloir honorer de votre présence l'inauguration de l'Exposition des oeuvres de Vincent Van Gogh, qui aura lieu le Samedi 5 Mai 1951, sous la présidence de Monsieur Gaston Defferre, Ministre de la Marine Marchande

A l'issue de la réception à l'Hôtel-de-Ville, MM. les Maires seraient heureux de vous retenir à dîner à l'Hôtel du Forum.
Veuillez faire connaître, dès que possible, à M. le Maire d'Arles que vous répondez favorablement a cette invitation.

VINCENT
VAN GOGH
EN
PROVENCE

ARLES
MUSÉE RÉATTU

St-REMY
HOTEL DE SADE

MAI 1951

A M. Mauron
en bon souvenir et
avec grande estime.
St Rémy le 7 mai '51
V. W. van Gogh.

VINCENT VAN GOGH

Fig. e
Cover of the catalogue, Mauron Archives

Fig. f
Dedication of the catalogue to Charles Mauron, Mauron Archives

Laren N.H. le 8 octobre '51

Vincent van Gogh
Oud mensenpaar, Den Haag
Vieux couple, La Haye
Old couple, The Hague

Cher Monsieur Mauron,
Ma femme et moi aurons le plaisir de passer à St. Rémy la semaine prochaine (pour un ou deux jours). Je vous préviendrai quelques jours d'avance. Nous espérons avoir l'occasion de discuter votre mémoire si intéressante sur Vincent. Il y a peut-être lieu d'y ajouter encore quelque chose.
Au plaisir de vous voir, veuillez agréer, Cher Monsieur Mauron (et Mme Mauron) nos sentiments dévoués
V. W. van Gogh

J'ai prévenu le Dr Leroy.

Corrected with the original drawing
Copyright Ir. V. W. van Gogh

10 NEDERLAND
AMSTE[RDAM] 8 X 1951

Monsieur Charles Mauron
Maire
Saint-Rémy-en Provence
(B.d.R.)
Frankrijk

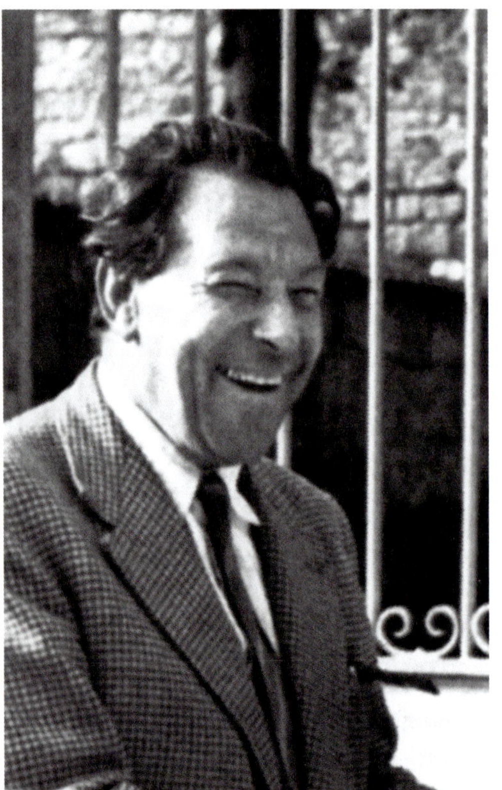

Fig. g
Postcard from engineer V.W. van Gogh addressed to Charles Mauron, 8 October 1951, Mauron Archives

Fig. h
Marc-Edo Tralbaut – photograph published in vol. IV of his *Van Goghiana* collections (Antwerp, 1967)

Arles, where Jacques Latour was present and, in the catalogue, a study by Charles Mauron titled "Vincent et Gauguin"; then, in 1957, the Van Gogh exhibition at the Musée Cantini in Marseille, prepared by Jacques Latour and completed by Marielle Latour, accompanied by a lecture from Charles Mauron on "Van Gogh et Monticelli". On a more personal note, the 1951 event allowed Charles Mauron to forge a warm friendship with the engineer Van Gogh and his wife Nelly (1897–1967), rooted in their shared interest in the psychoanalytic interpretations of Van Gogh, which they discussed during the painter's nephew's visits to Saint-Rémy, starting in Octobre 1951 (fig. g). In 1953, Charles Mauron published his major study in the review *Psyché*, entitled "La structure de l'inconscient chez Van Gogh". In March of the same year, together with his wife and the Latours, he was invited to the centenary celebrations, where he concluded the series of official lectures in Amsterdam with a talk on "Vincent and Theo". The Antwerp exhibition in May 1955 should also be mentioned, where Charles Mauron addressed "The Personality of Van Gogh",[18] at the invitation of another Van Gogh aficionado, the Belgian Marc-Edo Tralbaut (1902–1976) (fig. h), who has left us an impressive collection of documents and biographical research, "Van Gogh le mal aimé",[19] and who lived for a long time on both sides of the Alpilles.

It is hardly surprising to see, from the 1950s onwards, an increasing concentration of artists in and around the Alpilles. Coming from other regions of France or from abroad, many of them sought to settle here to capture the unique light and the striking contrasts of the landscape. At that time, the scenery remained much as Vincent had discovered and painted it. However, not all were landscape artists; there was also a particular atmosphere, a certain serenity that drew them here. The region was appealing, and a new form of cultural and artistic tourism began to emerge. Saint-Rémy, whose economy had once been predominantly agricultural, increasingly defined itself as a tourist town.
In 1963, the town decided, by mutual agreement, to form a twin city relationship with Zundert, Van Gogh's birthplace. This alliance marked the beginning of many events centered around the painter. The following year, a delegation from Saint-Rémy, including the dance group La Respelido led by its president Renée de la Comble, traveled to attend the inauguration of a monument in his honour by Her Majesty Queen Juliana of the Netherlands. The bronze sculpture, created by the sculptor Ossip Zadkine (1888–1967) (fig. h), depicts the two brothers, Vincent and Theo, and is installed on the Van Gogh square, not far from their birthplace. The pedestal, made of Saint-Rémy stone, was a gift from the municipal council.[20] It contains, in a finely crafted metal box by the local artisan Mr Chieusse, a small amount of soil from the Saint-Paul de Mausole garden. On this occasion as well, the Provençal town also offered a mosaic by the Catalan artist Josep Franch-Clapers (1915–2005), depicting the Alpilles landscape dominated by the Romanesque bell tower

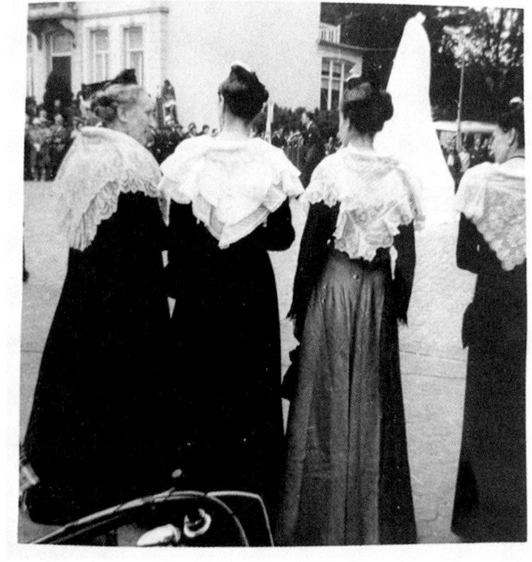

Fig. 7
The Respelido group in Zundert before the inauguration of the monument on 28 May 1964

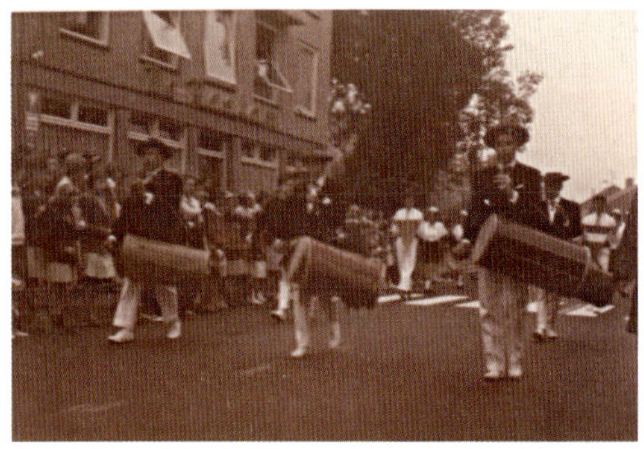

Fig. 8
Parade of tambourine players from Saint-Rémy in the streets of Zundert

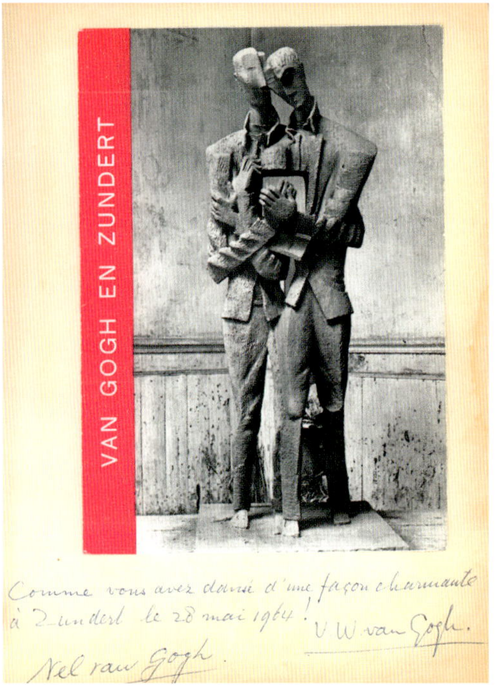

Fig. 9
Autograph entry of M.M. van Gogh in the Respelido guestbook

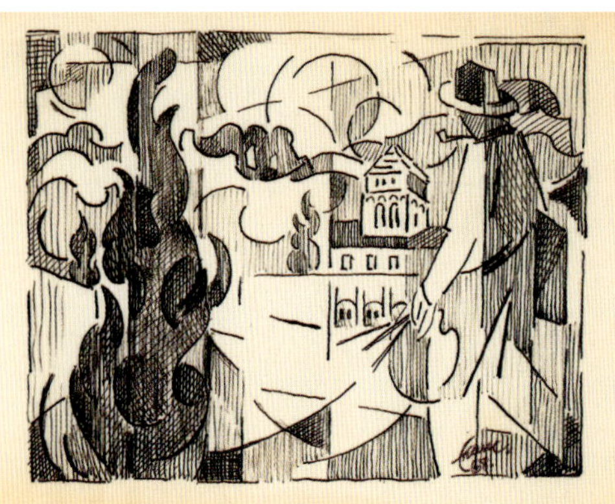

Fig. 10
Joseph Franch-Clapers, Mosaic project for Van Gogh © Musée des Alpilles – Ville de Saint-Rémy-de-Provence / Fabrice Lepeltier, *L'Œil et la Mémoire*

of the Saint-Paul monastery. It was in Zundert that the first contacts were made with Ossip Zadkine for the creation of a piece for Saint-Rémy. The internationally renowned French sculptor of Russian origin had already created a series of sculptures of Van Gogh, expressing his admiration for the Dutch artist. The curators of the Musée des Alpilles and the archaeological site of Glanum met with the sculptor, and the town placed the order in April 1965.[21] He crafted a faithful portrait of Van Gogh, continuing the reflection on the close bond between the two brothers, as expressed in the Zundert monument: it shows Vincent holding a letter from Theo. "The idea of placing the bust right in the town and in the very street that Vincent painted moves me deeply, and I find it infinitely more fitting and would cherish it dearly" wrote the sculptor to the mayor on 7 June 1966, after the latter had discussed the research done to select the most appropriate location.[22]

In August 1966, Saint-Rémy celebrated both Van Gogh and its twinning with Zundert with a week of festivities blending culture and local traditions. The programme included lectures, concerts, and bullfighting-related events (races, *bandido*, cattle contests, and a comedic bullfighting evening). On 15 August, the

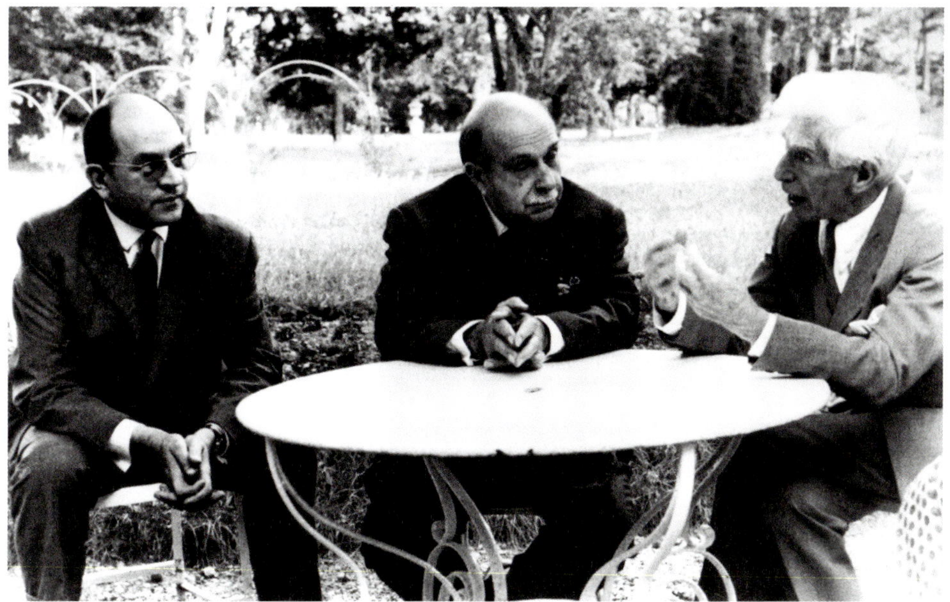

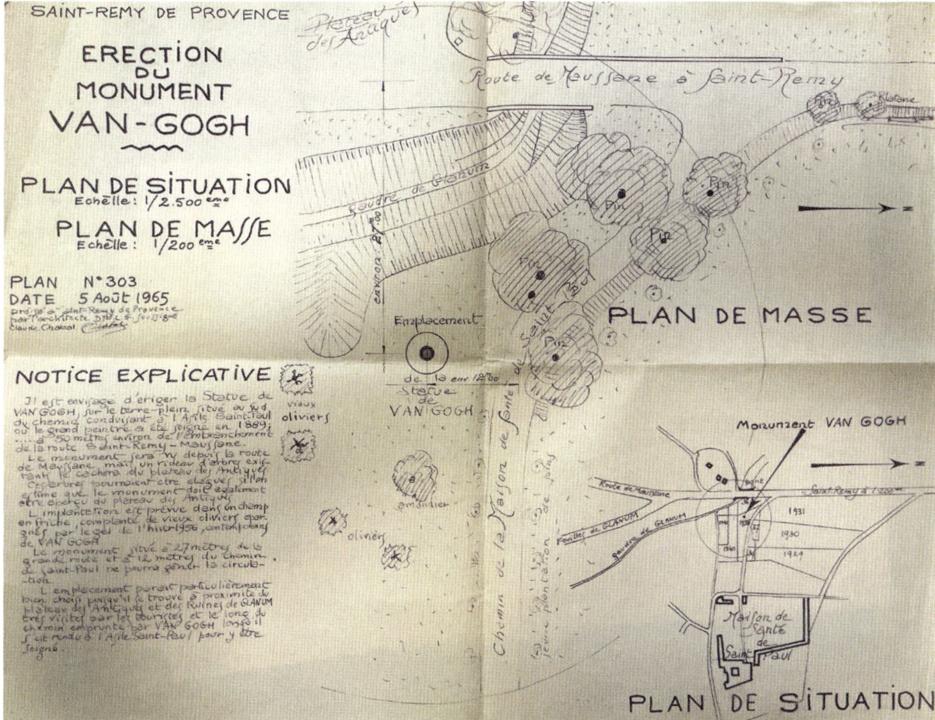

Fig. 11
From left to right: Marcel Bonnet, assistant curator of the Musée des Alpilles, Henri Rolland, Director of Antiquities, and Ossip Zadkine discussing the project in the grounds of the Hôtel des Antiques in August 1964 © Bibliothèque Joseph Roumanille, fonds Marcel Bonnet

Fig. 12
Claude Chabal, Location and ground plan for the erection of the Van Gogh monument, 5 August 1965 © AMSRDP

Carreto Ramado paraded with its thirty horses and mules, while the Saint-Roch festival took place in the Jardins district. Every day, there were cycle races, belote tournaments, pétanque matches, and gala balls adding to the festive atmosphere. To enhance the festivities, the Antiques, the pines of Saint-Paul, and the chapel of Notre-Dame-de-Pitié were illuminated by the Lombard Establishments. This initiative, spearheaded by the president of the festival committee, Mr Mathieu, was well received, though many lamented that this lighting was not maintained throughout the entire tourist season. A Dutch delegation of over seventy people came to Saint-Rémy for the celebrations. Mayor Manders, his aldermen, Mr Koeken and Mr Mertens, along with several other dignitaries, were officially welcomed at the town hall. However, it was the Damesshowdrumband, a battalion of fifty-six majorettes, that stole the spotlight with their number and their attire: fur-lined hats, capes, gloves, and boots perfectly suited for the blazing sun. They paraded through the town all the way to Saint-Paul and attended all the ceremonies alongside the Respelido group.[23]
On 13 August, a touching ceremony inaugurated the "Avenue Docteur Edgar Leroy". Having passed away the previous year, Dr Leroy truly deserved this public tribute, especially since he once remarked: "Everyone makes use of Van Gogh, but no one truly serves him";[24] on the contrary, he had significantly contributed to preserving the painter's memory. At 6 p.m., the bust was unveiled, finally placed in the alley leading to the cloister, in the presence of the artist Ossip Zadkine. In his speech, Mayor Louis Vigne expressed his pride, highlighting that "the mayor of a town that kept Vincent van Gogh's name on its registry for over a year, a town whose only stay by Van Gogh, a few square centimetres of paint, a few words, would have sufficed to make its name eternally glorious, fulfils a sacred duty of gratitude".[25]
These days of great popular rejoicing left a profound mark on the inhabitants of Saint-Rémy and helped strengthen the ties between the region and the painter. On 3 November 1986, on the occasion of the inauguration of the Van Gogh exhibition at the Metropolitan Museum of Art in New York, Mayor Henri Richaud reminded everyone that "this long-standing tradition of commemorating Vincent van Gogh, upheld by successive municipalities, has not wavered when the representatives of the Metropolitan Museum of Art in New York [Ronald Pickvance and Emily Walter] came to Saint-Rémy to draw from the very sources of Vincent's inspiration in preparing the catalogue for this exhibition. They found, almost untouched, the stones, the trees, and the light of the Alpilles that Van Gogh immortalised, and which the people of Saint-Rémy, who have the privilege of seeing them constantly, hold dear for the admirers of Van Gogh who visit regularly to appreciate the Saint-Rémy terroir". Gradually, Van Gogh's name became inscribed in Saint-Rémy's history, associated with the town's tourism promotion, and commemorations now punctuate the festive calendar.

The Van Gogh Centenary Celebrations

The centenary of the painter's death was organised as early as 1988, when the city welcomed Mr Becht, the director of culture for the "Van Gogh 1990" project launched by the Dutch Ministry of Culture. Mr Becht, highly interested in the exhibition held in Saint-Rémy in 1900, with photographs by Frédéric George then displayed at

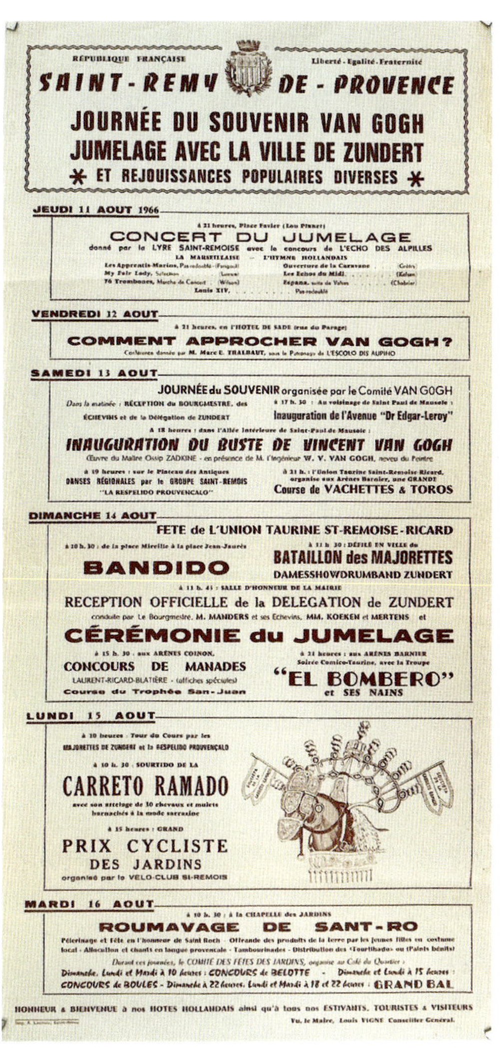

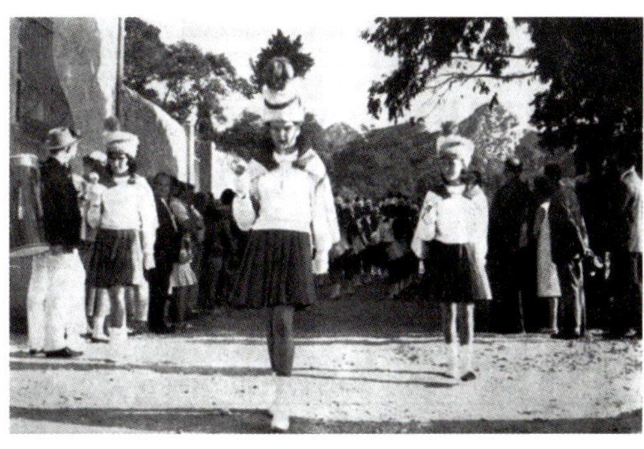

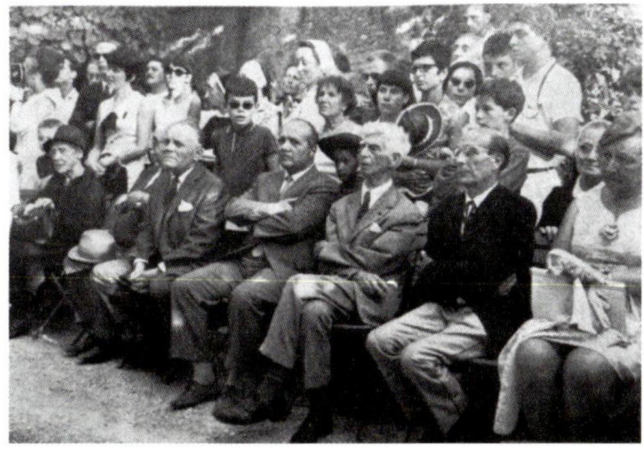

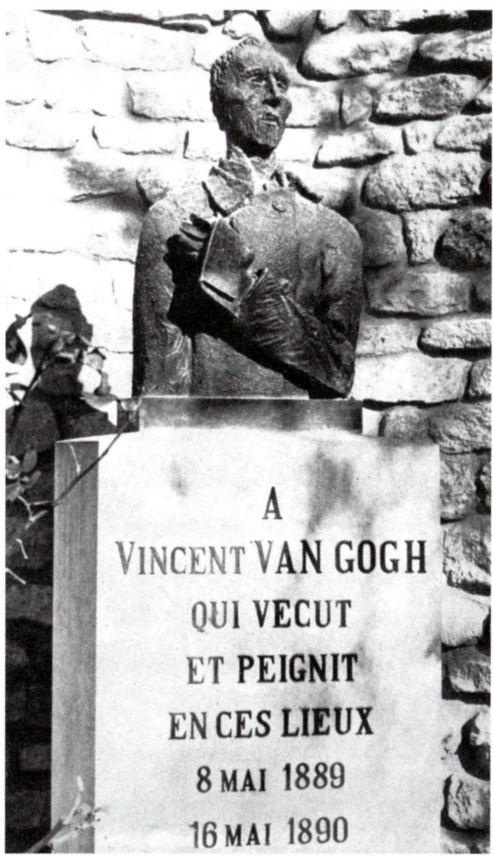

Fig. 13
Poster of the programme of festivities from 11 to 16 August 1966, Imprimerie Lacroix, Saint-Rémy © Musée des Alpilles – Ville de Saint-Rémy-de-Provence / Fabrice Lepeltier, *L'Œil et la Mémoire*

Fig. 14
Arrival of the majorettes at Saint-Paul, photograph by Zoé Binswanger. Saint-Rémy-de-Provence, Official Municipal Bulletin no. 3

Fig. 15
Unveiling of the bust, photograph by Zoé Binswanger. Saint-Rémy-de-Provence, Official Municipal Bulletin no. 3

Fig. 16
The bust in the Allée de Saint Paul, photograph by Zoé Binswanger. Saint-Rémy-de-Provence, Official Municipal Bulletin no. 3

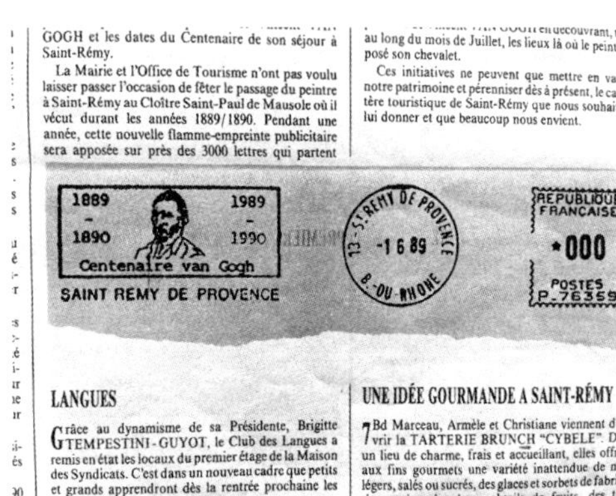

GOGH et les dates du Centenaire de son séjour à Saint-Rémy.

La Mairie et l'Office de Tourisme n'ont pas voulu laisser passer l'occasion de fêter le passage du peintre à Saint-Rémy au Cloître Saint-Paul de Mausole où il vécut durant les années 1889/1890. Pendant une année, cette nouvelle flamme-empreinte publicitaire sera apposée sur près des 3000 lettres qui partent

au long du mois de Juillet, les lieux là où le peintre a posé son chevalet.

Ces initiatives ne peuvent que mettre en valeur notre patrimoine et pérenniser dès à présent, le caractère touristique de Saint-Rémy que nous souhaitons lui donner et que beaucoup nous envient. ■

LANGUES

Grâce au dynamisme de sa Présidente, Brigitte TEMPESTINI-GUYOT, le Club des Langues a remis en état les locaux du premier étage de la Maison des Syndicats. C'est dans un nouveau cadre que petits et grands apprendront dès la rentrée prochaine les langues étrangères.

UNE IDÉE GOURMANDE A SAINT-RÉMY

7 Bd Marceau, Armèle et Christiane viennent d'ouvrir la TARTERIE BRUNCH "CYBELE". Dans un lieu de charme, frais et accueillant, elles offrent aux fins gourmets une variété inattendue de mets légers, salés ou sucrés, des glaces et sorbets de fabrication artisanale, des cocktails de fruits, des thés

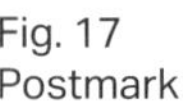

Fig. 17
Postmark

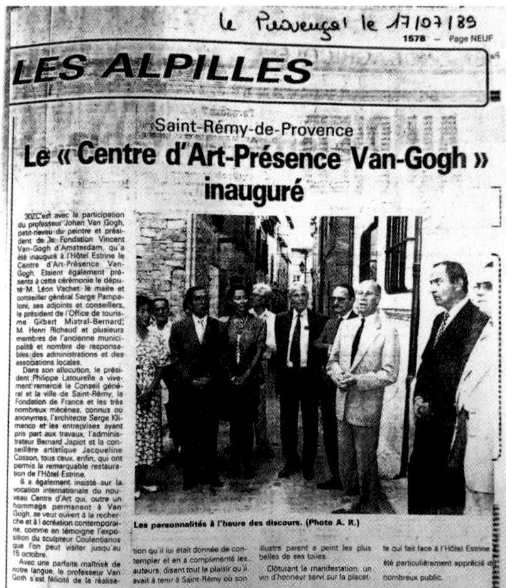

le Provençal le 17/07/89

1578 — Page NEUF

LES ALPILLES

Saint-Rémy-de-Provence

Le « Centre d'Art-Présence Van-Gogh » inauguré

30ZC'est avec la participation du professeur Johan Van Gogh, petit-neveu du peintre et président de la Fondation Vincent Van-Gogh d'Amsterdam, qu'a été inauguré à l'Hôtel Estrine le Centre d'Art-Présence Van-Gogh. Etaient également présents à cette cérémonie le député M. Léon Vachet, le maire et conseiller général Serge Pampaloni, ses adjoints et conseillers, le président de l'Office de tourisme Gilbert Mistral-Bernard; M. Henri Richaud et plusieurs membres de l'ancienne municipalité et nombre de responsables des administrations et des associations locales.

Dans son allocution, le président Philippe Latourelle a vivement remercié le Conseil général et la ville de Saint-Rémy, la Fondation de France et les très nombreux mécènes, connus ou anonymes, l'architecte Serge Klimenco et les entreprises ayant pris part aux travaux, l'administrateur Bernard Japiot et la conseillère artistique Jacqueline Cosson, tous ceux, enfin, qui ont permis la remarquable restauration de l'Hôtel Estrine.

Il a également insisté sur la vocation internationale du nouveau Centre d'Art qui, outre un hommage permanent à Van Gogh, se veut ouvert à la recherche et à l'acréation contemporaine, comme en témoigne l'exposition du sculpteur Coulentianos que l'on peut visiter jusqu'au 15 octobre.

Avec une parfaite maîtrise de notre langue, le professeur Van Goth s'est félicité de la réalisation qu'il lui était donnée de contempler et en a complimenté les auteurs, disant tout le plaisir qu'il avait à tenir à Saint-Rémy où son illustre parent a peint les plus belles de ses toiles.

Clôturant la manifestation, un vin d'honneur servi sur la placette qui fait face à l'Hôtel Estrine a été particulièrement apprécié du nombreux public.

Les personnalités à l'heure des discours. (Photo A. R.)

Fig. 18
"Le 'centre d'art présence Van Gogh' inauguré", *Le Provençal*, 17 July 1989

the Musée des Alpilles, requested that the municipality lend the exhibition to the Amsterdam foundation. This interest helped to enhance the commune's brand image beyond national borders.[26] In parallel with the major exhibitions held in Amsterdam and other key cities linked to Van Gogh, a variety of artistic events took place in Saint-Rémy: a photographic exhibition, guided tours, a film festival, an exhibition of young Dutch painters, a theatrical performance, and a painting competition…

It was on the occasion of the centenary that a trail of the locations painted by Van Gogh was created, inviting everyone to admire the landscapes where the painter had set up his easel. Visitors could find a reproduction of a painting accompanied by a brief excerpt from the correspondence between the painter and his brother Theo. A postal stamp featuring the artist, along with the dates of the centenary of his stay, was also issued.

In July 1989, in the presence of Johan van Gogh, the painter's great-nephew and president of the Vincent van Gogh Foundation of Amsterdam, the Présence Van Gogh Art Centre opened its doors in the restored Estrine Hotel, with the aim of paying tribute to the artist and his desire to see "living painters no longer so unjustly unknown". Mr Philippe Latourelle, the association's president, has always been fully committed to making this venue a privileged space for research, exhibition, and contemporary creation. In 2007, the designation "musée de France" was granted to the Présence Van Gogh Art Centre, which then became the Musée Estrine, entirely dedicated to 20th-century painting. The collection, gradually assembled in the creative lineage of Vincent van Gogh, is now regarded as national public heritage.

Indeed, in affirming its support for artists, the town commissioned René Coutelle (1927–2012) to create a new work in homage to the painter. The sculptor carved, from a limestone block weighing over 3.5 tonnes, a symbolic ensemble

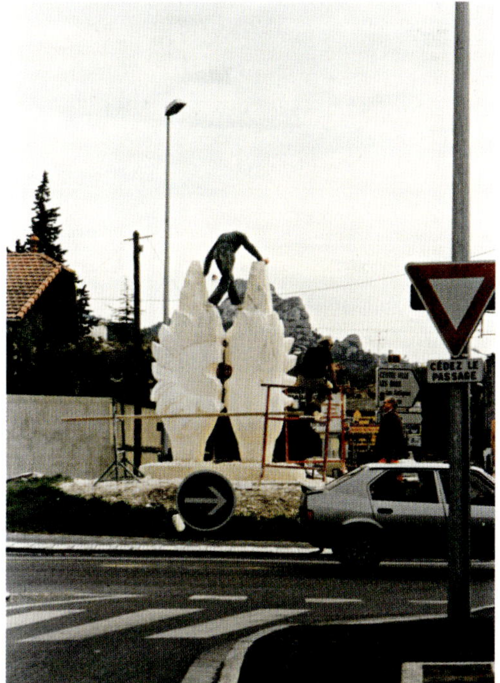

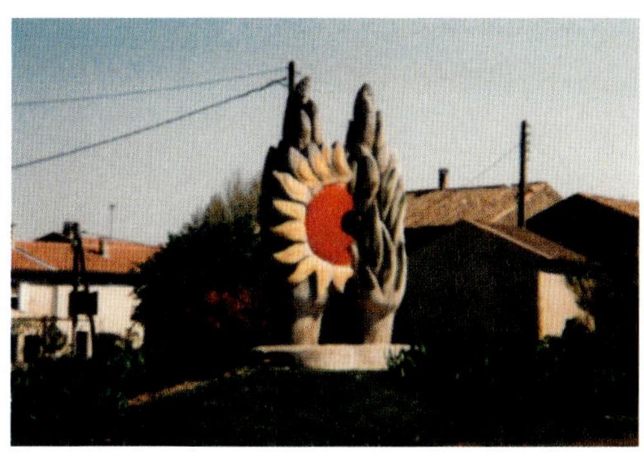

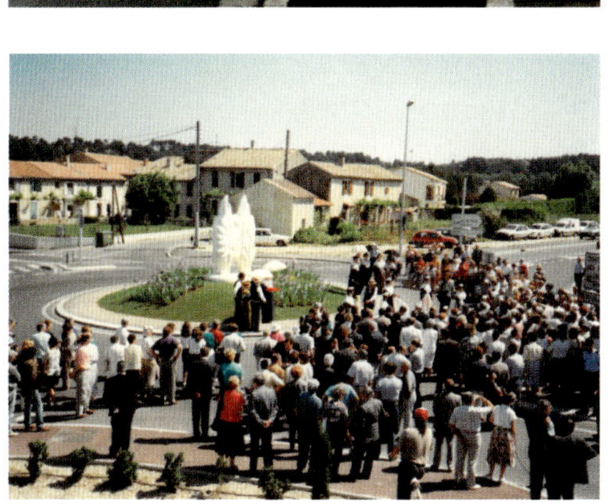

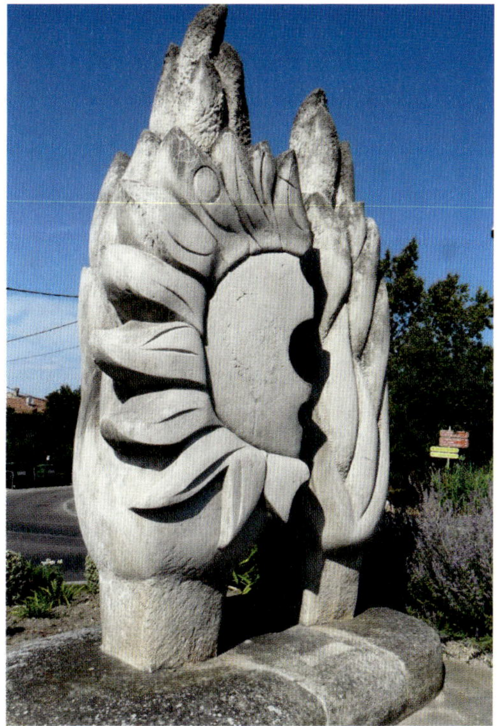

Fig. 19
The artist René Coutelle hard at work on the sculpture *Homage to Van Gogh*

Fig. 20
Unveiling of the sculpture on 16 May 1990

Fig. 21
The sculpture vandalised

Fig. 22
The sculpture today, weathered by time

comprising a sun, a cypress, and a sunflower. Titled *Hommage à Van Gogh*, this monumental statue was inaugurated at the roundabout on the Avignon Road on 16 May 1990, the anniversary of the painter's departure. A crowd had gathered well in advance in front of the monument, whose whiteness was softened by a lawn that had miraculously sprouted the previous day—courtesy of the technical services—and blue irises freshly imported from Holland.[27]

A few years later, some individuals deemed the stone too white to pay proper homage to the master of colour, and they did not hesitate to paint the sculpture yellow and red. Whether an act of vandalism or a poor taste prank, it cast a spotlight on the forgotten piece at the centre of the roundabout. The stone quickly regained its luminous grain, but the isolated artwork has over time acquired a greyish patina, nearly obscuring its original purpose.

The Stolen Bust

On the morning of 1 February 1989, the newspaper *Le Provençal* headlined "Van Gogh Unbolted!"—a shocking catchphrase, commensurate with the audacity of the theft that had occurred a few days earlier. While Arles was under heightened surveillance due to a new Van Gogh exhibition, another piece vanished during the night of 29 to 30 January: not a painting, but the very bust by Ossip Zadkine, installed in the Saint-Paul alley. In the early morning, the gendarmes could only note the facts: the four fastening bolts had been carefully sawed through, leaving only an empty stone pedestal.

A year after the theft, with the investigation yielding no results, the municipality requested a replacement

Saint-Rémy

Bientôt un nouveau buste de Van Gogh

Dans le cadre des journées parlementaires qui se sont tenues à Arles, les députés et sénateurs se sont rendus à Châteaurenard, passant jeudi par les Baux et Saint-Rémy.

Une brève halte a permis à MM. Chirac, Pasqua, Juppé, Pons, et à leurs amis, d'admirer le site des Antiques où les attendait la municipalité de Saint-Rémy.

Après que M. Prades, directeur de l'Office du tourisme, eut retracé devant les personnalités l'histoire des monuments romains, M. Serge Pampaloni a pu s'entretenir avec M. Chirac d'un sujet qui lui tenait à cœur : le buste de Van Gogh, œuvre du sculpteur Zadkine, volé comme on le sait dans l'allée de Saint-Paul. Ce que l'on ignore peut-être, c'est que le moule ayant servi à la Fonderie existe encore... et qu'il est la propriété de la ville de Paris !

C'est très volontiers que le maire de Paris a donné son accord pour que ce moule soit utilisé pour couler un nouveau buste, et il faisait savoir le soir, par l'entremise de M. Léon Vachet, qu'il se proposait d'offrir à Saint-Rémy cette statue qu'il viendrait lui-même inaugurer.

Bonne nouvelle donc pour tous ceux qui déploraient la disparition de cette œuvre artistique, précieux témoignage du séjour de Van Gogh à Saint-Paul-de-Mausole.

Notre photo :

Les parlementaires sur le plateau des Antiques. (Photo A.R.)

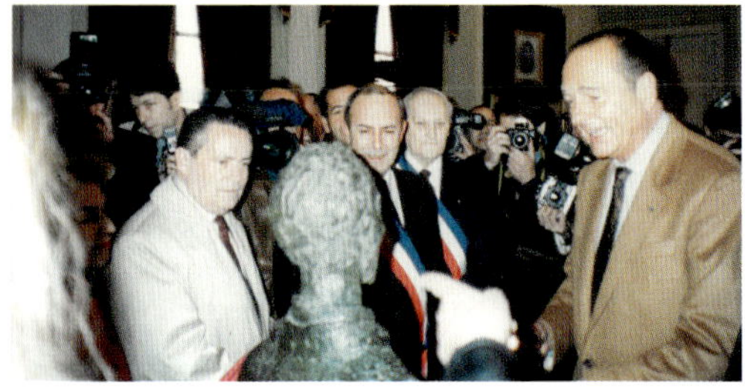

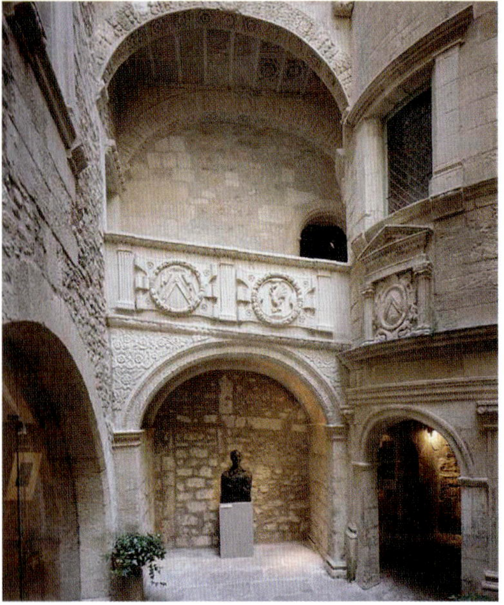

Fig. 23
"Bientôt un nouveau buste de Van Gogh", *Le Provençal*, 26 March 1990

Fig. 24
Mr Chirac and Mr Pampaloni at the official reinstallation of the bust in the town's reception hall © Mme Crudo

Fig. 25
Second cast of Zadkine's bust of Van Gogh in the inner courtyard of the Musée des Alpilles

St-Rémy

LE BUSTE VOLÉ DE VAN GOGH RETROUVÉ AU PAYS-BAS

Aujourd'hui dans

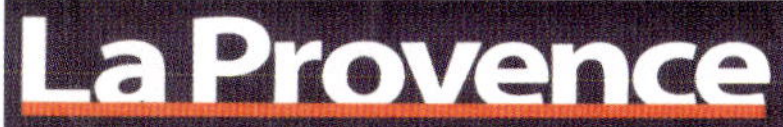

Fig. 26
Headline in *La Provence*, 24 May 2009

Fig. 27
Article in *La Provence*, 11 October 2009

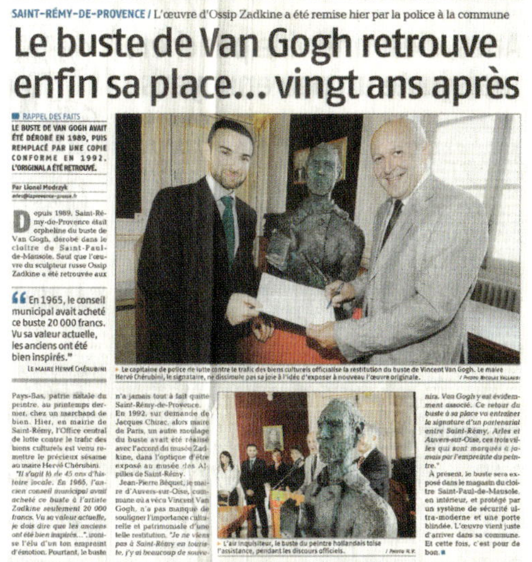

ALPILLES

Dimanche 11 Octobre 2009
www.laprovence.com

SAINT-RÉMY-DE-PROVENCE / L'œuvre d'Ossip Zadkine a été remise hier par la police à la commune

Le buste de Van Gogh retrouve enfin sa place... vingt ans après

RAPPEL DES FAITS

LE BUSTE DE VAN GOGH AVAIT ÉTÉ DÉROBÉ EN 1989, PUIS REMPLACÉ PAR UNE COPIE CONFORME EN 1992. L'ORIGINAL A ÉTÉ RETROUVÉ.

Par Lionel Modrzyk

Depuis 1989, Saint-Rémy-de-Provence était orpheline du buste de Van Gogh, dérobé dans le cloître de Saint-Paul-de-Mausole. Sauf que l'œuvre du sculpteur russe Ossip Zadkine a été retrouvée aux Pays-Bas, patrie natale du peintre, au printemps dernier, chez un marchand de bien. Hier, en mairie de Saint-Rémy, l'Office central de lutte contre le trafic des biens culturels est venu remettre le précieux sésame au maire Hervé Chérubini.

"Il s'agit là de 45 ans d'histoire locale. En 1965, l'ancien conseil municipal avait acheté ce buste à l'artiste Zadkine seulement 20 000 francs. Vu sa valeur actuelle, je dois dire que les anciens ont été bien inspirés...", ironise l'élu d'un ton empreint d'émotion. Pourtant, le buste n'a jamais tout à fait quitté Saint-Rémy-de-Provence. En 1992, sur demande de Jacques Chirac, alors maire de Paris, un autre moulage du buste avait été réalisé avec l'accord du musée Zadkine, dans l'optique d'être exposé au musée des Alpilles de Saint-Rémy.

Jean-Pierre Béquet, le maire d'Auvers-sur-Oise, commune où a vécu Vincent Van Gogh, n'a pas manqué de souligner l'importance culturelle et patrimoniale d'une telle restitution. *"Je ne viens pas à Saint-Rémy en touriste, j'y ai beaucoup de souvenirs. Van Gogh y est évidemment associé. Ce retour du buste à sa place va entraîner la signature d'un partenariat entre Saint-Rémy, Arles et Auvers-sur-Oise, ces trois villes qui sont marquées à jamais par l'empreinte du peintre."*

À présent, le buste sera exposé dans le magasin du cloître Saint-Paul-de-Mausole, en intérieur, et protégé par un système de sécurité ultra-moderne et une porte blindée. L'œuvre vient juste d'arriver dans sa commune. Et cette fois, c'est pour de bon.

"En 1965, le conseil municipal avait acheté ce buste 20 000 francs. Vu sa valeur actuelle, les anciens ont été bien inspirés."
LE MAIRE HERVÉ CHÉRUBINI

Le capitaine de police de lutte contre le trafic des biens culturels officialise la restitution du buste de Vincent Van Gogh. Le maire Hervé Chérubini, le signataire, ne dissimule pas sa joie à l'idée d'exposer à nouveau l'œuvre originale.

L'air inquisiteur, le buste du peintre hollandais toise l'assistance, pendant les discours officiels. / Photo N.V.

LE TÉMOIGNAGE de Frédéric Piwowarczyk *capitaine de police à l'Office central de lutte contre le trafic des biens culturels*

"NOUS L'AVONS CHERCHÉ DANS TOUTE L'EUROPE"

Le policier était hier à Saint-Rémy-de-Provence pour restituer le buste de Van Gogh.

Le jeune homme peut avoir le sourire. Il a fait partie de l'équipe de policiers qui a tenté de retrouver le buste de Van Gogh, sculpté par Ossip Zadkine. Un travail de longue haleine. *"On l'a cherché dans toute l'Europe, mais on ne connaît toujours pas le parcours exact de l'œuvre, même si on peut dire qu'elle a bien voyagé. Un temps, nous l'avons crue en Italie, une autre fois en Belgique, mais finalement, elle était cachée au Pays-Bas"*, affirme Frédéric Piwowarczyk. Dans le milieu du trafic d'œuvre d'art, tout est en fait affaire de réseau, selon le policier. *"Nous avons activé plusieurs de nos contacts, qui nous ont permis de remonter la piste, et à faire rendre le buste par son possesseur. Ce dernier n'a pas voulu décliner son identité, mais n'a pas fait d'histoire au moment de la restitution"*, explique-t-il, satisfait.

Au retour de son escapade provençale, le policier va maintenant se consacrer aux affaires en cours. Et ce n'est pas ce qui manque. *"Nous sommes dans une situation similaire aux années 1980, avec une recrudescence des vols de reliques dans les églises et les chapelles*, reconnaît-il. *Ceux qui trafiquent ce genre d'objets peuvent ensuite être poursuivis pour profanation."*
L.M.

L'ACCORD

TROIS VILLES DÉSORMAIS UNIES

Arles, Saint-Rémy-de-Provence et Auvers-sur-Oise ont profité de l'événement pour signer, hier, une charte de coopération culturelle et touristique "Vincent Van Gogh". Cet accord va favoriser les échanges, notamment scolaires, entre ces trois communes, autour de la mémoire et de l'œuvre du peintre hollandais.

▶ Lire aussi en page 5.

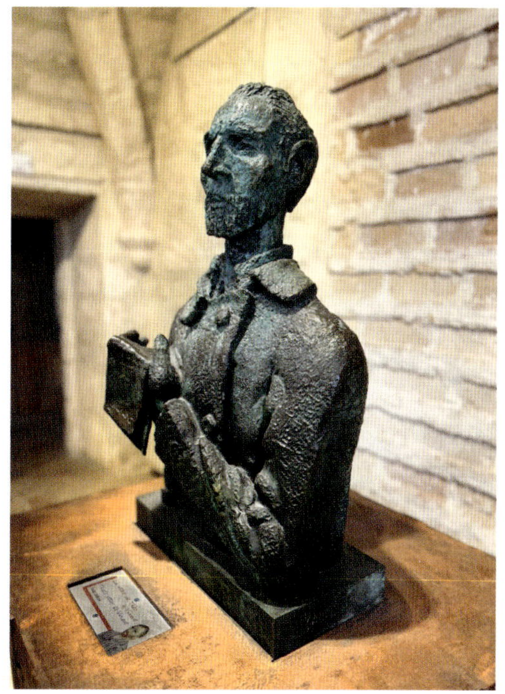

Fig. 28
Installation of the bust at Saint-Paul de Mausole

for the missing bust, the original plaster cast of which is preserved at the Musée Zadkine in Paris. It was during the parliamentary sessions of the RPR party in Arles that Messrs Chirac, Pasqua, Juppé, and Pons took a brief detour to the Antiques. Mr Pampaloni, the Mayor of Saint-Rémy, managed to speak with Mr Chirac, then Mayor of Paris, and secured a promise of a new bust. Thus, twenty-six years after the first casting, a second mould was exceptionally produced by the Susse foundry, followed by a new bronze casting. The new bust, generously offered by the City of Paris, was personally presented by Jacques Chirac during an official ceremony in February 1993. In order to ensure its safety, this second bronze version is now installed in the inner courtyard of the Musée des Alpilles.[28] A rare occurrence in the history of stolen artworks: in 2009, the bust that had been stolen two

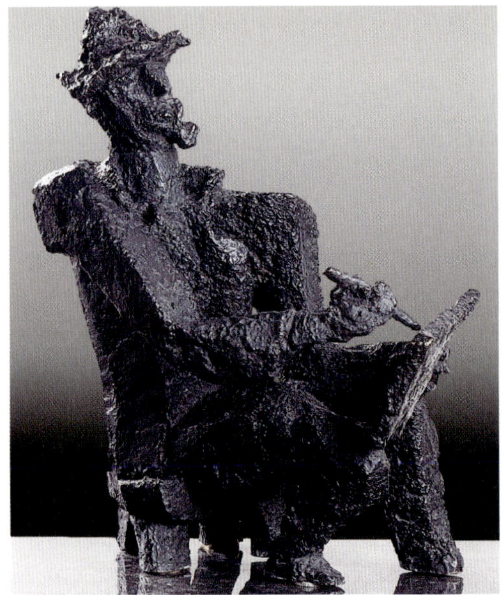

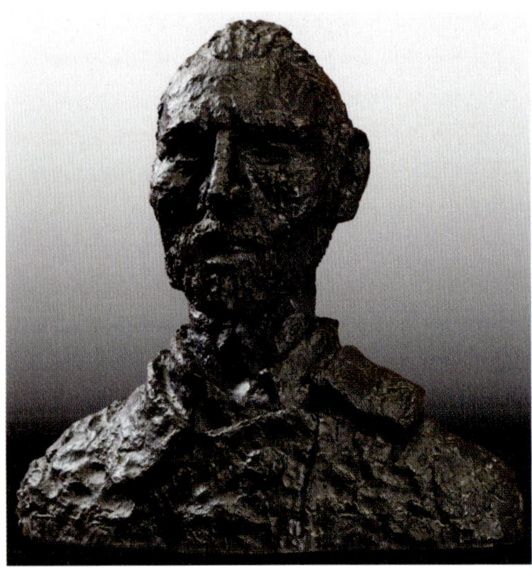

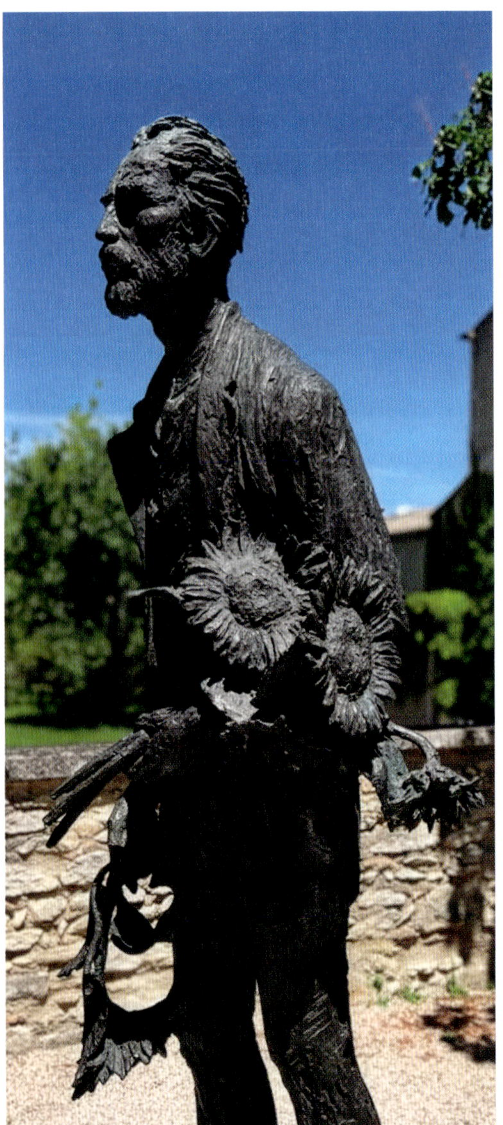

Fig. 29
Ossip Zadkine, *Van Gogh drawing*, Musée Estrine collection © Fabrice Lepeltier, *L'Œil et la Mémoire*

Fig. 30
Ossip Zadkine, *Bust of Van Gogh*, Musée Estrine collection © Fabrice Lepeltier, *L'Œil et la Mémoire*

Fig. 31
Gabriël Sterk, *The Sunflower Thief*, bronze statue

decades earlier reappeared. It was found in the north of the Netherlands, in Zwolle, at the home of a private detective who claimed to have removed it from the garage of a suspicious "businessman", wary of the bronze's origins and fearing legal trouble. The artwork was eventually willingly returned to the French Embassy in The Hague. Little is known about the extraordinary journey of the stolen bust. The Dutch police believe that the sculpture was used as collateral and a means of exchange in criminal transactions.[29] On 10 October, a representative of the Central Office for the Fight Against the Trafficking of Cultural Goods, Captain Frédéric Piwowarczyk, handed the original bust back to Mayor Hervé Chérubini, in the presence of Mr Jean-Pierre Béquet, Mayor of Auvers-sur-Oise, and Danièle Pourtaud, Deputy for Heritage of the City of Paris. The bust was once more installed at Saint-Paul de Mausole, this time indoors and under strict protection.
It is worth noting two other bronzes by Ossip Zadkine in Saint-Rémy-de-Provence, both acquired and preserved by the Musée Estrine. In 2004, the Dutch sculptor Gabriël Sterk, after creating an imposing statue of Cézanne for the city of Aix-en-Provence, decided to pay tribute to Vincent van Gogh. He then created *The Sunflower Thief*, a bronze sculpture over two meters tall, depicting Vincent on his way back to his studio, carrying the sunflowers he intends to paint with Gauguin. Initially offered to the City of Arles, the work was declined. Thanks to the decisive intervention of Dr Boulon, a physician at the Saint-Paul clinic, the Institute of Saint-Joseph—owner of the monastery—managed to acquire it. The sculpture was placed in the cloister walkway, with the artist personally determining its location.

The Vincent van Gogh Legacy

The hospital room, transformed into a museum since 1929, initiated the Van Gogh pilgrimage. The painter's stay is mentioned in a brochure published by the tourist office as early as 1948, and is now part of the history of the Saint-Paul de Mausole site. Visitors tour not only the room and the fields painted by Van Gogh, but also the remarkable cloister from the 11th and 12t centuries, a masterpiece of Provençal Romanesque art. However, the place, which impresses visitors with its great serenity, remains a psychiatric hospital.
Among the events related to Van Gogh that have enlivened the small capital of the Alpilles, we must mention the filming of at least two movies. One can only imagine the astonishment of the locals when, in 1955, the entire crew of a major Hollywood production settled there for several weeks. At its head was the director Vincente Minnelli, who had come to shoot *Lust for Life*, or *La Vie passionnée de Vincent van Gogh*, and, in the leading roles, Kirk Douglas, recipient of the Golden Globe for Best Actor, and Anthony Quinn, who would earn the Oscar for Best Supporting Actor. The rehearsals with the stand-ins, followed by the actual filming with the American stars, were closely observed by the people of Saint-Rémy.
The filming took place in Saint-Paul but also in the Jardins district, notably at Le Touret, for a scene in which Kirk Douglas, portraying Van Gogh, searches for an inspiring spot to paint amidst the almond trees and olive groves.[30] Released in France in 1957, the film had been shown at the Variétés cinema, and the locals were delighted to spot, even if briefly, the fields of petunias and olive trees from their neighbourhood. The film crew had made a habit of visiting

the Café des Arts, whose reputation for warm hospitality and delicious cuisine was already well-established. The guestbook of the establishment preserves a precious memory of that visit: on two pages, the two mischievous actors sketched each other in their respective roles. More recently, it was the biopic by Julian Schnabel, *At Eternity's Gate*, starring Willem Dafoe, nominated for an Oscar in 2019 for his portrayal of Van Gogh, that was partially filmed in Saint-Rémy. The film crew chose the cultural centre and the park of the clinic as natural settings for the film. On this occasion, employees and patients from both clinics, as well as adult residents of the specialised care home Les Iris, had the opportunity to watch the filming and meet American movie stars. Some even appear on screen for a brief moment as extras.

THE SAINT-PAUL HEALTH HOUSE

Dr. Jean-Marc Boulon

In 1995, Dr Boulon, a physician at the Saint-Paul health house, proposed to the institution's management and the nuns of the Saint-Joseph congregation to realise a dream expressed by Vincent van Gogh: to found an association of artists in the Midi region. Once the institutional agreements were secured, the association was founded under the name Valetudo, referencing the goddess of health and the ancient spring that fed the Gallo-Roman city of Glanum. Since then, this art therapy project—fully integrating art and culture into the care pathway—has enriched the mission of the Saint-Paul clinic. The association's workshop-gallery, located at the heart of the Van Gogh cultural centre managed by the Vivre et Devenir association, provides a space for female patients suffering from mental health issues similar to those of Van Gogh to create and exhibit their artworks.

For the tenth anniversary of the association, the premiere of Anne-Marie Cellier's play *Vincent ou l'âme bleue*, featured in the Avignon festival, was presented in the Van Gogh field behind the cloister and left the audience enchanted by the text and its performance.

On the occasion of the 20th anniversary, Vincent Willem van Gogh came to read, in the chapel, a few letters exchanged between his great-grand-uncle Vincent and his great-grandfather Theo. It was a moment of profound emotion, etched in the memory of all those present. The most moving instant was undoubtedly the reading of the letter that Theo wrote to his wife Jo—a unique and heart-wrenching letter in which he recounts the final moments of his brother Vincent, who died in his arms, and his burial, with only a few close friends, including the painter Émile Bernard. In 2025, Sister Nicole, a nun of the Saint-Joseph Institute, during the Saint-Rémy book festival, performed alongside Dr Boulon a few pages from the novel he co-wrote with Anne-Marie Cellier: *Van Gogh. Quatre saisons à l'asile Saint-Paul*.

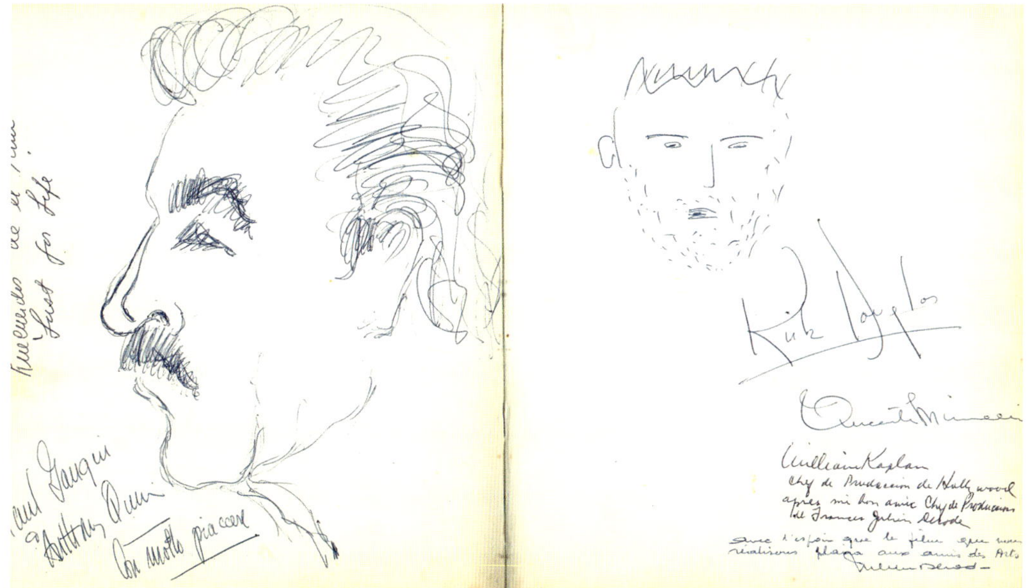

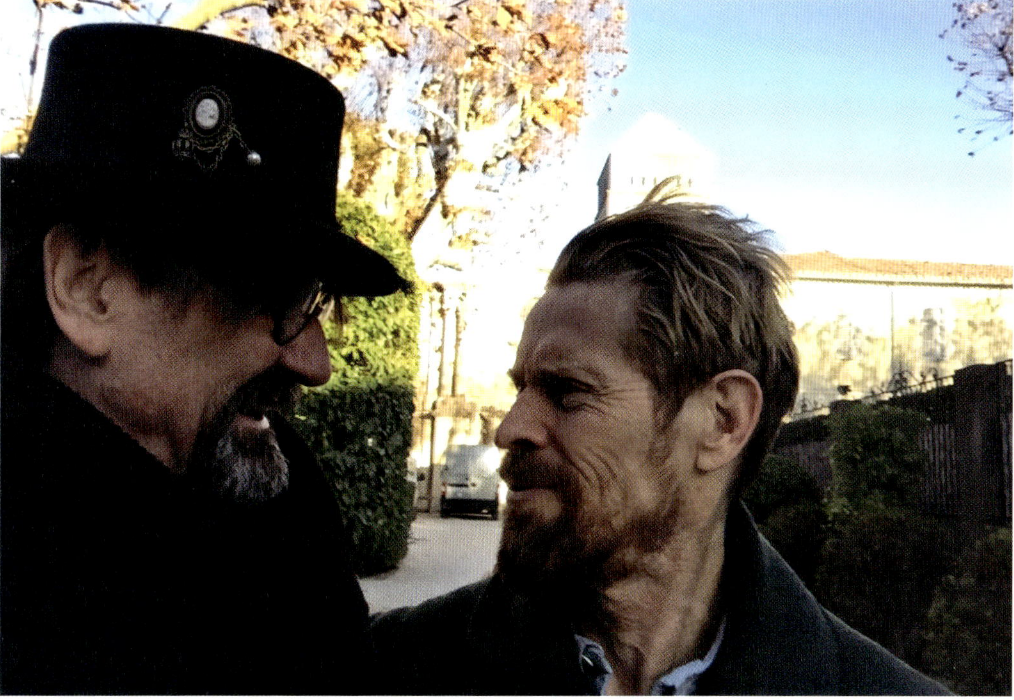

Fig. 32
Entries by Anthony Quinn and Kirk Douglas in the Café des Arts guestbook, private collection

Fig. 33
On the set of the film *At Eternity's Gate*

Saint-Rémy in Van Gogh's European Radiance

The painter's global renown has fostered tourist circuits that extend beyond Saint-Rémy. The town had partnered with Arles as early as 1951, but each city promoted the myth in its own way, depending on the opportunities. It must be acknowledged that the "Little Rome of the Gauls" has been more widely associated with the painter's stay in Provence, while the memory of Van Gogh has been maintained in Saint-Rémy by the local associations at Saint-Paul and the Musée Estrine.
In 2009, under the impetus of Martine Lagrange, Deputy Mayor in charge of culture, heritage, and communication, the town renewed its commitment and signed a cooperation charter with Arles and Auvers, the other two French towns where the artist stayed, in favour of cultural, educational, and touristic exchanges.
This partnership laid the foundation for the "Van Gogh Route", expanded to a European scale and realised through the creation of a dedicated website. Since then, the Van Gogh Europe network has been established: the town co-signed a letter of intent in Amsterdam in 2012 with the main French and Dutch stakeholders.
It has since strengthened to offer a sustainable and high-quality tourist experience, highlighting both the artist's work and the territories that inspired him.
At the level of Saint-Rémy-de-Provence, the collective "Van Gogh Saint-Rémy" brings together Saint-Paul de Mausole, the Musée Estrine, the tourist office, and the town, along with the Musée des Ailpilles.

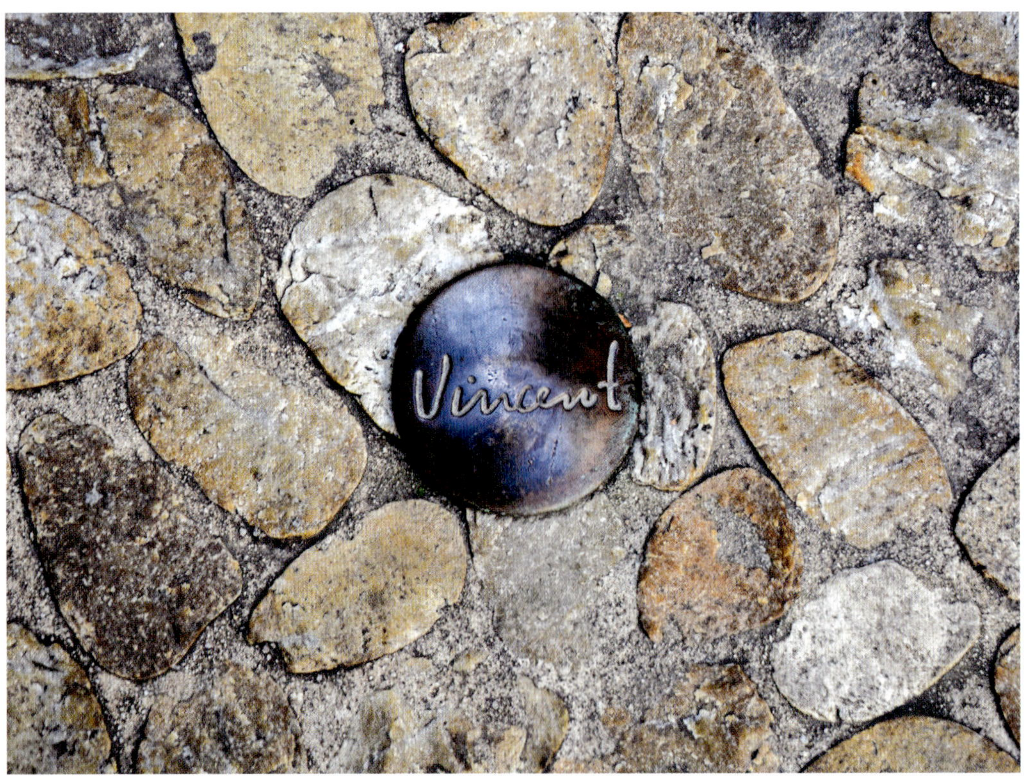

Fig. 34
Signpost on the Van Gogh route

In 2013, the Vallée des Baux-Alpilles Community of Communes decided to support the exploration of the region through the painter's stay and embarked on the renovation of the plaques along the walking trail. LEADER funding enabled the development of the "Van Gogh Natures" app, designed to provide contextual information for each artwork in its original setting. Ground signage connects the Musée Estrine—the Van Gogh interpretation centre—with Saint-Paul de Mausole. The various cultural institutions in the town have agreed to offer a programme aimed at highlighting the relationship between Saint-Rémy-de-Provence and Vincent van Gogh as a living patrimonial treasure, a source of knowledge and cultural development.

For the commemoration of the painter's 125th death anniversary, the Van Gogh Europe network united around a common cultural programme. During the Museum Night, the Musée des Ailpilles invited Philippe Monnier, from the association La Couverture Verte, to paint an interpretation of the famous painting *The Starry Night* using fluorescent pigments, on the Favier square plunged into darkness and before an enthralled audience. This performance was repeated in 2022, a year when the town's cultural institutions once again united to offer a programme dedicated to Van Gogh, including the dance show *Le Van d'un dernier été* by choreographer Simhamed Benhalima. With the Musée Estrine, and then the tourist office as its representative, the town is still part of the Van Gogh Europe network, which now unites four countries—the Netherlands, Belgium, England, and France—twenty-two cities, twelve remarkable sites, and ten museums. The Musée Estrine and the Musée des Alpilles are featured alongside prestigious institutions such as the Musée d'Orsay, the Van Gogh Museum in Amsterdam, the

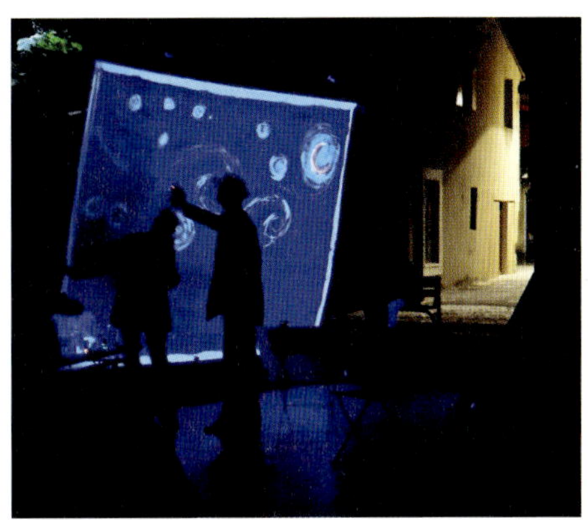

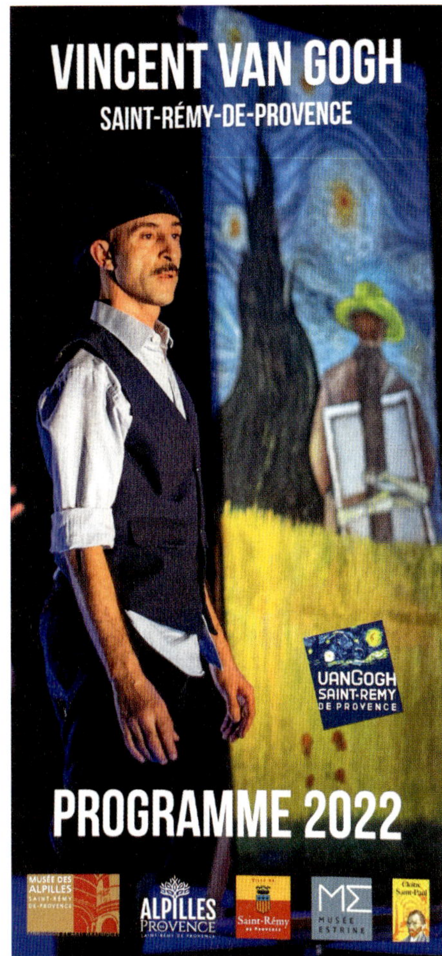

Fig. 35
Performance by Philippe Monnier for the 2015 Night of Museums in Place Favier

Fig. 36
The choreographer Simhamed Benhalima in the show *Van Gogh: A Last Summer*.

Kröller-Müller Museum in Otterlo, Van Gogh's birthplace in Zundert, and the National Gallery in London. By fostering cooperation, project sharing, and mutual support among its members, the network aims to make Van Gogh's cultural heritage accessible to the widest audience, with the ambition to inspire, unite, and engage present and future generations.

Through its many cultural and patrimonial initiatives, driven notably by the commitment of several residents of Saint-Rémy, the town has never ceased to keep Vincent van Gogh's memory alive. By offering everyone the chance to walk in the painter's footsteps, it continues today to keep his artistic and human legacy alive with new projects.

1 Louis Brès, "Aux Indépendants", *Le Sémaphore de Marseille*, 11 April 1905.
2 Letter 779 from Vincent to Theo, 9 June 1889.
3 M. Bonnet, *Deux ou trois choses sur… Vincent van Gogh*, brochure of the 1 May festivities, 1988.
4 Decree no. 1942-67.
5 Decree no. 1962-11.
6 Edgar Leroy, *La Folie de Vincent van Gogh*, in collaboration with Dr Victor Doiteau, Paris: Æsculape, 1928.
7 Edgar Leroy, "Van Gogh et le drame de l'oreille coupée", in collaboration with Victor Doiteau, Paris: Æsculape, July 1936.
8 Jean de Beucken, *Un Portrait de Vincent van Gogh*, Liège: Éditions du Balancier, 1938. Used as a "please insert" at the time, Charles Mauron's text was inserted at the start of the book from subsequent editions. Since 1936, Jean de Beucken (1905–1981) came regularly to Saint-Rémy, to the Mas de Berne.
9 In the *Armana prouvençau pèr 1946.*
10 See the speech made by Charles Mauron at Edgar Leroy's funeral, published in volume III of the collections *Van Goghiana* by Marc-Edo Tralbaut (Antwerp: Antwerpen Pierre Pere, 1966).
11 Much later it became the tourist office and was presided over by Dr Leroy.
12 The well-known ups and downs of his stay in Arles (especially the famous petition), are echoed by anecdotes from Saint-Rémy, in particular from the amateur painter Henri Vanel (1857–1947), who practised rifle shooting at two of Vincent's canvases (Jean de Beucken, *Un Portrait de Vincent van Gogh*, *op. cit.*, 1953, p. 20).
13 Son of the painter who lived in Eygalières, Alfred Latour (1888–1964)—who was also a member of the Resistance—Jacques Latour, born in 1918, is believed to have died in 1956 from the after effects of the abuse he suffered in captivity.
14 See "Un tresor à l'Oustau de Sado", memories of Louis Durand, aged sixteen at the time, who kept his father, Brigadier Jean-Baptiste Durand, company during long night watches (in the anthology by Marcèu Bonnet, *La Mount-Joio de Sant-Roumié e de l'Escolo dis Aupiho*, Saint-Rémy: Barnier, 2003).
15 Marielle Latour, "Les liens posthumes de Van Gogh avec la Provence", *Arts & Livres*, no. 118, 1984. Daughter of the Lyonnais engraver Philippe Burnot, Marielle Latour (1918–1993) ran the Musée Cantini in Marseille from 1957 until her retirement, in 1984.
16 In total, 7,305 paid entries and 1,513 free entries (journalists, students from teacher training colleges and fine arts schools, pupils from secular and private schools in Saint-Rémy, middle schools in Tarascon and Orange, and high schools in Marseille, Avignon and Aix-en-Provence; residents of the hospice, etc.).
17 Compiled by Madeleine Jauneau, assistant at the Musée de Lyon, with the help of Vincent Willem van Gogh, it opened with a text by Edgar Leroy, "Vincent van Gogh au cœur de la Provence", which was also published in the Saint-Rémy review *Lis Aupiho*, no. 1, April 1951.
18 Charles Mauron's texts on Van Gogh have been collected in their entirety in the volume *Van Gogh. Études psychocritiques*, Paris: Librairie José Corti, 1976.
19 Published in Lausanne in 1969 by Edita.
20 Resolution no. 1964-64.
21 Resolutions nos. 1965-76 and 1966-48.
22 Official Municipal Bulletin no. 3, 3rd quarter, 1968.
23 *Ibid.*
24 Diary of Jean Baltus, 6 February 1941.25 Speech by Louis Vigne, 13 August 1966.
25 Speech of Louis Vigne, 13 August 1966.
26 "La fondation Van Gogh à Saint-Rémy", *Plein Feux*, no. 11, November 1988, p. 3.
27 *Le Provençal*, 18 May 1990.
28 *L'Iris*, municipal newspaper, no. 19 (March–April 1992).
29 Jean-Pierre Stroobnats, "Un bronze de Zadkine sauvé par un détective privé", *Le Monde*, 23 May 2009.
30 Louis Gros, *Où êtes-vous jardins de mon enfance?*, Tarascon: Imprimerie de La Tarasque, 2012.

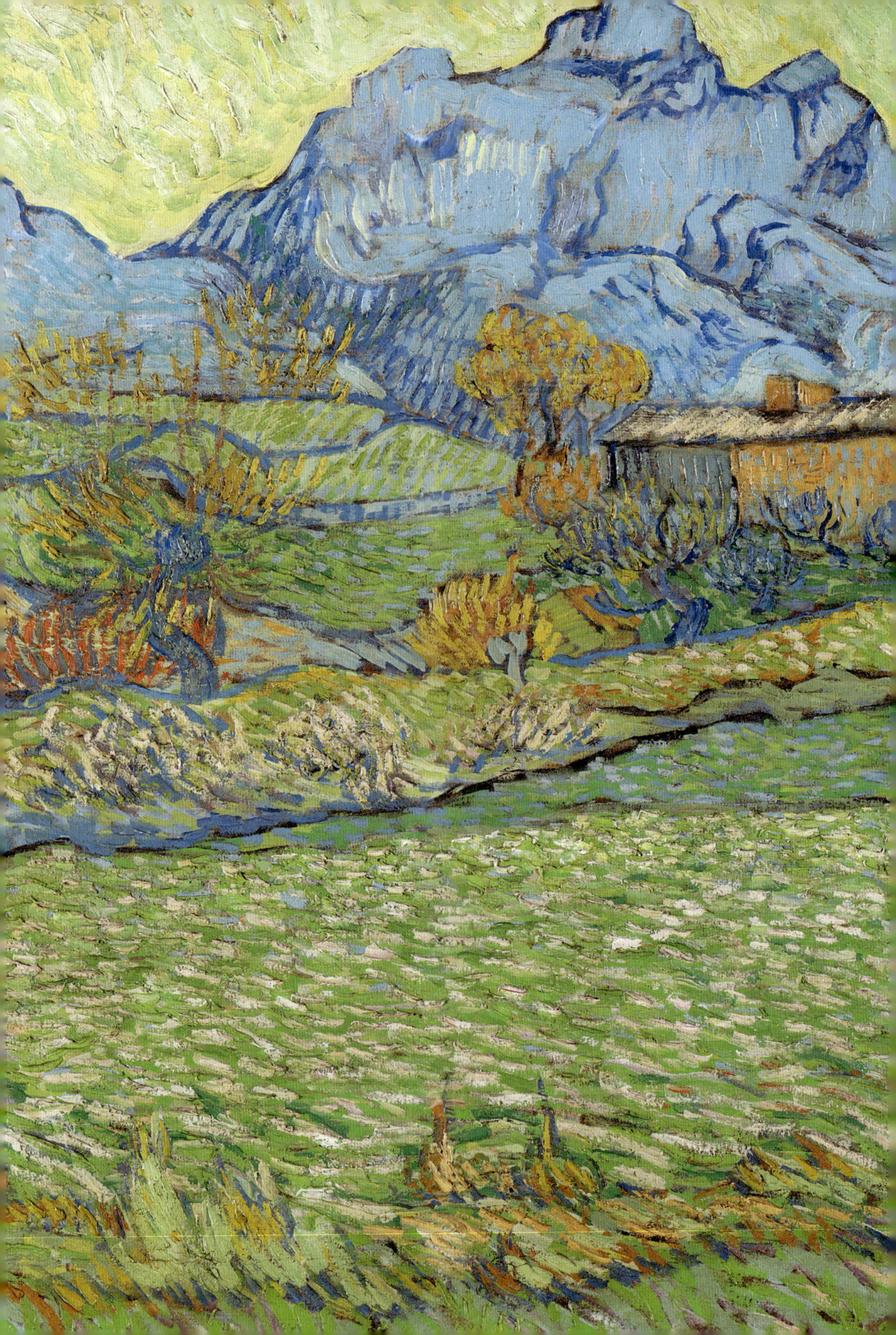

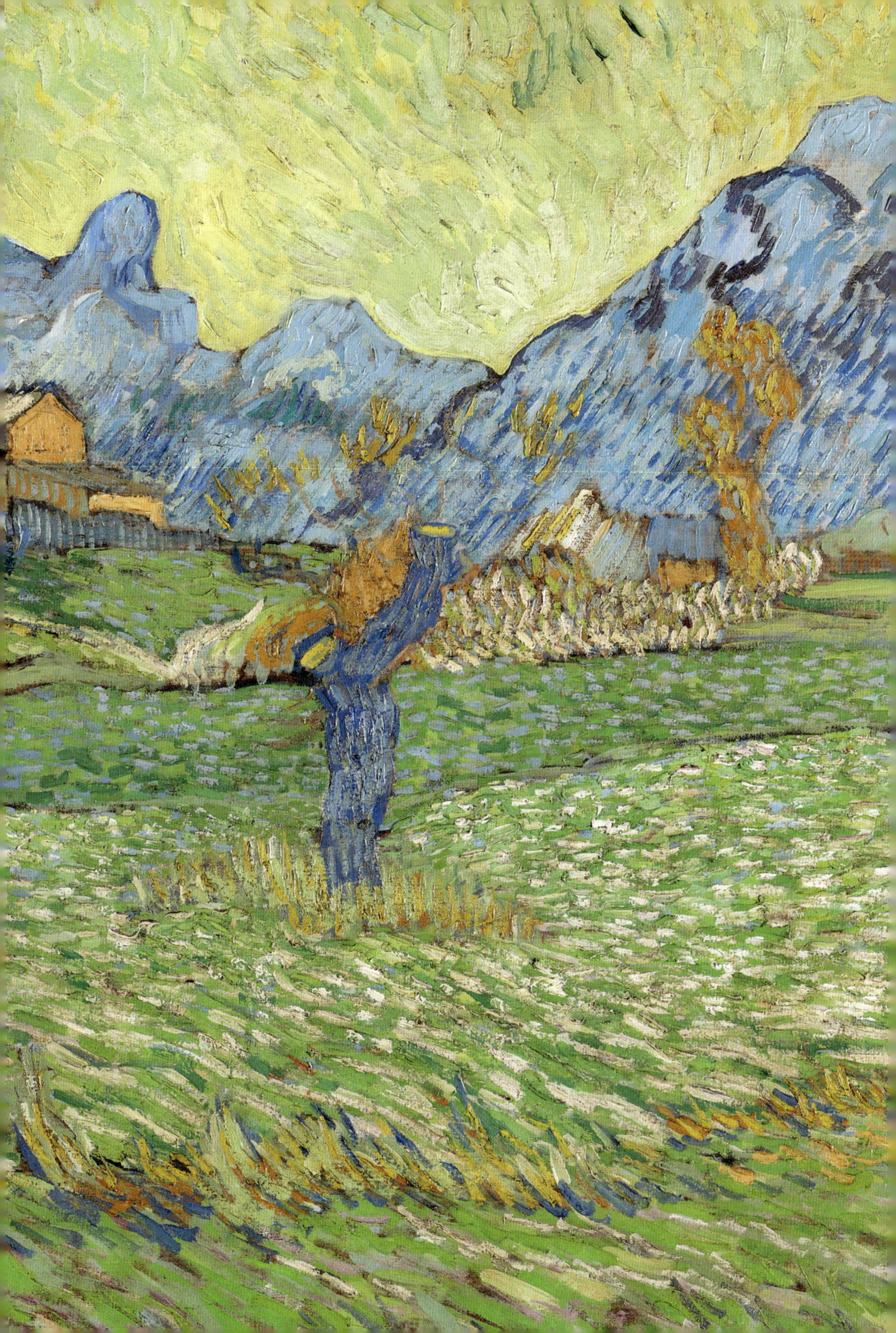

Photo Credits

p. 2 Foto Scala, Firenze

p. 4-5 Collection Kröller-Müller Museum, Otterlo, the Netherlands. Photography by Rik Klein Gotink.

p. 20 Foto Scala, Firenze

p. 23 Bridgeman Images

p. 26-27 DeAgostini Picture Library/Scala, Firenze

p. 31 Collection Kröller-Müller Museum, Otterlo, the Netherlands. Photography by Rik Klein Gotink.

p. 34 Superstock / Bridgeman Images

p. 34 Photo © Stefano Baldini / Bridgeman Images

p. 35 Collection Kröller-Müller Museum, Otterlo, the Netherlands. Photography by Rik Klein Gotink.

p. 36 Album/Scala, Firenze

p. 37 Album/Scala, Firenze

p. 41 Van Gogh Museum, Amsterdam (Vincent Van Gogh Foundation)

p. 42-43 Collection Kröller-Müller Museum, Otterlo, the Netherlands. Photography by Rik Klein Gotink.

p. 46 Bridgeman Images

p. 47 New Picture Library/Scala, Firenze

p. 48 Christie's Images / Bridgeman Images

p. 52 Album/Scala, Firenze

p. 56 Mary Evans/Scala, Firenze

p. 57 Foto Scala, Firenze

p. 59 Foto Scala, Firenze

p. 60 Photo Art Resource/Scala, Florence

p. 61 Christie's Images, London/Scala, Florence

p. 64 Copyright The National Gallery, London/Scala, Florence

p. 66 Foto Scala, Firenze

p. 67 Photo Scala Florence/Heritage Images

p. 68 Photo Scala Florence/Heritage Images

p. 70 DeAgostini Picture Library/Scala, Florence

p. 72 Album/Scala, Florence

p. 72 Photo Scala Florence/Heritage Images

p. 73 DeAgostini Picture Library/Scala, Florence

p. 73 RMN-Grand Palais / Hervé Lewandowski/ Dist. Photo SCALA, Florence

p. 74 Bridgeman Images

p. 75 Digital image, The Museum of Modern Art, New York/Scala, Florence

p. 75 Brooklyn Museum / Frank L. Babbott Fund and A. Augustus Healy Fund / Bridgeman Images

p. 80 Copyright The National Gallery, London/Scala, Florence

p. 82-83 DeAgostini Picture Library/Scala, Florence

p. 85 Collection Kröller-Müller Museum, Otterlo, the Netherlands. Photography by Rik Klein Gotink.

p. 88 RMN-Grand Palais / Patrice Schmidt/ Dist. Photo SCALA, Florence

p. 89 Van Gogh Museum, Amsterdam (Vincent Van Gogh Foundation)

p. 90-91 Album/Scala, Florence

p. 93 Bridgeman Images

p. 93 Photo Scala, Florence

p. 95 The Solomon R. Guggenheim Foundation/Art Resource, NY/ Scala, Florence

p. 96 Collection Kröller-Müller Museum, Otterlo, the Netherlands. Photography by Rik Klein Gotink.

p. 100 Bridgeman Images

p. 105 Bridgeman Images

p. 108 Album/Scala, Florence

p. 116 Photo © Stefano Baldini / Bridgeman Images

p. 128 The Phillips Collection, Washington, USA / Acquired 1949 / Bridgeman Images

p. 130 Museum of Fine Arts, Boston. All rights reserved/Scala, Florence

p. 134 Collection Kröller-Müller Museum, Otterlo, the Netherlands. Photography by Rik Klein Gotink.

p. 136 Collection Kröller-Müller Museum, Otterlo, the Netherlands. Photography by Rik Klein Gotink.

p. 137 Superstock / Bridgeman Images

p. 150 Photo Scala, Florence

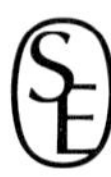

Silvana Editoriale

General Director
Michele Pizzi

Editorial Director
Sergio Di Stefano

Art Director
Giacomo Merli

Editorial Coordinator
Ramona Follo

Graphic Design
Annamaria Ardizzi

Copy Editing
Sara Clamor

Layout
Diego Mantica

Production Coordinator
Antonio Micelli

Editorial Assistant
Giulia Mercanti

Photo Editors
Silvia Sala, Barbara Miccolupi

Press Office
Alessandra Olivari, press@silvanaeditoriale.it

ISBN 9788836660223

Cover

Vincent van Gogh, *The Olive Trees*, June 1889, oil on canvas, 73 × 92 cm, New York, Museum of Modern Art

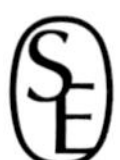

Silvana Editoriale S.p.A.
via dei Lavoratori, 78
20092 Cinisello Balsamo, Milano
tel. 02 453 951 01
www.silvanaeditoriale.it

Reproductions, printing and binding in Italy
Printed December 2025

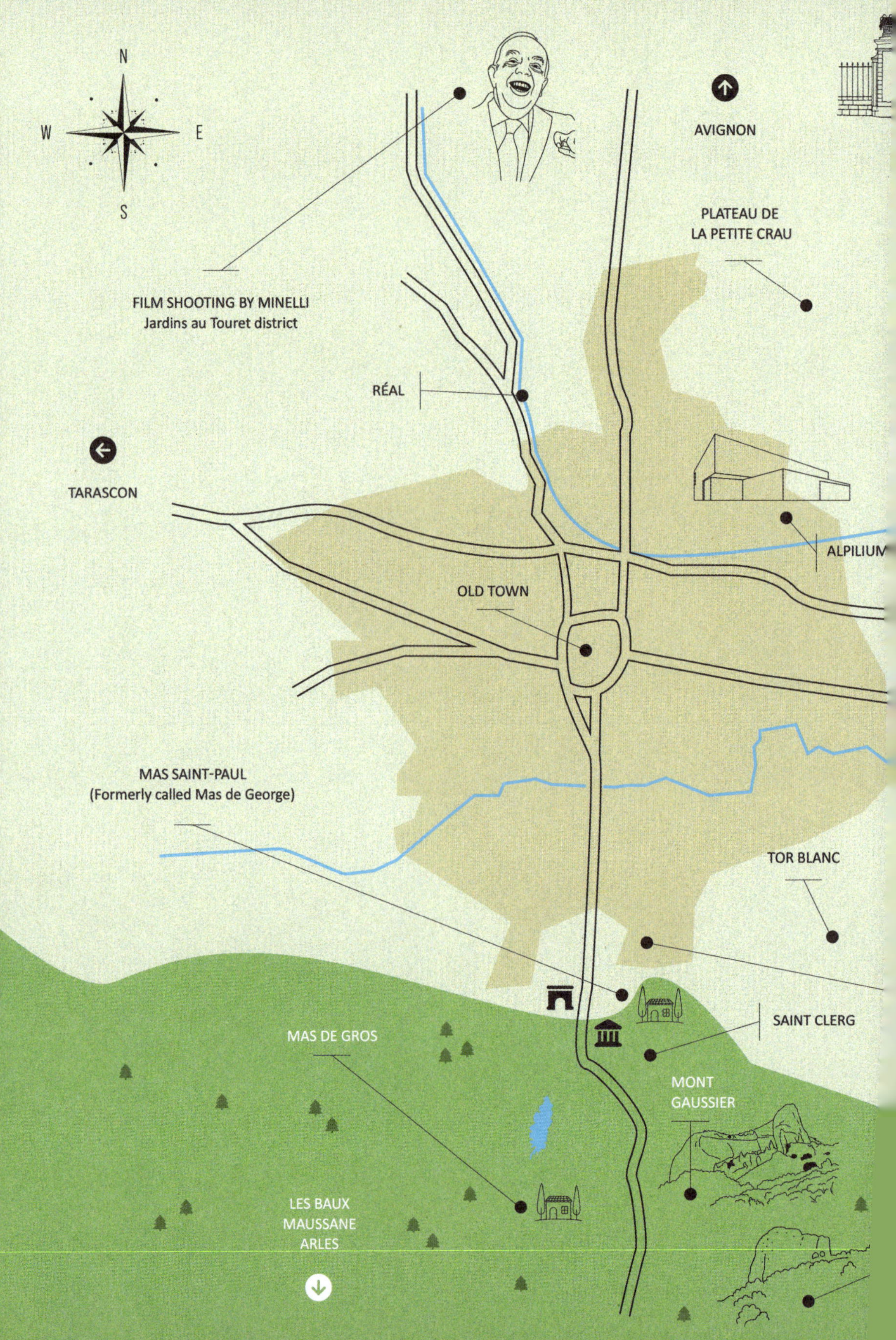
N
W
E
S
AVIGNON
PLATEAU DE
LA PETITE CRAU
FILM SHOOTING BY MINELLI
Jardins au Touret district
RÉAL
TARASCON
ALPILIUM
OLD TOWN
MAS SAINT-PAUL
(Formerly called Mas de George)
TOR BLANC
SAINT CLERG
MAS DE GROS
MONT
GAUSSIER
LES BAUX
MAUSSANE
ARLES